BB

D1326929

The Atlantic Ocean

by the same author

THE MISSING
OUR FATHERS
PERSONALITY
BE NEAR ME

The Atlantic Ocean
Essays on Britain and America

ANDREW O'HAGAN

faber and faber

First published in 2008
by Faber and Faber Limited
3 Queen Square London WC1N 3AU

Typeset by Faber and Faber Limited
Printed in England by CPI Mackays, Chatham ME5 8TD

All the following pieces are copyright of the author, but he wishes to thank the editors
of the publications where they first appeared:

'Scotland's Old Injury', 'The American Dream of Lee Harvey Oswald', 'The Killing of
James Bulger', 'Saint Marilyn', 'Tony and the Queen', '7/7', 'On the End of British
Farming', 'Cowboy George', 'Four Funerals and a Wedding', 'Celebrity Memoirs', 'On
Lad Magazines', 'On Hating Football', 'Poetry as Self-Help', 'My Grandfather's Ship',
'After Hurricane Katrina', 'The Faces of Michael Jackson', 'The American Way of
Sorrow', 'On Begging', and 'The Garbage of England' first appeared in the *London
Review of Books*. 'England's Flowers' first appeared in the *Guardian* Weekend
Magazine. 'The Glasgow Sludge Boat' first appeared in Granta. 'Tony and the Queen'
and 'England and the Beatles' first appeared in the *New York Review of Books*.

A CIP record for this book
is available from the British Library

ISBN 978–0–571–23885–9

10 9 8 7 6 5 4 3 2

for my daughter Nell

Contents

Introduction: The Atlantic Ocean

OCTOBER 2007

When you grow up by the sea you spend a good deal of time looking at the horizon. You wonder what on earth the waves might bring – and where the sea might deposit you – until one day you know you have lived all that time between two places, the scene of arrival and the point of departure, like a ghost on the shore. When I look back at my childhood on the Ayrshire coast, I recall a basic devotion to the idea that human nature and national character are as unknowable as the weather's rationale. Nevertheless, in those years I yearned to know whatever I could know and I fell in love with the Atlantic Ocean, imagining I saw it as somehow suspending very wonderful promises about freedom and democracy. That water had once made the world seem reachable, made life seem plausible, and standing there I watched the infrequent ships and thought of the Ireland my people had come from and the America so many of us were coming to be absorbed by. They were each out there, the past and the future, the great hunger and the maddening feast, and the Atlantic itself seemed capable of whispering these stories into the coves.

I was born on 25 May 1968. It was the high point of a certain kind of idealism – Paris witnessed the biggest of its student riots that day – and by the time I came to stand by myself on the beach at Saltcoats I was merely a representative ghost. The country at my back, and the Britain beyond, had already given up both its industries and its idealisms and much of its community to a brand-new notion of the individual. That is who we were at the end of the 1970s. I was a post-industrial Scottish child, wide eyed in the Winter of Discontent, and the ocean I looked out on was no longer streaked with ships fresh from yards on the Clyde or with vessels hot for the British Empire. My mother's father, Charlie Docherty, had once glided down that waterway on the *Captain Cook*, a ship bound with tons of merchandise for Sydney Harbour. Michael O'Hagan, my father's father, had sailed the other way round on HMS *Forfar*, which was torpedoed off the west of Ireland and sunk in the winter of 1940.

That was life beneath the waves. Breaking through them in my younger days, when the coast was clear and the air smelled of vinegar, was a pack of nuclear submarines based at Faslane. The Cold War was very neighbourly round our way: from my perch on the sea wall the Atlantic would now and then show evidence of the world that Britain was turning towards. Those submarines – *Resolution, Repulse, Renown, Revenge* – arrived with stealth and ascended like shadows to darken the old horizon: their fearful weapons systems were American and suddenly so were we. For a few ominous months in the early 1980s, of course, the Atlantic was the star of the show in an old-fashioned and bloody demonstration of outmoded imperial selfhood, the battle for the Falklands. Yet in the days of *Revenge* and *Repulse* – or vengeance and repulsion – the famous 'task force' came on like a tribute fleet, a horrible anachronism, steaming with alacrity towards the frozen nether regions of the South Atlantic, the vessels as ghostly in their own way as the lost ships of my grandfathers.

I have beside me as I write a group of postcards from the early days of our fifty-first statehood. They sit on my desk like snapshots of the Thatcher revolution, each one pointing in some way towards America and a burgeoning comedy of death and celebrity and inequality. They point to a future coalition of the willing: an evangelical lust for Christian ideals spanning the oceans; a capacity for wonder at the depth of feeling attached to one's own righteousness. They show cruise missiles and closed coal mines, Princess Diana and Greenham Common. And you can't look at the cards without thinking them a cultural presentiment of a very special relationship: a new kind of America and

Britain is inscribed in the images of Ronnie and Maggie. Most of all the cards are stepping stones across the sea: we observe in them what we learned from America about masking our guilt at how Christians behave when it isn't Sunday. They show the progress of popular sentiment and the forming of an instinct for gross spiritual compromise – they show how far we will go in order to love the marketplace. That's right: they show the birth of New Labour.

We must, at some level, have been greatly impressed by the simple brutality of the dollar, the way it could change old civilisations, just as Ronald Reagan smiled his smile and held his nerve and bankrupted the Soviet Union. After the 1980s, and the birth of Cool Britannia, it was well understood that the Argie-hating *Sun* would come out for New Labour, and when it did the relationship felt right and proper, for the meaning of democracy had changed in those years to become a treatise against outsiders and a passionately sentimental ideology. And so we woke up in the era of Tony Blair to find that Britain was not a comforting land on which to rest our ambivalence. It was a place where every politician had cut his cloth to suit the fashion of the times, cut it in the US style, so that we dressed ourselves no longer with an austere but fair sense of who we could be as a nation but with a belligerent certainty about who we are not. We learned to hate our enemies not for their criminal acts but for their metaphysical differences. 'You are either with America or you are against us,' said George W. Bush, and Britain was already by then another country. And so was America. By the time I had written the last of these essays, America was no longer a place admired by the world. People tried to blame America's enemies for that – foreign and domestic, left and right – but the sadder truth is that it was America's friends that did her harm. Even yet, as the idiots who supported that bad and stupid war scan the room for exits and blame the left for their greater wrongs, we find that Blair's version of brotherhood cost America dearly. He can say what he likes, and so can those soulless people in his government who stood silent to save their jobs, but Britain was the bad brother that goaded its sibling into psychosis.

It is easy for people to say that opposition to this kind of America – to this abuse of an idealistic, generous, open notion of America – is the same as blanket anti-Americanism. I won't even bother with that, because I know, and readers of these essays will know, that it is quite another America I would want to befriend into decency. I am talking about the one that gave me belief as a child, the one that seemed to provide a fair chance and a good laugh, the one of the best movies and the perfect novel. I am talking about the America once imagined by Scott Fitzgerald, the one that many people have broken their hearts trying to hold on to, the one commensurate with our capacity for wonder. Let the lazy snipers seize their opportunity and call those of us appalled by Dick Cheney and Donald Rumsfeld anti-American, for they know nothing of America that is worth defending. Let it be said that America lost its friends and gained an ally – for that is the story of a modern tragedy.

Jay Gatsby watches the beautiful green light at the end of Daisy's wharf, and the Atlantic waters that lapped under the beams there and under that famous green light were the waters of my own Atlantic too; they had come from the shores of a hopeful and once idealistic Britain. We share many things and I have always believed in our brotherhood, which is why it is sad to see us fall hopelessly together into that element that Scott Fitzgerald knew by heart: an utterly terrible grandness of delusion.

I found my way to London and began writing essays and books in the 1990s. I wanted to raise a smile and raise my game and sing some new notes if possible. I bow before the traditions that made this kind of writing and many of them are resolutely Scottish. It was the *Edinburgh Review* under Francis Jeffrey that first demonstrated how a very good journal could be more important every few weeks than several decent novels, and I believe I found that same quality of hospitality at the *London Review of Books*. As a novelist, I have perceived no contradiction between one literary activity and another and have cared for the great journals all my life: they contain a tincture of the very lifeblood of the culture, and the best ones find it natural to civilise our politics while taking steps to finesse our understanding of society. The best ones add to our stock of liveliness while proving anxious to upgrade the power, the precision, and the beauty of the language. They resist cant and play with fire. The essay and the long reported piece are forms with the most daunting exemplars in the traditions of both Britain and America, and I argue for the forms, not for myself, when I say we must fight at all costs to uphold their status.

This book opens with an essay about Scotland. I am now and then accused of being disloyal to Scotland – or of not liking it very much – by people who consider it an insult for authors to do anything other than praise the place where they come from. The Scottish writers I grew up loving and learning from – Robert Burns, James Boswell, Robert Louis Stevenson, John Galt, whether at home or abroad – would immediately have dismissed this for the terrifying nonsense that it is. A healthy literary culture would never expect its writers to reproduce the conceited forms of self-congratulation that every nation has at its disposal. There are those who like writers best when we are at our most agreeably banal. Yet it is our job to interrogate the culture as much as ourselves, and to enjoy a drink in the pub afterwards. Anything less constitutes a mockery of tradition, an insult to what one might call an international sense of discovery, a completely unforgivable slap in the face of the thoughtful reader, and a betrayal of the writer's talent. There will always be those who view the honest attempt to write carefully as something equal to a tantrum of self-importance, and there is nothing very much I can do about these people, who require writers to embody some patriotic principle. They are not my kind of readers or writers or pass-keepers: we are citizens of the world before we are subjects of any nation, and novels are not editorials and essays are not policy. Scotland is rich in both innocence and experience, and I begin this collection with an essay about my native land that might demonstrate how naturally a certain passion of regard can sometimes live beside a quantity of dismay.

'I will not serve that in which I no longer believe whether it call itself my home, my fatherland or my church,' wrote James Joyce in *A Portrait of the Artist as a Young Man*, 'and I will try to express myself in some mode of life or art as freely as I can.' But the buckling of freedom's meaning and the perversion of journalistic ethics have themselves become large parts of life in the last few decades. Nowadays, an emetic populism is taken to stand for common sense; a communal blaming and a self-pity is held in our culture to answer most persuasively to the call of truth. The common reader, wherever she exists, has never been so common, and George Orwell would whiten to address the mob that now scans the *Daily Mirror* and each night flicks between the bouts of gladiatorial combat happening on every other channel.

A kind of political idealism fell about the beaches of my youth like so many echoing and departing voices, and many of the essays in this volume take up the story from there. To me a book of essays might be bound by an atmosphere as much as by a theme – as any volume of prose or poetry might be – and so I make no great claims for this book's utility as a summary of relations between Britain and America. Rather, the book might constitute a journey into the space between us, both a comedy of errors and portrait of a marriage, as both an argument about empire and a slow drama about the meeting of fame and ordinary life. The shots fired by Lee Harvey Oswald may have marked the beginning of an ending for particular public hopes and certain private dreams, but so in another way was the killing of James Bulger and in another way again the mountain of flowers that gathered in the streets for Diana.

It was writing about the death of that Liverpool toddler that gave me my start at the *London Review*. We had all seen the pictures of the child being abducted from the Strand Shopping Centre and later the footage on television of the two ten-year-olds – at that time called Boy A and Boy B – being hounded by a mob holding up nooses as the children's van arrived at the court. I thought at the time that those images represented a new moment in the history of the community I grew up in, the northern working-class, which seemed for the first time hand-in-hand with the tabloids in a grim attempt to force unreason on top of unreason. Nobody was talking about the boys' back-grounds, the economic conditions of their lives or their educa-tion or their neighbourhood. They were simply exceptions, 'Devil Dogs', and their own community rose up to say they should be put down. John Major then said the second most chilling sentence ever spoken by a British prime minister. 'I think it is time for us to understand a bit less and condemn a bit more.' (The first most chilling was from Margaret Thatcher, his predecessor, who said 'there is no such thing as society'.)

I said to my editor I could recognise so much about the boys: their way of talking, their backgrounds, how they inclined towards one another as they walked. I was twenty-five, but my childhood seemed near to hand: it was filled with the essential dangers and abuses and lacks that had run to quite a different course in the cases of Boy A and Boy B, but that didn't stop me from wanting to understand the world that made them and sustained them and now rejected them. 'Confessions of a Liter-ary Journalist', said the *Guardian* when it reprinted the piece I wrote for the *London Review*. But liberal opinion was split in two over the Bulger case, and no amount of confession, no attempt to identify the sources of the boys' terrible act, could stand muster against the barrage of tabloid hate that rained down on them. I kept thinking of those two ten-year-olds who lived a mile or two from the silent docks of Liverpool, two boys who dogged school and watched American horror films rented by their parents about murderous dolls that must be destroyed. Around those boys we watched the beginning of a new social marriage in Britain: the conjoining of tabloid spite with underclass sentiment, a precursor of a new kind of populist energy that would run free and wild in the Blair years. I believe it started there, with the nooses and the moral panic, with the

indecent joy of condemnation and the CCTV. It will be remembered that it was the British newspapers who appealed to Lord
Justice Morland to have the names and pictures of the two boys
released and he did so with the public's support. At this point
one had to face the fact that Britain was a very different country from any in Europe: those terrified boys, who had done a
terrible thing, aged ten, not only faced the full rigours of an
adult trial but had their faces printed on the front page of the
Daily Mail at the end. Even today it is difficult to imagine any
other judge in Europe being successfully pressed by the media
to name Jon Venables and Robert Thompson, thus seeing three
lives destroyed instead of one.

The conjunction of killing and celebrity is not so modern if
you think of Jesse James or the Brothers Kray. But not everybody in the Wild West – or, indeed, in the Wild East End – could
have shared the ultramodern propensity to see other people's
suffering in the media as something of an enhancer of one's
own general feelings of well-being. While we were becoming
like a part of America, many of us learned how to forget the
idea of a common decency. Slowly, in the years that stretch
from the first term of the America-loving Thatcher to the last
term of the America-loving Blair, we saw a grand entrench-
ment of those rich and those poor. American's influence on
Britain, so good in many ways, put a stretch on this polarisa-
tion – Reagan's notion that a good society was a place where
some stayed poor so that others could be richer – and for all
New Labour's handsome talk about a 'classless society', we now
know that deep inequality is a condition we take for granted.
The have-nots make it worse by seeming so much to revel in
their deracinated culture, so glued to Sky TV and sugary products they do not see how they are becoming a by-product of
richer people's happiness. This is something of the culture I
grew up in and the point is not to condemn but to understand
it, as John Major said we should not.

Several essays here try to map the way we have drifted
towards the American manner of society. When I saw those

poor people – and I mean *poor* people – stranded in the Super-
dome in New Orleans after the hurricane, I immediately
packed a bag and crossed the Atlantic. There was no doubt in
my mind. There is still no doubt. It was about us, too. We share
an experience we can scarcely put a name to: many millions of
people now exist for whom life used to be defined by work and
is now defined by leisure. I'd say the complex losses and gains
involved in that alteration hover over these essays. Leisure made
us enjoy ourselves more, but who *are* they, these selves that are
enjoying to death?

The aftermath of Hurricane Katrina might have shown the
world that the dream once described by Martin Luther King
was cold in the glare of Bush's America. Michael Jackson continues to get whiter, and poverty in Britain is thought by some
to be a lifestyle choice. We have lived together through the un-
lessoning of Vietnam and come out the other side with a higher regard for the power of media images and a smaller regard
for human life. I have been moved by interest and by accident
into the way of these developments and I wanted my own personal accounts of them to settle here together.

Writers of a certain kind – the unwise kind, you might say –
should put on their shoes and go outside. There is something
intoxicating about the odour of pencil shavings and cut lilies,
but I always felt that outside was the place to test the weather-
proof nature of one's style and I have wanted to know how far I
can press for the unobvious disclosure. In time I may grow to
hate the outside world, but this book is a record of a natural
inclination to see the writer hard at work in the open air and at
the water's edges, finding out just what it might be that a writer
can find. In that sense the volume is also a story about the
parameters of style, the American manner of reportage in conversation with the British, laying down a plan for the Atlantic
mode.

All representative ghosts have their natural haunts, and I feel
my generation was built to feel with a measure of instinct how
non-fiction could be as written as fiction. But there are still

controversies around this topic and I've been known to run
into them. They featured even in my childhood and could be
found in the those dusty copies of the *Edinburgh Review* and
Blackwood's magazine that fired my dreams of literary possibility as a boy. When I think of grand attempts to shape real life
into art I don't think first of Kansas and *In Cold Blood*, I think
of James Boswell's fantasia of Johnson's life and the brilliant
Edinburgh mimics who wrote for the great journals. Reality is
not what it was, for writers no more than for the producers of
sellable television shows, and I suppose that is something I take
too much for granted. In any event, these pieces were written in
the belief that journalism, as much as fiction, might work best
when the style and the content are united. Material often speaks
in its own way and it is the job of the writer to capture that way
of speaking and to preserve it. This will sometimes mean
throwing everything of yourself onto the page, allowing your
own experience and your own ego to enliven the subject, but it
might mean erasing yourself as completely as actuality allows,
so that the material can properly survive your attempts to make
excuses for it. There are stories – especially ones that feature
extreme talk or behaviour – whose reality would be ground to
dust by authorial intrusion, by a writer nervous of his material
who was also anxious somehow to separate himself from its
existence on the page or its validity in life. But that is bad writing. Our only responsibilities are to accuracy and the literary
value of the thing – a writer who very obviously considers, as he
writes a piece, what his friends will think of him when they read
it is not a writer one can trust. It's not a question of being brave
or being right, but of sticking to the material.

Some time after publishing one of the pieces in this book, the
one about New Orleans, I discovered that some readers had
found it to be somewhat unfair to its subjects and to America
itself. I was told that some Americans had found it so too, and
that the fault – if it is a fault – was mainly to do with my seeming absence from the piece. I felt shocked at this discovery
because it appeared, for me at least, to betray a lack of faith in

what writing is about. The New Orleans piece may have any number of failings, and, as with everything here, I wish I could go back and make them right, but I doubt that any of them are to do with my failure to appear more often as myself, and to somehow correct the opinion of America configured by the reporting. I actually liked Sam and Terry, the two men in the piece, and I recorded the facts of their journey to the South with faith, but the material demanded that it be allowed to speak for itself. My dalliance with them in the act of gathering stuff for the piece was immaterial when it came to remaking their world in a literary sense. Their journey had drama and dialogue – and it may have had political relevance too, or social ramifications – but none of that would have been enhanced by my adding my own voice to their scenes. For good or for ill, one must sometimes let the story be the story, and my own attendance at Sam and Terry's rescue effort was not the story.

There is a fourth wall in journalism as much as in drama: writers take it down as and when it suits them, though in British journalism, as opposed to American, addressing the reader directly is considered good manners. George Orwell, for instance, with all his brilliance, would act as valet to every thought a reader might have, which might, at the same time, explain why Orwell is both so congenial to be with and why none of his non-fiction narratives is as beautiful as those collected in Joseph Mitchell's *Up in the Old Hotel*. Though they may not have known it themselves, the people who wanted me to be more present with Sam and Terry were really asking me to find a way to make Sam and Terry less like themselves, to launder them somehow by being a good liberal journalist who can explain or otherwise relieve the anxiety that is created by the men's way of talking and being. My critics weren't going that far, they weren't asking for a censor, but they needed help in coping with these two men and the picture my account of their world gave of America, and they wanted that help to come not from their own imaginations but from mine.

All I can say is Sam and Terry are not Everymen and their

America is not the only one: I wanted readers to be in proximity to the relentless tension of their lives and this meant establishing a style for the piece that might precisely meet that content. There are other pieces here where the author is forever coming to the front of the stage to explain why the sisters will not be going to Moscow, but the story about Sam and Terry depends on the idea that a journalist, as much as any writer, may on certain occasions be present everywhere but visible nowhere. I cared about the piece as writing, not as a social experience, though I think I always knew in my bones that some readers would want more of the latter. But editorialising would have killed Sam and Terry stone dead; I knew that more than anything. Perhaps people wanted me to say more about myself because it would have meant saying less about Sam and Terry: they were a discomforting pair, and the call for 'balance' is very often a masked desire that the thing being described just wasn't described or even seen to exist.

Writing is not a character test and writers aren't gods: you can charm your way into a reader's affections with displays of good counsel and little arias of decency, but it will almost always in the end be like adding sugar to a dish that can be known for its own flavours. You will find many personal pieces in this book – pieces where the author is the character and the character is the point – but now and then the presence of the actor is most keenly felt when he is offstage. John Hersey wrote *Hiroshima* without once denouncing the savagery of those who invented the atom bomb or without once giving rise in the reader's mind to the image of a good man scratching diligently in a notepad. He found a way to tell the story which perfectly served the story, and his example might tell us what we mean when we say that too much modern reporting is banal – it is the banality that comes when a writer imagines that he and his great conscience are more interesting than the story. Now and then they are, but the trick is to know when the story is working for itself.

In Britain over the last two decades, some of us might say that pop culture and pop politics have been under the spell of an American kind of allure. It's not a singular story – the same could be said of what used to be East Berlin – but in Britain we may have embraced the rise of the Christian Empire of America in ways that seemed purely natural and purely brave, if you followed Tony Blair. He felt he was right and saw it as an act of statesmanship to go to bed with the moral ambitions of George W. Bush, but in a sense Blair's record as the people's prime minister had already predicted such an event. Our own empire was gone. The shipyards had closed. We no longer exported Britishness to the world, so why wouldn't an ambitious, populist politician of the new millennium see it as natural – an act of survival, even – that we should instead swallow our pride and our reason and take a hand in exporting American democracy?

Several of these essays try to follow these arcs as they span the Atlantic Ocean: you might call it the people's journey from a pride in having pride to a dependence on dependence. The culture of self-help that seemed so to dominate the airwaves – including the airwaves of high culture, movies, poetry and the novel – was born in the suburbs of America as surely as Oprah Winfrey. Before long we were watching the leisured underclasses throwing chairs at one another on *Jerry Springer*, and then we had it too – every day on the *Jeremy Kyle Show*.

Culture as social balm.

Spite as entertainment.

Shouting as argument.

Dysfunction as normality.

Desires as rights.

Shopping as democracy.

Fame is the local hunger in so much of this and I find I have looked for it on both sides of the water. Sometime between the death of Marilyn and the death of Diana we learned to call it celebrity and began to feel it in our bones, this new open trade in alienation across the Atlantic. I remember the moment the Scottish light-entertainment heroine Lena Zavaroni went off to sing for Gerald Ford at the White House. It was the first time I realised someone like us could achieve fame. We couldn't have known then that, within ten years, this small girl would be writing private letters saying, 'I have lost myself', 'I am in a black hole', and that she would be dead by the age of thirty-four, killed by complications associated with anorexia nervosa. Her hunger for fame went physical, and over the years I came to see her as a patron saint of British celebrity. The rise of celebrity in Britain is actually the rise of a populist ethos.

As we clapped in our Scottish living room for Lena Zavaroni on *Opportunity Knocks*, I was convinced – being the youngest and the most starry-eyed – that the 'Clapometer' in London would pick up the noise and help Lena to win. *Opportunity Knocks* made the public the star: we made her success possible. And that is still the signature of phone-and-text competitions today. 'If I am a star,' Marilyn Monroe once said, 'then it is the public who made me a star.' And it is that power which became a kind of contagion in Britain at the end of the twentieth century. Margaret Thatcher may have wrecked our former sense of community, but she created a temperament for other forms of mass communion based on spite, many of which seek to mobilise collective feeling at 54p a minute.

This is the theatre of the new celebrity and its front-of-house staff is the tabloids. It is sometimes hard to be sure, when reading those papers with their trigger-happy eruptions of populist zeal, whether the issue at hand is a celebrity's big bottom or the exposure of a paedophile. Is one being invited to win a million pounds, or being told about the terror in Darfur or encouraged to gape at a woman's breasts or laugh at someone's downfall? It all comes at you with the same aggressive common sense and unassailable male joy. The wiles of celebrity make the public feel powerful and imperial: we can decide on the fame of ordinary people, which makes us feel very real and does something politics cannot do – it makes us feel together.

I remember walking through those flowers along The Mall after Diana died, thinking, *This is the revolution we've been waiting for: the country and the press got the god-like victim it wanted, and now come the observance and the vigils and the flowers*. It could only end in prayers. We wanted a celebrity to die in the cause of our need to feel that our own feeling of normalcy is everything. People were overwhelmed by the local power of that sentiment and they gathered together and bawled in the street.

A few years after that I was working on a novel and one day I visited a classroom of thirty girls. I gave out pieces of paper and asked them to write down what they wanted to be. It was the question we were always asked at school, and we would write 'astronaut' or 'hairdresser'. (Something that could take you to America.) Seventy per cent of the papers I'd given out to the girls contained a single word. 'Famous' was no longer an adjective; it was a job and a condition of being.

You used to have to be chosen. You used to have to be chosen over others, lifted up, made special. That is what being famous was all about: the glow of her chosenness, the heat of his recognisability. Producers and directors and editors and talent scouts chose you – they married you to the means of production – and then the public chose you in their turn. But the means of production have altered for ever, and now people can broadcast themselves in ways that make the old entertainment models seem as antique and ghostly as the music hall. Young kids make a record in their bedroom and they play it on MySpace. Girls create an audience and a network of contacts on Facebook, letting the world assess them and join them and make them famous. Everyone can make a spectacle of himself nowadays: home computers are increasingly built for that, for iLife, which isn't the same as any life that went on in this country before the dawn of the twenty-four-hour media cycle. Every bedroom is a potential studio and every person with Wi-Fi is a potential star. They are already the stars of their own lives. And perhaps that is where television has ceded most to the new technologies: togetherness will not in the future be served by a diet of programmes for our collective experience, but by each of us acting as producer and crew and star of our own show, which we then share with selected others. Our transit to Narcissus will be complete when our screens become mirrors: one star, one audience, the same person, oneself.

We have gone well past Andy Warhol. I saw that in New Orleans, when those two men from North Carolina showed a post-9/11 hunger to be heroic and be on television. At least they weren't on *Jerry Springer*, though in many ways they would have done well there. I flew home from Atlanta that time with a bag full of notes and a head full of recognitions: parts of the Britain I was going home to are not at all unlike the world of Sam and Terry. It was filled with people like one or two of the boys I grew up with, workless for years but holding out for fame or glory in the media or a famous win on the Lotto. People like that often went to Iraq and died fighting battles ordered and run by 1960s idealists.

As a writer I care about America, and care about its carelessness. But I know I will always be captivated by the green breast of the New World as imagined by Scott Fitzgerald, the old island that once flowered for the eyes of Dutch sailors. 'For a transitory enchanted moment,' he writes in *The Great Gatsby*, 'man must have held his breath in the presence of this continent.' And when I read that sentence I always think of my great-grandfather Hector Lavery, a fishmonger from Glasgow, who was crossing the Atlantic at the time Fitzgerald was writing his book. Arriving in Manhattan Sound on the SS *Columbia* in 1923, Hector and his wife Elizabeth and their child must have looked out and seen something of what the novelist had in mind. They had left a whole lot of life back in Glasgow – this was new life and the country must have seemed made for them. Sixteen liners narrowly avoided colliding at the piers that day before depositing 18,558 passengers on American soil. 'There were more than thirty-five nationalities represented by the immigrants who landed yesterday,' reported the *New York Times*, 'and some of them spoke such strange tongues that no one so far has been found who can understand them.' I like to think of my relatives' Glasgow and Irish voices with Atlantic salt on their tongues. When I look at their documents, I see they signed them with an X. The invisible worlds suggested by those bleary marks have spurred me in my attempt to find ways of writing these stories over the years. There is work to be done in our own hand, and I suppose I am still on that spit of Ayrshire coast, a scene of arrival and a point of departure.

Scotland's Old Injury

OCTOBER 2002

In Westminster Abbey a number of years ago, I stood for over an hour talking to Neal Ascherson. It was one of those freezing January evenings – cold stone, long shadows – and we adopted our BBC faces in Poets' Corner, looking at the memorials and marble busts on the walls. I noticed Ascherson was taking his time over an inscription to the poet Thomas Campbell, and some words of Campbell's began to echo somewhere in my head, two lines from *The Pleasures of Hope*:

> 'Tis distance lends enchantment to the view,
> And robes the mountain in its azure hue.

Not good lines, but they seemed good enough as I watched Ascherson watching. He gave the impression there was something new to be said about Campbell.

'Come with me,' I said. 'I want to show you something.' Leading Ascherson across the Abbey, round an altar, down a spartan side-chapel, I pointed through some slats to the Coronation Chair. 'They took it eight weeks ago,' I said, 'the Stone of Destiny.'

'How did they remove it?' Ascherson asked.

'They gouged it out. They broke the chair. It's a thirteenth-century chair.'

Ascherson looked at me, then looked again at the dimly lit chamber. He was smiling but I couldn't tell if he was pleased or not. The Stone of Destiny had been taken back to Scotland, and I remember wondering, as we stood in the Abbey, if Ascherson thought the Scots would be delighted to have their Coronation Stone back after seven hundred years. 'It was borne on the back of a polished military Land Rover,' he writes in *Stone Voices*.

The onlookers on the pavement were sparse, and did not applaud. They seemed uncertain about what reaction was expected of them; whatever it was, they refrained from it . . . They found this mournful pageant a bit alienating, and in a way it was meant to be. For the Queen, the Stone still remains her personal property; she had sent her son the Duke of York to escort it to Edinburgh Castle, where it would be deposited 'on loan' between coronations, visible to her subjects for £5.50 a peep.

Ascherson is interested in relics, interested in what they mean, and he's not short on native instinct when it comes to endowing even the most common stones of Scotland with an uncommon mystical power. His book *Stone Voices: The Search for Scotland* is a haphazard work of auto-geography, one man's attempt to map his feelings about his own country, to send his affections first through the prism of history and then through the mincer, to hold up his own experience, his own devotions, to argue with time and battle with his own ambivalence, and above all, in the end, to have a go at telling a story about what it's like to spend your life married to a scenic fiction: Scotland the Brave.

'Normally, people inclined to faith rather than to reason tend to affirm the authenticity of a relic,' he goes on, 'not to deny it.'

In Scotland, it was the opposite. It had become important and alluring to many people to believe, in the teeth of all probability, that the Stone placed in Edinburgh Castle was a fake.

Why was this? And what was the connection between the unexpected coolness displayed by the Edinburgh crowds and these compulsive denials? It was the fact that over time the Stone's importance had become essentially that of the grievance it evoked. What mattered about the Stone was precisely its absence: the fact that it had been carted off by an English king in an act of plunder which was also intended to be a symbolic act of conquest. Not the Stone, but the presence of the Stone at Westminster served to define one of the underlying realities of the English–Scottish relationship, and it continued to do so even after the 1707 Treaty of Union fused the two king-doms into one 'Great Britain'.

A half-hearted nation will want to hold fast to its grievances, and in that sense Scotland has done well. The nation's brick-work is cemented with resentments, from ruined monastery to erupting tower block: blame, fear, bigotry and delusion, their fragments powder the common air – and always the fault is seen to lie elsewhere, with other nations, other lives. Scotland is a place where cultural artefacts and past battles – the Stone of Destiny, Robert Burns, *Braveheart*, Bannockburn – have more impact on people's sense of moral action than politics does. The people have no real commitment to the public sphere, and are not helped towards any such commitment by the dead rhetoric of the young parliament. Yet the problem is not the parliament, it's the people, and the people's drowsy addiction to imagined injury – their belief in a paralysing historical distress – which makes the country assert itself not as a modern nation open to progress on all fronts, but as a delinquent, spoiled, bawling child, tight in its tartan Babygro, addled with punitive needs and false-memory syndrome.

Neal Ascherson has been through many long nights with this heart-scorching beast of a nation, yet, in spite of what he knows, he most often manages to play the part of the good father, coddling Scotland into a state of temporary sleep with the singing of old lullabies. As you would expect, the voice is tuneful and there is often an intelligent, estranged ring to what he writes. His book hovers over the hills and waterways of Scot-land, staring down at the rutted marks of former glaciers and the footprints of deer, but all the while there are questions whispered under his breath: do I belong here? Is Scotland authentic? And most stirring of all: when was Scotland?

The first of his journeys is to mid-Argyll, the place Ascher-son's family come from. At some non-negotiable level of him-self, he feels connected to those Bronze Age monuments, to these standing stones and circular cairns that punctuate the fields. In the manner of Hugh Miller, stonemason and essayist, the grain of Ascherson's thinking is apt to spark off these heathen formations, these 'ritual spires of condensed fear and memory', as he calls them, and a melancholic attitude accompanies the notion that the modern age can do damage to such configurations on the headland. Some of the stones have holes in them, peepholes, you might say, into those spots of time that matter to the author. We find him stopping to look at the stones as he makes his way to the Oban hospital where his mother lies ill. Marion Campbell, the novelist, historian and poet, an old friend of the Aschersons, was lying in a bed near by. 'Later in the ward,' Ascherson writes,

> I was talking to my mother about the Ballymeanoch stones, and the one that fell, and saying that nobody seemed sure when it had fallen. A muffled voice came from behind me. 'Well, I know!' said Marion, suddenly awake. 'It was in 1943, and a Shetland pony was sheltering up against it from the storm when it broke off. Must have terrified the poor beast.' She paused, and then said: 'Nobody would believe now that I remember the stone when it was up, and how I used to look through the hole.' She slept again, and later that afternoon they came to put screens around her bed. They tried to drain her lung, but it was too late. She must have known how ill she was.

There is a sense of belonging in all this, a sense of belonging to a place and a people, a love of nature, and one's own nature, and of what Joyce called the 'ineluctable modality of the visible'. I think Ascherson is less interested in origins, in where stones or people or nations come from, than in what happens to them, in how they are seen or how they see themselves, in what survives, and in the ways that one thing leads to another, which can become a fairly gentle way of describing your own personal history, too.

John Smith, the late Labour leader, believed a devolved Scottish parliament was 'the settled will of the Scottish people'. He died too young and is buried now on the Isle of Iona, in what is thought to have been the graveyard of the Scottish kings. There's a large oval stone lying over his grave, and it seems right, in the Ascherson way, for this man to be linked with the rudiments of some timeless, unknowable Scottish material, and tied to a notion of Providence. In 1845, just before the potato failure, the cholera epidemic reached Argyll; the village of Allt Beithe lay in the hills around Tarbert, and one day it was noticed that none of the villagers had been seen for a while.

'A rescue party set out, and went first to the hamlet of Baldarroch, where they found only the dead lying in their houses.' Climbing on, they reached Allt Beithe. There 'they found everyone dead or dying except for a baby, Archibald Leitch,' a little boy of two. He was carried back to Tarbert and brought up by relatives, and in time grew up to be a boat-builder – and, Ascherson points out, John Smith's great-grandfather.

When people write Scottish history, they do so, if they're at all sure of their market, with a certain degree of patience and hope, and with as good an eye for questions of destiny as for questions of fabulation. Scottish people respond to the idea that there is a Story of Scotland, and writers who can make that story a stormy marriage of internal and external strife – of deep feelings and strong weather, true love and ancient rocks – are answering to a need that is taken for granted in Scotland. Where documentary evidence is lacking, rocks can replace papers; people read their ancestral stories into the scattered stones, and even where there are papers, people have traditionally shown a tendency to make for the rocks if there is no supporting evidence for what is written. In this respect, Ascherson takes his cue from Hugh MacDiarmid – 'There are ruined buildings in the world, but no ruined stones' – and that is a poetic truth with a mighty appeal for Ascherson's generation of Scottish politicians. It appeals to those who are more taken with essence than experience, those who, for good reasons not bad, wish for an overarching grandeur, a galvanising truth, something in the Scottish character that can live up to the landscape. It is part of what Ibsen called 'the saving lie': the presentation of every sort of necessary, ancient virtue, which, taken together, might seem to compensate for the nation's terrible smallness of vision. Scotland is presently – and quite horrendously – failing the test of its own modernity. Much of its life is, by and large, a mean-minded carnival of easy resentments; it is a place of bigotry, paralysis, nullity and boredom; a nation of conservatives who never vote Conservative; a proud country mired up to the fiery eyes in blame and nostalgia. It's not nice to think about, but it's there, this kind of Scotland, and everybody knows it's there.

Ascherson's book is not an uprooting kind of work – it is soft, and soft-hearted, finding perfect cover in the hardness of rocks. It's difficult not to fail when dealing with the failure of Scotland, so much wells up, and one's deepest hopes are such a pitiable hindrance, but the time has surely come for calling a shovel a shovel. In place of 'Heartless Midlothian' and 'Young Mortality' – as yet unwritten accounts of the country's vast self-pity, arrested development and the way out of that – we are served with another 'Portrait of the Artist as a Reluctant Patriot'. Ascherson must know that Scotland does not live by the remnants of grandeur alone, it lives by lies, by lies stronger than truths, by fictions stranger than facts. Behind the great myth of Scottish self-observance, behind the chant of 'Wha's like us?', lies the fact that modern Scots don't ever quite look at themselves, and know nothing of what they are like. Wha's like us? The answer is nobody – especially not ourselves.

Ascherson's 'Search for Scotland' has trouble with the notion of 'us', but it has just as much trouble with notions of trouble. He draws his cutlass halfway, only to put it back again, to fix his eyes on the middle distance and ruminate on the efficiency of old songs, his hands sweating as they rest on the sheath that guards his blade. He has a lot to say about his forebears, but what might his own great-grandchildren contemplate when they look back to the Scotland of his day? 'Webs of mutual support', he says, the 'apparently indelible colouring of Scottish society'. He goes on:

Scotland has survived and still exists as a chain of small collective loyalties: 'Society People' singing in the hills or clansmen enlisting with their chieftain, colonists on the Vistula or private partnerships in Bengal, crofting townships in Assynt or mining villages in Fife.

When Scotland's last deep coal mine at Longannet flooded and closed down for ever in March 2002, a man called George came home from the pit to find his telephone ringing. 'Dinnae worry, big man, we'll see you're no stuck for work.' This is a nation at home in hard, stony times. It will find its own way in the world.

This is a cold, hard jet of pure nonsense. I'm happy for the chieftains, and happy for George, but Ascherson has witnessed the slow altering of several European societies, and witnessed too much of Scotland, overall, to allow such fetid and unimaginative resignation to stand at the end of his inquiry. I begin to worry that the great explicator of velvet revolutions has dithered too long in the purple heather, and has forgotten to ask what life is actually like over in Greenock, Buckie, Cumnock and Cowdenbeath. A chain of collective loyalties? A nation at home? You must be joking.

A people so addicted to the notion of belonging must surely live in fear of strangers, and, even more so, in fear of the stranger in themselves. In his better pages, Ascherson knows this, and he sometimes puts his powers of clarity to the task of expressing it. One of the first pieces of business in the new Scottish parliament was to be the repealing of Clause 2a, the one about 'promoting' homosexuality in schools and public libraries. An unholy alliance was forged in Scotland to oppose this removal, this 'routine detail of political hygiene'. With the backing of the brain-numbing *Daily Record*, the nation's tabloid newspaper, Cardinal Winning of the Catholic Church joined forces with the Presbyterians and was soon enjoying the financial backing of Brian Souter, a bus-line millionaire and born-again Christian, to 'Keep the Clause'. Souter used his millions to petition every home in Scotland. Of the people daft enough to respond to the campaign, six people out of seven voted to keep the clause and attacks on homosexuals increased immediately. Though the parliament held its nerve and repealed the clause, it put in a few sentences about heterosexuality and family life being the best thing since sliced bread.

Ascherson mentions Scotland's 'grim and persisting record of religious intolerance and discrimination'. He was able to say this without having the benefit of the Scottish Executive's most recent survey, which led to a leader in the *Guardian* this month declaring that the Scots were possibly the most racist group in Europe.

'There was a dogged public assumption that racial prejudice was an English problem to which the Scots – for reasons of social history, for reasons of superior native intelligence – were immune . . .'

But this was a prettified version of history. The Lithuanians coming to Scotland had at first run into a wall of hatred from the Scottish working class who perceived them, not entirely without reason, as cheap foreign labour brought in to collapse miners' wages. The Italian community was utterly unprepared for the ferocious anti-Italian riots which flamed through Scottish towns and cities in July 1940, when Fascist Italy joined the war on Hitler's side. But the central flaw in this self-congratulatory myth, the grand denial of the blatantly obvious, was the matter of the Irish.

With some verve, and some nerve, Ascherson tells a story of his own prejudice, of how he thought his young sister might have caught impetigo swinging on the gates of a Catholic school. But there are no jokes in Ascherson's book. 'Here was I,' he writes, 'a much-travelled journalist with left-wing opinions and a Cambridge history degree. And, nevertheless, for almost all my life I had never questioned that if you touched a railing used by small boys of a particular religion you would probably acquire a disfiguring disease.' He mentions other disfigurements along the way – murdered asylum seekers, lacerated Celtic fans, and land abuse, in one form or another – making his sonorous, ballad-singing conclusions about the strain of commonality in the Scottish seem all the more absurd.

You come to wonder why Ascherson won't attempt to understand Scotland's victimology. Why doesn't he relate the sociopathic elements in that small country to what he knows about the hungers of small nations elsewhere in Europe? These are matters most of us aren't equipped to explain. His book sets up an expectation of something new, and he is sometimes good at describing ailments, but when the call for new ideas and interpretations looms, he escapes into powerless long passages about deforestation, the Picts and the Gaels, seventeenth-century Scots in Poland, or the Covenanters, leading you to feel that Scotland's best journalist is becoming one of those writers whose main aim is to ensure polemic never gets in the way of positive thinking. That kind of thing is the opposite of Ascherson at his best, a fact you're reminded of when you come to passages like the following:

> The Scottish trauma is to do with self-doubt (sometimes masked in unreal self-assertion), with sterile speculations about national identity and – as I guess – with suspicions of 'otherness' which so often poison relationships between Scottish neighbours. But above all, the trauma shows itself in a chronic mistrust of the public dimension. The invitation to 'participate', especially to offer critical comment in public, touches a nerve of anxiety. This derives partly from the instinct that to disagree with another person before witnesses is to open a serious personal confrontation; the English or American assumption that 'free, open discussion' is non-lethal and even healthy is not widespread in Scotland ...
>
> The deep geological fault running underneath national self-confidence is still there ... and from time to time it makes itself felt. When it does, the confident few who lead political change feel misunderstood and betrayed. In Bertold Brecht's words about the leaders of the former East Germany, they feel tempted to dissolve this people and appoint another one.

Free-falling anxiety about Scottishness has a tendency, among Scots, not only to turn into hatred of others, but into hating bad news about the country itself, and seeing critics as traitors. There are few European nations in which intellectuals are so willing to serve as soft-pedalling merchants of 'national character', handmaidens to the tourist industry: broadcasters, academics, lawyers, some of the poets too, sell pride and tears, spiritual laxity and pawky good humour in place of inquiry.

I recently went to New York to take part in something called Distilled: Scotland Live in New York, a business and tourist junket masquerading as an arts festival, the highlight of which was a march by five thousand kilted bagpipers up Fifth Avenue. 'We want to show our solidarity with New Yorkers in their time of terrible suffering,' said the Lord Provost of Edinburgh, 'and remind you that Scotland is an excellent place to visit and invest in.' Whisky poured from the bar, commercial blether mixed with the unruly sentiment of the expatriate, and deals were made, palms were greased. I spoke to a man who deals in computer jobs in the Clyde valley. 'We're all New Yorkers now!' he shouted over his tumbler of Dewar's.

Alyth McCormack, an amazing singer of Gaelic music, got up on stage to sing a song about the Highland Clearances. The song is grave and bleak and full of historical complications and human wrongs, but you couldn't hear the woman and the song she sang. The business crowd and the cultural delegates of Scotland and New York were shouting at one another, their red faces all compliant, their glasses full, and the volume increased, the laughter bellowed out, until it became quite a thunder of ill consideration, and the sound of McCormack's voice just disappeared, and the business of land clearance or human loss was nowhere present in these people's minds. Meanwhile, over by the windows, in the tartan glory of 23rd Street, other people stood and they stared out at the missing towers, and some of them pointed to the view of the Statue of Liberty and the view of Ellis Island. As I made for the exit, I wondered if any of those at the windows were prompted by the drowned-out music to look for the ghosts of their ancestors standing on the quay.

'This race,' E. B. White wrote in his 1946 essay on New York, 'between the destroying planes and the struggling Parliament of Man: it sticks in all our heads.' Yes it does. And that day – Tartan Day in America – it mingled for me with thoughts of my own about what Scotland wanted to be in the world. Growing up in what the novelist John Galt wonderfully called The West – the West Coast of Scotland – we used to look from the beach and we'd feel happy we were on America's side and safe in the bowl of the Ayrshire hills. Our Scottish Enlightenment had fed into their Constitution, via Francis Hutcheson and Thomas Jefferson, and the music playing on the local radio – West Sound – was all country music about personal freedom and broken trust and breaking hearts.

In *Stone Voices*, Ascherson tells of his own visit to America the year before. 'Tartan Day is about liberty,' said the right-wing Republican Senator Trent Lott on that occasion, borrowing the Braveheartish banter that now stands for modern Scotland in Washington and Hollywood. Lott mentioned the Scottish clansmen who 'were our clansmen, our brothers', as if American kinship were the only kind that counts, the only context in which a small and ancient country might understand its own worth. The Scottish ministers (and Sean Connery) mugged for the camera, shouting 'Freedom!'

Scotland should have outgrown its own pantomime by now. 'Ending the war in Ulster,' Tom Nairn wrote in *After Britain*, 'entailed a fundamental rearticulation of the United Kingdom's unitarist tradition, founded on a post-Thatcher recognition that – in the language of the "Downing Street Declaration" – Britain no longer retained "a selfish strategic interest" in retaining control over any part of Ireland.' The constitutional plates have moved under Scotland, too – the nation itself has outgrown its own people – and Britain is not what is was. Some hatreds will tend to outlive their original occasions, yet traditional Scottish resentments about 'foreignness' must surely perish if the country is properly to awake in Europe.

Ascherson's most invigorating chapter is about the Scottish Empire – the subject of so much Nationalist bad faith over the years – and there can be no argument, now that the old style is gone, about how well Scotland did from the Union. All considered, it did better than England. There is, as Nairn puts it, a 'tantalising sense of redemption which always informs nostalgia', but the Scottish people cannot afford to get stuck there any longer, and Scotland must go on now to establish its role in bringing about a new United Kingdom within a new Europe. In the manner of Stephen Dedalus, we might do better to see Scotland's conscience as 'uncreated'; for while we must admit that Ascherson's stones are interesting, they are not as interesting as people. Nationalism in Scotland is a place where good men and women busy themselves shaking the dead hand of the past, but the naming of a tradition is not the same as the forging of a nation, and modern Scotland, now more than ever, needs a new way of thinking, a new kind of relation to the old, a way to live, a way to make itself better than the badness that's been and the badness to come. The question of what the past amounted to can lie about the grass.

The American Dream of Lee Harvey Oswald

DECEMBER 1995

When Gary Gilmore faced his executioners one cold morning in 1977, there was a serious, anxious, bearded reporter-type standing only a few feet away. Before the hood was placed over Gilmore's head, the man walked over to the chair, and took both of the killer's hands into his own. 'I don't know why I'm here,' he said. Gilmore looked up and replied sweetly: 'You're going to help me escape.'

The man's name was Lawrence Schiller. And he did help Gilmore escape: he took him to the world, over the tops of the Mormon hills and the mobile homes of Utah, he flew with the story of Gary Gilmore. He produced the television film, sold the interviews, oversaw pictures, advised on chat shows and specials, became the reporters' reporter, the producers' producer, and he later brought in Norman Mailer to write the book. He showed himself to be the king deal-maker and media broker, the chief documenter, of grand-scale American tragedy. Wherever there has been sensational news in America over the last thirty years, there you will invariably find Lawrence Schiller.

Schiller has helped all manner of American figures escape in this way, through the portals of recorded history, into legend. Marilyn Monroe, during the filming of a bathing scene in her last, unfinished film *Something's Got to Give*, suddenly disrobed on the set, at the studios of Twentieth-Century Fox. Just as she did so, there appeared a young man with a camera. On assignment for *Life* (expecting to take some pretty pictures of the actress in performance) his eyes nearly popped out of his head. Marilyn, he was alert enough to know, had not been photographed naked since the late 1940s, when she accepted fifty

dollars to pose nude for a calendar. Schiller's exclusive photographs were syndicated around the world. And Norman
Mailer later wrote the book.

When O. J. Simpson wanted to tell the world of his innocence, and the globe's media scratched at the door, there was
only one man with the skill to breeze into his cell. Lawrence
Schiller came in with his beard, his anxiety and his notepad,
and he helped Simpson write a book called *I Want to Tell You*, a
book that had nothing to do with Norman Mailer, but which
sold uncontrollably during the Simpson trial. Schiller has had
one of the strangest – and most strangely necessary – jobs in
America. He understood the power of syndication in a way no
one else did; he felt the need for made-for-TV movies while
others still haggled over cinema releases and back catalogues;
he saw the point of cable; he knows how to cut up a story, how
to apportion it, and how to pin down exclusivity. And he has,
from time to time, introduced himself as a new sort of figure in
the world of books. The Producer.

So it was with a certain inevitability, as the KGB archives
were opened up to the West in 1992, that Lawrence Schiller
would find himself in Moscow. The new documents would bear
on many things, but Schiller, as usual anything but slow on the
uptake, knew they might tell us something we needed to know
about Lee Harvey Oswald, perhaps the most mysterious and
most tragic American figure in the age of Schiller. If the gods of
reason were attentive, it would make sense for him to be reunit-
ed with his sparring partner and sometime mate, Norman
Mailer. Surely, if he was to help Lee Harvey Oswald to 'escape',
there was only one writer in America who could reliably meet
the task.

But there were problems to be overcome. Schiller and Mailer
– odd partners in the worlds of show and tell – had not always
got on. 'When it comes to lying,' Mailer warbled to gossip
columnist Liz Smith of the New York *Daily News* in the mid-
1980s, 'Larry Schiller makes Baron von Munchausen look like
George Washington.' Yet at the beginning of this new book

there is an appreciation: 'To Larry Schiller, my skilled and wily colleague in interview and investigation, for the six months we laboured side by side in Minsk and Moscow, and then again in Dallas, feeling as close as family (and occasionally as contentious).'

In a way, Norman Mailer has been staring for most of his life into the face of Lee Harvey Oswald. Mailer's characters have always been parts of himself, and part and parcel of the America of his time. If Marilyn Monroe was his dream lover – 'every man's love affair with America' – and Ernest Hemingway his idea of a self-like literary champ, it might also be said that his astronauts, his boxers, his single-minded karmic killers, his existential heroes, Greenwich Village idiots, his political ogres and saints, his high-minded Trillings, turncoat Podhoretzes, his self-authenticating graffiti artists, and his cursed, totalitarian generals, were also travellers in Mailer's inner cosmos.

It could be said to be natural, Mailer's interest in Lee Harvey Oswald. 'Natural' in the sense that he has always, as a writer, been interested in people who broke rules and took chances, who lived urgently and died violently. He has also set himself the task of shadowing those who, like himself, were greedy for action, and who forged their celebrity in the heat of extreme activity. But his relation to Oswald is even more proximate than that. Oswald may have killed the president, and Mailer, much more than any writer of his generation, has always tended to see himself as an American president manqué. In 1959, in his *Advertisements for Myself*, he wrote that 'like many another vain, empty, and bullying body of our time, I have been running for President these last ten years in the privacy of my mind, and it occurs to me that I am less close now than when I began'.

In the summer of 1960, the year after he wrote that, he visited John F. Kennedy at home in Hyannisport. He was there on behalf of *Esquire* magazine, to interview the young Catholic who sought the Democratic nomination, and Kennedy took him very seriously. In fact, he had mugged up before meeting the novelist. He knew that Mailer was hurt over the critical mauling he'd received for *The Deer Park*, and so, on meeting him, Kennedy named that novel as his favourite book of Mailer's. The *Esquire* piece came out, very much in favour of Kennedy, and was called 'Superman comes to the Supermart'. *Esquire*, at that time, was not without influence, especially among the young, especially among the young of New York. When Kennedy scraped home in that state, and so won the nomination, Mailer claimed that he was the cause of the victory, and later claimed to have inadvertently won him the presidency.

So you might well say that Mailer had a bit of a vested interest in President Kennedy, and another sort of vested interest in the mind of an outsider like Oswald. He has the good novelist's sense of correspondence, the inventor's joy at the magic of possibility, and he looks into Oswald's eyes with the thrill of one who imagines those eyes to have fixed on his one-time subject, JFK – very probably through the telescopic sights of a bolt-action Mannlicher-Carcano. *Oswald's Tale* is many things, but it is not another framing of the question 'Who Shot Kennedy?' Mailer wants to know what sort of person Oswald was:

> Before we understand a murderer – if he is one – we must first discover his motive. But to find the motive, we do well to encounter the man. In Oswald's case, that could be no simple task. How many young men are as timid and bold as Lee Harvey Oswald? . . . to understand a person is to comprehend his reasons for action. The conceit arose that one understood Oswald.

The understanding of Oswald begins in Moscow, and it is a good place to start. He travelled there in 1959 on an Intourist visa, and almost immediately tried to cut himself free of America. He wanted to relinquish his American citizenship, but the Consul refused him, and he spent his first weeks there in a state of utter frustration. He tried, a little half-heartedly, to commit suicide in his bathroom at the Berlin Hotel, but was saved by

Rimma, the first of several uncertain Russian girlfriends. The authorities eventually decided he could stay, but he remained under KGB surveillance and was moved to Minsk, to work in a radio factory.

Minsk in the late 1950s looked quite new: its stately apartment buildings of yellow stone, its wide avenues, were all built on top of the earlier Minsk, which had been destroyed by the Germans twice – once when they came in, and again when they retreated back to Poland three years later. Mailer draws up an intimate picture of family life: there are a great many women – women keen on men who were cultured and kind and not cheap – messing around in shared kitchens, trying to keep things clean, making things to eat, worrying over illness and injury.

Marina Prusakova worked in a pharmacy. She had come from Leningrad, and had a few boyfriends, some of whom remember her with affection, some of whom say she was a good-time girl. What is clear about Marina – even before she met Oswald – is that she was no good at housework or cooking. She lived with her aunt and uncle, and they would sometimes despair over her messiness, her lateness and her lack of direction. On 17 March 1961 Marina went to a trade-union dance with her friends from the Medical Institute. She wore a red dress and white slippers. She was asked to dance by an American – at first, she thought he might come from one of the Baltic countries – who called himself Alik. She liked him; he was very polite, sweet and reserved. He was well dressed. She took him to meet her aunt, who liked men to be polite; and soon enough Marina and Alik were married. At the wedding they all sang 'Chattanooga Choo-choo'.

Mailer recognises the virtue in attempting to understand Oswald through his marriage. He is not the first to have done so: he acknowledges and borrows from Priscilla Johnson McMillan's *Marina and Lee*, though he is able to add to that mostly American account thanks to the KGB transcripts. The newly married couple's apartment was bugged, and their early

married life, their frequent strife and their makings-up are doc-
umented here. Mailer and Schiller interviewed everyone they
could find who knew them. Oswald was a lazy worker, and was
much resented at the radio factory, not only for putting his feet
up on the desk, but for the special treatment he received as a
foreigner. He hated the job, but he didn't seem to notice that his
apartment was bigger than anyone else's.

The surveillance reports on Oswald make poor reading. If he
was an American agent (as many suspect), we can only assume
from these reports that he was no more effective in this capacity than he was as a builder of radios. He walked around, looked
into shops, picked up a book, failed to buy it, walked back
home. Oswald was a dissipater; he was not a great student in
Russia, an ideologue or a planner. He was a ditherer; he wasn't
at all sure who he was, or what he wanted to do. Furthermore,
he was dyslexic. 'His orthography is so bad at times,' Mailer
points out, 'that the man is not revealed but concealed – in the
worst of his letters he seems stupid and illiterate.' But Mailer
argues that this should not be allowed to hide something else
about him: 'Considering that he was still in his very early twenties, it is . . . not inaccurate to speak of him as a young intellectual.' Mailer is keen, keener than any writer has been before, to
reveal the nuances of Oswald's character, and the reach of his
mind. He serves notice on the common way of seeing Oswald –
as an incompetent, shifty, stupid and impotent rat – and
encourages us to think of him not only as having intelligence,
but as having other qualities that might cause him to be liked
here and there, and to be loved, as he sometimes was.

The stuff gained by Mailer and Schiller in their Russian
interviews is more interesting than the stuff emerging from the
lifeless files of the KGB. The absence of revelations in the KGB
documents is more than made up for by Mailer's imaginative
use of the new detail they contain. He uses it to fill out
Oswald's time in Minsk, to give word of his troubles, and the
changing shape of his mind. Cold War Berlin seemed dank and
sinister in Mailer's novel *Harlot's Ghost*; the Minsk of *Oswald's*

Tale seems bright and tells us quite a bit. The Cold War antics are vaguely comic. The interviews with older Russians bleed lavishly into the story: we feel we know Oswald better, and are newly acquainted with some possible motivations, by seeing the world he lived in during those confused years. It gives us clues, and deep background, to the hows and whys of Oswald's state of mind as he plunges forward – or backwards – to his American end.

Russia was his bid for the solvent, invisible life. When Russia failed him, something seems to have died in him; something new was born. He eventually wrote to the American embassy, looking to have his passport back. It took many agonies, much red tape, but eventually it was returned. He'd fought the bureaucracies of America and Russia in turn, and he'd beaten them, but he'd left himself with no open roads after all that. He took a reluctant Marina and child back to Texas, with a head full of scrap, and perhaps some ideas we can't yet speak of. Mailer ends the Russian part of his book – the firmer and slower-paced part – having provided a portrait of a man in crisis, a man unsure of his next big move. But let us leave Lee Harvey Oswald, for the time being, crossing the ocean, and scribbling some lines on the Holland–America Line notepaper: 'I wonder what would happen if someone would stand up and say he was utterly opposed not only to the government, but to the people, to the entire land and complete foundation of society.' You might say that shards of motivation were coming together, to make a window of opportunity.

On 4 May 1901, at about eight o'clock in the evening, the building which stood at 411 Elm Street in Dallas was struck by lightning. It burned all night, and the Southern Rock Island Plow Company, which owned the property, was forced to abandon it. The owners built a new seven-storey building on the same site, of modern design, with arched windows on the sixth floor. In 1963, the building was being leased by the Texas School Book Depository Company, a private textbook-brokerage firm.

I walked along in the too-hot afternoon, in the summer of 1995, and kept thinking how inordinately white the pavements were. The streets around Dealey Plaza looked like they'd only recently been scrubbed. The former Book Depository stood there like a warning, like a symbol of something not too bright or happy-making. It was one of those buildings that one knew something about; it sat in the memory, though I, for one, had never been to Dallas before. But I knew this building very well. It looked like it hadn't changed all since 1901, though many things had changed round about it. It stood up, blank and indifferent, in the hot afternoon, and I thought of Bates's hill-top house in *Psycho*.

The building is owned now by Dallas County; they use it as an administration building. It is full of offices and workspaces, except on the sixth floor, which is kept for something special. The whole floor is kept for what is called, by those who keep it, 'the memory of a nation'. It is known, by those who don't keep it, as Oswaldworld. But the places that make up Oswaldworld are more than one: they include the houses he rented in Dallas, the streets along which he supposedly made his escape, the place where he shot Tippett, the police officer, and the area of the cinema where he was arrested. It also encompasses the police garage where Oswald was shot; the post office across the road where Jack Ruby mailed his postal order minutes before; the spot where Ruby's Carousel Club stood. It is a whole bunch of bricks and sticks and marks on the ground, but it is even more than that. It is also a place in the mind – perhaps a place in the minds of everyone in America. Oswaldworld is the place where national chaos is; it's the place where good presidents get shot by nobodies. It's also the place where certainties break down, or fail to hold, and where absurdity and unknowable violence are unleashed from the margins. In the mind of just about everyone alive in America – and in places beyond America – there is a little corner marked Oswaldworld. There in Dallas, I could see it plainly in front of me. It had been appropriately housed.

Just a few streets over from the old Book Depository building there is a place called the Conspiracy Museum. The guys working there are weird: experts in who-did-what-to-whom-and-why in 1963; twentysomethings with an amateur grasp of ballistics; muggers-up on the constituent parts of the CIA, the internal workings of the FBI, the gripes of the Mafia; young men with strong views on the presence of shadows on the grassy knoll. They charge seven dollars for the low-down on who really shot Kennedy. A guy with a baseball cap and a moustache is speaking to tourists: he edits a fanzine for 'dudes obsessed with the case'. I hear him speaking to a bunch of tourists from Pennsylvania, emitting a sort of mantra – an Oliver Stone-like loop of verbal fact and fiction – that seeks to pound his guests out of their confusion. He even has theories about the people who run the Book Depository museum, the thing on the sixth floor, round the corner. 'They don't know what they're doing,' he says. 'It's all a whitewash. The people over there aren't even qualified to speak of this thing.'

There are other guys, perhaps related, who sell conspiracy mags and buttons on the grassy knoll. They sell maps and plans, too, and speak like born-again Christians. They have a way of saying the word 'truth' that makes you feel like a liar, or a believer in lies. They walk up and down in shorts: they seem to like being there, so close to something big, and you're almost surprised to see them stowing away dollar bills. They look up at the windows of the former Book Depository, counting up to the corner window of the sixth floor, and they look at you quizzically, saying, 'No . . . no, it couldn't have been.' As one of them says this, I notice there are tracks on his arms.

When you come out of the lift at the sixth floor you're immediately confronted by a giant photograph of what the floor was like on 22 November 1963. The roof beams are the same as the ones you see above your head, but the place in the photograph is not all corporate and red, as the space is now – it looks grimy, and is covered with boxes of books. I hear a voice beside me say: 'He was a real people-person.' There is a display on the wall of things-from-1963: a poster for *Psycho*, a programme for a new musical starring Richard Burton and Julie Andrews called *Camelot*, an advertisement for *Who's Afraid of Virginia Woolf?* There is a row of books from the time: Barbara Tuchman's *The Guns of August*; Betty Friedan's *The Feminine Mystique*; *The Rise and Fall of the Third Reich* by William Shirer. On every side you can hear Kennedy's voice: 'Let the word go forth . . . that the torch has been passed to a new generation of Americans.' It is repeated over and over.

There are panels of pictures, with text, all around. This must be what is meant by a multimedia presentation, for there are videos going, radios blaring, and looped bits of speeches and snatches of the Inaugural Address. As I walk past, I catch a spread from *Life* about racial turbulence in Birmingham, Alabama. The headline says: 'They Fight a Fire that Won't Go Out'. I take a few steps, and hear JFK's voice grow louder, drowning out a previous speech of his: 'I look forward to an America that will not be afraid of grace and beauty.'

As you make your way from panel to panel, you notice a sense of dread in yourself. Like station stops on a terrible journey (dare I say it, like Stations of the Cross), each of these displays, with their separate titles – 'The Kennedy White House', 'Turmoil at Home', 'The Trip to Texas', 'Reception in Dallas' – increases that dread. I looked at pictures of them arriving in Dallas, moving through the streets; I saw Jackie in her famous outfit, waving to people, the children smiling back. The Texas Book Depository Building emerges in the corner of the next screen; the cars move slowly, you can hear the voices of radio announcers and snatches of Kennedy's speech wafting from the front of the room, from the earlier part of the exhibition. You know that when you turn the next corner, and see the next panel, it will show the assassination. As you turn the corner, you can already hear the shots, you can hear Walter Cronkite announce the death of the president at a panel some way in front of that, and distantly, down the far end of the sixth floor, you can hear the 'Funeral March' as recorded in Washington.

As I turn, I see everything is dark. There are flickering pictures on a TV screen of the President's Lincoln turning into Elm Street, and running past the front of the building I'm standing in myself. I see him lurch in his seat, and feel it might all be happening now, outside, on this sunny day.

This clamour of memorial sounds, this cross-current of hard images and bits of life, this blend of recorded seconds in the unfolding of a prime historical moment – they are all part of what they call the 'Memory of a Nation'. And being a nation that knows how to harness and punish verisimilitude, and tease out bitter emotion, this exhibition is astonishingly unlike anything of its kind I've ever seen. There is, in fact, nothing of its kind. It is a pure exercise in the heightening of reality, in the Disneyfying of a cataclysmic moment in real life, a moment full of mystery and importance but also full of banality and pointlessness and stupidity. The sixth floor offers visitors the thrill of presidential assassination, the thrill of communal mourning, the thrill of whodunnit, the thrill of revenge, the thrill of national pride, the thrill of having been there, and the gloom of being none the wiser. As I stood by the corner window of the sixth floor, beside the sniper's nest, looking through the window, down through the trees, I almost expected a motorcade to appear beneath the leaves. You can't help but feel you are momentarily at the centre of another sort of universe. I stood at the window alone. It was like a movie set, smaller than I'd thought, and maybe like a model. It must all have looked so possible from here, so terribly likely. It was hard to think of it. On 22 November 1963, Lee Harvey Oswald crouched here, lifted his rifle, peered through a telescopic sight stamped 'Hollywood' – a detail seldom referred to – and shot the president. Everybody in the world would know where they were.

The Killing of James Bulger

MARCH 1993

The abduction and murder of James Bulger, a two-year-old boy from Liverpool, has caused unprecedented grief and anger. Hours before the two ten-year-old boys accused of the crime arrived at South Sefton Magistrates Court, a large, baying crowd had formed outside. As a pair of blue vans drew up, the crowd surged forward, bawling and screaming. A number of men tried to reach the vehicles, to get at the youths inside, and scuffles spilled onto the road. Some leapt over crash barriers and burst through police cordons, lobbing rocks and banging on the sides of the vans. Many in the crowd – sick with con-demnation – howled and spat and wept.

Home Secretary Kenneth Clarke has promised measures to deal with 'nasty, persistent juvenile little offenders'. Those two little offenders – if they were the offenders, the childish child-murderers from Walton – were caught on camera twice. First, on the security camera at the shopping precinct in Bootle where they lifted James, and again by the camera of a security firm on Breeze Hill, as they dragged James past – the child clearly in some distress.

Watching those boys on camera brought into my head a flurry of pictures from my own boyhood. At that age, we were brimming with nastiness. I grew up on a scheme in the last of Scotland's new-town developments. There were lots of chil-dren, lots of dogs and lots of building sites. Torture among our kind was fairly commonplace. I remember two furious old teachers driving me and my six-year-old girlfriend Heather Watt home early one morning. In recent weeks we had been walking the mile to school in the company of a boy, smaller and younger than ourselves, a fragile boy with ginger hair called

David. I think we thought of him as 'our boy'. We bossed him. Occasionally, when he didn't walk straight or carry our bags or speak when we wanted him to, we'd slap him or hit his hands with a ruler. We had to pass through fields to get to school, with diggers going and 'workies' taking little notice of us, though from time to time they'd bring over empty lemonade bottles which we could exchange for money or sweets at the chip shop. We must have looked innocent enough, holding hands, Heather and I, walking the younger boy to school.

Over time, we started to hit the boy hard. Our way to the school was dotted with new trees, freshly planted and bound to supporting stalks with rubber belts. We got into the habit of removing belts every day: we began to punish David with them whenever we thought he'd 'been bad'. Just a few hits at first on top of his shorts, not so's you'd notice. It got worse, though, and on the last morning, when we were caught by the two old lady teachers, we were beating his bare legs with the coiled-up straps. Though we'd set out on time that morning we were late, having spent the best part of half an hour on top of an out-of-the-way railway bridge practically skinning the screaming boy's legs.

That incident caused a scandal in our square. My mother was employed as a cleaner in another local primary school with David's mother and – although I remember crying and being confused and not quite knowing what we'd done wrong – I could see that we'd caused a lot of embarrassment. Up until the age of ten, I'd both taken part in and witnessed many such incidents. Some of my brothers had reputations for being a bit wild; other boys said they'd 'do anything'. I watched them do any number of crazy things to other kids around the squares, and I watched the other kids do some brutal things in return. One time, the whole family had to sit in front of a children's panel. That's what happens in Scotland if a child under sixteen commits an offence: the social work department calls in the whole family in an effort to assess what the real problem is and decide whether the child should be in care – which in my

brother's case would have meant a residential List 'D' school. In
the event that didn't happen, but it took a long time for the
community – especially our teachers – to forget what he did.
With a friend, he'd burnt down a wing of our local Catholic
secondary school.

It's not that any of us were evil; even the more bookish and
shy among us were given to a bit of destructive boredom and
stupid imagining. Now and then it got out of hand. The boys I
hung around with in my pre-teen years were always losing the
head. During the good weather, the light nights, what started
off as a game of rounders or crazy golf would end up as a game
of clubbing the neighbour's cat to death. A night of camping on
the playing fields could usually be turned into an opportunity
for the wrecking of vegetable gardens, or the killing of frogs and
people's pet rabbits. Mindless stuff. Yet now and again people
would get into things that you sensed were about to go over the
edge, or were already over it. My memory tells me that that
point was much more difficult to judge than I'd now like to
think.

My friend Moggie began taking music lessons at the house of
a woman who lived in the next square. She started going out
when she was supposed to be teaching him, leaving him to
baby-sit her child, who was not yet a year old. Moggie would
have been about seven or eight. One day I was in with him,
bashing uselessly on her old piano, when he shouted me to the
front of the living room.

'I'm biting the baby,' he said. 'D'you want to?'

The baby was lying on a white towelling nappy and Moggie
was bent over her, biting her arms and then her legs and then
the cheeks of her face. He said he did it all the time and that the
baby liked it. He said it was like tickling. I didn't want to do it
but said I'd stay and watch. Another game he played was to put
on a record, hoist the baby onto her legs and shake her in time
to the music. She obviously wasn't walking yet, but he would
jostle her and jam her legs on the carpet. Her head would jerk
about and she would cry. Some time later, the bite marks were

discovered and Moggie was barred from the house, although everyone – including the baby's parents – said that she had been bitten by the dog. I got to stay, since the woman reckoned I was sensible. Another boy who came to that house used to swallow handfuls of the woman's pills (she always had a great variety lying around, so much so that her daughter was eventually rushed to hospital after eating a load). Moggie joined the navy and the pill-swallower was at the edge of a mob of boys who killed someone at a local Cashline ten years later. In the years that I hung around it, that house (and there were many others like it) had been the site of a large number of life-threatening games, solvent-abuses and youthful experiments gone wrong.

Something happened when we all got together, even when we were that young. We were competitive, deluded and full of our own small powers. And, of course, we spoke our own language. We even had our own way of walking – which wasn't unlike that of the two boys on the video – dragging our feet, hands in our pockets, heads always lolling towards the shoulder. That culpable tilt gave the full measure of our arrogant, untelling ways. As only dependants can be, we were full of our own independence. The approval that really mattered was that of the wee Moggies and Bennas and Caesars we ran around with. There were times when I'm sure we could've led each other into just about anything.

Just William-type adventures – earning pocket money or looking for fun – would more often than not end in nastiness or threats to each other or danger to other people, especially to girls our own age and younger boys. There was badness in it, a form of delinquency that most of us left behind. The girls with whom I read books and coloured-in, with whom I regularly played offices, were the victims of verbal taunting, harassment and gang violence when I ran around with boys. We all carried sticks and were all of us baby arsonists who could never get enough matches. We stole them from our houses, stole money out of our mothers' purses with which to buy them and begged them from construction workers. I can remember pleading

with my mother to buy me a Little Big Man action doll from
Woolworth's and then burning it in a field with my pals. Most
of our games, when I think of it, were predicated on someone
else's humiliation or eventual pain. It made us feel strong and
untouchable.

If all of this sounds uncommonly horrific, then I can only
say that it did not seem so then; it was the main way that most
of the boys I knew used up their spare time. There was no
steady regression towards the juvenile barbarism famously
characterised in *Lord of the Flies*. We lived two lives at once:
while most of the stuff detailed above went on, we all made our
first communions, sang in the school choir, did our homework,
became altar boys and some went to matches or played brilliantly at football. We didn't stop to think, nor did our parents,
that something dire might result from the darker of our extra-
curricular activities. Except when that murky side took over,
and your bad-bastardness became obvious to everyone.

Bullies who had no aptitude for classwork – who always got
'easily distracted' scribbled in red ink on report cards that never
made it home – had unbelievable concentration when it came
to torturing minors in the playground, or on the way home. For
many of the pupils bullying was a serious game. It involved
strategies, points scored for and against, and not a little detailed
planning. It was scary, competitive and brought out the very
worst in those who had anything to do with it. Kids who were
targeted over a long period we thought deviant in some way, by
which I mean that they were in some way out of it – maybe serious, bright, quiet, keeping themselves to themselves. When I
was nine, there was a particular boy who lived two squares up.
For years I'd listened to boys telling of how they'd love to do
him in. I sort of liked him but, even so, I joined in the chase
when we pursued him in and out of the scheme and across
fields. This stood high in our repertoire of time-fillers. 'Where's
Broon?' – the boy's name was Alan Brown – took its place in a
list of nasty games that included snipes (skinning each other's
knuckles with cards after each lost game), kiss, cuddle and

torture (with girls), blue murder (the same, but sorer) and that kind of thing. If anyone came to the door when these games had gone too far, our mothers and fathers went ape. Belted and sent to bed, many of us would get up after dark and stare out the window, over the square, into each other's bedrooms. We grinned and flashed our torches, trying to pass messages. The message, I remember, was always quite clear: it meant see you tomorrow.

Even the youths who came from happy homes enjoyed the childish ritual of running away. When parents, sick with anxiety, came to the door or to school looking for their children, we'd never let on. We'd help eleven-year-old absconders get together the bus fare to a bigger place, all of us filling a bag with stolen tins and chipping in coppers for some hero's running-away fund. Of course, they'd always be caught and brought back, but not before we'd enjoyed the parental worry and the police presence in the classroom while the drama lasted. We all took and assigned roles in cruel little dramas of our own devising. Our talk would be full of new and interesting ways to worry or harass our parents, especially our fathers, who we all hated. Stealing his fags or drink brought a great, often awesome, feeling of quid pro quo.

I found many girls to be the same in that respect: I had a twelve-year-old table-tennis friend Alison, who told us she'd been crushing old light bulbs in a bowl and sprinkling them into her father's porridge. We thought that was great. Some of us knew how to stop it, though, while others just kept it up. A couple of my boyhood friends assiduously built bridges between their mindless, childish venom – their bad-boyish misdemeanours – and adult crime. Not many, but some.

Around the time of our cruelty to the boy David, the local news was full of the disappearance of a three-year-old boy called Sandy Davidson who'd last been seen playing on one of the town's many open construction sites. Guesses were that he'd either fallen into a pipe trench and been covered, or that he'd been abducted. He was never found. We thought about him, in class we prayed for him, and when we weren't out looking for something to get into, we tried to figure out what had happened to him.

Our mothers' warnings to stay clear of the dumps taught us that Sandy's fate could easily have been our own. And in silent, instinctive ways I'm sure we understood something of Sandy's other possible end, the one that wasn't an accident. We knew something of children's fearsome cruelty to children, and we lived with our own passion for misadventure. Though we knew it neither as cruelty nor as misadventure. No one believed that Sandy was playing alone at the building site that day. We didn't know it then, but as many of us grew older we came to think it not inconceivable that Sandy had come to grief at the hands of boys not a lot older than himself, playing in a makeshift sand-pit. All of these things have returned with the news of James Bulger's murder. More than once this week, a single image has floated into my head: a grainy Strathclyde Police picture of a sandy-haired boy, with its caption 'Have You Seen Sandy?'

England's Flowers

MAY 1998

For a long time England used to go to bed early. It was a country then of chimneys and cocoa-drinkers. Rich Tea was the favourite dip. In the evening, people would listen to well-spoken liars on the radio; they would polish their own shoes, and go up the stairs early. There were flowers on the wallpaper, flowers on the carpet. There were flowers on the china and on the lamp shades. The bedspread was usually an acre of roses, their redness quite faded in the wash.

The people of that country breathed flowers in their sleep. And, sometimes, their dreams – much like the old ballads – were pastoral dramas shaded in green. The flowerbed of England was love-bower and grave. The typical house in the typical street: a mouth of flowers, an English garden. How small the world is in the English memory: everywhere an outpost, a colony, a dominion; and in every field there was a flower-decked corner of home, where a soldier's bones made it forever England. Prime ministers and poets have made much of England's flowers. And the people have, too. Flowers put them in mind of who they like to be; the old houses, the old soil.

But what is the Elizabethan garden now? The empire is gone: there's more of the world in England now than there is of England in the world. The supermarket is a global bazaar; the television set is a mobile room with a view. England could never be that old thing again. But the love of flowers has grown somehow. It's as if the people were keen for the scent of that other England, that place of shelter and communal worth, of blooms as symbols of national feeling. It's as if they yearn, from time to time – usually in times of disaster and dismay –

for a childish liberty of flowers, like Wordsworth's sacred nurs-
eries of blooming youth:

> In whose collegiate shelter England's Flowers
> Expand, enjoying through their vernal hours
> The air of liberty, the light of truth.

And maybe there's a longing for something more: a runaway
sense of popular pride, a more fevered application of Wordsworth's floriation, such as that of Alfred Austin, with his 'Who
Would Not Die For England!'

> So across the far-off foam,
> Bring him hither, bring him home,
> Over avenues of wave,
> English ground, – to English grave;
> Where his soldier dust may rest,
> England's flag above his breast,
> And, love-planted, long may bloom
> English flowers about his tomb.

England's flowers. What a commodity. Wrapped in plastic at
the palace gates. Yet most of those flowers were not English.
Most flowers sold in England now are not from this place. They
are products of other debatable lands and they have their own
stories.

This is the story of one bunch. Their existence began in
1970. They are a breed of the most popular white lily, *Lilium
longiflorum*. With lilies, the shortest route from breeding to
market is eight years. In 1978 the first of our breed of lilies was
produced by Herut Yahel of the Israeli agricultural research
group. Nowadays, Israel produces ten to fifteen million of these
bulbs every year.

Dudu Efron is a bulb manufacturer. He stood talking under
an orange tree, a half-year after Diana's death. It was a normal
March day in the Israeli desert and Efron stood fanning himself
with a mobile phone. 'The Arabs hate everything we produce,'
he said, 'but sometimes business is stronger than politics.' He

was talking about the fact that many Israeli flowers end up in the Persian Gulf. They go to Holland first. 'The flowers, they lose their identity at the market. And, if the price is right, the Arabs will buy them.' He laughed under his moustache. 'Yes,' he said, 'there is a little something of Israeli soil in the houses of our friends, the Arabs.'

Efron was born in Jerusalem and grew up on a kibbutz. Agriculture and politics were mixed up in the life he remembers. 'The farmers in the kibbutzim were heroes. They protected the borders. The Israeli people thought they were noble. Now people think farmers are dirty. Stupid.' For twenty years Efron was a wheat grower, then he planted potatoes, and for the past few years he has been producing bulbs. Especially lily bulbs. Three years ago he produced the bulbs for our bunch. He froze them, then sold them to Haviv Sela.

Sela's farm is a baked cluster of sheds. There is also a house; a heap of sandshoes in the yard; a broken pot on the window; a goldfinch outspoken on the clothes line. The palm trees have hot leaves; a patch of sand encircles the bottom of each tree. Thirty years ago all of this was desert. Now, they grow white lilies from the soil. The farm is just outside the village of Amioz. 'We are making our history by single years, not centuries,' said Sela, out in the field with his blue cap. He rolled three bulbs in a brown hand. They can be used three, maybe four times, he said. Every June, he will pluck all the bulbs out of the fields, scrub them clean, leave them to dry for a while, and then place them in a giant freezer for sixty days. 'This makes the bulb think it has been through winter.' Once this is done, he will start planting them again. Each bulb to be planted four inches down in the soil. Sela's soil – the soil he calls 'my land' – is a difficult shade of red.

The bulbs for our bunch were put into the soil on 9 December 1997. This was the bulbs' third time pregnant: they produced two sets of flowers last year, and had since spent most of October and November in a pretend Siberian winter. Here again in the soil, they began to sprout. They were sprinkled with two minutes of water eight times a day. They had artificial light at night. The light came down in two-minute bursts. As the flowers grew, the men and women on the farm, who are all from Thailand, would weed the field by hand.

By January, young, green shoots had broken through the soil. Waxy leaves were showing. By February, the flower heads were formed. The cells were turgid with water, bloated with radiant energy. The heads were deep green; they tapered to white at the ends. By March, the stems were twelve inches high. Stout. And two weeks on, they had grown to their height: twenty-two inches. Sun-fed, water-made, chemically charged, carbon dioxide-breathing lilies. White lilies. They swayed easily in Sela's field. Full of life. The blue sky above, the red earth below.

Soon, it was time to cut them. Sela took out a small knife. He clipped each of our stems just a half-inch above the dirt. Thousands of stems were harvested this day: Wednesday, 11 March. Each of our stems had several flowers. Long heads, tight shut. They were carried from the field and placed in buckets of water. For five hours they stand outside in the sun. (This is an important time: if they aren't allowed to take in water and sun for this period of time, and just breathe, the flowers may never open.) Sela harvested our bunch at ten in the morning. They sat out in buckets until three o'clock. The buckets were then put into the big fridge. They are meant to stay there for not less than sixteen hours. Our bunch went in for the cold night. Meantime, Sela's family came about the yard. A cock crowed. Mrs Sela drank Diet Coke from a big plastic bottle. 'I don't like to feed my body rubbish,' she said. The uncut lilies moved in the long field. Acres of them. The lilies of the field.

> I am the rose of Sharon and the lily of
> the valleys. As a lily among thorns, so
> is my love among the daughters.
> (Song of Solomon 2: 1–2)

> And why take thought for raiment? Consider
> the lilies of the field, how they grow: they toil

not, neither do they spin: And yet I say unto
you, That even Solomon in all his glory was
not arrayed like one of these.
  (Matthew 6: 28–9)

Fable says the white lily sprang from the milk of Juno. But
Christian fable makes the larger claim upon them: they are
everywhere in the Bible. They represent virtue, celestial beauty and purity. To the Greeks and Romans it was a medicinal
flower. The bulbs were sometimes crushed and made into oint-
ment. The fragrant petals were used as a balm. In the Middle
Ages, the white lily was associated with the Virgin Mary (the
flower is included in many paintings of her), and also connected with Saints Dominick and Louis. Naturalists are certain lilies
grew plentifully in the Israel of the Bible. Yet they disappeared
somehow. No one reported seeing a colony of lilies in Palestine
until 1925. On a fine September morning M. N. Naftolsky, a
well-known plant hunter who was that day leading a party of
students from the Hebrew University in Jerusalem, found a
flock of white lilies growing wild in the mountains of Upper
Galilee. This, he knew, was the lily of the fields, the lily of the
valley, the lily among the thorns. It had found a way to survive
the various ravages of the land.

Sela's cultivated lilies spent the night at two degrees Celsius.
He brought them out of the fridge at 8 a.m. on 12 March. It was
an especially warm Thursday. Our lilies looked all lushly green.
They smelled of trees and soil. The flowers were still clamped
shut.

Sela's seven Thai workers were in the packing shed. Chen
Singsai is separating the good from the bad. He does this all day.
'You must be careful not to give too much water,' he said. 'Too
much water: the leaves go yellow.' Singsai comes from a village
600 miles from Bangkok. 'We have to work many more hours
for the Mother's Day.' He hopes to learn things about farming,
things he can take back to his own village one day. He has been
in Israel for seven years. His wife, like him, is working at the
bench and, just like him, she is sitting on a column of upturned

plastic tubs. 'We have been working the sixteen hours,' says Mr Singsai. The pay is reasonable. He is able to send something home to his mother. 'Not bad life,' he said. All the Thai women who work in these sheds have covered their faces. Even in the heat they are covered. 'They want to be white,' says Singsai. 'Like lilias.'

Our stems were put on to a machine. It was a kind of sorting machine. At the end, the stems were cut to size by a rotary blade. Many of the leaves were stripped. The man working that end of the machine stood in a pile of mashed plants. A patch of greenery tattooed on to the floor. 'Many flowers,' he said, 'and looking the same.'

Someone else took each bunch of five stems and placed them in plastic bags. At 9 a.m. our bunch was packed, with some other bunches, into a pink-and-yellow box, a carton with the word Carmel printed on it. At 11 a.m. a truck came to the farm. The cartons were loaded up. A lazy dog lay at the farm's gate. It was panting. It closed its eyes to the dust clouds. The too-hot morning; the rumble of trucks. The flowers were on their way to the packing house at Mabuim. This place is run by Agrexco – the company behind Carmel – and is one of fifteen packing houses in Israel. Agrexco is the main exporter of Israeli fruit and flowers. Liav Leshem, one of the company's young product managers, responsible for flowers, was driving on one of the Negev's new dual carriageways. He had one of those hands-free mobile phones. The phone rang every other minute. He spoke Hebrew to the office; English to customers calling from Holland and Germany. He wore a watch that was lodged in a sweatband. He drove past a spray-painting of Princess Diana. Someone had put a moustache on her. The graffito shimmers in the heat.

'It is hard,' said Leshem. 'we are dealing here with a very perishable thing. Flowers die too early if you don't look after them, give them the right conditions. At every stage of the flowers' journey, we keep the right temperature. It is very hard. There are three ways in the world to lose money – women, gambling and agriculture. Women is the most enjoyable; gambling is the quickest; and agriculture, well, agriculture is the surest.'

Agrexco was founded in 1957. Forty years later its turnover was $600 million. Year upon year the company grows: it is one of the biggest suppliers of roses and lilies and gerberas to the English market, and it feeds vegetables into all the main supermarkets. 'England wants more of the flowers now,' says Leshem. 'The supermarkets are taking over. They've increased their orders for next year. They like the quality, and we move fast.'

He was moving fast as he said this. Field after field fell away. 'Why are the white lilies so expensive?' he said. 'I'll tell you: because you have to freeze the bulbs after each planting. They demand a lot of irrigation in the ground. You cannot pack too many in a box, so the transportation costs are high. Very high. We send them all by air. But people love the lilies. Mysterious ... lilies in England. They use them in the marriages and in the deaths, no? England is our biggest market. What is the difference between a wedding and a funeral? In a wedding, two people are buried.'

The packing house at Mabuim is across from a cluster of new dwellings. They are middle-income houses; nice terracotta roofs. Three hundred growers – one as far as the Gaza Strip, 120 kilometres away – send their produce to this warehouse. More than 250 million flower stems a year pass through here. Millions of white lilies.

Our bunch arrived at Mabuim at midday on Thursday morning, 12 March. They were left in the fridge there for an hour. Then they were stamped. The label has the grower's barcode on it, the plant's name, and the serial number of the country and the customer. The cartons were loaded on to a pallet.

Our bunch went into a truck – bound for the Agrexco terminus at Ben Gurion Airport – at one o'clock. Each carton was passed through a bomb-detector machine before being loaded. A young Israeli driver stood by the machine. He was trying to blow a smoke ring through a smoke ring.

There are no accents in Israel. There is no dialect. There are many different kinds of voice, but only one steady inflection. Unlike other small countries – Denmark or Ireland, say – where the accent can change from street to street. 'The heart of the people is more ready for peace now,' says Leshem. 'More time, more blood on the soil, but eventually peace will come.'

Leshem's boss is called Gidon Mazor, a handsome, easy-smiling man in a cotton shirt. 'My father,' said Mazor, 'was a vegetable man. My father pushed me towards the flowers. It was a way of keeping me at home. And my own son is now in the business too.' He speaks as if companies such as Agrexco add to the big idea of Israel. Their idea. They show the country working. Another of Leshem's young colleagues said it is all just great: 'Britain, which left our country in such a mess in 1948, is now dying for our flowers. They can't get enough of them. Our lilies are the best in the world. We breed them to last long, and to stand up.'

Mazor is just as pleased that the company is doing well. But he is more cautious; in his eyes, he looks like he knows more of what success means, and more of what failure means, too. He can guess at the price of things. He has an older businessman's impatience with the trumpets of certainty. 'Things are better than ten years ago. Not good enough yet, but improving all the time.'

In the Agrexco terminal at Ben Gurion, the loading bay is like the set of a ballet production. Box after box is lifted on to cargo pallets. The forklifts' pas de deux. A symphony of horns and shouts and rubber doors flying open; bells ringing, engines revving up. The sound of tyres gripping the chilled Tarmac. Everything is cold for the flowers and the cherry tomatoes. Our bunch came in. The carton was placed on a pallet with the other things bound for London. Hundreds of boxes for London that day. Our pallet truck is dragged away by a yellow tractor. Checked for bombs. And soon it is beyond the coolness of the loading bay. Out on the Tarmac. Being lifted into the plane, a Boeing 747 with all the seats ripped out. Like a giant garage. Hot, but just the right temperature above the clouds. Five planes leave every day; each carries 110 tonnes of Israeli produce. The fruits of the soil. The lilies of the field. The plane flew overhead at 7 p.m.

Beeri Lavi spent two years working in Kenya. He helped to set up an irrigation system. He then managed the farms of the president of the Ivory Coast – growing mangoes, pineapples, avocados – and he took what he had learned back to Israel. He now runs Agrexco's operation in London. 'The English mentality about flowers is all change,' he said. 'They want variety. New kinds of flower. The lilies are in the supermarkets now, and not only for death. The narcissus was our first flower. That is the one we brought here first. England loves it. Now it wants everything. They want all the flowers.'

Lavi knows that the English used to buy fewer flowers. 'There was no money, and it is not a religious country, like Italy. There is less of Easter, less of Christmas. You were spending less on the graves. I was giving advice to the growers. I said, "Give them more pinks, more light blues, orange, and plenty of white. The English wants soft colours." And you want them cheap; for children to buy.'

The warehouse in Middlesex was Britishly messy. The men at their forklifts were hurried and cursing. Robbie Williams was revving them up on the radio. Our pallet came from Heathrow just after midnight on Friday, 13 March. Our carton was loaded into a cage. It was bound for London's New Covent Garden Market.

Roy Stevens was two hours away from waking up. He would soon wash and shave and drive to Vauxhall. He would come in the middle of the night, set out his wholesale stall and try against the clock to sell those flowers. Those flowers that are dying all the time. Our bunch of lilies was going to Mr Stevens: the first of the English buyers.

The English are funny about flowers. (Not the British: Scots get into trouble for not being flowery enough, although they are catching the bug; and the Welsh prefer vegetables.) But the funniness has changed. It has become postmodern. The old way of thinking about flowers in England was to do with homeliness, domestic security, heritage, national pride. That was the cultural atmosphere then.

But the new oddness about flowers is often to do with estrangement. That's how it seems. Flowers in England, more and more, can seem to give voice to an alien feeling; something of urban disconnectedness. They might speak of a distance from the old steadiness: your parents' easy belief in home and garden, and the English rose. Some people think the new uses of flowers announces a revival of that same English community; but those grotesque piles of wrapped flowers glinting by the roadside might only say the very opposite. Their cellophane might say it. They are condomised symbols of how it used to be. People don't touch the flowers; they don't know them. Their softened colours speak boldly of a lack. And the more they are piled, the more certain you become: the England they conjure is dead on the air.

You often see those flowers now. They don't mark soldiers – they mark the fall of people in ordinary life. People who are heroic only in the matter of their having met a surprising death: a car out of nowhere; a gang of crazy youths. Those flower shrines started to appear these last few years: at the sites of football stadium disasters; at the spot where a child was killed. And now they are everywhere in England. They are anonymous expressions of sympathy, from one passer-by to another. People come with those flowers as if it were an old-fashioned thing to do: laying flowers at the spot where some piece of random violence took place. As if to say, 'We didn't used to live like this'. As if to say, 'Let these flowers remind you of what is best in us'.

The people bending there, they act as if they know the flowers on the road could just as easily be piled for them. It is an odd – and oddly compulsive – piece of stage business in the televised culture. Many people use flowers much as they always did. But everything is touched by the new floriation. England suffers bouts of false-memory syndrome. It thinks it remem-

bers flowers, and an age of innocence; it recalls an open-air festival of clean living, and no murders. It knows of a world that
was never here, a time when everybody was one, and it marks
that time's passing with cellophaned flowers. The pinning of
flowers on the palace gates looked like a quiet revolution. It
looked like people saying something large in one voice. But it
was all in the mind, and all in the mind of television. The flowers were just flowers, and the people bored.

New Covent Garden Market is a gigantic cave of flowers; it
lights up while London sleeps. The perfume near knocks you
over. Forty or more large wholesalers, their flowers and plants
spilling over, lying out in boxes, stacked in high bins. Lilac
orchids, red amaryllis, yellow narcissus, pink ranunculus, frost-
ed eucalyptus, a world of roses, a globe of tulips. Lilies.

'A bit wet outside,' said Helen Evans, one of the market's
employees. All the stand-holders know her. She moves in a cloud
of winks and jokes and early-morning hellos. She has noticed
the strangeness and importance of the English drama about
flowers. It may be to do with memory, or the culture. 'But the
weird thing,' she said, 'is that they don't buy a lot of flowers. They
spend less on flowers than almost every country in Europe. The
overall retail market is worth £1,240 million per year; about £22
per person a year. But that is not high. The English love flowers
– they may think a lot about them – but they don't buy them in
a big way.' The Swiss spend £102 per person; the Germans £57;
the Dutch £47; the French £40. But the English market is growing bit by bit. The market has doubled since 1986.

As for our bunch of white lilies, the lid was off the carton,
which sat on the wet concrete. Each stem of the bunch looked
pert. They seemed a darker green in the English light. They lay
in the stand of S. Robert Allen Ltd, one of the market's big
wholesale firms, and were surrounded by blooms from everywhere. The traffic is conducted by Roy Stevens. 'We live by the
weather,' he said. 'Too hot, and the flowers are dead on the street;
too rainy, and the people won't bother stopping for flowers. It's
like that in Britain. I mean, who's going to allow themselves to be

dragged out looking for flowers on Cup Final day?'

'That lovely lady Princess Di going so suddenly – it was flowers everywhere. We noticed the rise in demand right away. Bang! All the white flowers were gone. You could just feel it. People needed flowers. And we sold everything we had.'

Betsy Kelly is seventy-nine years old. She has been selling flowers since 1930. A small, ambling bundle of cardigans and hats, Betsy is usually too busy to smile; she is famous at the market, as her father was before her, in the old Covent Garden of horses and carts. In all the fluorescence of the new place, Betsy is a star. A curmudgeonly one, for sure, with her waving hands, her rolling eyes, her air of being bothered by this or that nonsense. But Betsy knows her own game. She walked around our box of lilies like someone inspecting a gangrenous leg. Her lips were thinned: one could almost hear her good clock ticking, and see her thoughts, her cold ruminations on pounds, shillings and pence. For all these years, she has got up early, at four or five, and gone down the market to see what's what. Her husband died five years ago. She looked at the lilies, lifted our bunch, scratched her hat, and bought them. She looked around when asked a question. 'I've forgotten much more than you'll ever know,' she said.

Kelly's Flowers is quite far along the Commercial Road. The middle East End. A shop at the heart of Stepney. The road is filled with garment wholesalers and Indian takeaways. People trudge to the hospital. Rows of old houses sit neatly by the road. Layers of flowery wallpaper lying deep in the walls, deep in the modern emulsion. Some of the houses are being taken down. Mrs Carrington is another old lady from here. She told a story of playing as a child in some of those houses. Some of them lay less than half demolished more than half a century ago. 'Most of them had their roofs open to the sky,' said Mrs Carrington. 'We fashioned tables and chairs from bricks and boards that lay around in plenty. We would unearth broken pieces of crockery that served as plates, and once, to my joy, I found the bottom half of a blue glass vase. I stood it up in the middle of my table.

I filled it with the weeds that grew through the floorboards. Those houses were dark and smelly. But here we lived our pretend lives.'

Betsy Kelly was in the back of her shop. She beetled away at her flower arrangements. One of them had a glittery message embedded in red carnations. It just said 'Mum'. Betsy had brought our lilies back to the shop. They were soaking in buckets in her large fridge. They had spent the weekend in there. It was now five days since the lilies were picked on Sela's farm. They were still very fresh. The heads had whitened some more, and they had softened, too. The flesh of the lily was tender now. There was the beginning of a sweet perfume.

'My mum and dad had the shop,' said Betsy, 'and they had stalls as well. One up Petticoat Lane and one by the London Hospital. All their lives. You didn't have staff in them days. You just came in as a girl and worked. That was the times. The stuff was different. It was nearly all English-grown. The only bit of stuff that we ever got really was from France, or Holland, but not much. It's all the foreign stuff now.'

Betsy has been in the present shop for thirty-two years. She and her husband took it over when old Mrs Kelly became ill. 'We kept her,' said Betsy. 'She had whatsit – Alzheimer's – and in them days the family kept them. Different kettle of fish. We never got much support. Families did it all. When I was at school, I thought I would be a gym instructor. But my mother wanted me in the shop. People were more flower-conscious then. Visiting the hospitals and that; nowadays, they'd make you laugh. It's a wonder they go in at all. In them days, they visited the graves more. But this is us now. Do I still like flowers? Well, I suppose really, it's a way of life, know what I mean? I don't suppose for one minute I would like any other trade. I don't think I would like to pack up work 'cause I think to myself, after the hectic life I've led, if I was to pack up work I'd just go senile, and that wouldn't be me.'

Most nights in the week Betsy gets home after 8 p.m. She lives in Brentwood, out in Essex. Her two sons come in and out.

'Everything's a cost,' said one of them. 'It's a wonder anybody can make a shilling out of flowers now.'

'It was special, once upon a time,' said Betsy, 'the old Covent Garden Market. You had the personalities. You had the people. They were florists, flower-sellers. Today, it's all big business. Ask the old ones there now. Ask Tom. Ask Roy. Ask Ken. Any of the old ones will tell you: it was a pleasure to go to the old market. But it's all going multinational. They're killing the small trader. My mother stood in Whitechapel Road. My aunt beside her. Selling flowers. They worked bloody hard. You know St Clement Danes, the church, in Fleet Street? The vicar's wife when I was a girl was Mrs Pickford. And she used to have teas for the flower girls. Just young women. Between the two wars. And once a year Mrs Pickford took all the girls to Brighton. Everything was colourful in them days. Not just the flowers, the people.'

On Tuesday, 17 March, Betsy put the lilies out in the shop. Our bunch was beginning to open: some of the ends were pouting, some were puckered up. One of the ten stems was showing a white tongue. Two tongues. The leaves beneath were very green. Our bunch sat out for two days. The shop was packed on Thursday. Mother's Day was coming up. There were men looking out of place, children shaking their little fists of pound coins. Queues all day. Betsy's assistant, Sue, was plucking and wrapping, counting and cutting, laughing and teasing, and answering the phone.

At 2.30 p.m. a gentleman came in. His brother Amos had died. He had been ill for a long time. 'More merciful than tragic.' Mr Copping wanted to leave flowers at the rest home. Sue took our bunch of lilies from the bucket. She laid them on paper, added some daisies, a few white carnations, a bit of spray. She rolled them together, and charged him £20. Mr Copping walked out into the afternoon; the shop-bell rang at his back.

Amos Copping was dead aged sixty-nine. He had never been to Israel. The only time he was ever abroad was during his National Service. He'd spent part of a year in Hong Kong. His wife was dead, too. Mr Copping's body lay in Tadman's Funeral

Parlour on Jubilee Street and Stepney Way. It was to this address that his brother came with the bunch of flowers. He sat a while in the chapel with Amos. The flowers were placed in a white vase. Mr Copping noticed that there was a picture of the pope in the chapel. The coffin, the pope, white lilies, and the brother. The remains of Amos Copping were buried the following Tuesday. His daughters and his brother were there. 'More merciful than tragic,' they said.

After that, our flowers stayed on at Tadman's. They were placed on a small table in the hall. The carpets there are ever so blue. Everything is scrubbed. The thing you notice is how clean it all is. Spick and span. The air smells of anything but death. 'Everybody notices the smell,' says Maureen Tadman. 'It's the flowers and the scented candles.' The carpets look like they are hoovered on the hour. 'No,' she said. 'We don't use air fresheners or what-you-call-it, Shake'n'Vac. No. It's the natural smell. It's the same with the boys' appearance. They have to look smart. Appearance is so important.' The Tadman family has been doing funerals since 1849. The office wall is lined with old pictures of the Tadmans. Men with dark eyes and dark clothes. 'Wag' Tadman, the founder, in a portrait taken around the time of the Boer War; Alfred William Tadman, his son, 1882–1935, a man in a tall hat, his moustache so carefully clipped. The two boys he had: Cornelius and Alfred, 1914–96 and 1902–80, a couple of characters, upright in their portraits. All dead now, and down in the City Cemetery at Manor Park.

Maureen Tadman was dressed in black. She wore owlish glasses. Her demeanour was somewhat melancholy, but now and then she let go of her natural reserve, and a smile lit up her face. 'With a death,' she said, 'you really want to do things correctly.' She only employs tall men. And she's serious about their smartness. 'How would you feel if someone was burying you covered in earrings and ponytails?'

She is conscious of the role she has in other people's stories. She is there at the end of many a life, neatly dressed, efficient, doing things correctly. And she sometimes wonders about those lives too: what they did, how they did it. 'Here in the East End, marriage, birth and death mean everything to the people. They live their life a certain way. They are caring, traditional, and the tradition says that neighbours and friends will show support at the time of a death. And the number of floral tributes is evidence of that. It wouldn't be a true East End funeral without them.'

One of the funeral directors at Tadman's, Jason Saddington, said you see some funny things when you're driving a hearse. 'You don't see people taking off their hats any more. They just stare. And somebody might cross themselves. The younger folk just stare, and sometimes they rub their chest, like they're embarrassed or something.'

Mrs Tadman twisted her wedding ring around its finger. 'I always ask the boys to treat the bodies the same as if they were their own family. We all have our dignity.' Jason went up a ladder and washed the windows. 'It's a man's world, this,' said Mrs Tadman, 'and you need to work that extra bit hard if you're a woman. My own mother was buried by the firm. Aunt Ethel, too. And when it comes my turn, yes. I wouldn't want anybody else doing mine. Every person that comes in that door is not a number; they're people, and you must always remember that.'

A week later, our lilies were amazing. The white petals were wide to the world. An unopened stem had softened and drooped. It looked like a green silk purse. With their yellow stamens, their moist leaves, the flowers had a powerful scent, something of old earth and the Dead Sea. Life and other business went on around them, and the lilies slowly began to wilt. The whiteness turned to brown; the petals dried and shrivelled up. The fragrance vaporised overnight. Our flowers died about three weeks after Mr Copping.

They were placed in a bin out the back. On a windowsill there, back against the light, was a tin of air-freshener and a tub of Shake'n'Vac. Each container was covered with pictures of flowers. Live flowers under the sun. The freshness of some other day.

Saint Marilyn

JULY 2004

New York – contrary to popular opinion and Frank Sinatra – is never a city that doesn't sleep. It sleeps soundly in fact. You walk the streets on certain nights and suddenly you can feel quite alone under the buildings. It's not that the place is deserted, there are things going on – taxi-cabs, homeless people, late-night walkers, the police – but they can seem to proceed at that hour like things out of step, like odd yearnings of the imagination, or unexpected items in a gasoline-smelling dream of urban ruin.

I stopped one night in front of the Ferragamo shoe shop on Fifth Avenue. The light from the shop was so strong it seemed like daylight spilling over the pavement. I felt drenched in the uncanny whiteness. And there in the window, draped on transparent mannequins or laid on silver boxes, were some of the dazzling relics of the late Marilyn Monroe. 'A pair of stilettos by Salvatore Ferragamo, scarlet satin, encrusted with matching rhinestones.'

There's no place like home, I thought.

'Estimate: $4000–6000.' And further along a hand-knitted cardigan, 'with a brown geometric pattern and matching knitted belt. Worn by Marilyn Monroe in 1962 and featured in a series of photographs by George Barris taken on the beach in Santa Monica, California. Estimate: $30,000–50,000.' In the corner of the window there stood a halter-neck dress from the movie *Let's Make Love*. I thought of Marilyn and Yves Montand posing for the cameras with their unhappy smiles. 'Estimate: $15,000–20,000.' The Monroe things had been to London, Paris and Buenos Aires, and were now back in New York for auction at Christie's. Ferragamo took the opportunity for a cute bit of public-relations flimflam. The cold air from the ice rink at Rockefeller Plaza – underneath Christie's salerooms – seemed to be blowing in one great frosty whoop down the avenue.

The people who stopped put both hands on the Ferragamo window and the white light made each one a little blonder. One woman said 'beautiful'; the glass misted up in front of her mouth. I walked on a few blocks. There was a midnight service going on at St Patrick's Cathedral. A long queue stretched all the way down to the altar, where a glass case stood by itself, with a casket inside, containing the relics of St Theresa of Lisieux. A hundred years ago the Carmelite nun Thérèse Martin died, and she died, according to a woman I spoke to at the end of the queue, 'with a heart as big as the world itself'. The last words of St Theresa are not open to doubt. 'I am not dying,' she said. 'I am entering into Life.' She was canonised in 1925.

I joined the line at St Patrick's and followed it down and when it was my turn I touched the glass and walked away. Men to my side were crying and whispering. The relics of St Theresa were travelling the world too: last year Russia and Europe, this year America, from New York to Tucson, Arizona, with a spell over Christmas at the Church of St Jane Frances de Chantal in North Hollywood.

The Christie's sale of Marilyn's relics raised $13,405,785. The Ferragamo ruby shoes were bought for $48,300 by the son of the man who made them, while Lots 51 and 40, the Santa Monica cardigan and the dress from *Let's Make Love*, sold for $167,500 and $52,900 respectively. The big wow of the auction, as expected, was the Jean Louis sheath dress, covered in tiny stones, worn by Marilyn at John Kennedy's birthday tribute in 1962, when she sang 'Happy Birthday'. This went for over a million dollars. The man who bought it (owner of a memorabilia shop called Ripley's Believe It or Not) thought he'd got a great bargain. The Kennedy dress smashed the previous world record for the sale of a female costume: a blue velvet Victor Edelstein dress belonging to Princess Diana that sold for $222,500 in June 1997. The actor and peroxophile Tony Curtis, who must have forgotten that he once said kissing Marilyn was like kissing Hitler, got out of his seat at the auction to tell reporters that Marilyn would have been thrilled. 'She'd have enjoyed the fact that people still love her so much,' he said.

The sale of Marilyn Monroe's personal property – a plastic cup, a group of blankets, a plexiglas tissue-box cover, a piece of paper with the words 'he does not love me' written in pencil, to name just a few of the 576 lots that were auctioned – may represent the most interesting event to occur in contemporary art since the death of Andy Warhol. Indeed it takes Warhol's deification of celebrity past its absurdly logical conclusion: why pay more for a representation of Marilyn Monroe, even an Abstract Expressionist one like De Kooning's, or a mass-produced one like Warhol's, when, for a not dissimilar price, you can own a little something of Marilyn herself? The Christie's sale goes so far ahead of Warhol's thinking that we ironically end up back where we started, with the basic principle of authenticity. The threat – the joy – was always that Pop would eat itself in the end, and it has done. The old superstition about High Art, 'Rembrandt actually touched this canvas,' can now be applied to the personal belongings of the century's most famous woman – this object actually touched Marilyn – and thus our era's tangled worries with the meaning of fine art are for a moment resolved. Pop culture became its opposite number: the ordinary minutiae of the extraordinary life came to seem as formally expressive as *Guernica*. The designer Tommy Hilfiger pays a fortune for two pairs of jeans Marilyn wore in *The Misfits*. He frames them and hangs them up in his apartment. He gets the pleasure of Charles I pacing a banqueting hall replete with Van Dycks. Hilfiger gets to feel he has captured the thing that is truly seen to capture his time. The spirit of the age is a bundle of famous rags.

But what of poor Marilyn herself? What is she? And who was she before all this came to pass in her adopted name? What was it about her that allowed it to happen? And who are we that love her so much? These questions rise and fall like the sound of

distant applause as you read the Christie's catalogue. And occa-
sional answers can seem to spring from the pictures and
descriptions of the objects themselves. The book is a slick and a
morbid affair: the clothes are really nothing without Marilyn in
them; many of the photographs show her coming out of a film
premiere, or sitting hopefully in another tiny apartment. Her
possessions, you feel, are there to soften and furnish, to ease and
to deepen, the life of a woman who is barely in possession of
herself. But without her they seem like tokens of the purest
emptiness.

Marilyn's books and stockings and strings of pearls come to
ground you in a vivid life that is gone; her existence was so
much about projection and luminous performance that you
can hardly bear to imagine the macabre earthiness of her leav-
ings. It's a bit like contemplating Ophelia's soaking garments
and weedy trophies pulled from the weeping brook; they are
cold, modern remnants of desire and the misfortunes of fortune; tokens of the twentieth century's obsession with the
nuances of fame and public death.

*Madame Bovary. The Sun Also Rises. The Unnameable. The
Fall.* Marilyn's auctioned books are like scripts primed for her
long afterlife. And one of the others, *Dubliners*, contains the
story that captures something of the eerie and magical grip that
personal effects can hold for the living. Her gloves and candle-
sticks resemble those in Joyce's 'The Dead': rows of framed
photographs before a pier glass; we might imagine these objects
that once belonged to a beautiful, sad young woman can tell us
something strange and true about our own lives. The people
who queued to see her things around the world were apt to say
such a thing. The eternal-seeming fabulousness of a great
movie star – like that of a princess – might serve for a while to
transform even the dowdiest of realities. That is the myth, any-
way. And Marilyn Monroe was nothing if not a sacrifice to the
potency of her own mythology. Even her pet dog's tag and
licence (estimate, $800–1200; final bid, $63,000) become items
of great interest, symbolic pieces of the life of someone who has

entered into Life. Frank Sinatra gave her the dog. She called it
Mafia. Right now a person is looking at the licence and thinking
they grasp the meaning of the twentieth century. And who is to
say that person is wrong?

Norma Jeane Mortensen was born on 1 June 1926 in the charity ward of Los Angeles General Hospital. Her mother Gladys
Baker was now and again mad, leaving her daughter troubled
but free to dream up an alternative life, and to develop her vital
allure reading movie magazines. Norma Jeane had a keen sense
of how to conquer people's affections – especially those of men.
She wore lipstick. She wore short skirts. She told a sad story of
her upbringing. And after a spell modelling and flirting and
screwing and practising her walk, waiting in line with the other
girls at Schwab's Drugstore on Sunset Boulevard, Marilyn
emerged with a brazen sense of how to enliven the Fifties.

Marilyn invented a persona – The Girl – that would at first
seem to release her from the bad things of her childhood, but
which later became like one of her childhood ghouls, leaning
over her, making her all sex, and suffocating her. The Girl was a
fiction and a mask – 'Mae West, Theda Bara and Bo Peep all
rolled into one,' said Groucho Marx – which served to turn a
case of ordinary, everyday wishing into a triumph of calculated
stardom. There is hardly a single area of Norma Jeane's life that
wasn't fluffed up to enhance Marilyn's exotic stature. The Girl,
the resulting character, would seem to carry vulnerability and
sexual freedom to a new place in the movies, but in real life, in
the decompression chamber of overblown ambitions, the person who called herself Marilyn Monroe could only unravel in a
miasma of loneliness and uncertainty and pain. And worst of
all, even this, her bad times, her suffering, came in the end to
add to the myth of her specialness. In her own lifetime she
became the patron saint of sex; and afterwards, in her very
modern martyrdom, she made us feel that an engulfing sadness
does not in any way preclude a giant success. Marilyn's fans find
the combination fatal. And so unfortunately did she.

Encyclopedias exist to bring a constant proliferation of

knowledge to rest for a time in one place. Adam Victor's attempt on the universe of Marilyn Monroe – life, Life, After-life, scholarship, clothes, gossip, filmography, addresses, hospitals, drama coaches, superstitions, favourite toys – is truly mind-boggling. It may represent the triumph of detail over proportion, but still, all in all, it serves as a complete concordance to the many Marilyn narratives yet published. Here is a part of the entry on Marilyn's honeymoon with Joe DiMaggio:

> After a night at the budget CLIFTON INN motel in Paso Robles (and a meal in the restaurant of the Hot Springs Hotel, or at the Clifton Inn according to some versions), Joe and Marilyn drove in his dark blue Cadillac to a mountain lodge outside Idyllwild, near PALM SPRINGS, loaned to them for the occasion by Marilyn's attorney, Lloyd Wright. Here they had the uncommon luxury of two weeks alone together.

The upper-case names have entries to themselves. Just as the Christie's sale of Marilyn's knick-knacks did better than adjacent sales of German Art and the Ancient Jewels of Persia, so Victor's encyclopedia, a mini-Bible of our times, will do better than many a Complete Guide to This and That, or Encyclopedia of the Other.

There are more biographies of Marilyn Monroe than of any other person in the history of show business. Around seven hundred have been published in English alone, with a dozen or so new ones every year. It is even possible to suggest a typology of writings about Marilyn. It starts off with studio biographies written by publicists, and a kind of memoir by the screenwriter Ben Hecht (later published as *My Story* by Marilyn Monroe), featuring the well-spun tale of Norma Jeane's abused childhood, and the white piano she saved from her mother's house – a piano that sold for three-quarters of a million dollars at the Christie's sale. There were also early biographies by Marilyn's friends (the columnist Sidney Skolsky, the poet Norman Rosten) and her enemies – *Marilyn, the Tragic Venus*, based on the incriminating fibs of Hollywood scribe Nunnally Johnson. There have been plenty of biographies by people who worked for Marilyn, by her housekeeper Eunice Murray, her cleaner Lena Pepitone, by a fan called James Haspiel who used to stand outside her apartment, by one or two guys who slept with her, by any numbers of guys who wanted to sleep with her, and by a tittle-tattle lifeguard at the Ambassador Hotel in Los Angeles. Her half-sister Bernice Miracle wrote a fairly tender little book called *My Sister Marilyn*. Then to top it all there was *The Secret Happiness of Marilyn Monroe* by her first husband, James Dougherty.

In fact, you can easily top that too. There has been spurious tome after tome on the subject of her untimely death. Come on down, the Murder Cover-up Theorists. Anthony Summers wrote *Goddess*, an exhaustive, exhausting and paranoid account of how *everyone in the known world* wanted Marilyn dead. He also did the actress the supreme disservice of publishing a picture of her on the slab. There have been many of these sensational books, which mainly show how both Kennedys bugged her, buggered her, drugged her, killed her, collaborated with the Mafia, were set up by the Mafia, were punished by (or in league with) the Teamsters, or the Cubans, or the Rat Pack, and that every intelligence agency in the United States was busy tailing Marilyn or burning her phone records or laying plans to snuff her out.

Monroe's mother blamed her daughter for being born, and the child grew up with a dark memory of people screaming in the hall, of departures and uncertainties, and of men taking advantage of her loneliness and dependence. Even Marilyn seemed to realise that dressing up – going on show – was a way of providing an answer to the gaunt face of her mad mother in the Rockhaven Sanitarium. It might even be possible that Marilyn's efforts to dispel America's fears about sex were somehow related to her attempts to dispel her own fear of madness. At any rate her grandmother Della Mae Hogan died in a straitjacket. Gladys lived until the 1980s in a Florida loony bin. And

Marilyn presented herself to the world as a beacon of confidence, an angel of sex, while all her life she was troubled with the idea that her mind wasn't right.

It was Marilyn's misfortune to think that serious acting could save her from self-doubt. In 1955, after showing America and the world how to relax about sex by allowing her skirt to blow over her head in *The Seven Year Itch*, Monroe ran away to New York to become somebody else. But The Girl would always follow her. She threw a press conference to reveal 'the new Monroe':

> Cocktails were served for about an hour as guests awaited a 'new and different' Marilyn. Shortly after six, the front door opened and Marilyn blew in like a snowdrift. She was dressed from head to toe in white. A fluttery white mink coat covered a white satin sheath with flimsy, loose spaghetti straps. She wore satin high heels and white stockings. Her long, sparkling diamond earrings were on loan from Van Cleef & Arples.
>
> Marilyn seemed disappointed when people asked what was new about her. 'But I have changed my hair!' she protested. Her hair did seem a shade or two lighter. Asked to describe the new colour, Marilyn replied in a child's voice: 'Subdued platinum.' The crowd received Marilyn with good-natured amusement. They responded as though she were one of her comical, ditzy blonde film characters . . . 'I have formed my own corporation so I can play the kind of roles I want,' Marilyn announced . . . She declared herself tired of sex roles and vowed to do no more. 'People have scope, you know,' said Marilyn. 'They really do.'

This sad tableau is one of a pair. She came to England the following year to star in *The Prince and the Showgirl* with Laurence Olivier. At the initial press conference one of the straps on her dress broke with suspiciously good timing, whereupon she announced that she would very much like to appear in a film adaptation of *The Brothers Karamazov*. 'Which one would you play?' shouted one of the reporters. 'Grushenka,' said Marilyn, 'that's a girl.' 'Spell it,' said another hack.

Marilyn was cursed – or blessed – with an instinctive ability to intellectualise sex and at the same time to sexualise intellectuals. But in time this would constitute a schism in her everyday life: on the way up she tried to please men who only wanted her for sex, and at her height, at the pinnacle of her New York period, from 1955 until her death in 1962, she tried to please men who thought she was better than that. Fundamentally she swithered between giving and wanting: in time she would surround herself with intellectuals who thought they might harness her vulnerability and somehow turn her into a great actress or a happy person. Yet there was something in the material of her early life that made such achievements very difficult: fulfilment remained but a flickering, costly, benighted dream. In some chiefly unhelpful way she didn't know who she was.

A dozen years ago I went to look at Marilyn Monroe's grave. She is buried just beyond Hollywood at a place called Westwood Memorial Park. It was a very quiet place on a hot summer's day. As I walked over the grass the only real sound was coming from a bell that hung from a branch of a tree over the grave of Natalie Wood. A water sprinkler in the corner of the park made a placid arc over gravestones and shrubs. Not a bad place to live out one's afterlife, I thought. Down a lane called the Walk of Memory you pass Darryl F. Zanuck and Dean Martin, Peter Lawford and Fanny Brice. What I remember most is the atmosphere of the cemetery: the place was more than just a repository of famous bones; a giant investment of common wishes lay deep in the polished stonework. American wishes. The world's wishes. Yet the only scent that moved through the air was the scent of everyday boredom. It could have been any car park in America: a place where children might play on a vapid afternoon, the sun coming down, the future unknown. Yet in that same atmosphere there was something of America's allure to the impressionable world – it was a mood that travelled invisibly over the surface of the manicured grass, a liturgy of success, the psalm of America, with Marilyn as its tragic muse. How could we fail to follow that compelling sound to the ends of the earth?

Tony and the Queen

NOVEMBER 2006

Very good monarchs must surely dislike innovation, if only to acknowledge the fact that innovation must surely dislike them. It may be said that Queen Elizabeth II has been especially skilled in this respect, having fought every day since her coronation on 2 June 2 1953, to oppose any sort of change in the habits of tradition and to preserve the British monarchy from the encroaching vulgarity of public feeling.

When people say they love the Queen that is often what they love – her stoical, unyielding passivity – and one has to look to Elizabeth's great-great-grandmother, Queen Victoria, to find a monarch who might match her, and even beat her, as an idol of intransigence. 'The Queen is most anxious to enlist everyone who can speak or write to join in checking this mad, wicked folly of "Woman's Rights,"' wrote Victoria in her journals, 'with all its attendant horrors on which her poor feeble sex is bent, forgetting every sense of womanly feeling and propriety.' Victoria always had the habit of expressing her views in the third person, and the above was written in 1870, a year, it might help us to remember, when everyday British women were just being allowed by law, for the first time, to keep the money they earned. Being in touch with one's subjects, female or otherwise, was not seen to be a very necessary part of the job back then, and it might stand as one of the more limpid ironies of monarchy that the sovereigns who are most out of touch are usually the ones most loved.

Nevertheless, one might pity the present queen. Where Victoria only had women's suffrage and Charles Darwin to rub up against, poor Elizabeth had Princess Diana, and there we entered a whole new phase in the life of an endangered species.

There was always a question about how far Queen Elizabeth could go in the twentieth century without coming a cropper due to new waves of populism gone awry, and in Diana Spencer she met the near-hysterical embodiment of that tendency. In her famous *Panorama* interview with Martin Bashir in 1995, the one where she outed her husband as an adulterer, Diana looked down the camera lens as if she were looking through the sights of an automatic weapon. Here are some examples of how she spoke in that interview about her role within 'The Firm':

DIANA: I remember when I used to sit on hospital beds and hold people's hands, people used to be sort of shocked because they said they'd never seen this before, and to me it was quite a normal thing to do. And when I saw the reassurance that an action like that gave, I did it everywhere, and will always do that.

BASHIR: What was the family's reaction to your post-natal depression?

DIANA: Well, maybe I was the first person ever to be in this family who ever had a depression or was ever openly tearful. And obviously that was daunting, because if you've never seen it before how do you support it? . . .

BASHIR: What did you actually do?

DIANA: Well, I just hurt my arms and my legs; and I work in environments now where I see women doing similar things and I'm able to understand completely where they're coming from . . . .

BASHIR: Once the separation had occurred, moving to 1993, what happened during that period?

DIANA: People's agendas changed overnight. I was now separated wife of the Prince of Wales, I was a problem, I was a liability (seen as), and 'how are we going to deal with her? This hasn't happened before.'

BASHIR: Who was asking those questions?

DIANA: People around me, people in this environment, and . . .

BASHIR: The royal household?

DIANA: People in my environment, yes, yes.

BASHIR: And they began to see you as a problem?

DIANA: Yes, very much so, uh huh.

BASHIR: How did that show itself?

DIANA: By visits abroad being blocked, by things that had come naturally my way being stopped, letters going, that got lost, and various things.

BASHIR: So despite the fact that your interest was always to continue with your duties, you found that your duties were being held from you?

DIANA: Yes. Everything changed after we separated, and life became very difficult then for me.

BASHIR: Who was behind that change?

DIANA: Well, my husband's side were very busy stopping me.

Obviously, the elder royals and their familiars had completely missed out on the Oprah-isation of the universe. If they hadn't, they might have learned the new first rule of successful leadership: enjoy your inscrutability if you must, but don't ever stand in the way of a confessional heroine. If stopping Diana was something of a thankless task while she was alive, the effort would come to seem suicidal for the British monarchy in the summer of 1997, after Diana died in that Paris tunnel. William Shakespeare himself could scarcely have imagined, in the days after the crash, a royal household with more out-of-touch advisers than the Windsors had on twenty-four-hour call, each of them sharing a gigantic unawareness of the difference between a pest and a mass phenomenon. But it is said that much of the intransigence was coming from the Queen herself, who, despite all her experience, disported herself that summer like a person lumbering in a dark cave. She was somehow unable to see what the infants and the dogs in the street could see, that the old style was unsuited to the virulent new mood – and that if something had to give, or someone, it was most likely going to be the woman whose head appears ready-severed on Britain's postage stamps.

The English director Stephen Frears's account of that summer, *The Queen* (starring Helen Mirren as the unheeding head of the afflicted nation), offers a modern history play no less entertaining than it is unsettling. It may say something wild about present times that the gravest constitutional business can best be played out as situation comedy, but there are enough laughs in *The Queen* to make you think so. If one chose two dysfunctional families struggling with image problems, big appetites and tearful neighbours, it would be difficult to slide a cigarette paper between the Windsors and the Simpsons, yet Frears's movie pays Britain's first family the supreme compliment of taking it seriously, and it's hard not to feel that the results will enjoy a long and fruitful reign in the affections of moviegoers.

We first discover Tony Blair (Michael Sheen) cheesy-smiling his way into Buckingham Palace fresh from an electoral landslide. As is customary when seeking the Queen's permission to form a government, the prime minister goes down on one knee and listens to the Queen's invitation, though the first of many boons in Peter Morgan's script shows Blair getting in first with the words and generally doing a schoolboy's impression of a powerful man, which is exactly right. 'In the end, all Labour prime ministers go gaga for the Queen,' says his wife Cherie (Helen McCrory), who, when called upon to curtsy before Her Majesty, barely manages a resentful, crooked-heeled half-dip. We quickly see that Tony Blair will appear at the dead centre of the piece, a decision that not only honours the facts but focuses one's attention on the real subject of the film: the sudden needs of the British people and their fin-de-siècle emotionalism. The real Tony Blair – at least the chipper, Bambi-like, pre-Iraq Tony – understood this fairly recent and fairly shocking aspect of Britishness as well as Diana did (his every other move seemed to say 'I feel your pain'), and the lack of that understanding on the part of the British monarchy gives the film its drama, just as it gave King Tony the orb and sceptre for a fortnight.

Helen Mirren has the Queen down to a T: everything, from the slightly bow-legged, corgi-perturbed walk to the school-marmish fussiness over gloves and pens and handbags. It may take a brilliant actress to play a brilliant actress, and Mirren allows one to feel that Queen Elizabeth II harbours no little innocence about the worlds that are rumoured to exist beyond her role. Though her hair is always primped and her tweeds immaculate, Mirren's Queen can barely hide the extent to which her life of service has come to seem an affliction. And when news comes in the night, to her bedroom at Balmoral, of Diana's death, it is obvious from the tiny, near-invisible mechanics of Mirren's performance that the sovereign might be clinging to a narrow understanding of duty as a way of express-ing both her anger at Diana and her copious reluctance to learn anything new about the world.

Stuck in the Scottish Highlands with a bunch of stag-hunting yes-men, the Queen watches on TV as the London palaces are islanded in flowers. They think it will pass in a jiffy – that the people will return to their senses – but Blair comes on the phone with the news that Her Majesty's people need her in their time of grief. '*Their* grief!' she exclaims, seeing Blair as both a public-opinion-mongering idiot as well as a quisling lawyer too full of himself to comprehend the weight of history. Despite the tabloid headlines, she refuses to return to London and denies permission for the ensign at Buckingham Palace to be flown at half-mast. (The objection being that even the Queen herself, when dead, would not be afforded this honour.) Invariably standing behind her at such times is her husband Philip, the Duke of Edinburgh (James Cromwell), whose bum-bling, ossified attitudes could easily, any day of the week, make Lady Macbeth look like Coretta Scott King. Even the Queen looks modern next to him.

The Queen Mother is just baffled by developments, and Frears shows her sipping from a tumbler of gin as a shadow falls for the first time on her daughter's seamless reign. 'You are the greatest asset this institution has,' she says. 'One of the greatest it has ever had.' Prince Charles, meanwhile, played with broken, ashen-faced confusion by Alex Jennings, secretly drinks of the New Labour cup, knowing, or feeling in the midst of panic, that it must contain the elixir that will enable him to survive his late wife's popularity.

Blair got it right from the first. It may, as the film shows, have been his vicious henchman Alastair Campbell who invented the phrase 'the people's princess', but Blair's deployment of it the morning after Diana's death, and his clearly heartfelt chiming with the nation's feelings, made him come to seem like the Queen's only hope. Against all the instincts of her breeding, she finally came to London and addressed the people under a low-ered flag, speaking, as New Labour wince-makingly suggested she should, 'as your Queen and as a grandmother'. When it came to Diana's funeral, and that medieval-seeming display of public grief, the Queen sat in Westminster Abbey looking much like a painted warhorse marching to new orders. 'I think,' says Blair in the movie, 'when you look back, you will see that this was actually a very good week for you.'

'And an even better one for you, Mr Blair,' says Mirren's Elizabeth at her most acidic.

Blair's premiership was initially a throbbing pop concert of focus-grouping, news-spinning, rabble-rousing, and being 'on message'. One of the beauties of *The Queen* is that it shows not only what the British sovereign had to learn from Mr Blair but ultimately, and perhaps even more poignantly, what Mr Blair had to learn from her. 'Some day they will try to get rid of you,' she says to him, as he sits across from her at the end of that summer, trying in his Tonyish way not to gloat. 'And quite sud-denly.' This proves to be one of the film's prophecies, and a great, crowd-pleasing joke – I saw the film both in London and in New York, and at each screening the audience burst into applause at this point. Why? Schadenfreude, I suppose. But also because Blair's populism ultimately is no match for the Queen's resilience: if he is a concert, she is a museum, and she has seen ten prime ministers come and go. The film persuades us that Blair might secretly have enjoyed his little stint at 'saving the monarchy'. Yet as I write, it is King Tony who is standing on a cliff with the nation's finger pressing on his back.

Elizabeth II's run-in with the vox populi was, in the end, no real threat to her. As soon as she spoke to her people 'as a grand-mother' they seem to have felt both relieved and assuaged, as people sometimes do after an hour of chair-throwing on *Jerry Springer*. If Jonathan Swift had been alive at that hour, he might have viewed it as a great, short battle between two kinds of silli-ness: the Queen's anachronistic severity versus the people's lachrymose self-indulgence. But here is a film that succeeds by giving ample weight to both, and we end up feeling a little of the Queen's pain, as her late daughter-in-law might have said.

7/7

People began laying flowers on the steps of St Pancras Church the morning after the 7 July bombings, and within a day or two the steps had been transformed into a slope of glinting paper, the flowers strangely urban behind the police cordon. It was also a slope of words: handwritten messages, emails, shop-bought cards and pavement script. The church's columns were chalked with words too, and the Word of God – a King James Bible, 'User's Guide on Back' – appeared to float unabashed on a sea of London scrawls.

For a few days after the explosions, the atmosphere was bad on the buses. Passengers were looking into every face as they sat on a Number 30 from King's Cross, and if the face happened to be brown, they looked to their bag or backpack. That is how fear and paranoia work: they create turbulence in your every-day passivity; everyone was affected after the bombings, and the botched follow-up on 21 July in ways that won't quickly go away. In the realm of paranoia, the second bombings were more powerful than the first, for they made it clear how very gettable we are, even in a culture of high alert. To anyone with imagination (or who knows anyone who's ever had a second stroke), the most recent attack brings a dimension of constant threat. No one needed to die for this to take effect: 7 July showed us what death on the bus or the Tube looks like; the second attack showed that these images wouldn't be allowed to remain just a bad memory. Sitting upstairs on the Number 30 a few days after 7 July, I found myself thinking: in this seat, would it be a leg I'd lose, or an arm? Would I die instantly? Or would I be one of those walking around afterwards in a daze? The London bomb-ings are an ontological disaster for anyone who commutes in a big city: the blasts have taken the steadiness out of people's expectations and replaced it with a more or less hysterical dependence on the size of their luck. That sort of thing is OK from a distance, but it can punish your spirit on the down escalator at nine o'clock in the morning.

When the Number 30 passed a statue of John F. Kennedy in Marylebone Road, a teenager looked up at his mother. 'It all started with him,' he said.

'I know what you mean,' his mother said. 'He was the first to get this amount of coverage.'

In Hyde Park rows of old ladies were sitting in the rose garden. In their white skirts and sandals, they had an air of seen-it-all about them, pointing to beds of flowers and thinking nothing of cellophane. And maybe they had seen it all: by the boating pond, fixed to the bandstand, was a plaque engraved with yet more London words. 'To the memory of those bandsmen of the 1st Battalion of the Blues & Royals who died as a result of the terrorist attack here on 20 July 1982.'

The remains of the Number 30 bus were covered in blue tarpaulin and removed from Tavistock Square a week later. In the days when the street was blocked off, when Upper Woburn Place became a forensic scene and a no-man's-land, I found myself quietly hankering after the openness of Tavistock Square, and several times that week I came down to look at the barricade and puzzle over the idea that the square had gone. I wondered if the street had not lost its life too, as often happened in the Second World War, when people would arrive to mourn both the dead and the place where they used to go. Among many things, the bombings gave those of us who are attached to the city a sense of what it might be like to be very old, to see a graveyard at the corner of every street, a bar where some dead friend used to drink, a bench where you once got a kiss.

There's an essay by Cyril Connolly, 'One of My Londons', in which he writes of London as a city of prose. At the point of writing the essay, Connolly found it hard to be in London for more than a few days at a time, so freighted with former lives

were the streets around Fitzrovia, so haunted by memory and
well-honed sentences. The square that is formed by King's
Cross, Lamb's Conduit Street, Tottenham Court Road and Warren Street is one of my Londons, and the very centre of that
London is Tavistock Square. If London is a city of prose, then
this is the capital's capital, a square of reason and memory and
imagination. My home's home.

The *London Review of Books* had its offices in Tavistock
Square for almost ten years. We were housed in a couple of
rooms on the third floor of the BMA building, Entrance C,
where the great blue door is now shattered and the windows
pierced. The paper bears no deeper connection than that to this
terrible event, and the pictures of Entrance C spattered with
gore will alter every Londoner's sense of London, not just those
who knew the doors and the square they open onto. Yet proximity is the currency in a culture of bomb-fear: those of us who
used to come to that place every morning might be allowed to
pause for a second in our own way. The *London Review* sent out
prose, and poems, from that building every fortnight, and one
day a young man came to the door with a bomb strapped to his
back.

Standing in the square the other day, trying to ignore the
statue of Mahatma Gandhi – it's not hard to ignore, both
because of its ugliness and the minatory nature of his peace-
ableness – I reached for the answer. But the answer, of course,
was there all along: more thought. More argument. For Blair to
deny that the invasion of Iraq influenced the bombers is an
insult to both language and morality. For Islamic extremists to
pretend that their cause will not be set back in Britain by tar-
geting buses and tube trains is a murderous delusion. Blair's
war has been a drafting exercise for young jihadis, and the
efforts of the young jihadis will be a drafting exercise for the
British National Party. Welcome to Endgame England.

Several of the victims of the bus bombs were taken into the
forecourt of the British Medical Association, where they were
attended to by as many doctors, and where two passengers died.

I was always amazed by the length and circuitousness of the corridors in the BMA building, which made one feel like a lost blood cell travelling through the arteries of some giant corporate body. Our office seemed so small and tight compared to all that expanse, but it was to those rooms, with their windows looking down on Tavistock Square, that Salman Rushdie once delivered his review of Calvino's *Invisible Cities*, and where it was edited, cared for, 'washed and ironed', as the editors would say. 'Why,' he wrote, 'should we bother with Calvino, a word-juggler, a fantasist, in an age in which our cities burn and our leaders blame our parents? What does it mean to write about non-existent knights, or the formation of the Moon, or how a reader reads, while the neutron bomb gets the go-ahead in Washington, and plans are made to station germ-warfare weaponry in Europe?' He went on: 'The reason Calvino is such an indispensable writer is precisely that he tells us, joyfully, wickedly, that there are things in the world worth loving as well as hating; and that such things exist in people, too.'

Those were the same rooms where Tony Blair arrived breathlessly one day before catching the train at Euston. The piece he delivered may have required more ironing than Rushdie's, but it too, in October 1987, found its place in the paper's pages. He wrote that Mrs Thatcher 'will wield her power over the next few years dictatorially and without compunction' and further predicted that 'the 1990s will not see the continuing triumph of the market, but its failure'. And it was into those same rooms that Ronan Bennett came with one of the longest pieces ever published in a single issue of the *LRB*, a report on the civil and legal injustices perpetrated by the state in its desperate pursuit of those guilty of the Guildford bombings. Argument in the long run is louder than bombs, even if, as often happened in my day at the *London Review*, people would ring up to cancel their subscriptions when they violently disagreed. It was mostly after we'd run a piece by Edward Said. 'I refuse to read pieces written by murderers,' one of them said.

'And we're happy not to publish them,' I said.

'Said is happy to see Israelis bombed,' she said.

'No,' I said. 'Professor Said is happy to make arguments, and we are happy to publish them.'

But it was Tavistock Square itself that was on my mind. It is understandable that condemnation, in such a case as this, will precede contemplation, but perhaps less bearable that we live at a time when it will overthrow honest thinking altogether. The square is a living testament to the opposite view. More than a hundred years before people were phoning to complain about Edward Said's right to write, Charles Dickens was furnishing his new house on the same site, and furnishing his new novel, *Bleak House*, with characters who struggled to agree about how to live in the world and what to believe. Peter Ackroyd provides a nice picture of the novelist in the agonies of trying to complete his new house, sitting disconsolately on a stepladder while 'Irish labourers stare in through the very slates.' A later visitor, Hans Christian Andersen, saw a magnificent eighteen-room house, filled with pictures and engravings. But nothing is simply one thing, not even the reputation of a great house, and Dickens's pile on Tavistock Square drew ire from George Eliot. 'Splendid library, of course,' she wrote, 'with soft carpet, couches etc., such as become a sympathiser with the suffering classes. How can we sufficiently pity the needy unless we know fully the blessings of plenty?'

The commentators spoke almost by rote about how the bus explosion on Tavistock Square was 'unimaginable', and it was pretty unimaginable, all the more so in a place where so much had been imagined and where people had lived, indeed, fully in accordance with their empathetic capacities. We used sometimes to have a drink after work at the County Hotel, which looks out to Upper Woburn Place with a rather doleful quiver about its nicotine-stained jowls. Everybody who came into that bar – railwaymen from Euston, dancers from the London School of Contemporary Dance – carried a very large sense of particularity about them. Maybe it was the lighting. In among the half-pints of bitter and the curly sandwiches, something in the atmosphere of that bar, with its giant 1940s radio, made everyone seem discrete and minutely alive, not like the hordes of Southampton Row. Everybody smoked cigarettes in those days. There was no television and nobody had a mobile phone. They served lemonade out of bottles. It was heaven to me.

Dorothy Richardson lived at 2 Woburn Walk, the narrow passage next to the County Hotel. It was a 'flagged alley' in 1905, a 'terrible place to live', she wrote. Nearly under the shadow of St Pancras Church, Richardson's flat stood above a row of shops (as it still does), a stonemason's, in her case, while across the alley, at Number 18, W. B. Yeats had one of his London addresses. Richardson recalled seeing him standing at the window on hot summer evenings, breathing the 'parched air'. In his biography of the poet, Roy Foster reports that 'the flat at Woburn Buildings was scraped and repapered in an effort to remove insect life, though WBY still returned there for his Monday evening entertainments'. It appears that Dorothy Richardson was never invited; she and Yeats never actually spoke, though years later she remembered them almost bumping into each other in Tavistock Square. 'For memory,' she wrote, 'we stand permanently confronted either side of that lake of moonlight in the square.'

Like Hasib Hussain, the Number 30 bus was a stranger to Tavistock Square. But the eighteen-year-old who wasted his own life and twelve other people's on that bus knew something about the poetry of Yeats. The bomber had seven GCSEs, including one in English, and Yeats was one of his topics. Heaven knows what was on his mind when he set off his terrible backpack that morning, and one can only be sad that it wasn't Yeats, a one-time neighbour to his terrible, beautyless act, or his poem 'Easter 1916', a distillation for me of the saving power of two-mindedness, the great theme of old Bloomsbury.

On the End of British Farming

MARCH 2001

This last while I have carried my heart in my boots. For a minute or two I actually imagined I could be responsible for the spread of foot and mouth disease across Britain. On my first acquaintance with the hill farmers of the Lake District, on a plot high above Keswick, I had a view of the countryside for tens of miles. I thought of the fields that had passed underfoot, all the way back to Essex, through Dumfriesshire, Northumberland or Sussex. Later I would continue on my way to Devon, passing through other places waking up in the middle of the worst agricultural nightmare in seventy years. My boots are without guilt, but in all the walking here and there, in the asking and listening, I came to feel that British farming was already dying, that the new epidemic was but an unexpected acceleration of a certain decline.

In the last few weeks nearly 100,000 head of livestock have been condemned. The industry has lost £300 million. A freeze still holds on the export of livestock. Country footpaths are zones of reproach and supermarkets are running out of Argentinian beef. The Agriculture Minister is accused of doing too much and doing too little. The questions surrounding the foot and mouth epidemic – Where will it all end? How did it all start? – might be understood to accord with anxiety about every aspect of British agriculture today. The worst has not been and gone. It is yet to come. Still, one thing may already be clear: British farming hanged itself on the expectation of plenty.

One day not long ago I was in the Sainsbury's superstore on the Cromwell Road. Three of the company's top brass ushered me down the aisles, pointing here, gasping there, each of them in something of a swoon at the heavenliness on offer. 'People want to be interested,' said Alison Austin, a technical adviser, 'you've just got to capture their imagination.' We were standing by the sandwiches and the takeaway hot foods lined up in front of the whooshing doors. Alison swept her hand over the colourful bazaar of sandwich choices. 'This is a range called Be Good to Yourself,' she said, 'with fresh, healthy fillings, and here we have the more gourmet range, Taste the Difference. We have a policy of using British produce where we can. With carrots, for example, we want to provide economic profitability to the farmer, using the short carrots for one line of produce and the bigger ones for another.'

The Cromwell Road branch of Sainsbury's is what they call a 'flagship store'. It's not only a giant emporium, it is also grander than any other store in the chain, selling more champagne, fresh fish, organic meat and Special Selection food. Six varieties of caviar are available all year round.

'People are gaining more confidence in sushi,' said Peter Morrison, Manager, Trading Division. 'We have joined forces with very credible traders such as Yo! Sushi and we aim to educate customers by bringing them here.' Alison handed me a cup of liquid grass from the fresh juice bar, Crussh. There was something unusually potent about that afternoon – the thoughts in my head as I tilted the cup – and for a moment the whole supermarket seemed to spin around me. People wandered by. The place was a madhouse of bleeping barcodes. 'How do you like it?' one of them asked. I gulped it down and focused my eyes. 'It tastes like an English field,' I said.

The store manager guided me to the cut flowers. 'We are the UK's largest flower sellers,' he told me. 'The biggest year-on-year increase of any product in the store is in flowers.' The bunches before me were a far cry from the sad carnations and petrol-station bouquets that now lie about the country as tributes to the suddenly dead. The ones he showed me had a very smart, sculptural appearance, and they sold for £25 a pop. 'We have forty kinds of apple,' Alison said, 'and again, we take the crop, the smaller ones being more for the economy bags.'

'Someone came in on Christmas Eve and asked for banana leaves,' the keen young product manager over in fruit and vegetables told me, 'and you know something? We had them.'

You would have to say that Sainsbury's is amazing. It has everything – fifty kinds of tea, four hundred kinds of bread, kosher chicken schnitzels, Cornish pilchards – and everywhere I turned that day there was some bamboozling elixir of the notion of plenty. Their own-brand products are made to high standards: the fresh meat, for example, is subject to much higher vigilance over date and provenance than any meat in Europe. 'Some things take a while,' Peter Morrison said. 'You can put something out and it won't work. Then you have to think again, about how to market it, how to package it, where to place it, and six months later you'll try again and it might work.' We stopped beside the yoghurts. 'Now this,' he said, picking up a tub of Devon yoghurt, 'is made at a place called Stapleton Farm. We got wind of how good it was: a tiny operation, we went down there, we got some technical advisers involved, and now look, it's brilliant!' I tasted some of the Stapleton yoghurt. It was much better than the liquid grass. 'It's about the rural business growing,' Peter said. 'Real food is what people want. This couple in Devon' – he gestured to the yoghurt pots – 'started from virtually nowhere. Of course they were nervous at first about working with such a major retailer. But these people are the new kind of producer.'

Passing the condiments aisle I saw an old man standing in front of the Oxo cubes. He looked a bit shaky. His lips were moving and he had one of the foil-wrapped Oxo cubes in the palm of his hand. 'People go to Tuscany,' Alison was saying, 'and they eat Parma ham and they come back here and they want it all the time. So we go out and find the best.' You are always alone with the oddness of modern consumption. Walking under the white lights of Sainsbury's you find out just who you are. The reams of cartons, the pyramids of tins: there they stand on the miles of shelves, the story of how we live now. Cereal boxes look out at you with their breakfast-ready smiles, containing flakes of bran, handfuls of oats, which come from fields mentioned in the Domesday Book. We went over to the aisle with the cooking oils and Alison did one of her long arm-flourishes: 'When I was a child,' she said, 'my mother used a bottle of prescription olive oil to clean the salad bowl. Now look!' A line of tank-green bottles stretched into the distance. 'Choice!' she said.

Supermarket people like to use certain words. When you are with them in the fruit department they all say 'fresh' and 'juicy' and 'variety' and 'good farming practices'. (Or, as head office puts it, 'in 1992 Sainsbury developed a protocol for growing crops under Integrated Crop Management System principles. Following these principles can result in reduced usage of pesticides by combining more traditional aspects of agriculture and new technologies.') In the meat department there is much talk of 'friendly', 'animal well-being', 'humane', 'safe', 'high standards' and 'provenance'. The executives spent their time with me highlighting what they see as the strength of the partnerships with British farming which keep everyone happy. 'The consumer is what matters,' said Alison, 'and we believe in strong, creative, ethical retailing.'

Down at the front of the store again I put one of the gourmet sandwiches on a table and opened it up. The bread was grainy. The lettuce was pale green and fresh. Pieces of chicken and strips of pepper were neatly set out on a thin layer of butter. The open sandwich was a tableau of unwritten biographies: grains and vegetables and meat were glistening there, uncontroversially, their stories of economic life and farming history and current disaster safely behind them.

When I was a boy we had a painting above the phone table. It was the only real painting in the house, and it showed a wide field in the evening with a farm at the far end. The farmhouse had a light in one of the windows. The painting had been a wedding present, and my mother thought it was a bit dour and dirty-looking, so she did the frame up with some white gloss, which flaked over the years. I used to lie on the hall carpet and look at the picture of the farm for ages; the field was golden enough to run through and get lost in, and the brown daubs of farmhouse were enough to send me into a swoon of God-knows-what. I suppose it was all part of a general childhood spaced-outness, and it meant nothing, but it seemed very heightening at the time. The painting raised my feelings up on stilts, and made me imagine myself to be part of an older world, where people lived and worked in a state of sentimental peace. All rot of course. But lovely rot. Sometimes I would come downstairs in the night and shine my torch on the painting.

At one time it seemed as if all the farms around our way had been abandoned or pulled down to make room for housing. Past railway lines and beyond the diminishing fields we would find old, dilapidated Ayrshire farmhouses with rusted tractors and ancient wooden drinking troughs lying about in the yard, and we'd play in them for half the summer. Cranberry Moss Farm, McLaughlin's Farm on Byrehill, Ashgrove Farm, the Old Mains – nowadays they are all buried under concrete, except for the farm at Toddhill, which became a home for the mentally handicapped. In my youth they had been like haunted houses. There were echoes in the barns.

Those farms seemed as remote from the daily reality of our lives as the one in the wedding picture. We would never live there: computer factories and industrial cleaners would soon replace them as providers of jobs, and it was these new places, in our Ayrshire, that spoke of the lives we were supposed one day to live. We took it for granted – much too early, as it turned out – that farming was a thing of the past, a thing people did before they were sophisticated like us. We never considered the stuff on our plates; we thought the school milk came on a lorry from London. Never for a second did my friends and I think of ourselves as coming from a rural community; like all British suburban kids, we lived as dark, twinkling fallout from a big city, in our case Glasgow, and we thought carports and breeze blocks were part of the natural order.

But of course there was plenty of agriculture. It surrounded us. The farms had just been pushed out a wee bit – and wee could seem larger than it was, at least for us, shocked by the whiteness of our new buildings into thinking a thatched roof was the height of exotic. Everything changed for me with the discovery of Robert Burns: those torn-up fields out there were his fields, those bulldozed farms as old as his words, both old and new to me then. Burns was ever a slave to the farming business: he is the patron saint of struggling farmers and poor soil. But now, as I write, the situation of farming in this country is perhaps worse than it has ever been, and the countryside itself is dying. We are at a stage where it is difficult to imagine British farming surviving in any of its traditional forms; and for millions living on these islands, a long-term crisis has been turning into a terminal disaster.

The total area of agricultural land is 18.6 million hectares, 76 per cent of the entire land surface. According to an agricultural census in June 1999, there has been a decrease of 5.3 per cent in the area given over to crops, as a result of a decrease in cereals and an increase in set-aside. According to a recent report from the Ministry of Agriculture, Fisheries and Food (Maff), the 1999 figures show a drop in the labour force of 3.6 per cent, the largest decrease in a dozen years. 'These results,' the report continues, 'are not unexpected given the financial pressures experienced by most sectors of the industry over the last few years.'

Farmers' income fell by over 60 per cent between 1995 and 1999. Despite increases in production, earnings were lower in 1999 by £518 million. The value of wheat fell by 6.5 per cent and barley by 5.4. Pigs were £99 million down on 1998 and lambs £126 million down; the value of poultry meat fell by £100 million or 7.4 per cent; the value of milk fell by £45 million; and the value of eggs by 10 per cent or £40 million. A giant profit gap has opened up throughout the industry: rape seed, for example, which costs £200 a ton to produce, is selling for £170 per ton (including the government subsidy); a savoy cabbage, costing

13p to produce, is sold by the farmer for 11p, and by the supermarkets for 47p.

Hill farmers earned less than £8,000 a year on average in
1998–9 (and 60 per cent of that came to them in subsidies), but
late last year, when I first started talking to farmers, many were
making nothing at all, and most were heavily in debt to the
bank. A suicide helpline was set up and the Royal College of
Psychiatrists expressed concern at the increased number of sui-
cides among hill farmers in particular. A spokesman for Maff
said that agriculture was costing every British taxpayer £4 a
week. After Germany and France, the UK makes the largest
annual contribution to the Common Agricultural Policy, and
yet, even before the great rise in the strength of the pound,
British farmers' production costs were higher than anywhere
else in the EU, to a large extent because of the troubles of recent
years.

'Everything is a nightmare,' one farmer told me. 'There are
costs everywhere, and even the subsidy is spent long before you
receive it. We are all in hock to the banks – and they say we are
overmanned, but we don't have anybody here, just us, and children maybe, and an absolute fucking nightmare from top to
bottom.' The strong pound, the payment of subsidy cheques in
euros, the BSE crisis, swine fever and now foot and mouth disease, together with overproduction in the rest of the world's
markets – these are the reasons for the worsened situation. But
they are not the cause of the longer-term crisis in British farming: local overproduction is behind that, and it is behind the
destruction of the countryside too. For all the savage reductions
of recent times, farming still employs too many and produces
too much: even before the end of February, when diseased livestock burned on funeral pyres 130 feet high, some farmers were
killing their own livestock for want of a profit, or to save the fuel
costs incurred in taking them to market.

In Britain nowadays most farmers are given aid – a great deal
of aid, but too little to save them – in order to produce food
nobody wants to buy. The way livestock subsidies work – per

animal – means that there is an incentive for farmers to increase flocks and herds rather than improve the marketing of what they've got. As things are, subsidies save some farmers, but they are a useless way to shore up an ailing industry, except perhaps in wartime.

The evidence of what is wrong is out in the British land itself. It is to be found in the particularities of farming experience now, but also in a historical understanding of what farming has meant in this country. Farming – more even than coal, more than ships, steel, or Posh and Becks – is at the centre of who British people think they are. It has a heady, long-standing, romantic and sworn place in the cultural imagination: the death of farming will not be an easy one in the green and pleasant land. Even shiny, new, millennial economic crises have to call the past into question. How did we come to this?

In the eighteenth century, farmers were still struggling out of the old ways depicted in *Piers Plowman*, or the Bayeux Tapestry, where English farm horses are seen for the first time, bringing vegetables from the fields to the kitchen table. Jethro Tull, one of the fathers of modern agriculture, devoted himself to finding ways to increase yields – he invented the seed-drill, a machine that could sow three rows of seed simultaneously – and collected his ideas in *The New Horse Houghing Husbandry: or, an Essay on the Principles of Tillage and Vegetation* (1731). His ideas were widely accepted by the time he died at Prosperous Farm, near Hungerford in Berkshire, ten years later. Arthur Young, an agricultural educator and zealot of Improvement, set out in 1767 on a series of journeys through the country. *A Six Months' Tour through the North of England* gives a spirited first-person account of changing agricultural conditions. 'Agriculture is the grand product that supports the people,' he wrote. 'Both public and private wealth can only arise from three sources, agriculture, manufactures and commerce . . . Agriculture much exceeds the others; it is even the foundation of the principal branches.' But the new improvements came at a price and they changed for ever the relationship between the land and the people who tried to live by it. British peasant life was effectively over. 'The agrarian revolution was economically justifiable,' Pauline Gregg writes in *A Social and Economic History of Britain, 1760–1965*, but 'its social effects were disastrous. Scores of thousands of peasants suffered complete ruin. The small farmer, the cottager, the squatter, were driven off the soil, and their cottages were often pulled down.' The British countryside, in the face of all improvements, and with every prospect of sharing in the coming wealth of nations, became as Goldsmith described it in 'The Deserted Village':

> Ill fares the land, to hastening ills a prey,
> Where wealth accumulates, and men decay;
> Princes and lords may flourish, or may fade;
> A breath can make them, as a breath has made;
> But a bold peasantry, their country's pride,
> When once destroyed, can never be supplied.

In the spring of 1770 British cows were so disabled by starvation that they had to be carried out to the pastures. This business was known as 'the lifting'. *The General View of Ayrshire*, published in 1840, records that as late as 1800 one third of the cows and horses in the county were killed for want of fodder. By the end of winter in this period, according to John Higgs's *The Land* (1964), every blade of grass had been eaten and the animals were forced to follow the plough looking for upturned roots.

The social structure of the country had changed, the population had grown, the plough had been improved, the threshing machine had been invented, and crop rotation had taken hold. William Cobbett, in his *Rural Rides* – originally a column that appeared in the *Political Register* between 1822 and 1826 – captured the movements which created the basis of the farming world we know. Cobbett rode out on horseback to look at farms to the south and east of a line between Norwich and Hereford; he made an inspection of the land and spoke to the people working on it. He addressed groups of farmers on the Corn

Laws, taxes, placemen, money for agricultural paupers, and the general need for reform.

In one of his columns he describes meeting a man coming home from the fields. 'I asked him how he got on,' he writes. 'He said, very badly. I asked him what was the cause of it. He said the *hard times*. "What times?" said I; was there ever a finer summer, a finer harvest, and is there not an old wheat-rick in every farmyard? "Ah!" said he, "*they* make it hard for poor people, for all that." "*They*," said I, "who is *they*?"' Cobbett yearned for a pre-industrial England of fine summer days and wheat-ricks, and yet his conservatism did not prevent him from becoming an evangelist of Improvement. As for 'they' – Cobbett knew what was meant; he later called it 'the Thing', and sometimes 'the system'. He railed against everything that was wrong with English agriculture: low wages, absentee landlords, greedy clergymen, corruption; and he was prosecuted for supporting a riot by these same agricultural workers the year after he published *Rural Rides*. Cobbett saw how self-inflated governments could sit by and watch lives crumble. His discriminating rage has the tang of today. 'The system of managing the affairs of the nation,' he wrote in *Cottage Economy*, 'has made all flashy and false, and has put all things out of their place. Pomposity, bombast, hyperbole, redundancy and obscurity, both in speaking and writing; mock-delicacy in manners, mock-liberality, mock-humanity . . . all have arisen, grown, branched out, bloomed and borne together; and we are now beginning to taste of their fruit.'

Rain was running down Nelson's Column and Trafalgar Square was awash with visitors inspecting the lions. An American woman stepping into the National Gallery was worried about her camera lens. 'This British weather will be the end of us,' she said, as her husband shook out the umbrellas. In the Sackler Room – Room 34 – children with identical haircuts sat down on the wooden floor; they stared at the British weather of long ago, spread in oils with palette knives, and they, too, asked why it was always so fuzzy and so cloudy. One group sat around Turner's *Rain, Steam and Speed – The Great Western Railway*. The instructor encouraged them to express something about the atmosphere of the picture. 'Does it make you shiver?' she said. 'It's like outside,' one of the children replied. But most of them were interested in the hare running ahead of the train. 'Will it die?' one of them asked. 'Where is it running to?'

The future. You feel the force of change in some of these weathery British pictures. Over the last few months I kept coming back to this room, and sitting here, further up from the Turners, looking at Constable's *The Cornfield*. We see an English country lane at harvest time where nothing is unusual but everything is spectacular. Corn spills down an embankment, going to grass and ferns, going to pepper saxifrage or hog's fennel, dandelion and corn poppy, down to a stream. Giant trees reach up to the dark, gathering clouds. At their foot, a small boy lies flat on his front, drinking from the stream. He wears a red waistcoat and has a tear in the left leg of his trousers. A dog with a marked shadow looks up and past him with its pink tongue out. The sheep in front of the dog are making for a broken gate that opens onto the cornfield. A plough is stowed in a ditch; the farmer advances from the field; and in the distance, which stretches for miles, you see people already at work.

The picture has philosophical currency: people will still say it is an important part of what is meant by the term 'British' – or at any rate 'English'. This is the country delegates sing about at the party conferences, the one depicted in heritage brochures and on biscuit tins, the corner that lives in the sentiments of war poetry, an image at the heart of Britain's view of itself. But here's the shock: it no longer exists. Everything in Constable's picture is a small ghost still haunting the national consciousness. The corn poppy has pretty much gone and so have the workers. The days of children drinking from streams are over too. And the livestock? We will come to that. Let me just say that a number of the farmers I spoke to in the winter of 2000 were poisoning their own fields. The Constable picture fades into a new world of intensive industrial farming and environmental blight.

The Cornfield is said to show the path along which Constable walked from East Bergholt across the River Stour and the fields to his school at Dedham. Last October I made my way to Dedham. It was another wet day, and many of the trucks and lorries splashing up water on the M25 were heading to the coast to join a fuel blockade. On the radio a newscaster described what was happening: 'The situation for the modern British farmer has probably never been so dire, and a further rise in the price of fuel could kill many of them off.'

Before leaving I had rung a pig farmer, David Barker, whose farm is north of Stowmarket in Suffolk. Barker is 50 years old. His family have been farming pigs in Suffolk for four generations; they have lived and worked on the present farm since 1957. He owns 1,250 acres and 110 sows, which he breeds and sells at a finishing weight of 95 kilos. Among his crops are winter wheat, winter-sown barley, grass for seed production, some peas for canning, 120 acres of field beans, 30 acres of spring oats and 100 acres of set-aside.

'Five years ago I was selling wheat for £125 a ton and now it's £58.50,' David Barker said. 'I was selling pigs for £90 and now they're down to £65. And meanwhile all our costs have doubled: fuel, stock, fertiliser. There's hardly a farmer in East Anglia who's making a profit. The direct payments from Europe have declined also because they're paid out in euros.'

'What about swine fever?' I asked, innocent of the epidemics to come.

'There are over five hundred farms that haven't been able to move pigs since August,' he said. 'Immediately, this becomes an agricultural nightmare. The pigs are breeding, the feed is extortionate, and you end up relying on things like the Welfare Disposal Scheme, where pigs are removed for next to nothing. Gordon Brown's bright idea: they give you £50 for a pig that costs £80 to produce.'

'What can be done?' The stormy weather was making his phone crackly.

'Well, this government has no interest in farming,' he said. 'People in the countryside in England feel they are ignored and derided and, frankly, it appears that the government would be much happier just to import food. This is the worst agricultural crisis in dozens of years. We're not making any money anywhere. Take milk: the dairy farmer receives 7p in subsidy for every pint; it takes between 10p and 12p to produce and it costs 39p when it arrives at your door. A lot of farmers are giving up and many of those who stay are turning to contract farming – increasing their land, making prairies, to make it pay.'

'Is that the only way to reduce costs?'

'Yes. That, or by going to France.'

David Barker used the word 'nightmare' at least a dozen times during my conversation with him. He told me about a friend of his, another Suffolk farmer, who, earlier in the swine-fever debacle, had sold his 250 pigs into the disposal scheme, losing £30 on each one. Barker himself was waiting for results of blood tests to see if his pigs had the fever. 'If it goes on much longer it will ruin me,' he said.

When I arrived at Nigel Rowe's farm near Dedham only the weather was Constable-like. Out of his window the fields were bare and flat. 'European pig meat is cheaper to produce,' he said, 'because we have higher standards and higher production costs. As soon as foreign bacon gets cheaper by more than 10p per kilo the housewife swaps. That is the rule.'

I asked him if he felt British supermarkets had been good at supporting bacon produced in Essex or Suffolk. 'The supermarkets have been very clever at playing the different farming sectors off against each other,' he said. 'The Danish model is very centralised – they are allowed to produce and market something called Danish Bacon. We are very regional over here, very dominated by the tradition of the local butcher. Supermarkets want the same produce to be available in Scotland as you get in Sussex. Only the Dutch and the Danish can do that, and some of these foreign producers are so powerful – the Danish producers of bacon are much bigger than Tesco.'

Nigel has 2,000 pigs. But he's not making money. As well as working the farm he has a part-time job as caretaker at the local community centre. 'In the 1970s we were all earning a comfortable living,' he said, 'and when I was at primary school in the 1960s at least thirty of my schoolmates were connected with farming. Now, in my children's classes, there are three. I had 120 acres and I had to sell it recently to survive. I also had to sell the farm cottage my mother lived in in order to stay here. That's what I was working on when you came – a little house for my mother.'

He looked out the window at the flatness beyond. 'The arithmetic is simple,' he said. 'When I started in this game it took five tons of grain to buy the year's supply of fuel for the tractor. Now it takes 500 tons. What do you think that means if your acreage is the same? The government seem hell-bent on the old green and pleasant land, but they won't get behind the people who keep it that way.' Nigel sat in his living room wearing a rugby shirt and jeans speckled with paint from his mother's new house. 'They're not thinking straight,' he said. 'Our product needs to be marketed – branded, with a flag, which is presently not allowed. It's all wrong. We have to import soya as a protein source for our pigs now because we can't use other animal meat or bone fat. But this country imports tons of Dutch and Danish meat fed on bone fat.'

As we walked out of the living room I noticed there were no pictures on any of the walls. We went outside to the pig sties. The rain was pouring down, the mud thick and sloppy on the ground, and one of Nigel's pigs was burning in an incinerator. As we looked out I asked him what had happened to the land. 'The subsidies from the Common Agricultural Policy have got out of hand,' he said, 'because they are linked to production rather than the environment. Did you know the rivers around here are polluted with fertiliser and crap? We're seeing a massive degradation of rural life in this country. Bakers and dairies have already gone, onions have gone, sugar-beet is gone, beef is pretty much gone, lambs are going.'

Before we went into the sty he asked me if I was 'pig-clean'. 'I'm clean,' I said, 'unless the fever can come through the phone.' Hundreds of healthy-looking pink pigs scuttled around in the hay and the mud. He picked one up. 'Farming is passed down,' he said, 'or it should be. A farm is built up for generation after generation, and when it starts to slip and go – you feel an absolute failure. That's what you feel.'

We went around the farm and Nigel explained how things work. The notebook was getting very wet so I put it away. 'You feel a failure,' he said again, looking into the wind. 'The other night I was at a meeting: 140 farmers at a union meeting paying tribute to four hill farmers under forty-five who'd committed suicide.' He leaned against the side of the barn. 'We are no longer an island,' he said, 'everything's a commodity.'

Charles Grey, the leader of the Whig Party, won a snap election in 1831 with a single slogan: 'The Bill, the whole Bill and nothing but the Bill.' The Reform Act, which was passed the following year after several reversals and much trouble from the Lords, increased the British electorate by 57 per cent and paved the way for the Poor Law and the Municipal Corporations Act; this in turn killed off the oligarchies which had traditionally dominated local government. The misery and squalor that Cobbett had described in the late 1820s worsened during the Hungry Forties; it was not until after the repeal of the Corn Laws, and the subsequent opening up of trade, that British farmers found a brief golden moment. By the end of 1850 Burns and Wordsworth and Constable were dead, and the countryside they adored was subject to four-crop rotation and drainage. Something had ended. And the Census of 1851 shows you what: for the first time in British history the urban population was greater than the rural. Yet the cult of the landscape continues even now as if nothing had changed. Today some parts of East Sussex look like Kansas.

In 1867 it became illegal to employ women and children in gangs providing cheap labour in the fields. This was a small social improvement at a time when things were starting to get difficult again: corn prices fell; there was an outbreak of cattle plague; cheaper produce arrived from America; refrigeration was invented in 1880 and suddenly ships were coming from Australia loaded with mutton and beef. At a meeting in Aylesbury in September 1879, Benjamin Disraeli, by then Earl of Beaconsfield, spoke on 'The Agricultural Situation', and expressed concern about British farming's ability to compete with foreign territories. 'The strain on the farmers of England has become excessive,' he said. The year before, he claimed, the Opposition had set 'the agricultural labourers against the farmers. Now they are attempting to set the farmers against the landlords. It will never do . . . We will not consent to be devoured singly. Alone we have stood together under many trials, and England has recognised that in the influence of the agricultural interest there is the best security for liberty and law.' British farming struggled to compete in the open market until 1910, when the Boards of Agriculture and Fisheries and Food were established and the state became fully involved in supporting it. No one was prepared for what was coming next: squadrons of enemy aeroplanes would darken the fields, and out there, beyond the coast, submarines were about to reintroduce the threat of starvation.

The year 1914 was yet another beginning in British farming. John Higgs argues that the war found agriculture singularly unprepared:

> The area under crops other than grass had fallen by nearly 4.4 million acres since the 1870s . . . and the total agricultural area had fallen by half a million acres. When the war began the possible effects of submarine attacks were unknown and there seemed no reason why food should not continue to be imported as before. As a result only the last two of the five harvests were affected by the Food Production Campaign. This came into being early in 1917 with the immediate and urgent task of saving the country from starvation.

This was the start of a British production frenzy, a beginning that would one day propagate an ending. Free trade was cast aside in the interests of survival, and agricultural executive committees were set up in each county to cultivate great swathes of new land, to superintend an increase in production, with guaranteed prices. The Corn Production Act of 1917 promised high prices for wheat and oats for the post-war years and instituted an Agricultural Wages Board to ensure that workers were properly rewarded for gains in productivity. Some farmers objected to having their produce commandeered for the war effort. One of them, C. F. Ryder, wrote a pamphlet entitled *The Decay of Farming*. A Suffolk farmer of his acquaintance, 'without being an enthusiast for the war', was quite willing to make any sacrifice for England which might be essential, but, as a dealer in all kinds of livestock, he knows the shocking waste and incompetence with which government business has been conducted, and thinks it grossly unjust that, while hundreds of millions have been wasted, on the one hand, there should be, on the other, an attempt to save a few thousands by depriving the agriculturalist of his legitimate profit.

Despite the words of the non-enthusiast, the war had made things temporarily good for farmers. But the high prices of wartime couldn't be maintained and in 1920 the market collapsed. This was to be the worst slump in British agriculture until the present one. With diminished world markets and too much grain being produced for domestic use, the Corn Production Act was repealed in 1921. British farmers were destitute.

In *A Policy for British Agriculture* (1939), a treatise for the Left Book Club, Lord Addison, a former minister for agriculture, tried to explain the devastation that took place during those years.

Millions of acres of land have passed out of active cultivation and the process is continuing. An increasing extent of good land is reverting to tufts of inferior grass, to brambles and weeds, and often to the reedy growth that betrays water-logging; multitudes of farms are beset with dilapidated buildings, and a great and rapid diminution is taking place in the number of those who find employment upon them . . . Since the beginning of the present century nearly a quarter of a million workers have quietly drifted from the country to the town. There are, however, some people who do not seem to regard this decay of Agriculture with much dismay. They are so obsessed with the worship of cheapness at any cost that they overlook its obvious concomitants in keeping down the standard of wages and purchasing power, and the spread of desolation over their own countryside. Their eyes only seem to be fixed on overseas trade.

There are those who argue that it was this depression – and the sense of betrayal it engendered in farmers between the wars – that led the government to make such ambitious promises at the start of the Second World War. Addison's policy, like many agricultural ideas of the time, was based on a notion of vastly increased production as the ultimate goal. 'Nothing but good,' he wrote, 'would follow from the perfectly attainable result of increasing our home food production by at least half as much again . . . a restored countryside is of first-rate importance.'

It was too early in the twentieth century – and it is perhaps too early still, at the beginning of the twenty-first – to see clearly and unequivocally that the two goals stated by Addison are contradictory. The vast increases in production at the start of the Second World War, and the guarantees put in place at that time, set the trend for overproduction and food surpluses – and began the process of destruction that continues to threaten the British countryside. The pursuit of abundance has contributed to the creation of a great, rolling emptiness. But in the era of the ration book, production was the only answer: no one could have been expected to see the mountains on the other side.

Two years before Addison took office Thomas Hardy died, and voices were raised in Westminster Abbey invoking his own invocation of the Wessex countryside:

Precisely at this transitional point of its nightly roll into darkness the great and particular glory of the Egdon waste began, and nobody could be said to understand the heath who had not been there at such a time. It could best be felt when it could not clearly be seen, its complete effect lying in this and the succeeding hours before the next dawn.

It was in Addison's time that glinting combine harvesters began to appear in the fields.

You hear the Borderway Mart before you see it. Driving out of Carlisle, beyond the roundabouts and small industrial units, you can hear cattle lowing and dragging their chains, and in the car park there are trucks full of bleating sheep arriving at a market that doesn't especially want them. Inside you can't breathe for the smell of dung: farmers move around shuffling papers, eating rolls and sausages, drinking coffee from Styrofoam cups. Some of them check advertising boards covered with details of machinery for sale, farm buildings for rent – the day-to-day evidence of farmers selling up. 'It could be any of us selling our tractor up there,' an old man in a tweed cap muttered at me.

The tannoy crackled into life. 'The sale of five cattle is starting right now in ring number one,' the voice said. A black heifer was padding around the ring, its hoofs slipping in sawdust and shit, and the man in charge of the gate, whose overalls were similarly caked, regularly patted it on the rump to keep it moving. Farmers in wellington boots and green waxed jackets hung their arms over the bars taking notes. One or two looked more like City businessmen. The heifer was nineteen months old and weighed 430 kilos. The bidding was quick and decisive: the heifer went for 79p a kilo.

'If you were here in the prime beef ring six or seven years ago,' the auctioneer said later, 'you would have seen the farmers getting about 120p per kilo. That is why so many of the farmers are going out of business. Four years ago, young female sheep would be going for eighty-odd pounds, and today they are averaging thirty.'

Climbing to Rakefoot Farm outside Keswick, you see nothing but hills and, in the distance, the lakes like patches of silver;

tea shops and heritage centres and Wordsworth's Walks serve as punctuation on the hills going brown in the afternoon. Will Cockbain was sitting in front of a black range in a cottage built in 1504. 'There are ghosts here,' he said, 'but they're mostly quite friendly.'

Will's father bought Rakefoot Farm in 1958, but his family have been working the land around Keswick for hundreds of years. 'There are more Cockbains in the local cemetery than anything else,' he said, 'and they have always been sheep farmers. Sitting here with you now, I can remember the smell of bread coming from that range, years ago, when my grandmother was here.' Will has 1,100 Swaledale sheep and 35 suckler cows on the farm. 'Seven thousand pounds is a figure you often hear as an annual earning for full-time farmers round here,' he said. 'Quite a few are on Family Credit – though not many will admit it. We farm 2,500 acres, of which we now own just 170, the rest being rented from five different landlords, including the National Trust. The bigger part of our income comes from subsidies we get for environmental work – keeping the stone walls and fences in order, maintaining stock-proof dykes, burning heather, off-wintering trees.'

'Can't you make anything from the sheep?' I asked.

'No,' he said. 'We are selling livestock way below the cost of production. Subsidies were introduced in 1947 when there was rationing and food shortages, and the subsidies continued, along with guaranteed prices, and now even the subsidies aren't enough. We've got the lowest ewe premium price we've had for years. In hill farming the income is stuck and the environmental grants are stuck too. Fuel prices are crippling us. We are in a job that doesn't pay well and we depend on our vehicles. We are responsible for keeping the landscape the way people say they are proud to have it – but who pays for it? The people down the road selling postcards of the Lake District are making much more than the farmers who keep the land so photogenic.'

Will Cockbain was the same size as the chair he was sitting in. Staring into the fire, he waggled his stocking-soled feet, and blew out his lips. 'I think Margaret Thatcher saw those guaranteed prices farmers were getting and just hated it,' he said, 'and now, though it kills me, we may have to face something: there are too many sheep in the economy. Farmers go down to the market every other week and sell one sheep, and then they give thirty or forty away. They're not worth anything. There are mass sheep graves everywhere now in the United Kingdom.' Will laughed and drank his tea. 'It's only those with an inbuilt capacity for pain that can stand the farming life nowadays,' he said. 'I like the life, but you can't keep liking it when you're running against the bank, when things are getting out of control in ways you never dreamed of, relationships falling apart, everything.'

On the walls of Will Cockbain's farm there are dozens of rosettes for prize-winning sheep. A picture of Will's son holding a prize ram hangs beside a grandfather clock made by Simpson of Cockermouth, and an old barometer pointing to Rain. 'This is a farming community from way back,' Will said, 'but they're all getting too old now. Young men with trained dogs are a rarity, and hill farming, of all kinds, needs young legs. We've lost a whole generation to farming. My boys are hanging in there for now, but with, what, £27,000 last year between four men, who could blame them for disappearing?'

'It's going to be a nightmare if they let farming go the same way as mining,' said another farmer, 'but still, we all vote Conservative up here. The Tories were much better to us.'

As early as 1935 there was panic in the Ministry of Agriculture about the possibility of another war. The First World War had caught British agriculturalists on the hop: this time preparations had to be made. And it was this panic and this mindfulness that set in train the subsidy-driven production that many feel has ruined (and saved) the traditional farming economy in this country, creating an 'unreal market' and a falsely sustained industry, the root of today's troubles. Before the outbreak of war, policies were introduced which favoured the stockpiling of tractors and fertilisers; there were subsidies for anyone who ploughed up permanent grasslands; agricultural workers were released from war duty; and the Women's Land Army was established. Farming became the Second Front, and the 'Dig for Victory' campaign extended from public parks to private allotments.

With the war at sea British food imports dropped by half while the total area of domestic crops increased by 63 per cent: production of some vegetables, such as potatoes, doubled. Farmers in the 1920s had complained that their efforts to increase production in wartime had not been rewarded by an undertaking of long-term government support. The mistake would not be repeated. Promises were made at the start of the second war, and in 1947, with food shortages still in evidence and rationing in place, an Agriculture Act was passed which offered stability and annual price reviews to be monitored by the National Farmers' Union. Parliament instituted a massive programme of capital investment in farm fabric and equipment, and free advice on the use of new technologies and fertiliser was made available. Water supplies and telephone lines were introduced in many previously remote areas. Farmers working the land in the 1950s and 1960s, though there were fewer and fewer of them, had, it's true, never had it so good. At the same time increased use of artificial fertilisers and chemical pesticides meant greater yields and what is now thought of as severe environmental damage: motorway bypasses, electricity pylons, larger fields attended by larger machines, with meadows ploughed up, marshes filled in, woods and grasslands usurped by acreage-hungry crops – what the writer Graham Harvey refers to as 'this once "living tapestry"' was being turned into 'a shroud . . . a landscape of the dead'.

Government subsidies and grants in wartime, cemented in post-war policy, prepared British farmers for the lavish benefits they were to enjoy after Britain joined the Common Market in 1973. Today, the Common Agricultural Policy gets a lashing whatever your view of the EU. One side sees quotas and subsidies and guaranteed prices as responsible for overproduction and the creation of a false economy. The other accuses it of being kinder to other European states and not giving enough back to British farmers, a view generally shared by the farmers themselves, but secretly abhorred by the government, which is handing out subsidies. The two sides agree, however, that the CAP doesn't work, and as I write a new round of reforms is being introduced.

In 1957, when the Common Market came into being, there was a deficit in most agricultural products and considerable variance in priorities from state to state – some to do with climate and dietary needs, some to do with protectionist tendencies. (British farmers who feel ill served by the CAP often say it was formed too early to suit British needs.) The CAP came into effect in 1964. It was intended to rationalise the chains of supply and demand across member states. This was to be achieved by improving agricultural productivity and promoting technical progress; by maintaining a stable supply of food at regular and sensible prices to consumers; by setting up a common pricing system that would allow farmers in all countries to receive the same returns, fixed above the world market level, for their output. Agricultural commissioners were given the right to intervene in the market where necessary, and a system of variable levies was established to prevent imported goods undercutting EC production. The vexed issue was the common financing system, which still operates today, and which means that all countries contribute to a central market support fund called the European Agricultural Guidance and Guarantee Fund, or EAGGF. All market support is paid for centrally out of this fund, with budgetary allocations for each commodity sector. Cash is paid out to producers in member states regardless of the level of a country's contribution to the fund.

One consequence of this protectionist jamboree has been an increase, across the board and in all member states, in the variety and quality of available products, from plum tomatoes and cereals to hams and wines and cheeses, with modern supermarkets now carrying a vastly increased range of produce at comparable prices. (This may have pleased British consumers but it hasn't pleased British farmers, who argue that supermarkets have exploited this abundance, breaking traditional commitments to local producers, and 'shopping around Europe' for supplies which could be got in Britain.) A second consequence has been the familiar overstimulated production and the creation of surpluses. It may even be that by continuing to offer not only guaranteed prices but production subsidies to boot, the CAP can be considered one of the chief instigators of the current crisis.

In the early 1990s European agriculturalists, seeing the need for the CAP to give direct support to an ailing industry – 'to protect the family farm', as they often put it – and to protect the environment, began to speak a different language. The European Commission, in its own words,

> recognised that radical reforms were necessary in order to redress the problems of ever-increasing expenditure and declining farm incomes, the build up and cost of storing surplus food stocks and damage to the environment caused by intensive farming methods. A further factor was the tensions which the Community's farm support policy caused in terms of the EC's external trade relations. Various measures have been adopted since the mid-1980s to address these problems, e.g. set-aside, production and expenditure quotas on certain products and co-responsibility levies on others. However, these proved inadequate to control the expansion of support expenditure.

A constant refrain during the Thatcher period was that measures like these would only serve to impede market forces. The bucking of market forces, however, was one of the founding principles of the CAP, and even today, when we finally see the bottom falling out of the system of rewards and grants for over-production, the tendency is towards 'relief' packages, which New Labour support through gritted teeth. It would appear that for a long time now British farming has been faced with two choices: a slow death or a quick one. And not even Thatcher could tolerate a quick one.

Consumers stand to save more than a billion pounds from the cuts in support prices; and the Blair government is largely in agreement with these proposals, although there are elements which, according to documents available from the Scottish Executive, it finds less than satisfactory:

> While the general proposals for addressing rural policy lack detail, they look innovative and offer possibilities for directing support to rural areas. The downside of the proposals is that the compensation payments look to be too generous, there is no proposal to make farm payments degressive or decoupled from production ... The Government has also declared its opposition to an EU-wide ceiling on the amount of direct payments which an individual producer can receive. Because of the UK's large average farm size, this proposal would hit the UK disproportionately. Elsewhere, there is uncertainty about how the proposals would work in practice. This includes the proposal to create 'national envelopes' in the beef and dairy regimes within which Member States would have a certain discretion on targeting subsidies.

A modern journey across rural Britain doesn't begin and end with the Common Agricultural Policy. Since the end of the Second World War, and escalating through the period since the formation of the EEC, what we understand as the traditional British landscape has been vanishing before our eyes. Something like 150,000 miles of hedgerow have been lost since subsidies began. Since the underwriting of food production regardless of demand, 97 per cent of English meadowlands have disappeared. There has been a loss of ponds, wetlands, bogs, scrub, flora and fauna – never a dragonfly to be seen, the number of tree sparrows reduced by 89 per cent, of song thrushes by 73 per cent and of skylarks by 58 per cent. 'Only 20 acres of limestone meadow remain in the whole of Northamptonshire,' Graham Harvey reports. 'In Ayrshire only 0.001 per cent remains in meadowland ... None of this would have happened without subsidies. Without taxpayers, farm prices would have slipped as production exceeded market demand ... Despite years of over-production, farmers continue to be paid as if their products were in short supply.'

I set out on my own rural ride feeling sorry for the farmers. I thought they were getting a raw deal: economic forces were against them, they were victims of historical realities beyond their control, and of some horrendous bad luck. They seemed to me, as the miners had once seemed, to be trying to hold on to something worth having, a decent working life, an earning, a rich British culture, and I went into their kitchens with a sense of sorrow. And that is still the case: there is no pleasure to be had from watching farmers work from six until six in all weath-ers for nothing more rewarding than Income Support. You couldn't not feel for them. But as the months passed I could also see the sense in the opposing argument: many of the bigger farmers had exploited the subsidy system, they had done well with bumper cheques from Brussels in the 1980s, they had destroyed the land to get the cheques, and they had done noth-ing to fend off ruin. When I told people I was spending time with farmers, they'd say, 'How can you stand it? They just com-plain all day, and they've always got their hand out.' I didn't want to believe that, and, after talking to the farmers I've writ-ten about here, I still don't believe it. But there would be no point in opting for an easy lament on the farmers' behalf, despite all the anguish they have recently suffered: it would be like singing a sad song for the 1980s men-in-red-braces, who had a similar love of Thatcher, and who did well then, but who are now reaping the rewards of bad management. As a piece of human business, British farming is a heady mixture of the ter-rible and the inevitable, the hopeless and the culpable, and no less grave for all that.

Britain is not a peasant culture. It has not been that for over two hundred years. Though we have a cultural resistance to the fact, we are an industrial nation – or, better, a post-industrial one – and part of the agricultural horror we now face has its origins in the readiness with which we industrialised the farming process. We did the thing that peasant nations such as France did not do: we turned the landscape into American-style prairie, trounced our own ecosystem, and with public money too, and turned some of the biggest farms in Europe into giant, fertiliser-gobbling, pesticide-spraying, manufactured-seed-using monocultures geared only for massive profits and the accrual of EU subsidies. A Civil Service source reminded me that even the BSE crisis has a connection to intensive agribusiness: 'Feeding animals with the crushed fat and spinal cord of other animals is a form of cheap, industrial, cost-effective management,' he said, 'and it would never have happened on a traditional British farm. It is part of the newer, EU-driven, ultra-profiteering way of farming. And look at the results.' Farms in other parts of Europe, the smaller ones dotted across the Continent, have been much less inclined to debase farming practices in order to reap the rewards of intensification.

The way ahead is ominous. In a very straightforward sense, in the world at large, GM crops are corrupting the relation of people to the land they live on. Farmers were once concerned with the protection of the broad biodiversity of their fields, but the new methods, especially GM, put land use and food production into the hands of corporations, who are absent from the scene and environmentally careless. By claiming exclusive intellectual property rights to plant breeding, the giant seed companies are gutting entire ecosystems for straight profit. It is happening in India, Algeria, and increasingly in places like Zimbabwe, and it is among the factors threatening to make life hell for the traditional farmers of Yorkshire and Wiltshire.

In 1998, in a leaked document, a Monsanto researcher expressed great concern about the unpopularity of GM foods with the British public, but was pleased to report that some headway had been made in convincing MPs of their potential benefits. MPs and civil servants, the document says, have little doubt that over the long term things will work out, with a typical comment being: 'I'm sure in five years' time everybody will be happily eating genetically modified apples, plums, peaches and peas.'

In 1999 the Blair government spent £52 million on developing GM crops and £13 million on improving the profile of the Biotech industry. In the same year it spent only £1.7 million on promoting organic farming. Blair himself has careered from one end of the debate to the other, swithering between his love of big business and his fear of the *Daily Mail*. Initially, he was in favour of GM research in all its forms: 'The human genome is now freely available on the internet,' he said to the European Bioscience Conference in 2000, 'but the entrepreneurial incentive provided by the patenting system has been preserved.' Other voices – grand ones – disagreed. 'We should not be meddling with the building blocks of life in this way,' Prince Charles was quoted on his website as saying. The government asked for the remarks to be removed. 'Once the GM genie is out of the bottle,' Sir William Asscher, the chairman of the BMA's Board of Science and Education remarked, 'the impact on the environment is likely to be irreversible.' The Church of England's Ethical Investment Advisory Group turned down a request from the Ministry of Agriculture to lease some of the Church's land – it owns 125,000 acres – for GM testing. More recently, Blair has proclaimed in the *Independent on Sunday* that the potential benefits of GM technology are considerable, but he has also introduced the idea that his government is not a blind and unquestioning supporter. 'We are neither for nor against,' said Mo Mowlam.

Poorly paid, unsung, depressed husbanders of the British landscape, keeping a few animals for auld lang syne, and killing the ones they can't afford to sell, small farmers like Brian Carruthers, the man who lives outside Keswick with his Galloway cows and keeps his children on Family Credit, or the pig farmers in Suffolk, told me they felt as if they were under sentence of death from the big agricultural businesses. I asked one of them what he planned to do. His response was one I had heard before. 'Move to France,' he said with a shrug. Graham Harvey is in no doubt about where the fault lies: 'In the early 1950s,' he writes, 'there were about 454,000 farms in the UK. Now there are half that number, and of these just 23,000 produce half of all the food we grow. In a period of unprecedented public support for agriculture almost a quarter of a million farms have gone out of business . . . It is the manufacturers and City investors who now dictate the UK diet.'

The government has been stuck in farming crisis after farming crisis, but it recognises – though until now somewhat mutedly – the accumulating evils of the subsidy-driven culture. Its public position is to undertake large-scale, environmentally friendly tinkering with European funding, attended by vague worries about changes in the world market. An unofficial spokeswoman for Maff told me there were much deeper worries than the policy-wonks would be heard admitting to. 'It is like the end of the British coal industry,' she said,

> but no one wants to be Ian McGregor. In the time since BSE 110,000 head of cattle have disappeared: it seems that farmers were burning them on their own land. It's a cultural thing, too: no one wants to admit that a certain kind of farming, a certain way of English life, has now run to the end of the road. People will supposedly always need bread. But there is no reason to believe it will have to be made with British ingredients. The disasters in farming aren't so temporary. And they aren't mainly the result of bad luck. No. Something is finished for traditional farming in this country. Not everything, by any means, but something – something in the business of British agriculture is over for good, and no one can quite face it.

The day before I set off for Devon there was a not entirely encouraging headline on the front of the London *Evening Standard*: 'Stay Out of the Countryside'. Just when it seemed there was little room for disimprovement in the predicament of

British farmers, news came of the biggest outbreak of foot and mouth disease in more than thirty years. Twenty-seven infected pigs were found at Cheale Meats, an abattoir in Essex, a place not far from Nigel Rowe's pig farm in Constable country. Infected animals were quickly discovered on several other farms. Suspect livestock began to be slaughtered in their hundreds. Such was the smoke from the incineration site in Northumberland that the A69 had to be closed for a time. British exports of meat and livestock (annual export value £600 million) as well as milk (of which 400,000 tons are exported a year) were banned by the British government and the EU. 'It is like staring into the abyss,' Ben Gill, the President of the National Farmers' Union, said. 'On top of the problems we have had to face in the last few years, the impact is unthinkable.'

The National Pig Association estimates that the relatively small outbreak of swine fever last year cost the industry £100 million. The last epidemic of FMD, which took hold in October 1967, led to the slaughter of 442,000 animals – a loss of hundreds of millions of pounds in today's terms, only a fraction of which made it back to the farmer in compensation. Last month's ban affected more than half of Britain's farmers and no one doubts that many of them will be ruined.

The county of Devon seemed dark green and paranoid when I travelled there the day after the ban was introduced. It seemed to sit in fear of the disinfecting gloom to come, and as the fields rolled by, I considered the ongoing assault on Hardy's Wessex, the trouble on all sides, and the sense of an ending. Yet I'd originally planned my visit there as an opportunity to gaze at a vision of farming success. Stapleton Farm, my destination, was the one named by the Sainsbury's executives on the day I walked with them around the flagship store on the Cromwell Road, as an example of the new kind of partnership that can exist between supermarkets and farmers. Stapleton produces the quality brands of yoghurt and ice-cream admired by Sainsbury's: their optimism seemed hard to recapture on the way to Devon that morning.

Stapleton Farm is not far from Bideford, near Great Torring-
ton, and there isn't a cow to be seen there. They use bought-in
milk to make the yoghurt and ice-cream that is so highly
regarded by the people at Sainsbury's. No livestock, no fields,
no manure, no tractors, just a small manufacturing unit that
couldn't be doing better. This is the enterprise Sainsbury's put
me onto when I asked about the partnerships with farming that
mattered to them. This is the new thing.

I found Carol Duncan in a Portakabin she uses as an office.
She was surrounded by Sainsbury's invoices and office sta-
tionery. Like her husband Peter, who soon arrived with a
marked absence of flat cap or wellington boots, Carol considers
herself a modern rural producer. 'I was absolutely delighted
when we managed to get rid of the very last cow off this farm,'
she said. 'That's the thing about cows, you know, they just poo
all the time.' Peter's father and his grandfather had run Stapleton Farm in the traditional West Country way; they had livestock and they worked the fields through thick and thin. 'But
from an early age I wasn't interested in that kind of farming,'
Peter admitted. 'I wanted to be inside reading books. And then,
when my time came, I was interested in the different things you
can do with milk. In the 1960s we farmers needed to diversify
and head ourselves to somewhere better. The traditional way
had been to stand around waiting for the government price
review. I wanted to make yoghurt and change things around
here. My father would say: "Who's going to milk the cows?"'

'He just wouldn't stop being a farmer, his father,' Carol said.

Peter laughed. 'Yes. But we started with three churns. Carol
was an art teacher and that kept us going through the difficult
years. We made yoghurt and started selling it to independent
schools.'

'That's right,' Carol said. 'If you're paying between £13,000
and £16,000 a year for a school, you want to make sure your
children aren't going to be eating rubbish. We had to fight for
our markets. In 1994 the price of milk in Devon went up by 29
per cent. We had to increase the price of the yoghurt by 5 per

cent and we lost some of our German contracts. I went out and fought to get them back. It was horrible: 200-year-old cheese-makers were shut down, and hardly a Devon clotted-cream maker was left standing. But there's too much milk. It's in over-supply. Six years ago we thought we were going out of business.'

'We started exporting our stuff,' Peter said, 'to Belgium especially. We supply an upmarket supermarket chain called Delhaize.'

'Until this morning,' Carol said. 'We've just been banned from exporting.'

'We're hoping it will only be a matter of weeks,' Peter said, 'but this is the sort of thing that can ruin people. We're praying it doesn't spread.'

There were a number of people coming and going outside the Portakabin window. They seemed different from most of the farming people I'd met: they were young, for a start, and they seemed like indoor types, a different colour from the field-workers I'd come across in Essex and Cumbria, Kent and Scotland. The Duncans have over thirty people working at Stapleton Farm – chopping, grating, mixing, packaging, labelling, loading. The buildings where the yoghurt and ice-cream are produced are old farm buildings that have been con-verted. They look typical enough among the high hedges of North Devon; yet inside each shed there are silver machines and refrigerated rooms that are miles away from the world of cows. Peter tells the story of the Sainsbury's development manager coming down to see them in 1998 as if he were relating a great oral ballad about a local battle or a famous love affair. 'The woman came down,' he said. 'I thought she seemed so fierce. They had already taken samples of our yoghurt away. They said they liked them. But when the woman came that day she just said, "I suppose you'd like to see these," and it was the artwork for the pots. They'd already decided we were going into busi-ness. I nearly fell off my chair.'

Carol laughed in recognition. 'Yeah,' she said, 'and they say, "How many of these can you produce a week?" So we started aiming for 10,000 pots a week in a hundred Sainsbury's stores. They were very pleased with the way it was going, weren't they, Peter?'

'Oh yes,' he said, 'and we were putting yoghurt into the pots by hand and pressing the lids on. It was incredibly hard work.'

'Then they wanted to double it,' she said.

'Oh yes,' he echoed, 'they wanted to double it. We had to get better machinery. So it was off to the bank for £80,000. Come February 1999 we were doing 50,000 to 60,000 pots a week.'

Carol swivelled in her office chair. 'We think Sainsbury's are geniuses,' she said. 'We just give them yoghurt and they sell it.'

Stapleton Farm processes all its own fruit by hand. All the milk they use comes from three local farms. Recently, they started giving the milk farmers half a penny more per litre, because of the hard time the farmers are having.

'It's been a music-hall joke for years,' Peter said, 'about farmers complaining. But now that the worst has come true the whole thing's beyond belief.'

In the face of all this seriousness, I remembered some lines of George Crabbe's, from 'The Parish Register' (1807):

> Our farmers round, well pleased with constant gain,
> Like other farmers, flourish and complain.

'The ladies who work for us all come from within three miles of here,' Carol said, 'and they're working for housekeeping money. The farms they live on are struggling and they are here to earn money to feed their kids. But it's a struggle for us too. Most of the people who work here take more away from it than we do, but it's our little dream.'

The Duncans' dream has been one of survival and self-sufficiency, and of being free of that last cow. But as environmentalists they may have trouble living with the price of their own success: expansion. The week I spoke to them they were reeling from having bought a £68,000 machine that wasn't yet working. Sainsbury's want them to produce more and more and they are aware of the fact that doing well entails spending more, so that demand can be met. They are now heavily in debt but also rejoicing at their own success. In the autumn of 1999 their contact at Sainsbury's suggested they have a go at making ice-cream.

'Oh God,' Carol said, blushing at the recollection, 'I didn't know how to make ice-cream. I just made a litre in my little kitchen Gelati and we sent it off. They said they had eighty samples to try. And they decided they liked ours the best. So that was it.'

'Yes,' Peter said, 'that was a visit to the bank for another hundred grand. We had about ten weeks to get the production into full swing. And in the first twelve months of production we sold £750,000 worth of ice-cream.'

Carol is more forthright, and I would say more conservative, than her husband. She obviously hates the idea of farming but likes the idea of country-related things: 'An art student wouldn't be seen dead near a farm,' she said at one point. 'Farmers just have the wrong attitude.'

'No,' Peter said, 'not all of them. The problem was the Marketing Boards, which gave farmers the wrong idea. They thought someone would just take their produce away and turn it into money. This has been the situation since the end of the war. No other country in Europe was like that. That is why we are so far behind.'

Carol heaved a huge sigh. 'I'm so pissed off about the foot and mouth disease. We had a whole lot of ice-cream going into Spain next week. Not now. I hope it doesn't spread to here.'

'Starting to do business with Sainsbury's feels a bit like being mown down by a bus,' Peter said.

'Yes,' said Carol, 'but I was so relieved when we got rid of that last cow and that old farm. That's the thing with a lot of the farmers around here: they have the potential to get into tourism, get into the farm cottages side, caravans and all that.'

Supermarkets want to be able to rely on volume. If Stapleton Farm's yoghurt continues to grow in popularity – which it will, as part of Sainsbury's Taste the Difference range for the more discerning shopper, costing 45p, against the Economy brand's 8p – then they will have to get bigger. The charm of Stapleton's smallness cannot last; the supermarket culture requires commitment and tolerance of the highest order from producers. 'I remember once thinking,' Peter said, 'that maybe yoghurt would end up being produced by about three factories in Europe. And it may go like that.'

'Our girls,' Carol said, 'have been brought up to believe that Europe is their oyster. And at this moment we are just what Sainsbury's wants.'

I asked the Duncans if they were worried about having all their eggs in one basket. What happens if people get fed up with Devon yoghurt? What happens if Sainsbury's find somewhere cheaper, or somewhere better able to meet the volume required? Or if it falls for the new kid on the block? Carol met my gaze evenly. 'We'll survive,' she said.

Before going into the factory with Peter I had to put on white boots and a white jumpsuit, sterilise my hands and pull on a hairnet. Peter stopped in the middle of a chilled room, with the sound of clicking going on further along the line, the sound of mass production. 'This was a cattle shed when I was little,' he said. 'I can remember it quite clearly.' We stood beside a pallet of strawberry yoghurts bound for Sainsbury's. It had the special label already attached. I asked him who paid for the Sainsbury's packaging. 'Oh, we do,' he said.

That afternoon Tim Yeo, the shadow agriculture spokesman, said that the government had responded in chaotic fashion to a chain of farming crises. 'I wish he would shut up and go away,' Nick Brown replied. 'He is trying to make political capital out of a terrible situation.' And when I was barely out of the West Country news broke of another farm where livestock was found to have contracted foot and mouth disease. The farm was in Devon. And the farmer owned thirteen other farms.

The most comprehensive guide to British farming performance is provided by Deloitte & Touche's *Farming Results*. 'Despite cutting costs and tightening their belts,' the report for autumn 2000 concludes, 'farmers have suffered the lowest average incomes since our survey began 11 years ago.' Several facts stand out, so unreasonable do they seem, and so shocking. 'In the last five years the net farm income of a 200-hectare family farm has plunged from around £80,000 to just £8,000 . . . Those farmers who have expanded their operations dramatically in recent times . . . cannot sustain profitability in the face of tumbling commodity prices.' 'The bad news,' says Mark Hill, the firm's partner in charge of the Food and Agriculture Group, 'is that we predict small profits becoming losses in the coming year. This is due to a further fall in output prices and yield plus rising costs of £25 per hectare in fuel alone.'

An equally gloomy drizzle was making a blur of Otford the day I visited. Hedges were loaded like wet sponges, the short grass squeaked underfoot, there was mud in the road and mud at the farm gate, with a cold whiteness in the Kent sky that darkened quickly in the afternoon. Ian and Anne Carter were sitting in the drawing room of their farmhouse. She is a Justice of the Peace, groomed to a fine point of civic order, wearing a blue suit with a poppy pinned to its lapel. She is well spoken, opening up her world in good clear Southern English, the language of the prep school and the Shipping Forecast, and her generosity seems to go perfectly with the rationale of the teacups. Ian stretched out his long legs like a teenager: he is likeably comfortable with everything he knows and everything he doesn't know; he is right as rain and habitually nice. They both shook their heads.

'You need to have 2,500 acres to make farming work nowadays,' he said. 'Not so long ago you could have 600 acres and second-hand equipment and send your kids to a good school and holiday in the South of France. That's all gone now.'

'Absolutely,' said Anne, 'there has been pressure from the fertiliser companies to use certain fertilisers. There are too many sheep owing to these awful subsidies. The whole countryside out there has changed almost beyond recognition.' Over the fireplace hangs a Constable painting: a portrait of one of Anne's ancestors. There is something darkly lively about the picture. For a while we all sat and stared into it. 'It's not at all famous,' Anne said, 'all the famous ones are out there being admired.'

A British Legion-type couple came to lunch. 'It's funny the way things go,' the man said, 'when you think of all those British companies that went to the wall. British manufacturing took such a hammering and now you see that a whole way of living and working has disappeared.'

'Do you think the land will eventually be nationalised and given to the National Trust?' his wife asked.

'You mean heritaged?' someone else said.

'Very interesting what's happened to *The Archers*,' Anne said. 'This year Nigel, who has the big house, Lower Loxley, is involved in some sort of shooting gallery. They didn't have that before. *The Archers* has become less and less farming and more sex.'

We braved the weather and walked several miles over the fields. Anne spoke about a spiritual connection she felt with the countryside and a hope she retained in the balance of nature. There were milky pools beside the trees, and when I walked with Ian he tried to give an account of why things had gone the way they had, a story of overproduction and subsidy distortion and diseased animals and the threat of bad seeds. It seemed less imposing that the land belonged to the Carters, and much more interesting, in an easy, uncomplicated way, that they belonged to the land thereabouts. They seemed to walk it knowingly. We stopped at the family chapel, dedicated to St Jude, in a building which dates from 1650. A book inside the chapel tells the story of the ownership of this piece of land – the lay ownership from 1066 to 1521, the removal of the house and the farm from a nobleman to one of the wives of Henry VIII. Across from the chapel is a disused cowshed that Anne's father built in 1946. Water dripped from the lintel, and an inscription is carved above. 'To the glory of agriculture,' it says, 'and the working man.'

Cowboy George

SEPTEMBER 2003

It's odd to think that Abraham Lincoln was killed by an actor, because most of the memorable American presidents to follow him were actors in their blood. Eisenhower excelled in the part of the sturdy veteran who'd come home to tidy the porch, and Nixon was every part in *The Godfather* rolled into one. But it took Ronald Reagan to drive the matter past the point of absurdity: president of the Screen Actors' Guild as well as star of *Bedtime for Bonzo*. The person who today seems most like a real president is Martin Sheen, who plays one in *The West Wing*. George W. Bush – the less-real real president – has settled for the part of a B-movie cowboy, and takes his role very seriously. Only the other day he was talking about 'riding herd' with the Middle East peace process.

Bush made Wild West philosophy a central plank of his 2000 election platform. In a documentary made by Alexandra Pelosi, we were able to see him spreading his most important message – the right way to wear a pair of Texan trousers, the right kind of Lone Star belt to hold them up. Some commentators have the idea that Bush's delivery is really an impersonation of Ronald Reagan impersonating James Stewart and John Wayne, but I think that elevates him too much: his mentality is clouded with lesser subtleties, occluded with hungers of a more brutal, mercenary, low-budget kind. He has the effective salesman's knowledge of how to play with people's sense of what is good about themselves, and he brings on tears in his pitch for the superiority of the American Way of Life. Cowboy simplicities about justice, evil and cowardice seem to suit the president's mindset, and they suit the mindset of the people running his intelligence.

James Woolsey, a former director of the CIA, wanted an invasion of Iraq much earlier than it happened. He was in London in 2001 gathering evidence about Iraqi weapons, and had this to say about the movie *High Noon* in a February 2002 article for the *Wall Street Journal*:

> Cowboys are normal people – some are impulsive, some are loners, some are neither. But what [the Europeans] are rejecting is not a modern-day cowboy, but rather a modern-day marshal, and marshals are different. They and their equivalents, such as GIs, have chosen to live a life of protecting others, whatever it takes. That's not being impulsive – it's deciding to be a shepherd instead of a sheep.

The extent to which cowboys are normal people, the extent to which normal people are normal people, were questions that came up all the time in the film-making career of John Ford, a career that lasted fifty years, and which one way or another says as much about home and landscape, belonging and solitude, war and peace, history and memory, America and Europe, as that of any American storyteller in any medium. Ford made some terrible films, and many of his good films have terrible things in them, and as a man he was almost certainly terrible all the time, but greatness is no hostage to goodness of character, and his hatefulness and sentimentality, his brutishness and intolerance, are no less bold or striking for being inseparable from his best achievements. Ford was the cowboy director's cowboy director, but his work can be seen both to extol and repudiate the settled notions of American virtue that quicken the pulse of the Bush administration. Like Bush and Co., he was all for America, but unlike them he knew that America was becoming a dangerous fantasy.

Rousing as their criticisms are, I can't go along with the ferocity of Ford's detractors (they seem to close their eyes to watch his films), but David Thomson makes a mighty-seeming case against him in his *Biographical Dictionary of the Cinema*. From the 1975 edition:

Ford's male chauvinism believes in uniforms, drunken candour, fresh-faced little women (though never sexuality), a gallery of supporting players bristling with tedious eccentricity and the elevation of these random prejudices into a near political attitude – thus Ford's pioneers talk of enterprise but show narrowness and reaction . . . The Ford philosophy is a rambling apologia for unthinking violence later disguised by the sham legends of old men . . . The visual poetry so often attributed to Ford seems to me claptrap in that it amounts to the prettification of a lie . . . Ford's visual grace, it seems to me, needs the flush of drink in the viewer before it is sufficiently lulling to disguise the lack of intellectual integrity . . . It is sometimes claimed that Ford is a superb visual storyteller; that he unerringly places his camera and edits his footage. But the same could be said for Leni Riefenstahl. The glorification of Ford's simplicity as an artist should not conceal the fact that his message is trite, callous and evasive.

Thomson doesn't like Ford's 'message'; he is not persuaded that his movies tell a story against themselves, or that their beauty is more than 'lulling'. He sees Ford's shortcomings everywhere: in his abuse of geology, his celebration of dumb machismo, his irresponsible ignorance about tribes and histories, and most of all in his evasion of 'truths' in favour of panoramas. In a later edition, Thomson sought to mitigate his dislike, but he made his case more damning:

In an age of diminishing historical sense in America, but of regular crises that dramatise our need to ask what happened (with Watergate, Vietnam, Iran-Contra etc.), I marvel that Ford's heady obscurantism has such defenders. But to take Ford properly to task may be to begin to be dissatisfied with cinema.
Adherence to legend at the expense of facts will ruin America – the work is well under way. And lovers of the movies should consider how far film has helped the under-

mining. Ford is not the only culprit: Clint Eastwood's over-praised return to the West, *Unforgiven*, begins as an attempt to see things afresh, but at last its rigour collapses and it becomes not the West but just another western. Still, Ford is the pioneer of this vision, and that is what I railed against in 1975.

The Searchers is still a riveting, tragic and complex experience, a movie in which Ford gives up many of his false certainties, and a story filled with disturbing, half-buried thoughts of race and failure. On the strength of that one film I would love to read a thorough life of Ford (such as Joseph McBride managed for Frank Capra, that other fragile hero).

The reasons Ford 'has such defenders' are amply supplied in the book McBride has now written about him, which shows how we might do better not to understand our enemies too quickly, how even idiots have art in them, great art even, so long as we don't ask them to mirror our certainties. Here is a Ford who is unearthed from the strange wonder of his films, and whose films are unearthed from the grave of their maker's reputation. Thomson was not entirely wrong: he just wasn't saying the only things to be said about Ford, and by calling for the attentions of a McBride he encouraged the writing of a book – this one – that may serve to damn his own unseeing-ness. It's not always best to meet a perceived blatancy with a blatancy: McBride shows spirit in his search for what lies beyond the unlovable in John Ford, which at the same time proves to be a search for the troubled lives that might be found among the shadows and voices and characters of Ford's amazing pictures.

John Feeney was born near Portland, Maine, but his people were from Spiddal, a village about eight miles outside Galway City. The west of Ireland is its own Monument Valley, and all his life Ford never stopped thinking about it: he signed the name Feeney to his last will and it is the name that would be inscribed on his coffin. 'If there is any single thing that explains either of us,' he said to Eugene O'Neill, 'it's that we're Irish.' Ford's great discovery was that many of the citizen soldiers who fought in the American Revolution were Irish immigrants: a finding, McBride writes, that 'roused in him a vital connection to American history and the nation's heroic ideals'.

Being Irish but not born in Ireland, Ford's imagination was married to a complex of nostalgias, and yet sentimentality was only the beginning of the story. Ford's feeling for Ireland and for himself gave him a way of dreaming about America and the frontier, a way of understanding power and modernity. 'For Britain, the Irish are the Indians to the far west, circling the wagons of imperial civilisation,' Fintan O'Toole writes in *The Lie of the Land: Irish Identities*. 'Once in America, of course, the Irish cease to be the Indians and become the cowboys.'

What Thomson misses when he looks at Ford is the elegiac element in his westerns, the way his static camera summons what Andrew Sarris has called 'his feelings of loss and displacement already fantasised through the genre'. The Old West is a vista of mourning, yet the films are about the funny and mysterious and sometimes savage ways that people survive there and go on to make lives for themselves. Hoot Gibson, a room-mate of Ford's when he started to make cowboy pictures, said Ford 'was worse Irish than me', and if he failed to take up his responsibilities as a debunker of American myths, that is perhaps because those myths lay close to his heart, and also because he had an instinct for making them newly beautiful.

Lindsay Anderson noted Ford's ability to make things 'poetically true', as opposed to true, but he also knew how to make his strong feelings – about the past, say, or about authority – enlarge the dimensions of his sometimes humdrum material, to the point where the best dramas pulsate with something entirely personal, the stamp of things essential to his life and surprising to the world. Ford visited Ireland in the nervous first years of its Free Statehood: on 2 December 1921 he crossed the Irish Sea from Holyhead on the *Cambria* – Michael Collins and Erskine Childers, on their way back from the Treaty negotiations in London, were making the same journey. The *Cambria* collided with a schooner (killing three men) and when Ford arrived in Galway he discovered his ancestral home was in flames. McBride tells the story well, drawing on a letter Ford wrote to Sean O'Casey in 1936:

> He wrote that upon arriving in Spiddal, he went directly to the thatched cottage of his cousin Michael Thornton, a country schoolteacher and IRA leader. Ford was astonished to find the Thornton home engulfed in flames. Michael's aged parents were standing in the road in silent anger watching truckloads of Black and Tans leaving the scene. Their son was later imprisoned by the British. Following his release, Michael Thornton worked for the Irish Free State before returning to his profession as a schoolteacher. Ford gave the name of his Thornton cousins to John Wayne's character in *The Quiet Man*, Sean Thornton.

The reverberations of this trip to Ireland and the power of the burning house go all the way into Ford's movies: it is the family home burned by the Indians at the beginning of *The Searchers*; the working-class dwellings torn down by corporate bulldozers in *The Grapes of Wrath*; the departing son is like those who have to leave their homeland in *How Green Was My Valley* or wander stateless like Ford's Mary of Scotland and like every cowboy he put on the screen. *The Quiet Man*, a sentimental favourite with the Irish, promotes a central myth among tribes of that sort: the myth of the man returning home to reckon with what he is made of. As much a keynote of the lachrymose paperback as of Joyce's *Ulysses*, as much a feature of Irish songs as of plays like Tom Murphy's *Conversations on a Homecoming* – the knock at the door, the traveller returned. If Ford's version is the most colour-saturated, it is also the one most infected with American anxiety about the high price of exile, the belief that for all that America can give (and materially it can give you everything) it can't guarantee you a culture of belonging.

Each one of Ford's films is about a man trying to find a people. Sometimes, he finds them among the half-cocked, drunken renegades of the wild frontier. At other times, as in his cavalry trilogy, the people sought are a company of men, a regiment where one can test one's bravery and honour and achieve one's rank. Sometimes it is among the Indian tribes, as in *Cheyenne Autumn* or in *The Searchers*, when the Natalie Wood character comes to live with her abductor. Ford was looking in green valleys and dust bowls and army units and Christian missions all his life: that is perhaps why he was, as a maker of westerns, the great visionary of empty space and plains rolling to the horizon – his life and his work were energised by the notion of an authentic home, a place that would be his, if only he could find it. In *Stagecoach*, all the main characters are trying to get to a new place, and with each turn of the wheel there is more of the past behind them, more danger overcome. A small family of roamers, they are looking for a real destination: not just Lordsburg, but some more significant point of arrival. The Ringo Kid (John Wayne) falls in love with good-time gal Dallas (Claire Trevor) during the journey, and he makes the grounds of their suitability for one another clear: each has lost their parents, and has no other home bar the one they might invent together. An interviewer asked Ford why he was so taken up with the theme of the family. Ford shrugged and said: 'You have a mother, don't you?'

If you want to understand the early history of American liberalism don't look at the experience of the parents, the immigrants, but at the aspirations of the children, the ones for whom America offered a tricky answer to the problem of belonging. The parents wanted a better life: they got on a boat. The children have a better life: they can't find a boat that will take them back to themselves. American patriotism isn't quite like other patriotisms: it is born of hysteria and Ford's cowboy films map the violence of unbelonging. John Wayne, Victor McLaglen, these men hunger for authority, for company, for routines and customs and native patterns: without them, they are cursed to

gun their way across the American landscape, killing Indians
for the crime of having a culture. Ford's depiction of the Indians often has a quality of frustrated envy about it, as well as
genuine fear. Himself a stranger, he had a good old-fashioned
dislike of other strangers. It was (and is) Hollywood's way to
reject cultures that fail to make themselves available for instant
understanding.

In *The Man who Shot Liberty Valance*, Senator Ransom Stod-
dard – 'Rance' – played by James Stewart, is one of those figures
whose efforts marked the passage from western lawlessness to
proper democracy. As a young man Rance is mugged by the
local personification of evil, Liberty Valance (Lee Marvin), who
strides around with a whip making everybody feel bad. Everybody except Tom Doniphon (John Wayne), who stands up to
Valance but feels bad for other reasons, and who burns his own
house down when the drink overtakes him. Rance comes into
this lawless town with his law books in his bag: he is looking to
be an attorney one day, but seeing as he's detained in Shinbone,
he takes a job, falls in love, and sets about trying to teach the
locals a thing or two about American values. Despite doing so
under a framed picture of Abraham Lincoln, Rance fails to
impress the town with talk of brotherhood and the Declaration
of Independence: what does it is his shooting and killing the
hated Liberty Valance in a duel. The irony is only deepened
when we eventually learn that it wasn't the academic Rance
who killed him: Tom Doniphon shot him from an adjacent
alleyway, but allowed the glory to settle on the man who would
eventually go on to a seat in the US Senate.

I've said nothing about the wonderful antics of the towns-
people in this film (especially the Falstaffian editor of the *Shinbone Star*, played by Edmond O'Brien), but the depth of the
allegory the film lays out makes it one of the wonders of the
western genre. Here is a way of understanding American history, the democratic personality, community, violence, and the
role of legend in getting from one era to another. When the
James Stewart character is an old man and returns to the town

to play the true story of how the state became governable thanks to somebody else's shooting of Liberty Valance, the new editor of the *Shinbone Star* won't print it. And then we have the famous line: 'This is the West, sir. When the legend becomes fact, print the legend.'

Today that could be the motto of CNN or Fox News. Ford's own personal chaos allowed him to understand something profound about America's relation to itself and its people's relation to the rest of the world: that the progress of the unbelonging will not be halted, that no culture is as strong as one built on the legend of tough policing and moral superiority. Liberty Valance was downed by the unstoppable wheels of civilised democracy in the form of James Stewart – except that he wasn't. He was killed by an invisible man with nothing to lose and a belt full of bullets.

By this time, Ford had his own Hollywood legend to contend with, and it wasn't subtle: the binge-drinking, woman-slapping, actor-baiting hero of the Naval Reserve, getting more right-wing by the second, and fulfilling his destiny as a man who would burst into tears at the first bars of an Irish song but refused to speak to his own son for the best part of the son's life. Ford's politics had been borrowing more and more from his splenetic side for years. Early on he had described himself as a 'socialistic democrat – *always* left'. But his Irish Republican cousinage, his belief in the Spanish Loyalists, his involvement with the Hollywood Anti-Nazi League, his picketing (afterwards denied) in support of the Los Angeles Newspaper Guild strike of 1938, did not stop him from later showing friendliness to the militant anti-communists in the industry or becoming one of the founder members of the Motion Picture Alliance for the Preservation of American Ideals.

Ford had come under fire while trying to film the war – the American landings in North Africa, the Battle of Midway, the landings at Omaha Beach – and though he received a Purple Heart and the results won Oscars, he never felt rightly rewarded for those efforts and all his life continued to campaign for more recognition from the naval and military authorities. The war years had pushed him further to the right, bringing him under the influence of hard-line anti-communists and burgeoning Cold Warriors. Back in Hollywood, he was ideologically pushed around by John Wayne and Ward Bond, both rabid Red-baiters. As a cowboy director, he made a virtue of being 'on both sides of the epic', rooting for the cowboys and the Indians (in his head they took it in turns to be the Black and Tans), but the Blacklist was one of the issues on which Ford's ambivalence faltered. His FBI file noted that his political activities 'were of a mild nature', but thought it likely that he was 'long a fellow traveller' with 'Communist Party Front groups'. As McBride says, he took 'some principled stands against the Blacklist', but he also did much to allay fears that he himself was suspect: at one point he named names in an almost casual way, but when the Committee mistakenly blacklisted Anna Lee, one of his favourite regular actors, he railed against it. He made a call and got her removed. McBride remarks:

> Although the story demonstrates Ford's loyalty to a friend in trouble, the fact that he could get someone off the Blacklist simply by picking up the phone raises disturbing questions. Why did Ford have such power? How often did he use it? Was it appropriate for *anyone* to be able to say if someone should or should not work? And by clearing Anna Lee, did Ford facilitate and tacitly approve the blacklisting of the woman with whom she had been confused?

At any rate, and however steep his contradictions, Ford was capable of shaking up a cocktail of native sentimentality and bullish American patriotism and pouring it into the ear of anyone who liked him. 'Your letter received,' he wrote to one of his relatives, 'with the discouraging news that the Reds – one John Huston – are seeking refuge in our lovely Ireland. This ain't good, he is not of the right wing.'

No artist would want his style to have to answer to his bad character, but bad character isn't always a hindrance to a perfect style: it may even be that the style could not exist were the artist merely a good person. This is the deepest mystery about John Ford: how could such crudeness as Ford undeniably had as a man not stand in his way as an artist? How could a man who prided himself on the possession of such reactionary certainties demonstrate such subtlety in his handling of America's psycho-geography, the dreams of its people and their long travels and longer regrets? The sky in Ford's movies is full of the romance of possibility: it seems to suggest a future for the world much better than that endured by the men and women rolling onwards in the covered wagons below.

How could a man so blurred with loathings and prejudices also be so open to human weakness, experience and variety? Henry Fonda's character in *The Grapes of Wrath*? John Wayne's mysterious bigot in *The Searchers*? Roddy McDowall's dreaming little boy in *How Green Was My Valley*? Claire Trevor's loose woman in *Stagecoach*? John Wayne's old soldier Captain Brittles in *She Wore a Yellow Ribbon*? James Stewart's ironical hero of democracy in *The Man who Shot Liberty Valance*? Margaret Leighton's fanatical religious zealot in *Seven Women*? What even the most elegant of Ford's detractors don't want to say, I imagine, is that John Ford was an artist in spite of himself – almost to spite himself. His films are beautiful and exciting in a way that might surprise those who imagine that beauty keeps its own company.

'The light,' Angela Carter wrote in a story about both John Fords, is 'the unexhausted light of North America that, filtered through celluloid, will become the light by which we see America looking at itself'. It comes down to this: Ford's rarity was to show America at the difficult business of becoming itself, and his talent for composition is one of the most magical, most painterly things in the history of the cinema. The militarisation of American democracy was not invented by Ford, merely described. In *Young Mr Lincoln*, he showed a president who could set out to reconcile oppositions and place universal toler-ance among the great American ideals. 'All his actions as a young man,' writes his biographer, 'are supercharged with our common knowledge of his destiny.' Yes indeed, Lincoln's destiny: to be killed by an actor who would step into his shoes.

Four Funerals and a Wedding

MAY 2005

When I was young people didn't die and they didn't pass away. They certainly didn't expire, or perish, though there was a woman in our street called Hazel who dabbled in spiritualism while her philandering husband went out to fix people's Hotpoint twin-tubs, and she quite often spoke of people who had 'crossed to the other side'. I thought that was sick. Hazel had a lot of anger in her, as people now say, and I felt that must explain her hazardous use of words. She'd met Sandy, her husband, when he drove one of the Alexander buses about the town of Elgin. She happened to be the clippy on the same bus, and she would often tell me about the beauty of those single-decker vehicles ('the Bluebird') and the handsomeness of Sandy behind the wheel. Now she was furious all the time, and took it out on her accordion, playing Strathspey reels until the red varnish flaked off her fingernails.

In our town it was all in the words. Nobody was ever 'dearly' anything, certainly not 'departed'. 'Deceased' seemed a bit high and mighty, even allowing for the fact that in Scotland every-one's station is slightly raised by their having enjoyed, if you will, the process of personal death. People in my childhood found the word 'death' unsayable, and got round it by saying, of someone whose corpse lay in the next room, that 'something had happened'.

'If anything ever happens to me,' my mother would say, 'you'll find the Liverpool Assurance policy book in the cupboard up above the stock cubes.'

'If something happens to me,' my grandmother said, 'don't put me up in that Dalbeth Cemetery. It's a cold place.'

And my father too. 'If anything ever happens to me you'll know what life's all about.'

'What do you mean "if"?' I would say. 'Why can't you just say "when I die"?'

'You think you're that smart,' my granny would say. 'But that's just a morbid thing, to use that word.'

'Death!'

'Don't say it! It's a horrible word.'

'Death!'

'Stop it,' my mother would say. 'I hate talking like this, but if something happens to me ...'

'What do you mean "if"? And what do you mean "something"? The thing that will happen to you is called death and there's no ifs or buts about it.'

'He's so pessimistic, him, isn't he?' my granny would say. 'Always had a dark side. Probably got it from his uncle John. He was like that as well. Morbid.'

'You're just trying to draw attention to yourself,' my father would say. 'If something ever happens to you, I suppose you'll want one of them statues to yourself up in the Glasgow Necropolis.'

'Yes,' I said. 'The sign could say: "Up here, something did happen to Andrew O'Hagan. Like each of us, he wondered if it would happen. And it did."'

Something happened to my second ever schoolteacher, Mrs Wallace. We saw her totally somethinged in her coffin under a huge crucifix of Jesus Christ, to whom, by the look of the nails and the blood running down his arms and toes, there might also have been a question of something happening. Mrs Wallace was a champion smoker and worrier of rosary beads. She took a liking to me, giving me the not entirely popular task of writing pupils' names on the blackboard if they spoke while she was out having a fag. I was so unremitting and keen with the chalk that Mrs Wallace figured me to be a potential candidate for the priesthood; she got me my first gig ringing the bell on the altar at St Winnin's, though a combination of sleepiness and professional jealousy on my part was to harm my chances of advancement in the eyes of Father McLaughlin.

Mrs Wallace's funeral was my first one, and in some senses no funeral could ever have the same intensity, not even my own in the event that anything should ever happen to me. I sat through the funeral mass, aged seven, in a state of shock, with all the pasty-faced solemnity of a Pre-Raphaelite mourner confronting the eternal, my intense concentration broken only for a second by the gentle passing of the family, who I knew instantly must be counted the stars of the occasion, each of them top to toe in respectful, chalk-free, something-comprehending black. My seniority in the diocese was not marked by an invitation to the graveside, but I did go there two years later, taking the bus to a populous cemetery in the small town of Stevenson. Mrs Wallace's spot was up against the right-hand wall, deep in the shadow of the Ardeer Explosives Factory. Of course, something has since happened to the factory and its cooling towers too, but I remember their real presence in that Stevenson graveyard. In a tangle of crosses and angels it said on the gravestone 'Mary Wallace', the chiselled words seeming to embody in some powerful and menacing way the mysteries of faith.

In the via Monserrato, a few weeks before the death of Pope John Paul II, the light seemed yellow against the rain, and Rome seemed a place not of eternities but of passing trade. Cardinal Cormac Murphy O'Connor entered the restaurant in his civilian uniform of open-necked shirt and windcheater, smiling to the waiters and taking his usual table. I didn't approach him, but took time to notice the high-spiritedness of his friends, happy to be in the company of the head of the English Catholics, a man not given to any obvious show of relaxation but, rather, seeming constantly anxious about being behind with business.

Nearby is the English College, or the Venerable English College, as its fan base likes to call it. Father Clive was waiting on the steps for me. He was in his late twenties, very neat, soft-toned and red-cheeked, and he welcomed me into the building in the manner of someone obeying time and tradition, naming the exact moment on his watch before telling me I was the latest visitor in a tradition of literary visitors stretching back to John Milton. He said it very kindly, but I wanted to laugh. However, something high in his red cheeks warned me neither to laugh nor to make any reference to *Paradise Lost*. I simply smiled and composed my wits and followed him over the black and claret tiles to the Martyr's Chapel.

'This is a fourteenth-century floor,' Father Clive said. 'The college is the oldest of all English institutions abroad.' He showed me a little pond in the garden where students swam in the hot months. They called it the 'tank' and it conveyed to me an image of passengers bathing in the swimming pool of a sinking ship. But the mood of the college did not suggest sinking: there is a form of religious devotion which can, at a certain time in the evening in a place such as Rome, seem to shape the very air itself, though I presume only Catholics could suppose so. In any event the English College had the kind of peacefulness that ancientness alone can bestow – the young men walked the hall knowing the world they walked in possessed the texture of meditation and martyrdom, of prayers uttered and strong beliefs confirmed. Yet round the corner in the Campo de' Fiori, the statue of Giordano Bruno stands high above a modern centre of bar snacks, designer scarves and trendy beers, a statue reminding those who care to be reminded that modernity has its martyrs too.

My paternal grandmother ran a fish shop in Glasgow that had nothing on the walls but a framed print of the dying Christ. She used to tell children that they should mind to behave themselves, because – and she'd point at the picture – 'that's what he got for being good'. My grandmother took the modern world to be a simple affront to her sense of right and wrong; Protestants were barbarians to her mind, and she refused to attend my cousin's wedding when he married one. I remember the conversation. My father said to her: 'Do you hate Pakis as well?'

'No, Gerald,' she replied. 'I don't hate anybody. I've never stepped inside a Protestant church in my life and I'm not going to start doing it now.'

I once wrote some words on a piece of paper and pushed them to her across the sofa. They said: 'You like authority more than freedom.' She just looked at me. I like to think that inside the moment that contained the look, she told me, without saying anything, that I was trouble. My father had once thrown a lemonade bottle through her window and that was a kind of trouble she could dislike but understand. Her look told me that my kind of trouble was worse. She looked away and crumpled up the paper and put it on the fire.

I was ten years old when John Paul II came to power. My granny instantly adored him, loving his feudal side without reservation and simply ignoring the freedom-upholding aspect. The only thing she was truly agnostic about was politics: she never mentioned that, and her only concern when it came to sports was whether Celtic were likely to beat Rangers. She had no worries about communism, though; she worried about poor people and she came from poor people, but that was it, except she might say that poor Protestants had brought it on themselves with a well-known aversion to a day's work. She didn't live long enough to see John Paul II's visit to Glasgow and his giant mass in Bellahouston Park. (She missed it by a year.) 'There is one Lord,' he said on that occasion, 'one faith, one baptism, and one God who is father of us all, all over, through all and within all.' She would have levitated with pleasure at that line, and the whole business of him saying it in Glasgow would have represented to her a victory far greater than anything achieved at Bannockburn.

The night before the pope died, Rome became a great character in its own fiction, seizing and displaying all parts of itself to the world's television cameras. But two rather complicated images of Rome came back to me. The first was of Dorothea Brooke stuck in the via Sistina while her husband worked all day in the Vatican Library. George Eliot gave us to believe that Dorothea felt bleached and drained of blood by the ruins, basilicas and colossi of Rome, those 'long vistas of white forms whose marble eyes seemed to hold the monstrous light of an

alien world'. For the new Mrs Casaubon, Rome's spiritual splendour, its role as historic centre, could only suck the colour from
the present day, and I wondered, looking at those two high,
lighted windows in the pope's apartments, whether there wasn't
something overblown and cinematic about the event of his
death, like the drama of the great operas which can sometimes
seem the wrong sort for the small human business at hand. An
old man was dying in those rooms; the pomp of history had the
will to rob the matter of its most present sadness.

'Dorothea all her life,' George Eliot wrote, 'continued to see
the vastness of St Peter's, the huge bronze canopy, the excited
intention in the attitudes and garments of the prophets and
evangelists in the mosaics above, and the red drapery . . .
spreading itself like a disease of the retina.' On the day of the
funeral the Church showed much of the strength that lies in its
hierarchical weave. The coffin had layers too, cypress and zinc
inside oak, and was flanked by scarlet cardinals who themselves
were flanked by purple bishops and black-clad dignitaries, in
the folds of which stood Cherie Blair with her mantilla blowing
in the wind, and further in again, the Bushes looking bored and
slightly vexed as they always do abroad, him especially, forever
scanning the middle distance for un-American mirages. Fold
within fold the dignitaries stood, queens, princes, heathen
courtiers, and in some dark pocket at the outer edge the future
king of England lowered his eyes to shake the hand of Robert
Mugabe.

We live in cultish times – not to say, occultist ones – in which
it seems not unreasonable for people, en masse, to weep in the
streets for public figures they previously cared little about.
Pope John Paul II was pretty much like that himself, creating
more saints than any other pope, and so it appeared natural
that thousands of mourners interrupted the funeral with cries
of 'Santo Subito!' The papers said the mourners were mostly
Poles, but in fact they were mainly Italians, giving him back a
little bit of what he gave them: an excited neediness for supra-
human entitlement. There was a great deal of clapping as

Cardinal Joseph Ratzinger offered his words of appreciation to the dead pontiff. Clapping is the way it is always done nowadays, clapping in church, clapping by roadsides, as if a surge of assent had no outlet bar through the palms. What is a saint these days but a celebrity whose fame is guaranteed for ever? And so we have it: applause, the currency of fame.

'Shhh, we are in a church,' Anita Ekberg says as she climbs to St Peter's dome in *La Dolce Vita*. 'This is where I want to write my name,' she says, and the photographers chase her up the steps with light bulbs popping. Ekberg at the top of St Peter's basilica, as much as her dip in the Trevi fountain, looking almost bleached with attention, is an image of public-personhood becoming a sort of religion. Her hat is blown off and she giggles as it falls down to St Peter's Square, to the place where the princes of the Church and the princes of the world now attend this funeral, watched in their turn by cameras from every corner of the earth.

The very best ironies live their lives inside other ironies. Henry VIII changed his relationship with the Catholic Church so as to enable himself to marry his chosen bride. (Sadly, something happened to her.) Five hundred years later, Prince Charles changes the date of his wedding to his chosen bride so as to attend the funeral of the head of the Catholic Church. We can be sure of only one dissimilarity between these two English royals: Henry wasn't forced into his decision by a fear of the *Daily Mail*. Charles, like Henry, has come to find fame despicable, and also to find himself shadowed by the public image of a dead former wife, but unlike his Tudor forebear, he appears to have no ability to force his will, allowing every potential show of principle to appear like a fluttering of small resentments.

It may be the chief characteristic of the Windsor dynasty, this ability to make grand things small. The Poet Laureate, Andrew Motion, wrote a poem for the wedding which rather effectively takes them out of the great tide of history and into the more local business of the heart,

which slips and sidles like a stream
Weighed down by winter-wreckage near its source –
But given time, and come the clearing rain,
Breaks loose to revel in its proper course.

This was nicely said, more nicely said than the matter was achieved, as Charles and Camilla came down Windsor High Street to the Guildhall in the style of two people going to a Saturday morning jumble sale, their hearts not yet very obviously revelling in their proper course but still detained by the weight of year-round wreckage. As they emerged from their car, a local steel band tried to add lightness, and cover a few boos, with a rendition of 'Congratulations', a song once sung by Cliff Richard to remind people that happiness is a feeling constantly under threat from the songs that celebrate it. 'Beautiful white dress,' the woman from the BBC said.

'Hardly white,' the person beside me said. 'She's got two huge children.'

'It wasn't quite white,' said Trinny, one of those women off *What Not to Wear*. 'More like oyster.'

There's a bit of bunting round the pubs and a few grannies waving Union Jacks and eating buns. No tea-trays. No street parties. In almost every respect it was like the suburban wedding of two elderly people who got it wrong first time around. Camilla did look happy: she's the sort of person who goes to lunch with her daughter and steals her chips and smokes her cigarettes, so she must be fine. She and Charles signed the register on a little table below a stained-glass window bearing the legend of George VI and the year 1951, when Charles was three years old and his mother was four years married, still a princess in a world before British steel bands and Cliff Richard.

'Here they come,' the BBC said.

'Oh, they look a bit awkward,' said James Whitaker, Royal Expert. 'Oh well. Never mind. She's finally got him in her grip.'

'I don't think I am wallowing in exuberant excitement,' said Piers Morgan, former editor of the *Daily Mirror*. 'I think there will be a sigh of relief among the public that there is now some legitimacy about this couple.' Mr Morgan managed to be consistently polite about the royal pair, quite forgetting, perhaps, the stuff about Camilla he'd included in his recent book of diaries, *The Insider*. At one point in the book he describes having lunch with William and his mother. 'Oh, Mummy, it was hilarious,' he has William say about a television show. 'They had a photo of Mrs Parker-Bowles and a horse's head and asked what the difference was. The answer was that there isn't any.' Morgan adds: 'Diana absolutely exploded with laughter.'

Everybody at the royal wedding was watching everybody else to such an extent that the BBC's female commentator, Sophie Raworth, dressed in a dutiful pea-green suit by Caroline Charles, entirely lost her footing when Piers Morgan pointed out that she was wearing exactly the same outfit as Virginia Parker-Bowles, the second wife of Camilla's first husband. Sophie was clearly put out that something so suitable for her own foxy self should be thought appropriate for Granny Frump, and went unprofessionally silent for a while. It used to be that the British public looked on these occasions with a subject's sense of inclusion, seeing very clearly their own role and their own station in the whole affair. Now, they watch as one might watch a freak show or a procession of soap stars, which is more or less the same thing.

'Eeeeech,' the person next to me said as the guests arrived. 'He's got super-posh hair! Like sparse candyfloss. Look at these people, they're so well bred they're practically wraiths. Look. No hips at all.'

'They don't look especially clean,' I said.

'Yes,' she said. 'That's super-posh. Like the Queen Mother, who didn't do anything about her little brown teeth. In that respect they're like the working-class people who love them.'

'They can't help it,' I said.

'Yes they can. They're just out of touch. Everybody's got fabulous teeth now. Diana had great teeth. These skinny men are all a terrible throwback.'

'With bad teeth.'

'Yeah. Toilet teeth. Eeeeeech! There's Trudi Styler. She's super-dirty. Look at her loving the camera. O, look at her. She just wants to lift up her skirt and do it.'

During the blessing in St George's Chapel, Grieg's 'Last Spring' from *Two Elegiac Melodies* bled into Wordsworth's 'Immortality' ode, and Camilla stood at the altar wearing a hat which briefly put one in mind of a cross between Julius Caesar and the Statue of Liberty, a combination appropriate, perhaps, to her position in the royal household. Generally speaking, however, the white suburban theme managed very well to survive the austere beauty of the fifteenth-century chapel. The groom cajoled his bride to remember her words, the young guests waved and blew kisses, the mother-in-law sat through the whole thing with a face like fizz, the buses waited outside to take everyone to the reception – 'pragmatic, pragmatic, pragmatic', the BBC said – and the people outside looked exactly like people who hadn't waited outside all night for a place at the front (as people did in their tens of thousands when Charles married Diana) but, rather, as if they'd stopped for a peek on their way to Sainsbury's. The royals walked out of the chapel to the theme-music from *The Antiques Roadshow*, or was it Handel's *Water Music*?

Saul Bellow seemed to me to possess more moral lustre than your average pope, but then I only read him, I didn't marry him, as five people did. The pope and Saul Bellow were enemies of nihilism in one form or another, and I would have given anything to hear a conversation between the two, the Pole so miniature in his certainties on the one side, and the novelist so grand with his Russian genes and his American talk, so large in his openness to being absolutely sure about nothing. Great writers are fonts of ambivalence, and the coverage of Bellow's death (a subject he had covered very precisely himself) seemed allied to his greatest efforts as a maker of life on the page. Bellow was better at seeing things – the true good and the true bad in things – than the routines of politics and religions would have allowed him to be. No one said it, but he was always at his least imaginative when he offered his political opinions.

Lying between the West and Connecticut rivers, the town of Brattleboro, Vermont, was built on modest profits from water and music. It was a resort town before the Civil War, famous for the 'water cure' at the Brattleboro Hydropathic Establishment, which drew on the pure springs along the Whetstone Brook. The town later produced reed organs – 'providing music for the whole of America' – but the once flourishing factories of the Estey Organ Company are closed now, the buildings empty in their acres, representing in that windowless way a complete view on another time.

Saul Bellow's funeral took place in the Jewish section of the town's large cemetery. Brattleboro has a complicated relationship with still waters, but the rabbi made reference to them in both Hebrew and English, via Psalm 23. Bellow's imagination was no stranger to the valley of the shadow of death; that same shadow picks out the true lineaments of Herzog or Citrine or Albert Corde – 'death,' Bellow said, was 'the black backing on the mirror that allows us to see anything at all'. Still, it is not easy to think of Bellow's grave, the people there putting a soul to rest whose excellence had lain in its modern restlessness.

A friend of mine tells me there were about sixty at the grave. The rabbi explained that Bellow had asked for a traditional Jewish burial – quite spare and simple. He also said that Bellow had wanted them to finish the job, that his funeral should not be merely figurative, that each person at the graveside was to throw a shovel of dirt onto the coffin. The family went first, using the shovel, then came Philip Roth, who threw the soil into the grave with his hands. Almost everyone else went up to pick up the shovel. 'What was remarkable,' my friend said, 'was that one was reminded of the sheer labour it takes to replace all that soil. For half an hour, it must have been, there was silence, as we dug into the mound and threw the earth onto the coffin.'

In Rome, as the wind fluttered the pages of Holy Writ laid on top of the pope's coffin, it seemed, for all the hosannas, that the coffin contained someone who had spent many years denouncing the reality of the world in favour of an elevated fiction. Yet, of the two men, of the two imaginations, who could argue that Bellow was not the real pro-lifer? It might be counted a shame, considering the size of his constituency, that the pope never saw the funny side of eternity, a side that even Bellow's minor characters were apt to cosy up to. But still it is hard to think of all that invention and hilarity encoffined.

Prince Rainier of Monaco believed in miracles. 'Either prayer works or it doesn't,' he once said. 'And I believe it works.' With these words he made his way to Lourdes in the mid-1950s in the company of his personal priest, an American, Father Francis Tucker, to pray to Mary the Blessed Mother for the safe delivery to him of a good and beautiful Catholic bride. Grace Kelly was the answer to his prayers: 'I want to thank you for showing the prince what an American Catholic girl can be,' Father Tucker wrote to the Hollywood star, 'and for the very deep impression this has left on him.'

When Kelly left New York on the SS *Constitution*, on 4 April 1956, she was turning her back, as the newspapers liked to say, on Hollywood dreams in order to live a real-life fairy-tale. But there were more than a hundred reporters on board the ship, a fact which begins to tell you how her tale was also a nightmare. Like Anita Ekberg's climb to St Peter's dome, Grace Kelly's wedding a decade earlier was a dramatic moment – a poetic moment, one might say – in the destruction of private life. In 1981, a year before she died, Kelly attended a gala event in London and stood next to Diana, the new Princess of Wales, who wept on the older princess's arm when they went to the loo. 'Don't worry, dear,' the former actress said. 'It will only get worse.'

Flags were tied back with black ribbons, coastal waters were off-limits to all shipping, the casinos were closed, and Monte Carlo's manhole covers were sealed against the possibility of terrorists the day they buried Prince Rainier. The fort above the bay sent cannon fire into the empty waters and half the principality's six thousand residents lined the road to the cathedral, the building where Rainier Grimaldi married Grace Kelly fifty years earlier and where he was soon to join her remains in the family crypt. Several of the dignitaries were suffering from Eurolag – Rome, London, Windsor, Monaco – but *Monaco-Matin* declared it 'an intimate but planetary funeral'.

The Grimaldis have brought more libel and invasion-of-privacy lawsuits than any other family in Europe. Where the cardinals in Rome had almost strutted for CNN, Monaco's female royals hid behind black lace headscarves, crying along-side Barber's 'Adagio for Strings', seemingly exhausted by loss and a lifetime's trial by cameras. Prince Rainier got his sweet Catholic girl and people got their fairy-tale, but strangely, under the arc lights and the pageant colours signifying seven hundred years of continuous reign, the Grimaldis looked done-in, as if they had come to realise that love was not the story after all. Prince Albert stared through the mass and I wondered if that look on his face did not acknowledge the fact that his life was not his own. The funeral was not a celebration of love but another reckoning with cruel fate. 'History is the history of cruelty,' Herzog said. 'Not love, as soft men think.'

This has been an odd fortnight for the authorities. New lights have appeared in the Vatican apartments. The tombs are sealed and Cardinal Ratzinger has mounted the throne as Pope Benedict XVI. In Brattleboro, Vermont, trains trundle past the cemetery and summer visitors begin to stand in line for the Estey Organ Company Museum. The casinos are open in Monte Carlo and private boats once again take their own chances with romance and death in the clear blue of the Mediterranean. The bunting is down in Windsor High Street, and children continue to rendezvous at the doors of Burger King and up the street and round the corner at the gates of Eton College. It's all nothing in the children's eyes.

The Glasgow Sludge Boat

DECEMBER 1995

The Clyde used to be one of the noisiest rivers. Thirty or forty years ago you could hear the strike of metal against metal, the riveter's bedlam, down most of the narrow channel from Glasgow, and at several other shipbuilding towns on the estuary. There was a sound of horns on the water, and of engines turning. Chains unfurled and cargoes were lifted; there was chatter on the piers. But it is very quiet now. Seagulls murmur overhead, and nip at the banks. You can hear almost nothing. The water might lap a little, or ripple when pushed by the wind. But mostly it sits still.

This quietness is broken, five days a week, by the passage of the two ships which carry one of the Clyde's last cargoes: human effluent, sewage, sludge.

Glaswegians call these ships the sludge boats. Every morning, they sail west down the river to turn, eventually, south into the estuary's mouth, the Firth, where they will drop their load into the sea. By this stage of the voyage, their elderly passengers may be dancing on the deck, or, if the weather is wet or windy, playing bingo in the lounge. Underneath them, a few thousand tons of human sewage (perhaps some of their own, transported from their homes) will be slopping in the holds.

There was a time when passengers and cargo set sail from the Clyde to New York, Montreal, Buenos Aires, Calcutta and Bombay in liners equipped to carry awkward things like railway locomotives and difficult people like tea planters. And now, almost alone upon the river, this: tons of shit accompanied by an average complement of seventy old-age pensioners enjoying a grand day out, and travelling free.

This morning it was the ladies – and several gentlemen – of

the Holy Redeemer's Senior Citizens' Club of Clydebank who
were taking a trip down the river. I'd watched them ambling on
to the boat from the wharf at Shieldhall sewage works, each of
them with a plastic bag filled with sandwiches and sweets. Now
I could hear the party arranging itself on the deck above me, as
I stood down below to watch the sludge being loaded into the
ship's eight tanks. It came from the wharf through an enormous red pipe, then into a funnel, and then from the funnel
into a hopper, which channelled the sludge evenly through the
ship's basement. It took about an hour and thirty minutes to
load up. As the ship filled – with wakeful passengers and tired
sludge – a little fountain of perfume sprinkled silently over the
hopper's top.

We were on board the *Garroch Head*, a handsome ship
named after the point near the dumping ground forty miles
downstream, and built on the Clyde, as was her sister ship, the
Dalmarnock (named after a sewage works). The *Garroch Head*
can carry 3,500 thousand tons of sludge, the *Dalmarnock* 3,000
tons. They are not particularly old ships – both were launched
in the 1970s – but neither seems likely to survive the century.
After 1998, the process of dumping at sea will be outlawed by a
directive from the European Union on grounds of ecology and
public health. And yet this quiet disposal, this burial of a city's
intimate wastes in ninety fathoms halfway between the islands
of Bute and Arran, once seemed such a neat and clean solution.

Until the 1890s, Glasgow's untreated sewage went straight
into the river's upper reaches, where it bubbled under the surface and crept ashore as black mud. Civic concern arose with
the stench; the population was still growing in a city made by
the first industrial revolution and popularly described as 'the
workshop of the world'. In 1889 the city's engineer, Alexander
Frew, read a paper on the sewage question to the Glasgow
Philosophical Society, and then addressed increasingly heated
questions about what was to be done. He opposed dumping at
sea, and suggested instead that the sewage be spread along
the banks of the Clyde, where it would come to form fine

agricultural land. The city rejected this scheme, though a feeling persisted that something *useful* (and profitable) might be done with Glasgow's swelling effluent; in London at that time, the Native Guano Company of Kingston upon Thames appeared to be setting a trend with this sort of thing. Glasgow's own brand, Globe Fertiliser, was popular for a short while. But here, science was ahead of the game – or behind it – with new artificial fertilisers that were more powerful and cheaper than the processed human stuff.

How did other cities arrange their disposal? A delegation went from Glasgow to Paris to find out, and there discovered a great tunnel on either side of the River Seine. Sewage poured out of pipes into these tunnels, which then poured into the Seine some miles from the city. The Seine, however, was clean when compared with the Clyde, because (as the delegation noted) the current carried the effluent away from the city to less fortunate towns further downstream, and then to the sea. The Clyde, on the other hand, was tidal; sewage went with the ebb and came back up with the flood – a mess that, like an unwanted stray dog, could not be shooed away. There was also another reason for the Seine's relative purity, which perversely had to do with Glasgow's greater progress in sanitation. Paris had 600,000 closets, or lavatories, but only a third of them were water closets; the rest were dry, their waste carried away by night-soil carts to fields and dumps. Glasgow, thanks to its climate and municipal reservoirs and pipes, had most of its lavatories flushed by water. It had wet sewage rather than dry, and much more of it to get rid of.

In 1898, nine years after the Paris trip, another delegation travelled south, this time to London, where they were shown the system of sewers, sewage works and, lastly, sewage ships which carried the capital's waste to its destination far out in the Thames estuary. They were impressed, and by 1910 Glasgow had a similar system in place – the second-largest (after London) in the world, with three great sewage works sending their produce down the Clyde in ships.

The passengers came later, just after the First World War, when a benevolent but cost-conscious Glasgow city council (then called the Glasgow Corporation) decided that convalescing servicemen would benefit from a day out on the Clyde. Cruising on pleasure steamers up and down the estuary and across to its islands was then Glasgow's great summer pastime; the sludge boats offered the city council the prospect of killing two birds with one stone. Their voyages were already paid for out of the rates. The servicemen could travel free. It was seen as an expression of socialist goodwill – allied with the enlightened Victorian municipalism that had given Glasgow its lavish water supply and so many public parks. The vessels were rebuilt to carry passengers, fitted out with more lifeboats and saloons, equipped with deck quoits. By and by, their traffic in convalescing servicemen died away, to be replaced, thanks to the charitable offices of Glasgow Corporation, by old people who couldn't afford cruises on the regular steamships, but who may have been encouraged by the doctor to take the air.

And so it was, in the summer of 1995, that I came to be travelling with the Clydebank Holy Redeemer's on top of 3,500 tons of sludge.

Everything – or everything visible to the passenger – on the *Garroch Head* was scrupulously clean. The wooden table and chairs in the lounge shone with polish; the urinals gleamed; the deck was as free of dirt as any deck could be. The haphazard filth and toxic stews of Glasgow were kept well out of sight. There was a sense among the crew that it was this opposition of cleanliness to filth that carried them and their ship forward on each voyage.

We sailed past the grass and rubble where the shipyards used to be – Connell's and Blythswood to starboard, Simons and Lobnitz to port – and I talked to a woman who was leaning on the ship's rail and enjoying the breeze. She was called Mary Kay McRory, she was eighty, and she had a big green cardigan pulled across her chest. Her eyes ran, but she laughed a lot as she spoke. She said the first time she had sailed on the Clyde was in

1921, when she had travelled as a six-year-old with her family on the steamer that took cattle and people from Derry in Ireland to Glasgow, and very seldom took the same ones back again. Mary Kay's father was escaping some bother in Donegal; he heard of work in Glasgow, came over and was employed right away as a lamplighter. Then he summoned his wife and the six children. 'We came away from Donegal with biscuits,' Mary Kay said. 'Everybody would throw biscuits over the wall to you. They were good biscuits. The food over there was good.'

She had worked as a waitress, when the city was still full of tea rooms, and then on the Glasgow trams for twenty-five years. I asked her if Glasgow had changed much, and she got me by the arm. 'Ye can say what ye like,' she said, 'but there's no poverty now, none.' She talked a lot about sanitation, about toilets and baths, in the way many old Glaswegians do. Those who remember lavatories shared with neighbours and trips to the public bathhouse tend to talk more about these matters than people like me who grew up thinking it was nothing special to have porcelain bits at the top of the stairs stamped ARMITAGE SHANKS.

Plastic bags were being rustled in the lounge. Out of them came the day's supplies: sandwiches of white bread cut into quarters and filled variously with slates of corned beef, chicken breast, shiny squares of gammon, salmon paste and cheese spreads. And then the treats to follow: Paris buns, Blue Riband biscuits, Tunnock's Teacakes, Bourbon creams. Some of the women dropped sweeteners into their tea and stirred melodically for a long time after. Others placed ginger snaps at the edge of their saucers, or unwrapped tight wads of shortbread, ready for distribution. Neat stacks of white bread and sweet acres of treats stretched on the table, in front of every passenger. All the mouths were going – shredding meat and sloshing tea – like washing machines on a full load.

This was not lunch for the Holy Redeemers; merely elevenses.

Sludge, in the particular sense of our sludge boat's cargo, comes about like this. The sewage pumped into Glasgow's three sewage works is twice screened. The first screening takes out large objects – lumps of wood, rags, metal – that somehow find their way into the sewers. The second screening extracts smaller, abrasive materials such as glass and sand. Then comes the first separation process, designed to make the organic component of the sewage sink to the bottom of the tank (just as sediment will settle in a bottle of wine). They call this the stage of primary settlement. The heavy stuff at the bottom is called raw sludge; the clearer liquid above is settled sewage.

The raw sludge is not ready to dispose of; it needs further modification and is subject to biochemical breakdown. Some of it goes through a process called digestion. Bacteria are allowed into the holding chambers, where they feed energetically on the proteins and carbohydrates, diminishing the organic matter until the sludge is fit to be spread on farmland or made ready for dumping at sea. Then, at the works near the wharf at Shieldhall, the sludge is 'settled' one last time, to increase the content of sinkable solids in the watery mix. The stuff in the hold has passed through many systems – biological and mechanical – and it will have no final rest from the biological, even at the bottom of the sea. It degrades there to feed marine life (the fishing near the dumping ground is said to be fairly good) and continue its journey through the ecosystem.

There has, however, been an awful lot of it dumped, and all in the same place. In the first year of the sludge boats, 213,867 tons were carried down the Clyde. In 1995, the figure was 1.8 million tons. The total for the century is 82.6 million tons. The seabed at the dump's centre is said to be damaged, its organisms contaminated. The EU has delivered its verdict. Glasgow needs a new venue for the sludge, and old ideas are being re-examined. Fertiliser, for example. Sludge is rich in nitrates (4 per cent), phosphate (3 per cent) and potassium (1 per cent), and full of nutrients – it could do a good job on the land, and farmers seem willing to try it for free. It is also well suited to grass-growing and is already being spread on derelict industrial sites to prepare them for reclamation. A new product range – sludge cakes, sludge pellets – will be tried on the waste ground that was once the Ravenscraig steelworks, the largest and last of Scotland's steel plants, where the soil has been poisoned by decades of metal wastes. Sludge used there could make a meadow grow.

We passed Greenock, which used to make ships and sugar, and then veered left into the Firth proper. The *Garroch Head* was going at a fair pelt now, and most of the passengers had their eyes down, playing a restive round or two of bingo. Some were nibbling still at the corners of buns and sandwiches. From the saloon porthole the water looked silver, as if some giant shoal of mackerel swam just beneath the surface. The islands of Great and Little Cumbrae stood out, like two large boulders only recently dropped into the sea.

We passed them. Up on the bridge, they were slowing the vessel down, ready to discharge their load. We had reached the dumping ground, and as soon as the position was right a crewman on the bridge flicked a switch and I heard a little rumble. The valves were opening. I thought I could feel the cargo starting to be pulled by gravity from its tanks.

I went down from the bridge to the deck nearest the water and saw the first of the billowing columns. Fierce puffs, great Turner clouds of wayward brown matter, rose up and spread in an instant over the surface. The waters of the Firth were all at once rusty and thick, and the boat was an island in a sea of sludge. This was all in the first few minutes.

We moved off, leaning to port, aiming to complete a full circle as the sludge descended. A group of pensioners stood in a row looking out, covering their mouths and noses with white hankies. All the worst odour of a modern city, until now stored and battened down, was released in this time-stopping, comical stench. I looked up at the coast and wondered for a second where it had all begun, because this was an ending, and the sense of an ending was as palpable and strong as the brew in the sea before us.

The ship turned about and headed home. Its emptying had taken ten minutes. Back in the saloon, the pensioners were dancing to a song called 'Campbeltown Loch, I Wish Ye Were Whisky'. My tea sat just where I'd left it, and I was happy to notice it was still quite warm.

Celebrity Memoirs

JANUARY 2003

If you want to be somebody nowadays, you'd better start by getting in touch with your inner nobody, because nobody likes a somebody who can't prove they've been nobody all along. Today's celebrities hack their cloth to suit the fashion of the times: the less you do the more you are doing, the less you know the more you are knowing, the less you wear the more you are wearing, and so say all of us. God loves a chancer more than he loves a trier, and the tabloid newspapers – who recognise no higher power than themselves – speak every day for a Britain that is perfectly in love with its cellphone democracy. This is William Cobbett's country no more, so let us sling a troubled thought among the Christmas books.

The sufferings of a celebrity, despite the enjoyments, despite the privilege, are supposed to embody the sufferings of us all. They remind us how we are all the same, that even Christ suffered pain, and suffered it for our sake. Is that the only sainthood we can know? You see it everywhere now: on *EastEnders*, in *Heat* magazine, on television chat shows and movies produced by Miramax. Pain is one of the new pleasures, abuse is the new nurturing. A hummable, weepable, narcissistic self-pity, hitherto only available in the speeches of Billy Graham and the recording work of Tammy Wynette, has, over the last few years, taken Britain by storm, and it is nowhere more evident than in the new style of celebrity autobiography.

Many modern celebrities call everyday people 'normals', and it was a proper normal, Dave Pelzer, who gave these plot-losing self-describers their narrative arc and their sad tone. Since it came out in 1993, *A Child Called 'It'* – a whole book of seismic wallowing – has inspired the famous with the notion that a brutal life story generously told could guarantee unlimited book sales. Suddenly, people didn't experience their childhoods, they survived them, they didn't live their lives, they 'came through' them, and right there, one small step for the mangled, one giant leap backwards for mankind, these authors grasped a powerful rationale for adult self-obsession and the eternal hungers involved in fame. They found they could set themselves up as a principality of wounds. Here's Pelzer:

> Standing alone in that damp, dark garage, I knew, for the first time, that I could survive. I decided that I would use any tactic I could think of to defeat Mother or to delay her from her grisly obsession. *I* knew if *I* wanted to live, *I* would have to think ahead. *I* could no longer cry like a helpless baby. In order to survive, *I* could never give in to her. That day I vowed to myself that I would never, ever again give that bitch the satisfaction of hearing me beg her to stop beating me.

And then, a hundred pages of thick ears and italicised selfhood later:

> I'm so lucky. My dark past is behind me now. As bad as it was, I knew even back then, in the final analysis, my way of life would be up to me. I made a promise to myself that if I came out of my situation alive, I had to make something of myself. I would be the best person that I could be. Today I am. I made sure I let go of my past, accepting the fact that that part of my life was only a small fraction of my life. I knew the black hole was out there, waiting to suck me in and forever control my destiny – but only if I let it. I took positive control over my life.

There was a point not long ago when Dave Pelzer's self-rescue manuals held the top three spots in the best-seller charts. In Britain, it is likely that one out of every fifteen adults will have read a Pelzer book, and the 'inspirational' style in general, with its page-turning mix of the brutal and the banal, its triteness of phrase and sentiment, has changed the memoiring business for good. 'Making something of yourself in the world', as Pelzer sees it, is the only way to rob a sad childhood of its dark victory over your experience. For the newer kind of celebrity, the contemplation of the Nobody years becomes a guaranteed way of justifying the Somebody years and all the excesses that Somebodyhood might involve. Fame finally gets to have an essential moral component: it is the work of self-preservation, a summit of reason, a resounding answer to the riddle of life, a compact of exemplary human capabilities, a reverie of the perfect comeuppance, the ideal riposte to familial abuse. Being famous comes to seem like the natural order's premier reward for martyrdom.

The relationship between sainthood and stupidity – think of Charles Bovary, a fool raised by what he endures, or Princess Diana, the patron saint of non-swots – is a connection that lies too deep for tears in these biographies. Yes, they are simple-hearted bids for approval, but there is also something vicious in the journeyings of self-glory that they represent, something rapacious and nearly vengeful in the attempt to position famousness as a corrective to the unfair balance of power in the average childhood. In every one of these books, the dedication is the key: in most cases they tell you everything, a hard haiku of explicitness, set before the swirling poetry of the difficult life.

The Scottish singer Lulu is Pelzer in a feather boa. 'To ma mammy and ma daddy,' she starts off. 'This would not have been possible with you here, but would never have been possible without you.' As dedications go, this is pretty scruffy, but you soon see how beautifully it encapsulates the trouble at the centre of our Lulu's life. Right away, before you're halfway down Garfield Street, the demons are stalking the tenements, made to appear in a puff of psychoanalytic smoke:

> Even when cut and bleeding, my mother kept goading him. I don't know what she wanted to prove. Maybe she was looking for attention. Or maybe she wanted to be punished. Some people would rather be beaten and abused than

ignored, particularly when they are lonely and hurting. There were nights when the fights would wake me, but I was always ready to be woken. I slept with my muscles taut and my teeth clenched. My heart would fly into my mouth. Blinking into the darkness, I'd look across at Billy. I didn't want him to cry. We'd huddle together, flinching as the fists landed. Neither of us wanted to believe our parents could hate each other so much.

And, of course, not long in bringing up the rear is the neediness, the attention, an obsession with fashion detail the like of which we haven't seen since Patrick Bateman was looking out his tie in *American Psycho*, and, then, of course, there's the friends. Lulu has more than your average head for vertiginous name-dropping: it's Elton this and John Lennon that, insecurity all the way, but this doesn't stop the portrait from becoming something of an anthem to Little Me-ism. Lulu is a Sixties being: one of the first of that generation of pop stars to be found cool on account of their class, their vowels, their cheek and their style. But thrillingly, Lulu – unlike so many of her starry pals – has held on to her hunger, and every paragraph of her autobiography is a battle to win ground from the hurters: every sentence sets out to convey the message that success is an essential part of the revenge strategy for the abused and the self-abused, all of which makes her a very contemporary kind of self-revealer. Lulu is a Scotch egg: ginger on the outside, hard-boiled on the inside, and a favourite at the parties of the resolutely unposh. Yet, in her own account, her life has been a rather sophisticated battle with her own gigantic feelings. Celebrity writers are obsessed with feelings:

> I just had this innate understanding that I *had* to keep working. With hindsight I can see it was a mishmash of Protestant work ethic, a sense of responsibility for people and a desire not to be forgotten. I didn't ask myself what I could do differently. That sort of introspection came years later when I learned how to get in touch with my feelings

and learned how to look after the world inside me, not just
the world outside. John was working harder than ever. He
had a growing client list and was making a real name for
himself as a celebrity crimper and 'top London hairdresser'
as the papers referred to him. I used to get annoyed with
him for never being home. I wanted more of his attention.

Following some bad times with the crimper and the loss of
her record company, Lulu has found popularity again by
singing with the boy band Take That, and now she is the beautifully nipped and tucked grande dame to a whole new generation of self-seekers, kids who, all over again, are in love with the
idea that someone from nowhere can take everywhere by
storm. Her new manager is the teen-wrangler Louis Walsh, who
can be regularly seen making and breaking young hopefuls on
Saturday-night television. Out of her troubles – and the overcoming of her troubles – Lulu has become poster-girl for a new
generation of the enduringly ambitious. Her latest album went
straight into the UK pop charts at number four.

Self-hagiography – and its popularity – probably has more to
do with needs than choices, but what happens when those
needs are shared by the people who know you best? In literature
this sort of thing has a heartbreaking history, if one thinks of,
say, Jane Welsh Carlyle, or Mrs Tennyson, or Vera Nabokov; but
what if Pamela Stephenson, the clinical psychologist married to
Billy Connolly, is the modern version? Here is a woman who
never fails, in her ultra-bestselling biography *Billy*, to take
advantage of her domestic arrangements, so that every semi-
recumbent position poor Connolly might assume becomes an
opportunity for the wife to conjure with the old psychic woes.
Dedication: 'To the Connolly and McLean families, in the spirit of healing through understanding; and to all families who are
divided by religious differences, or who struggle with abuse,
poverty or addiction.'

Of course, there must be advantages in living with a saint,
and spouses must get something out of it for themselves, but
Pamela Stephenson so effectively Pelzer-ises Billy Connolly that

you begin to wonder what it is about the lives of talented people that lends itself so readily to a thoroughly banal account of themselves. Stephenson gives us a Billy Connolly whose rage is no longer enjoyable; he is no longer the working-class guy who was a careful listener and a wry observer of shite and toil, but a thoroughly broken adult who is constantly running into the limelight as a way of escaping the emotional starvations and sexual abuses of his childhood. He is not really at home in Glasgow or Los Angeles; the stage is his only home, and it is not any joyful platform either, but a place where demons are routinely confronted, where voices from the past are finally (but repeatedly) given their answer, and for Stephenson, as for all these writers, the whole of show business is something larger than itself: it is not a job, but a display of courage; it is not to do with a developed gift, but a grievous vocation; it is not a wonderful effort to be good and special, but a fleeing from badness and a fight to be normal. If John Bayley made the world an unsafe place in which to be a spouse, then Pamela Stephenson goes one step further: she takes a person famous for his character and gives him the psychological boil-wash of his life, leaving him damp, colourless, wrung out, and softened; dragged into a basket waiting at the base of her hungry machine.

Like many sentimental narrative-makers, Stephenson is addicted to flashbacks that begin to kick in from a position of apparent glory: Billy is standing on a stage surrounded by applause; he is in attendance at a flash Hollywood party; he is negotiating the corridors of his vast castle, the centre of a world he has made for himself; and yet, as his biographer has it, the terrors of the past are always ready to encroach on his achievements, making them sickly and hysterical. Childhood has everything to do with the problem of fame, of course, but more subtly than this, and often in ways that offer permission to the talent rather than force depletion on the character. If fame is a kind of freedom for some people – a kind of release, and a revenge – it needn't mean that every interesting element of that person is a form of falsification, a deranged refusal of everything that was handed down. Stephenson turns Connolly into the sum of his abuses, a product of darkness alone, and she helps us to lose sight of his native defences and imaginative leaps, his power of communication, his handy way with blasphemy, his light-conducting naturalism in the face of some pretty bad odds. Connolly is funny, and his funniness is not merely some sensational consequence of his sadness. He has more versions of himself than his biographer can live with: his ability to inflect society and inflect himself derives from a culture much larger than the culture of drunk fathers who like to put their hands down their children's pyjamas.

But in the mind of celebrity survivalism, nothing could ever be so interesting as that:

> It's hard to know exactly why William molested his own son. He had the experience of being extremely religious and, since the Catholic Church was very strict about the sanctity of marriage, he saw no possibility of divorce from Mamie or remarriage at any point: however, that doesn't really explain why he chose this particular form of sexual expression. It wouldn't be the first time extreme sexual repression in an ostensibly religious person led to 'unspeakable' acts. As Carl Jung explained, denial of our shadow side will often cause it to rise up against us. Perhaps William himself had been sexually abused in childhood, as is so often the case with perpetrators. In fact, historical accounts of that culture and time would suggest that, in those overcrowded conditions, incest was extremely common.

And when Stephenson first meets Connolly, 'it felt as if we were joined at the wound'. The comedian is now surrounded by people who are hungry for his seriousness, and who have detained themselves with enough Jung to render all good comedy an illness. In a performer, rawness is not necessarily the enemy of polish, but Connolly's loved ones clearly want him to smarten up his ideas about himself, as if he was negligent before, as if solving the past in conventional ways requires much more of him than his genius. As psychic rescues go, *Billy* is the perfect modern celebrity's kind of thing; it might not be evident – not in the following paragraph anyhow – that low-fat self-regard is no less poisonous than self-doubt.

> It is August 2000 and the heavy green dining-room curtains at Candacraig, our Scottish home, have been drawn to hide the bright evening sunshine of a northern summer night. A few close friends, some of them known to the world as very funny people, have just seated themselves with us around the dinner table. The conversation gravitates to an uncomfortable discussion of the impetus for comedy, in reply to a question from one of the non-comedians at the table.
>
> 'For me,' interjects Billy at one point, 'it's about the desire to win. My audience becomes a crowd of wild animals and I have to be the lion-tamer or be eaten . . .'
>
> 'Oh, is that so?' Steve Martin challenges him. 'You don't think it's about a little hurt from Daddy?'

When you want everything, and get everything, maybe the fantasy of having nothing becomes your luxury. In show business, that kind of thinking has always, at the same time, been part of the reality and the campness of the industry. 'Hollywood's a place where they'll pay you a million dollars for a kiss and ten cents for your soul,' said Marilyn Monroe, someone for whom adult fame could seem like a poor betrayal of the richness of girlhood dreams.

These people's books always tell you what they've got – the cars, the attention, the castle, the hotels – but this is really just a kind of throat-clearing for the main announcement: I Have None of the Things that Normal People Have. As vanities go, this one is pretty hot, but it's now widespread enough to have become a pop cultural commonplace. Sentimental as a lollipop, no doubt, but at one stroke it turns the audience's envy into pity, the star's excesses into privations, and makes the generally bloated star feel like someone who lives at the very centre of the world's suffering. There's a price to be paid for fame, you see, and only the famous would understand. It's a Judy Garland-style balance sheet of profit and loss, now scripted into the deepest self-dramatisations of our celebrity culture; when you have everything you are insufferably lonely in your view of things on our small planet; and slowly, photogenically, you become a victim hounded by 'demons' and 'parasites'.

In the 1960s and 1970s, in the earlier days of British light entertainment and pop music and television, this was a hidden, unknown process, where worlds of dissociation and distraction engulfed young people before they knew what was happening to them, and the journey through famousness for someone like the singer Lena Zavaroni seems to me an entirely different order of drama, a properly personal disaster that involved a notion of community and a post-war idea of domestic life, leisure and the good society. She was the last gasp of the entertainment world that existed before global corporate sponsorship and MTV. But the meaning of publicity has changed everything: there is a new sort of narcissism in the dramas promulgated by the famous, an explicit revelling in fame for its own sake, in the branding of personality, and it is a development the world finds compelling.

'This book is dedicated to the walking wounded,' Geri Halliwell writes. (Halliwell too can now be found acting as a judge on one of the Saturday-night talent shows that have changed young Britons' notions of what it means to be alive.) And yet, despite the millions, the gear, the house in Hollywood, her story happens not to be an account of all the luck and the fun she is having.

> It would take a whole book on its own to really explain the recovery process I have been through. All I can do is try to convey how profoundly it affected my life . . . I can honestly say it has been the most painful thing I have ever done, and the most rewarding. I didn't know it at the time but the moment I picked up the phone and asked for help, I took my first step on the road to recovery. That simple step marked the end of years and years of denial because I was

confessing that I was powerless over food and that my life was out of control as a result.

I began to realise how dishonest I had been to myself and to my friends and family for so long, I was living a double life, giving the impression that everything was fine and that my eating problems were over when I knew that I had been controlling and bingeing. Now I just wanted to be honest. The first person I had to be honest with was myself. I had accepted I was powerless over food but now I had to look for the reasons. And when I did, I realised that my addiction was not the disease, but the symptom. Insane as it sounds, I even found a reason to be grateful for my problem.

Well, not as insane as all that. We have to assume that Geri is part of the generation that likes to think success is the answer to the principal questions of a young life, and that, after success, the only answer is failure, which serves to deepen the notion of success. She wants normality but also wants to say normality is a curse:

I came from a poor family and a broken home and had always felt like I was the odd one out, the token working-class girl in Watford Grammar School. But these things alone can't really explain my eating disorder. They do help to explain why I was so hungry for fame from an early age – after all, they are the classic conditions needed to produce a wannabe. I think the real explanation has its roots in the death of my father in November 1993 and the fact that six months later – still reeling from my loss – I walked into a London rehearsal studio and auditioned for the group that would become the Spice Girls.

Every one of these books should be called *Still Reeling from My Loss*. Waterstone's ought to have a wall for them: 'Still Reeling after All These Years'. The problem, you might imagine, is less to do with the ordinary to and fro of free school dinners and Dad being partial to the odd snifter, and more to do with the modes of behaviour common to a tribe of people who take more interest in the media's interest in them than they take in themselves or the people around them. Most of these celebrities spent too much time staring lovingly (then hatefully) into the media pond: if it's not the mirror it's the *Mirror*, and modern celebrities are covered in vanity, low-mindedness and deceit when it comes to the tabloid press, to say nothing of the press's own behaviour.

Geri Halliwell's old chum from the Spice Girls, Victoria Beckham, has a thing or two to say about the push-me-pull-you mechanics of the British press, but, first off, she's in a class of her own when it comes to dedications. She feels sorry for herself too, but she manages quite deftly, in dedicating the book to her family, to remind us all how effectively her sense of self has obliterated their reality:

> Mummy, Daddy, Louise and Christian. Over the last six years I have turned your lives upside down. And I don't just mean having to live behind security gates. As difficult as it has been for me, it has been even more difficult for you – not just coping with my personality, with its ups and downs, but your whole lives have been changed. While I have fame and the money that comes with it, all you have, apart from being proud, is the upheaval.

That's all I'm having to do with Victoria Beckham, except to say that she and her husband, David, in their relationship with the press, have taken the notion of abuse, the abuse of one set of human beings by another, to levels that make Billy Connolly's childhood seem like a chapter from *The Swiss Family Robinson*. They may be right to feel hunted by the press, but feeling hunted by the press is an aspect of self-hunting too: their famousness is an occasion for grief, and their grief is a constituent part of their fame.

The newspapers love abuse stories and they love the mixture of celebrity and populism that marries so easily in the culture now. People can vote these celebrities into being, they can read about their horrific lives in the papers, they can buy the books that give more details and which speak of the terrors of the press, they can move quickly onto the next serving of success and pain, voting new people on and new people off, and to Tony Blair and culture-surfers everywhere, it can seem like a nice way of having a democracy. Tony Blair asked for a meeting with one of the judges on *Pop Idol*, Pete Waterman, and sought his advice on how to harness the five-minute convictions of that generation. Not long ago, the winners of its predecessor *Popstars*, the group Hear'Say, broke up in a welter of tears and recriminations, speaking of horrific media manipulation, destroyed personal lives and abuse on the street.

Celebrity means nothing now without the notion of suffering. Fresh off the block, aged only eighteen, *Pop Idol* runner-up Gareth Gates is here with his autobiography, already hooked up with a ghost-writer of his former self, already reeling from the difficulties of being a success. These books know their market: again, this is not a youthquaking story of hard work, sheer pleasure, tradition and talent, but a tale of how Gareth struggled to make it with a speech impediment:

> I had a stammer from the moment I tried to put sentences together, which my parents recognised because my dad had a stammer up until he was 18, which he grew out of (my sister Charlotte has one too; sometimes it's hereditary). My stammer got worse over the years and at five I was referred to a speech therapist, but this didn't really help me. My stammer would make me completely unable to say a sentence properly, but I didn't want this ever to get in the way of what I wanted to do.

You would think talent was enough, but talent nowadays is not enough: it must answer a grievance, it must canonise its bearer. At the most visible end of tabloid fame, no talent at all will be fine, so long as the body itself is lovely, and makes itself available for whipping and anointing and self-explaining. Here's the facts. Ulrika Jonsson used to be the weathergirl on

TV-am. She had an affair with the England football manager. Over the last year she has had more newspaper and magazine articles written about her than were devoted to the war in Sudan, the elections in Brazil and the future of the Common Agriculture Policy combined. But Ulrika is familiar with her own agony and she is ready to share. (Dedication: 'To Cameron and Bo. Remember, if the worst comes to the worst, being screwed up can sometimes make you more interesting.') And so the past comes reeling back. The book is called *Honest*:

> I have been married, divorced, faithful and unfaithful. I have battled with depression and enjoyed moments of bliss. I have had an abortion, I have been raped and I have stripteased. I have loved myself and loathed myself. Throughout my life, my exterior and interior have done battle – not just on account of being born one nationality and living quite another, or indeed of having parents at opposing ends of the personality spectrum, but also on account of having lived my life very publicly for some fourteen years. At the age of 32 what had surfaced was a crisis of persona.

And that's where the story ends: you don't have to be good at anything, and you don't have to have done anything, except to have somehow been a celebrity and known what that costs. Readers will forgive you anything except your uncomplicated success.

On Lad Magazines

JUNE 2004

A spokesman admits that the cancellation of the Saturday-night sleeper from London to Aberdeen 'until the end of time' is a bitter blow for those who like to wake up on a Sunday morning to the munching of Highland cattle, but there can be no question of having the train back, say the men at Euston. They can't find a single soul who'll agree to work the shift.

'It was like an alcoholic bullet flying through the night,' a former guard says, poetically. 'You just couldn't cope with those guys on their stag nights. That's what did it. The buffet car was a cesspool. They were climbing into the berths with Christ knows who. It was madness. They'd pull the emergency cord. They'd fling the bog roll down the aisles. They'd vomit. Break guitars over each other's heads. You can't be having that on a nice train.' You'll find the same sentiment echoing around the hostelries of Dublin's Temple Bar, where stag nights have been banned, proprietors believing that the Ryanair generation has made a mockery of the art of running amok. Over on cheap flights from Prestwick and Stansted, these boys were often to be found floating trouserless in the Liffey at dawn, or staggering up Grafton Street, their T-shirts clinging to them with alcopops and spilled sambuca.

Britain's news-stands are heaving with magazines devoted to the rough magic of being a bloke. On first sight you think they are what my friends used to call scud mags; the girls who adorn the covers – legs wide, breasts atumble, nipples fit for pegging a couple of wet duffle coats on – tend to be among the nearly famous, a tribe of models admired by laddish editors for their friendly shagability and the hunger in their eyes. The market for male 'general interest' magazines has grown massively in the

UK, as if young men suddenly needed to be celebrated and serviced in a new way, as if there were a new demand among them
for reassurance about the wonders of male normalcy. They look
for all this in the way people like Tony Parsons have taught
them, in a spirit of soft-core irony and hard-core sentiment.
But apart from reassurance and a sort of avenging pride, what
are these magazines selling to their readers? With their grisly
combinations of sensitivity and debasement – 'How to Bathe
Your New Baby' v. 'Win the Chance to Pole-Dance with
Pamela!' – it may be time to consider whether these men's magazines aren't just the latest enlargement on the old fantasy of
men having everything they want to have and finding a way to
call it their destiny.

Stag & Groom Magazine is edited by a woman who has no
end of tolerance for the male love of male company. She has the
modern Lifestyle writer's addiction to life as it might be lived in
a pink paperback, and that means her men are allowed to be
very bad and also to know that their badness is quite lovable.
But maybe she's just having a monumental laugh. 'Stags!' she
writes in the editorial of the second issue:

> Are you doing all you should? Have you partaken of suffi
> cient extreme sports, fine dining and wild women to ensure
> that your sense of adventure is fully sated in advance of the
> big day? Have you, in short, succeeded in scaring yourselves
> silly enough to be ready for a little marital peace and har
> mony? No? Well, what the deuce are you waiting for, old
> boy? Get out there in the mud and allow your dearest
> friends to shoot seven shades of crap out of you. When
> you've finished, it's your stagly duty to adjourn to a fine
> establishment for haute cuisine, Courvoisier and Cuban
> cigars, perhaps followed by some clinical observations of
> the gentler sex at play.

The 'old boy' thing – as well as the advertisements for honeymoons in the Maldives and for Mayfair jewellers – might suggest *Stag & Groom*'s target readers are a level or two up the social scale from the alcopopoholics, but the thing about new laddishness is that it has something of Tony Blair's classless, open-palmed, universalising, 'we are all feeling this pain together' baloney (an attitude that understands courage to be a strong mixture of earnestness and easily available empathy), so the magazine will speak to every marriageable young fellow who is happy to see himself as just another upholder of simple truths about modern men and how we are. A gentleman's magazine of the old sort could rely on the notion that nobody confused gentlemen and guttersnipes, but it is fashionable now for grandees to drink pints and plebs to drink champagne, allowing *Stag & Groom* to do its thing in an untroubled way, talking about football and chest-waxing in the same quick breath, murmuring piously about the best man's duties and the wisdom of choosing the Lotus Elise as a wedding car, as if the trials of manhood were a holy pilgrimage, as if, indeed, the rites of male vanity were aspects of a religion into which we have all very recently been born again.

After reading a few issues of the newest men's weeklies, *Zoo* and *Nuts*, I began to wonder if the readers of these magazines might want to have sex with their chums. It's like men who want to sleep with their best friend's wife: why don't they just cut out the decoy? *Zoo* presents a world of men joined by the same desire, not for the same women (though they wouldn't say no), but for a community of leering men. All these magazines are, in the end, about providing a sense of belonging, but few are as blatant in their invitation to the fantasy of tribal kinship as *Zoo*, which runs a regular item called 'Guilty Wanks: Toss Off and Then Think About What You've Just Done'. The list underneath, detailing the people readers are ashamed of thinking about when they're having sex with themselves, includes the child pop group S Club 8, '*National Geographic* bare-breasted tribeswomen', Natalie Portman in the film *Leon*, and 'your best mate's girlfriend'. *Zoo* loves the notion that all men are the same at heart: dirty and funny and fucked-up and violent, slaves to their needs and not ashamed – the articles about football brutality snuggle up quite naturally with 'The Ten Sex-iest Rears in the World'. The editors borrow the notion of male universality from the spirit of Britain under Blair, but the unfunny barbarism of the magazine's content shows there are still differences between men, if only in degree.

You'll find that no pride is greater than the pride that comes with being thick. Britain is filled with people who are really proud of their stupidity. I'm surprised *Nuts* hasn't made this its rubric – 'We're Thick. And Everybody Else Is a Tosser' – yet, for all that, it wears its density more or less lightly. It favours stories about gangland hitmen (Brian 'The Milkman' Wright, 'during his drug-dealing days he always delivered'; John 'Goldfinger' Palmer, once 'one of Britain's richest men, owning a fleet of pri-vate planes, helicopters, boats and cars'), and every few pages there's a soap star in her knickers, usually followed by a report, written with barely contained excitement, about a massive pile-up on some notorious bend of a foreign racing track. A deli-cately positioned article called 'Please Smash Me in the Face!' accompanies photographs of a bloodstained skinhead with a face like a plate of steak tartare:

> Being thrown head first into a barbed-wire fence doesn't sound like much fun – but this senseless gibbon does it as his hobby. During a blood-spattered Backyard Wrestling match between shaven-headed fighter Karnage and his rival Sic, Karnage was repeatedly smashed in the face with a strip light then elbow-dropped onto a bed of barbed wire and cacti.

Alas, poor Karnage. The popularity of *Nuts* is, in some ways, as hard to understand as the success of the *Sun* – unless you take it for granted that a frightening percentage of young British men are sociopaths. In that sense, *Nuts* and *Zoo* are closer to their tabloid newspaper cousins than to other men's magazines: mostly, though, what they resemble are mad-dog football fanzines and the kinds of website that carry pictures of suicide victims.

The thirst for a beery men's magazine – not a girly magazine, but something that could both celebrate and make common cause with men's worst habits – was first attended to ten years ago with the inauguration of *Loaded*. The anniversary campaign last month featured billboards across the country showing a large-breasted girl with the words 'Loaded: Ten Years Fighting for Feminism' printed across her skimpy top. The cover of the June issue offers free beer and Durex, but my copy just contained a packet of Extra Strong Mints, which I'm trying not to take personally. *Loaded* tries to be bubbly about its degeneracy, but it's mostly just a jokeless, pulpless exercise in self-abuse. Of course it tends to like lagers and motors, fighting and hooligans, and imagines the rest of the world is fraudulent and missing out because it has other things on its mind. What's sad about the magazine is that, despite its defensive bluster, it has no convictions to be courageous about, and there's nothing in its contents worth attacking. It shows as many pictures as it can of coy girls concealing their nipples, and sandwiches these between rubbishy little sections flogging aftershave. *Loaded*, too, likes the notion that it's conducting a conversation with real men, a conversation that needs very few words. Yet the British lad magazine is not about men at all, or about the business of being a grown-up person; it's fuelled by a childish notion of hedonism – pills, thrills and bellyaches – which sees politics as a mug's game and wives as a curse. They may be right about that, but if so they are right in a fairly boring way: no man older than twenty-one wants to be told they're a failure unless they live like George Best. And that's *Loaded*'s central anxiety: it exhibits a very British smallness of style in its understanding of male recklessness, and its world of Saturday nights is really a lament for passions spent or never experienced.

So why are men's magazines in Britain so largely devoted to a tittering schoolboy's understanding of life and laughter? In America, where publications such as *Esquire* and *GQ* originated, men's magazines weren't scuzzy in the way ours are, and quite often they were venues for some of the country's best and most expensive journalism. *Playboy* and *Esquire*, particularly, could produce, and have, anthologies of first-rate political and cultural journalism, and even this month, when the newish British lad mag *Jack* flags on its cover 'A Speed Special Starring Fast Planes, Bikes and Women', the much-derided *Playboy* advertises a long piece by Gore Vidal on God and the state. *Jack* runs a piece about British wrestling in which even the writer seems completely bored with the subject:

> I ask Keith to tell me the difference between the British wrestler and the new breed of Americans who seem to have moved wrestling on a notch. Apart, of course, from one being built on steak puddings and the other on steroids. 'British wrestling is somewhere the family can go and have a good night out. It represents a typical good night's entertainment,' says Keith.
>
> When the ring is up the wrestlers hurry into the dressing rooms to get changed. The audience is already arriving. There will be 100 to 150 people, mainly made up of friends and family and a few obligatory old ladies sucking on boiled sweets. As the audience shuffle in carrying chairs I scan a borrowed running sheet.

Say what you like about the 1960s, and say what you like about America: the original *Esquire* would have sent George Plimpton to write about the wrestling, and would have given him space for 20,000 words. It's hard to know what *Jack*'s editors are offering readers, or how they look at the world: perhaps they're just fed up and *Jack* is a magazine for fed-up blokes, or a magazine edited by people who are badly hung-over from reading *Loaded*. In any event, when a men's magazine lacks care and conviction to this extent – when even its pieces on Italian football and foreign bloodbaths are stale – you begin to ask yourself if the British male it's supposed to attract isn't perhaps a little disastrous. Is he tired? Is he upset? Is he depressed?

Nostalgia and small-mindedness are among the most exhausting things to hum a tune about, but so is loneliness, and a lot of what you see when you look into these magazines is just men being confused about what to make of themselves. If you look closely at the stuff, you see how many of the men either writing or being written about associate ageing with isolation: the smell of fear rises out of the aftershave ads and the free sachets of facial scrub on every other page. Who am I? What am I becoming and can I stand it? *Esquire,* which tends to be the best-written of these publications, and which maintains its connection to its own traditions by running the odd piece you might care to read, has a copy of Jonathan Franzen's essays to give away with the current number. It still has some 'Sexy but Deadly' micro-celeb on the cover, but inside, the anxieties I've been talking about are more humanly displayed. Henry Sutton writes about being a 'Broken-Up Man'. It starts with him crying in front of his seven-year-old daughter:

> A friend of mine keeps ringing me up to say that being a bloke and getting divorced means I'm on a one-way ticket to a bedsit in Balham. 'You'll get screwed,' he says. Having spoken to a couple of lawyers, having realised how things are stacked against me legally, well, yes, I probably am going to get screwed. I'm screwed already. I'm 40. I'm totally broke and I'm almost homeless. How the fuck did I let this happen?

A few years ago Robert Bly celebrated the notion of men running into the woods to beat their own chests, but many of the newer bibles of male self-realisation unwittingly celebrate something else: the notion that men might flee to the big cities and grow their own breasts. At any rate, there is a very strenuous blend of women-envy in some of the magazines for men. Richard Wollheim has just finished telling us, in *Germs,* his frighteningly good memoir, about wanting to be a woman sixty years ago. 'I knew that what I wanted,' he wrote, 'was, not so much to have her, though I also wanted that, as to be her.' And later: 'The way to a woman's heart, I had come to believe, was along the hard, stony, arduous track of effeminacy.'

Another kind of men's magazine has been busy turning that
arduous track into the primrose path. *GQ*, like the others,
always has a glossy girl on the cover, but the magazine is actually quite gay, at least in the sense that the late Ian Hamilton used
the term. Hamilton thought it was gay to look left and right
when you crossed the road, and he thought it was gay for men
to blow-dry their hair. This went on for a while until one day he
made the point to Martin Amis that it was actually quite gay to
sleep with a woman. *GQ* is gay in that way: it appears to envy
women more than lust for them, and its pages are full of tips on
how men should depilate, breast-enlarge, slicken, tart up, and
generally make themselves a bit more attractive to members of
the non-opposite sex.

On one page, the film director Eli Roth, described as the
maker of the 'body-horror-in-the-woods' movie *Cabin Fever*
(nothing to do with Robert Bly), says: 'I'm a closet metrosexu-
al. I try to look like I've just rolled out of bed but the truth of
the matter is I have spent thousands of dollars on Kiehl's products. Plus, when girls come over, my stock of Kiehl's is the deal-
breaker for them spending the night.' Then there's an article
about the latest sex thing: from Japan obviously, and now big in
America, called *bukkake*, where men don't have sex with
women but all stand around together in a room and mastur-
bate over the girl. Then there's a piece about the joy of not
wearing underpants. The agony uncle makes Quentin Crisp
look like Charles Bronson, or is it Charles Bronson like Quentin
Crisp? 'Quilt covers or eiderdowns?' an anxious letter-writer
asks. 'Blinds or curtains? Carpet or wooden flooring? Wallpaper
or paint? Wall lights or free-standing lamps? Mirrored or
wooden wardrobes? I've just got my first house and need some
advice on how to decorate my bedroom. I don't want to put the
ladies off.'

'You could use sacks as blankets,' comes the reply, 'have bin
bags as curtains, spray graffiti on the walls, only have a torch for
a light – ANYTHING as long as you don't install mirrored
wardrobes.' Later on there's a two-page spread of the young

actor James Franco's lips. That's *Gentleman's Quarterly* for you: a magazine for men who want to have what women have – clean nails, hairless chests, fresh armpits and moist lips. A magazine for men clever enough to want to look like the kind of person they're supposed to want to sleep with themselves. And seeing as half the people who read *GQ* probably do sleep with themselves, this might just be considered sound editorial policy.

Since good-looking naked men started appearing on the covers of magazines aimed at men, the incidence of bulimia among British males has risen by 100 per cent. Bulimia sufferers are still more than 90 per cent female, and of the men a great proportion are gay, but the numbers are also going up for men in general, as if to confirm what the experts always said about the pressure exerted by images of the perfect on the imperfect. The June issue of *Men's Health* offers Britain's eager blokes the chance to 'Be Built like Brad Pitt'. The magazine shows men how to have sex, how to shave, how to book a holiday, but mainly – relentlessly – how to change the shape of their bodies, always accompanied by pictures of men with chests as broad and pert as the plains of Montana. Of course, women have been putting up with this sort of harassment for years, and perhaps the success of *Men's Health* – among those of us who love it, and the figures are rising – is God's way of torturing us with unguents, dumb-bells, fancy toothbrushes and canoes, to make up for years of magazines telling women about the needfulness of dieting if you want to keep your man, with helpful pictures of the smilingly skinny. I've heard men saying the men in *Men's Health* make them sick: they don't mean they disapprove of them, they mean they disapprove of themselves in relation to them, and that's a comeuppance. The threat of the male gaze has been making many women and gay men ill for years, but men's magazines show that the threat has now become general enough to be counted a cultural worry. All men now experience other men's looks, and that is one of the anxieties these magazines sometimes exploit and sometimes suppress.

All the men in *Arena Homme Plus* look like Greta Garbo, like Marlene Dietrich, or like women done up to look like Valentino. The editors declare that they edited the issue – 'The Boys of Summer' – with photographs of Hollywood legends pinned to the wall, and the resulting issue is perhaps the highest form of camp you'll encounter this season, unless you happen to be a roadie on Cher's next 'Farewell Tour' of Britain. Fashion is answerable to nothing but fashion, and male vanity has a million fresh occasions every day, so the fact that the men in *Homme Plus* dribble over one another and rest their hair-gelled heads on one another's shaved chests should be no great cause for worry. It's just a prettier version of the sort of thing that used to happen on the London-to-Aberdeen sleeper every Saturday night.

On Hating Football

JUNE 2002

I can tell you the exact moment when I decided to hate football for life. It was 11 June 1978 at 6.08 p.m. Scotland were playing Holland in the first stage of the World Cup Finals in Argentina. It happened to be the day of my tenth birthday party: my mother had to have the party after my actual birthday owing to a cock-up involving a cement-mixer and the police, but the party was called for that afternoon, and the cream of St Luke's Primary School turned up at 4 p.m., armed with Airfix battle-ships and enough £1 postal orders to keep me in sherbet dib-dabs for a month.

Things started to go badly the minute my father rolled into the square in a blue Bedford van. He came towards the house in the style of someone in no great mood for ice-cream and jelly, and within minutes, having scanned the television pages of the *Daily Record*, he threw the entire party out of the living room – Jaffa Cakes, Swizzle Sticks, cans of Tizer, the lot – all the better to settle down to a full ninety minutes with Ally's Tartan Army, now taking the field in Mendoza.

A full cast of Ayrshire Oompa-Loompas (myself at the head) was then marched upstairs to a requisitioned box room, where several rounds of pass-the-parcel proceeded without the aid of oxygen. I managed to eat an entire Swiss roll by myself and take part in several sorties of kiss, cuddle or torture before losing my temper and marching to the top of the stairs. From there, look-ing through the bars, I could see the television and my father's face. Archie Gemmill, at 6.08, wearing a Scotland shirt with the number 15 on the back, puffed past three Dutch defenders and chipped the ball right over the goalie's head. The television was so surprised it nearly paid its own licence fee, and my father, well, let's just say he stood on the armchair and forgot he was once nearly an altar-boy at St Mary's.

My school chums were soon carried out of the house on stretchers, showing all the signs of a good time not had, by which point my mother was mortified and my father was getting all musical. 'We're here to show the world that we're gonnae do or die,' he sang unprophetically, 'coz England cannae dae it coz they didnae qualify.' My birthday was spoiled, and I decided always to hate football and to make my father pay. I had a hidden stash of books in a former bread bin upstairs – the revenge of the English swot! – and I went out to the swing park to read one and to fantasise about becoming the West of Scotland's first international male netball champion.

Hating football was a real task round our way. For a start, my brothers were really good at it; the fireplace had a line of gold and silver strikers perched mid-kick on alabaster bases, and they turned out to be the only part of the fireplace where my father wouldn't flick his cigarette ash. For another thing, I went to a school where Mr Knocker, the teacher, was football-daft, and he'd sooner you packed in communion than afternoon football. But Mark McDonald – my fellow cissy – and I broke his spirit after he gave us new yellow strips to try on. We absconded from the training session and stretched the shirts over our knees, all the better to roll down Toad Hill in one round movement before dousing the shirts in the industrial swamp at the bottom. The destruction of footballing equipment was beyond the pale: we were too young for Barlinnie Prison, so we got banned to Home Economics instead and were soon the untouchable kings of eggs mornay.

My father gave up on me. Mr Knocker put me down for a hairdresser and a Protestant. But there was always my uncle Peter, a die-hard Celtic supporter – not like my brothers, but a real Celtic supporter, the sort who thought Rangers fans should be sent to Australia on coffin ships, or made to work the North Sea oil rigs for no pay – and Uncle Peter for a while appointed himself the very man who would, as he delicately put it, 'get all that poofy shite oot his heid before it really does him some damage'.

Game on. But not for long. Uncle Peter arranged to take me to see Celtic and Rangers play at Hampden Park. He was not unkind and had put some planning into the day out, but not as much planning as I had: for a whole week it had been my business to make sure that the only clothes available for me to wear to the treat were blue. For the uninitiated, I should say that Celtic fans tend not to wear blue, especially not to the football, and *never*, in all the rules of heaven and earth, to a Rangers game.

My uncle was distressed. He called me a Blue Nose to my face (strong words for a bishop) and when we arrived at the ground he made me walk behind him. He said that if Rangers scored and I made a noise he would throw me to the Animals (the stand in Celtic Park where men peed and drank Bovril was affectionately known as the Jungle). When Celtic lost the game 1–0 he called me a Jonah and said everything was lost with me and I should stick at school because I was bound to end up at university or worse.

Easier said than done. Academic distinction at our secondary school was mostly a matter for the birds, so the best a boy could do was to set his mind on surviving four years of PE without ending up in the Funny Farm (Mrs Jess's remedial class, only marginally more humiliating than being excluded from the school team). It was a wonderful education in the intricacies of human nature. I had pals, good pals, and as a resident smoker at the corner and a fearless talker-back to the nuns, I was in a position to feel confident about their loyalty when we came before Mr Scullion, the chief lion at the gym hall.

Not a bit of it. No sooner had Scullion given some Kenny Dalglish-in-the-making the chance of picking a football team than all affection and loyalty would fall away like snow off a dyke. First lesson: let nothing stand in the way of winning. My good-at-football erstwhile mate would choose one loon after another – a bandy-legged chaser here, a cross-eyed soap-dodger there – until the teams were nearly complete, except for me and Mark McDonald and some poor dwarf called Scobie left glistening with shame on the touchline. A new deputy headmaster came to the school; you could tell by looking at his hair that he was all brown rice and liberal experiment, so I wrote him a well-spelled note about reversing the method used for the picking of teams. I remember the day and the very hour.

'O'Hagan,' the PE assistant said, 'pick your team.'

I walked the few yards onto the field like General Patton contemplating the sweep of his 3rd Army over France. 'Scobie,' I said, 'McDonald.' And so it went on until every lousy player in the group had smilingly succumbed to an early invitation from the worst football picker in the history of St Michael's Academy. My hand-picked Rovers and I got beat 12–0.

When I was twelve, I had nearly run out of juice on the football-hating front; it was an exhausting business not playing the game. But then I had an idea of quite intense perversity. Even my friend Mark had to shake his head sadly and note that in the arsenal of anti-football weaponry my new device was just too much: for a moment he pitied my trophy-winning brothers, he truly felt for my Scotland-deluded dad. I had gone nuclear: Jacqueline Thompson's School of Ballet.

Ah, the pleasures of disownment. Before setting off to Dancewear in Glasgow to buy my first set of pumps, however, I was dragooned by the seething Scullion to take part in a hateful five-a-side against Kilwinning Academy. What happened? With only two minutes to go I ran into the ball with the ferocity of a POW making a dash for the barbed wire. Reader, I broke my leg. As I fell to the ground in agony I was sure the *sylphides* were coming to fetch me *en point*, but – after even more delusion – I woke up in Kilmarnock Infirmary wearing a plaster cast the size of Siberia, and my father drove me home in perfect silence. The years have passed now, but I can still see him smiling in the audience many months later, the night of Jacqueline Thompson's Christmas Dance Display at the Civic Centre in Ayr, as his youngest son came onto the stage, football boots and socks pristine, whistle in mouth, to make his first appearance onstage in a dance number called – I swear to God – 'Match of the Day'.

For long enough – 1982, 1986, 1990, 1994, 1998 . . . , oh how they trip off the tongue – I have comforted myself with the notion that my sense of defeat about football is entirely in keeping with my nation's performance on the field. But I am getting older now, and Scotland are not getting any better; being a Scottish person means growing into your sense of defeat, and like every other square-shoed man trying to get a bit closer to the bar, I find myself now occasionally looking towards football to offer a sense of nation-sized glory at least once before I pack up my pistols and grow a moustache. Imagine the horror. No sooner had Scotland failed to qualify than I was moved to treat my friends to John Steinbeck's comment to Jacqueline Kennedy: 'You talked of Scotland as a lost cause,' he said, 'and that is not true. Scotland is an unwon cause.'

Bloody hell. Better make mine a double. Five minutes later I was thinking about Ireland and five minutes after that, God bless us and save us, England. This is the hallmark of the truly hardcore football hater: he is a turncoat, naturally, and he will sometimes give in to sentiment, but at heart he is without grief or care about the prospect of victory or defeat, and all he really wants is for his birthday party to take place in a nice big room with tables and chairs.

Into the bargain come the jokes: like all would-be playground subversives, I was, more than anything else, a sniggering wreck, an absolute pest who would do anything for a laugh. For instance, I've never heard a joke about Scotland's crapness at football that I didn't find funny, and, by the same token, just the other week, when I saw the Tennent's lager advertising campaign for the World Cup – 'Och Aye Kanu,' it says over a Nigerian flag, 'C'mon the Tartan Argie' over an Argentine one, and 'Support Sven's Team' over Sweden's – I took the train back to London in a swoon of certainty about the wisdom of Scotland's dislike of England. Once you get into the swing of it, there's nothing so addictive as inconstancy; the only trouble comes when football-hating becomes a sort of love, when you find yourself not saving hours but dispelling days in your pursuit of understanding the whys and wherefores of the unbeautiful game.

I would, by the way, encourage anyone inclined to pursuits of that kind to keep their distance from the World Wide Web. The internet – a thing which at times seems designed for and by nut jobs of all stripes – is never madder than when hosting any sort of discussion about football by any sort of fan. Take the following which picks up the England–Scotland resentment theme just alluded to. Topic headline: 'I Wish You Would Stop Sponging Off Us':

Browser A: You are a twat. We want to be free of you inbreed half-breed Anglo-Saxon scum and one day we'll get rid of you and your German Queen.

Browser B: I am making it my mission in life to inform my fellow countrymen (English) what a bunch of pathetic cunts you Jocks are. Get ready to reap the whirlwind. Tourism will die.

Browser C: Yeh. England is your master, bow down, you subservient nation. And bugger the Argies as well.

I hate to cut out of the debate at such a crucial juncture, but you get the idea, and it does go on for thousands of hours. I have to say, though, perhaps surprisingly to some, that this kind of sophistication has yet to cause the generally football-appalled like myself to see the light.

I have this bunch of pals in London who are mainly Scottish but who play in a team called the Battersea Juniors. They are more persuasive in this regard. The team is a bit up and down, a bit part time, even for a Saturday league, but I went to see them recently with a view to turning them on to the virtues of figure-skating. It didn't entirely work out: a feature of the genuine egomaniac is that we can't ever truly understand other people's obsessions, but these boys were absolutely for real – I recognised their determination from my youthful days with Mr Scullion. 'You're a fucking pure tosser,' said Alan to the referee, a Christian who gives up his Saturday mornings for £10.

'You keep it shush!' said the referee.

Paul was trampled on by the home team and screamed like a pig and got a twisted ankle. Raymond was out of breath and shouted to me that he's been on a pizza and fags diet for the last six months and had just crashed his TVR Griffith into a central reservation.

'A low-slung car for a high-profile guy,' said Russell.

The linesman was smoking a gigantic joint and shouting down the phone to his girlfriend in the rain. A young English player called Kez was up and down the park: 'He's new to the team,' said the injured Paul, 'young, fast and talented – unlike us. Oh. My leg's fucked.' He stared into the mud and the driving rain. 'I wonder if I should take a sicky.'

Alan eventually got a red card. The referee said that repeatedly being called a 'knob' was like being accused of sexual deviance. Alan apologised. 'OK,' said the referee, 'I'll let it go this time, but any more of that and it'll go through.'

'Cheers, Ref,' said Alan. And when the Christian departed the field of play Alan turned to his team-mates. 'Knob,' he said.

Meanwhile, these last weeks, the World Cup has come to spread the values of commitment and fraternity at an international level. I remember my dad buying me and my four brothers Celtic strips one Christmas; my brothers doing keepy-up with the new balls and tearing off their pyjamas as quick as possible to don the green and white, and me, standing at the door, looking into all this carnage with eyes like My Little Pony. 'I *told you* he would hate it,' said my mother, who reached behind a green sofa, producing a Post Office set to gladden the heart of any housebound hooligan.

I phoned my father the other day in a fit of questionable delight after England beat Argentina. 'England are a shite team,' he said philosophically. 'They get one goal and they think they're the champions of the universe.' I tell him I've been

buying dozens of packets of Panini football stickers for my girlfriend's two boys. 'You lay them all out and stick them in the
book,' I said, 'and then you mark down the results and all the
information about the players and you can cross-reference
them and all that stuff.'

'Typical enemy of the game,' said my father. 'Turns everything into office work.'

Poetry as Self-Help

NOVEMBER 2004

People have been asking for books to help them since the invention of printing. Before printing, actually, in the days of scrolls and tablets: what is the Bible if not a self-help manual? William Caxton got in on the act early enough with *The Game and Play of Chess Moralised* (1474), a book which aimed to make people better than they used to be, not by bringing their souls nearer to God, but by bringing their pawns closer to the king, which many readers accepted would do for the time being. In what my headmaster used to call the interim period, self-help books have taken over the world, which is fast becoming a place where no one is safe from the threat of their own improvement. Nineteenth-century must-haves – *How to Be Happy though Married* (1887) and *How to Be Pretty though Plain* (1899) – have recently been, well, improved on, with the publication of such instant classics as *How to Become a Schizophrenic* by John Modrow (1992) and *How to Shit in the Woods* by Kathleen Meyer (1989).

There are people who will only read westerns or crime and others who prefer not to read any book unless, like the works of Maya Angelou, it manages somehow to have a self-help tinge. ('Self-Improvement' is now, quite often, a section in your local library.) The self-help preference has the ear of Oprah Winfrey, who publishes one of the most successful magazines in America, and there is a separate best-seller chart for books whose titles love a colon, books that will settle for nothing less than improvement for their readers. Currently riding high are *Why Your Life Sucks: And What You Can Do about It* by Alan Cohen, *When Children Grieve: For Adults to Help Children Deal with Death, Divorce, Pet Loss, Moving and Other Losses* by John James and Russell Friedman, and *Bodylove: Learning to Like Our Looks and Ourselves: A Practical Guide for Women* by the punctuation-crazed Rita Freedman. Publishing houses in New York, busy, as usual, looking for the hot new writing talent, will expect to find it in the medical journals and at psychoanalytic conferences, such is the demand for quasi-medical books which tell you how to deal with life's crapness. In the same way, editors are often to be found with their favourite children's authors, trying, over a glass of herbal tea, to persuade them to write something simple but heart-warming that might prove to have 'crossover appeal' in the adult market.

Britain didn't grow Elvis or Coca-Cola, but it grew Billy Fury and Irn Bru, and the great new self-help ethos has had little trouble finding local imitators. It may be an indirect part of Princess Diana's legacy to the British nation, the success of *The Little Book of Calm*, but self-help has had its main British impact on television. Trinny and Susannah have just come back with a new series of *What Not to Wear*, a show which aims, like all self-help, to make people smile by first making them cry. *Celebrity Fit Club* is not a million miles away, together with DIY shows and cookery programmes that provoke people into thinking their life's troubles can be vanished away with an apt deployment of cushions and fresh coriander. Nobody doubts it; everybody's buying.

This thinking has now been applied to the tired world of British poetry, which has long been in need of a specialist makeover, what with all those lisping ladies in tweed suits and National Health spectacles. The self-help treatment wouldn't have worked in poetry, though, if it hadn't been able to pass the Nigella test – you need somebody foxy and energetic to head up the whole operation, or it's dead before it starts. Thankfully, there's Daisy Goodwin, who has lovely dark hair and perfect teeth: just the person to encourage the use of poetry as a kind of mental flossing. The message is slick and pretty as an ad for Colgate: regular reading of poetry keeps you sparkling, even if it sometimes seems a bit of an effort. Keep it up and you will learn to enjoy the experience. It will help you in ways you never imagined. You will see the benefits into old age and beyond.

This has less to do with poetry, of course, than it does with marketing, and indeed it was T. S. Eliot – that toothsome Tom, so ready to lighten your load and share your pain – who gave us fair warning about the price to be paid for messing with popularity. 'We persist,' he wrote in 'Tradition and the Individual Talent',

> in believing that a poet ought to know as much as will not encroach upon his necessary receptivity and necessary laziness, it is not desirable to confine knowledge to whatever can be put into a useful shape for examinations, drawing-rooms, or the still more pretentious modes of publicity. Some can absorb knowledge, the more tardy must sweat for it. Shakespeare acquired more essential history from Plutarch than most men could from the whole British Museum. What is to be insisted upon is that the poet must develop or procure the consciousness of the past and that he should continue to develop this consciousness throughout his career.
>
> What happens is a continual surrender of himself as he is at the moment to something which is more valuable. The progress of an artist is a continual self-sacrifice, a continual extinction of personality.

Well: so much for that. The 'extinction of personality', in the sense that Eliot meant it, has long since become extinct, and the rest – knowledge, self-sacrifice, the development of a consciousness – are less interesting, in the minds of most of the new-style poetry-tasters, than the idea that poetry has a duty to give people a leg-up from one part of the day to another. Poets are now often low-paid providers of half-memorable speech, moral hygienists, caption writers, or purveyors of beauty and truth to a community of readers seeking quickly to heighten their emotions or beef up their wedding speeches. People reach out to poetry when they're feeling drowsy or needy or depressed; it's as if the Romantic dream of commonality has created a populist monster that can only tolerate the language of reassurance, as if Chatterton had indeed become the symbol of poetry: not of poets, as traditionally understood, but of poetry's battalion of soft readers, dreaming of a sensitive exit and a pretty corpse. Those who want a gust of emotion will usually go to a Richard Curtis film, or read one of Goodwin's suggested poems for people feeling out of sorts. And if they rent *Four Weddings and a Funeral* they can have both at once, without having to leave their own heads, however briefly. 'Accessibility' is the watchword; 'making poetry available to people who would never ordinarily read a poem'. Naturally, one can see the point of this noble effort, and I hereby propose three cheers for the non-elitists.

Goodwin's *Poems to Last a Lifetime* has chapter headings like 'Journey of Life', 'Missing You', 'Commitment Problems', 'Getting Older' and 'Memories', each of which offers a group of soothing and instructive lines, accompanied by the editor's friendly remarks, which not only show an interest in content over form, but, very largely, in emotional content over any other sort of content. In the section called 'Infidelity' there are six poems, starting with 'Story of a Hotel Room' by Rosemary Tonks. 'This poem should be read,' the editor writes underneath, 'by anyone about to embark on an affair thinking that it's just a fling. It is much harder than you know to separate sex from love.' Very often, an interest in what the poem 'says' will be accompanied by biographical information about the author. Underneath Robert Graves's 'Symptoms of Love', for instance, we learn this: 'Scientists have recently classified love as a form of psychosis. Robert Graves knew all about this. The poet once threw himself out of a third-floor window after his mistress Laura Riding. Miraculously, they both survived.'

In Goodwin's world, every poem is a caution, every stanza a warning, every line a piece of advice, and every word a note to self. 'The Compassionate Fool' by Norman Cameron is therefore not a poem in which the scheme of rhyme and half-rhyme, the sound of the words and the weight of the stanzas, is the bet-

ter part of the message; only an elitist would say that the shape
of the poem somehow carries the sense of ambush and psychological game-playing the speaker is describing. And if it does,
who cares? Who has the time to work with that? Cameron's
poem, for Goodwin's readers, is more immediately accessible,
though we might ask ourselves what exactly is being accessed.
'This brilliantly subtle poem,' Goodwin writes, 'was recommended to me by a friend when she heard I had been promot-
ed at work. She said it was a reminder that because I was now a
boss, I was fair game. "No one," she said, "will hesitate to stab
you in the back."'

Goodwin's poetry column in the *Mail on Sunday* has more
than three million readers, and her fans argue she is the best
thing that ever happened to British poetry: she is making people aware of modern poets they'd never heard of and informing
'the average reader' of poetry's relevance to their lives. Good-
winisation means that poetry has a chance to survive, though it
might also mean that difficult writing does not. Defenders
argue that scansion doesn't matter and difficulty can cry
Rapunzel-like from its ivory tower: so long as people are 'getting something' out of poetry, improving their outlook, then
nothing else matters. Like the positive, hi-energy mantra that
accompanies most self-help, this is almost exquisitely patronising. It's as if Goodwin were being lined up against William
Empson, only to emerge as the people's champion, spurning
Mount Parnassus's windy summits for the moonlit shores of
ordinary feeling and good sense. Nothing I could muster in my
attempts to patronise Goodwin could match her own sweet
skill in patronising her readers, her assumption that people will
settle for tinctures of elderflower cordial.

These are tough times for elitists. Display will always win out
over privacy, as if seriousness was boring, as if contemplation
was excluding, as if understatement was underhand, and as if
difficulty represented a kind of dishonesty. In this climate, the
'democratisation' of poetry is just another phoney enterprise,
like open government, a sop to that element in the national

atmosphere which says inclusion is everything. Poetry is often difficult, and its difficulty is part of the richness of what we have; it is a crime to make the unobvious obvious, an act of vandalism to render it trite, like turning Mozart into ringtones while calling attention to its improving qualities. Some people, of course, will call that democracy, but what does it leave you with? An increased audience for Mozart? A bigger sale for new volumes of poetry? No, I'm afraid not. Poetry sales haven't budged in the UK for years, though 'old favourites' are taking up more and more space in the bookshops, at the expense of new poets. But Daisy's picks are selling – Daisy's happiness-seeking audience is happy.

Self-help is often enough a flowering of self-pity, and those who propagate it are always ready to see the road to wisdom as one which must traverse the palace of excess emotion. And though its forms and its centrality in the culture are new, the tendency is old. Writers have often wished to brutalise the notion that poetry is not for everybody. Here's Cecil Day Lewis in 1947, trying to get them young:

> 'Poetry won't help you to get ahead in life.' This is the sort of thing superior persons say, or men who think the main object in life is to make money. Poetry, they imply, is all very well for highbrows and people with plenty of time to waste, but it's no use to the man-in-the-street. Now that's a very new-fangled idea. The man-in-the-street in ancient Greece would never have said it: he flocked in crowds to watch poetic drama; and so did the Elizabethan man-in-the-street, to see the poetic plays of Shakespeare and other dramatists of the time. Then think of the medieval minstrels and bal-lad-singers, who drew great audiences in village or castle to hear them recite poems. Think of the peasants in Russia, in Ireland, in Spain, in many other countries, still making up their own poems.

In his 'Lecture on the Uses of Poetry', William Cullen Bryant, the great American editor and poet, argued, a hundred years before Day Lewis, that poetry might exist as a pattern of thought and invention which works best when resisting the lure of a person's immediate concerns. 'One of the great recommendations of poetry,' he wrote,

> is that it withdraws us from the despotism of many of those circumstances which mislead the moral judgment. It is dangerous to be absorbed continuously in our own immediate concerns. Self-interest is the most ingenious and persuasive of all the agents that deceive our consciences, while by means of it our unhappy and stubborn prejudices operate in their greatest force. But poetry lifts us to a sphere where self-interest cannot exist, and where the prejudices that perplex our everyday life can hardly enter. It restores us to our unperverted feelings, and leaves us at liberty to compare the issues of life with our unsophisticated notions of good and evil. We are taught to look at them as they are in themselves, and not as they may affect our present convenience, and then we are sent back to the world with our moral perceptions cleared and invigorated.

The old 'Treasuries' were collections of poems presented for their own qualities as opposed to a series of specified emotional utilities. Volumes called *101 Poems to Get You Through the Day (and Night)* or *101 Poems to Keep You Sane* are more cynical objects, dreamed up by people who understand advertising and know how to make hay out of the culture's deficiencies. One would feel able to admire their ingenuity were they not now becoming set texts, defining, in a brand-new way, the function of poetry in British and American life. That is what plucks the comedy from this dark drama: it is a story that shows dumbing-down in free fall.

Peter Forbes edited *Poetry Review* between 1986 and 2002, so you'd be right to label him a friend to modern poetry. His magazine never shifted many copies but it always exhibited high standards: make way, then, with sniffles and genuflections, for *All the Poems You Need to Say I Do*, a scrofulous little collection

targeted at people who think poetry comes into its own at
funerals, or, in this case, weddings. Maybe Forbes has been
Goodwinised; at any rate, he has obviously been persuaded of
the self-helping role poetry has taken up. Last year, he edited
something called *We Have Come Through: 100 Poems Celebrat-
ing Courage in Overcoming Depression and Trauma*, a title not
only suitably long but pertinently broken-backed by that
shameless colon. 'If you're in the first throes of a new excitement,' Forbes writes here, 'or need to put a new relationship to
the test, or put a failure behind you, or have reached the point of
the great affirmation, you'll find a poem here for the occasion.'

As with Goodwin's new book, there's hardly a bad poem in
Forbes's anthology – that's not the point. These books are full of
excellent poems which suffer only by being corralled together
under a nauseating rubric. Forbes has exercised taste and
judgement in the matter of his choices (no one could argue
with Patricia Beer's 'The Faithful Wife' or Norman MacCaig's
'True Ways of Knowing'), but what cultural moment, or commercial hunger, is being serviced by the publication of such
sky-blue and touchy-feely anthologies of variously thoughtful
poetry with their invariably thoughtless introductions?

We're only a step away from the felicities of Patience Strong
and Helen Steiner Rice, from verses on greetings cards, words
intended for the heartsore and the nostalgic, words to soothe
and lull and never question. And that's the rub with all this
pukey anthologising: a certain kind of poem self-selects, a form
of address that offers a clear reflection of what the lovelorn, the
sinning, the abandoned, the bereaved already know. The self-
help poetry anthology likes Auden and Yeats, but nothing too
early and strange in Auden and nothing of Yeats and his gyres.
It likes Wendy Cope and Emily Dickinson, Sylvia Plath and
Anne Sexton, Robert Lowell and Thomas Hardy and the lullabies of Housman. It prefers poets whose speakers say how
they feel, and feel what they say, while never running out of
rhythm and never speaking in tongues. It likes Philip Larkin,
the unlikely patron saint of self-help, though it's amusing to

consider how untouched he would be to find his effusions on hopeless love, coming death and boredom deployed in a continuing effort to floss the minds of the readers of the *Mail on Sunday*.

I have now read a great many of these anthologies. There is no T. S. Eliot to be found in them. No Ezra Pound. No Wallace Stevens. Everything floats down to a gentle paradox, and here is ours: anthologists who sell emotional progress to their readers hate poetry that constitutes progress in itself.

It's tough news. I know it's tough.
Let me protect you.
Like the hard shells on Morecambe beach.
There, there.
We always get through stuff.
Together. Don't we?

My Grandfather's Ship

MARCH 1997

The early railways were rough maps of Victorian fancy. Trains and human hearts, in those days at least, were similar engines, chugging along on fresh steam or dank air. The Victorians cared about going forward: they meant to conquer all the worlds beyond their own, and no matter of geology, or history, or finance, was too big for their ambition, or too small for their genius. The story of the great railways is also the story of minor lives, and how they were made, or altered, or destroyed, with the coming of the new machines. People have been travelling from one great place to another for ever, in their heads, but to move over the distant world – to be carried quickly on wheels, or propelled fast over water, or carried supersonically through the air, or through space, to some faraway place – must count for a lot in what it means to be modern. The carriages that carried us, the sustaining vessels, have a central role in our recent tales. We are intimate with our modes of transport. These vehicles are now close to us by nature, by desire and by design. Transport promises a future, just as it carries the remembrance of selves and places and things passed. Ours is a world of pictures coming and going at speed. Few of us now live, or would care to live, with the guarantee of being in one place for ever. But the British live with these thoughts of expansion and speed just as their empire is shrinking to nothing.

Canada always seemed like a fair place to end up – the scramble westwards hastened by the demand for furs, and by the unholy business of the Gold Rush. The Great Canadian Pacific Railway, completed in 1885, was to bring 'Western Civilisation' to the simple parts of North America, and from there to the even simpler parts of the Orient. In 1887 the Earl of Harrowby reported that the Canadian railway was 'perhaps the greatest revolution in the condition of the British empire that had occurred in our time . . . It had brought the Pacific Ocean within 14 days of the English coast.' The company that built the railway wanted to expand the world until it met itself on the other side, and said hello, in English. They began to invest in a fleet of ships, urgent vessels, that would bind the glittering trade routes between England and Canada. The Canadian Pacific Railway sent its first president to London: he, too, spoke of civilising Australasia and the Orient, and he found able listeners at the Post Office, at the Chamber of Commerce and at the Colonial Office. The man came back to his company and ordered ships.

SS *Montrose* had been built by a Middlesbrough company called Sir Raylton Dixon and Co., and was launched in 1897. It was a steel vessel weighing 5,431 tons; it was 444 feet in length and 52 feet wide. It was neither a big ship nor was it especially fast. It made about twelve knots. The steamer's first owner was Elder, Dempster and Co., who ran it on behalf of a South African shipping company. The ship was intended to carry cargo, and was fitted out with giant refrigeration chambers, but these were replaced with berths and she spent her first few years carrying troops to the Boer War. In 1900 she carried the entire Dublin & Denbigh Imperial Yeomanry, along with their many horses, to the South African coast. The ship was later brought into service on the Beaver Line, a fleet of ships sailing between England and the prosperous shores of North America. The Beaver Line was bought up by the Canadian Pacific Railway in 1903.

Canadian Pacific ran advertisements in British newspapers telling of the new life; it sent an agent to London to spread the word, to farmers especially, that things could be better if you upped and offed to Canada. At the turn of the century a travelling exhibition van used to drive all over Britain, high and low, to the remotest villages and the primmest suburbs, passing on the good news about emigration to Canada. The CPR company records, and *Lloyd's List* for 1903, reveal the effects of this sudden drive over the hills and byways of pre-war British yearning: 'Evidence of the great "trek" to Canada has been very patent in the streets of Liverpool during the last few weeks. Crowds of emigrants have been thronging the streets, and outside offices of the several steamship companies engaged in the Atlantic trade there have been large numbers of people waiting while their tickets were procured.' A second-class cabin to Montreal, on SS *Montrose*, would have cost you seven pounds.

Nobody could claim the *Montrose* was especially plush. It was a steerage vessel: most of the passengers were quite content to bed down in loose bunks deep in the old refrigerators. The heating was fine, and people said the food was a version of adequate. The crossing could be rough. But the *Montrose* gained the reputation of being a worthy and serviceable little vessel: well run, trusty and as comfortable and quick as you'd get for the money. The passengers could pace the decks without fear of assault or disease (not as new a feature of the crossing as you might expect). Not long after it was bought over by Canadian Pacific, it had a Marconi wireless fitted on board. The man in charge of SS *Montrose* in 1910, Captain H. G. Kendall, had been second officer on another old Beaver Line ship, SS *Lake Champlain*, which had been the first merchant ship in history to be fitted with a wireless. Now the ships were not so alone at sea.

For several years after 1910 one of the popular songs in the music halls of Great Britain went like this:

> Oh Miss le Neve, oh Miss le Neve
> Is it true that you are sittin'
> On the lap of Dr Crippen
> In your boy's clothes,
> On the *Montrose*
> Miss le Neve?

Had she not been the victim in the case, Mrs Belle Crippen, a music-hall chanteuse herself, would have been among those to sing such a song. As it was, she had the least fortunate role in that weird tragedy of unfortunates, the Crippen case, which is perhaps the best remembered of what Orwell once called 'the old domestic poisoning dramas'. Dr Hawley Harvey Crippen, a bespectacled, respectable man who lived in North London, killed the lady, cut her up and buried her in the coal bunker. He then took up with his lover, a young thing called Ethel le Neve. Like many murders before and since, the one carried out by Dr Crippen came to be seen as a reflection on and of its time. All manner of local customs, fashions, ways of speaking, ways of believing, ways of wanting, seemed to come together in that horrible tale.

The *Montrose* was in port at Antwerp on 20 July 1910. It was due to sail to Quebec. There were reports in all the papers that a warrant had been issued for the arrest of Dr Crippen and his paramour. They had been spotted at a Brussels hotel, but were lost track of soon after. SS *Montrose* set off from the quay. Kendall, the ship's captain, takes up the story:

> Soon after we sailed for Quebec I happened to glance through the porthole of my cabin and behind a lifeboat I saw two men. One was squeezing the other's hand. I walked along the boat deck and got into conversation with the elder man. I noticed that there was a mark on the bridge of his nose through wearing spectacles, that he had recently shaved off a moustache, and that he was growing a beard. The young fellow was very reserved, and I remarked about his cough.
>
> 'Yes,' said the elder man, 'my boy has a weak chest, and I'm taking him to California for his health.'

The fairly Sherlockian Kendall retired to his cabin to scrutinise the *Daily Mail*. There he found Scotland Yard's descriptions of Crippen and le Neve. He then arranged for 'Mr Robinson and son' to take meals with him at the top table.

He thought the boy Robinson ate things a little delicately. The *Montrose* dining room was considered a pleasant place to be, but the two passengers who'd caught the Captain's eye seemed anything but easy. Kendall and the older gent roamed the deck together; the wind blew up once, revealing a revolver in Mr Robinson's pocket. That was enough to confirm Kendall's worries. He went below and gave his wireless operator a message to be sent to Canadian Pacific's office in Liverpool. 'One hundred and thirty miles west of Lizard . . .' it said, 'have strong suspicions that Crippen London cellar murderer and accomplice are among saloon passengers . . . Accomplice dressed as boy; voice, manner and build undoubtedly a girl.' Kendall later recalled 'Mr Robinson sitting on a deck chair, looking at the wireless aerials and listening to the crackling of our crude spark-transmitter, and remarking . . . what a wonderful invention it was.'

Inspector Dew, from Scotland Yard, got the message and jumped on a faster boat, the *Laurentic*. He expected to overtake the *Montrose*, and land at Newfoundland before the slower boat arrived. He wired Kendall to apprise him of his plan. There are two versions of what happened next. One has Inspector Dew coming onto the *Montrose*, being introduced to Mr Robinson by Captain Kendall and then grabbing the passenger with the words: 'Good morning, Dr Crippen.' Dew thereafter put the man, and his girlish son, under arrest. The other version of Crippen's last moment of freedom on the *Montrose* has him cursing Captain Kendall, and placing a hex on the ship, as well as the spot they stood on. This version has something on its side: the *Empress of Ireland*, captained by the resourceful Kendall, sank four years later near the same spot, with great loss of life.*

The *Montrose* was soon forgotten again. It continued, though, to ferry a less fearsome cargo of émigrés and holiday-makers across the cold water of the Atlantic. In the summer of 1914, the *Montrose* stood again in Antwerp, next to another of the Beaver Line ships, the *Montreal*. The latter ship was full of coal, but its engines had been removed for repair. Suddenly the German advance began, and both ships found themselves

---

* Over 1,000 died, though not Kendall, who lived to be ninety-one.

crowded with Belgian refugees. They had to leave the harbour in haste: *Montrose* would have to drag the listless *Montreal* out to sea. The new war refugees lay about the deck; some sat cheek by jowl in the dining room; many more were packed into the old refrigerators and the saloons. The *Montrose* managed to drag the *Montreal* as far as the Nove, and then our ship continued on its way to Gravesend.

SS *Montrose* tired very young. She was sold to the Admiralty at the end of October 1914. It was felt that the best way to make the ship serve the war was to fill her holds full of cement, and to sink her as a block ship, just outside Dover harbour, where she might prevent the too-easy arrival of German U-boats. The work of cementing was still in progress a few days after Christmas that year, when the *Montrose* broke from her moorings and drifted away until she foundered on the Goodwin Sands. The watchmen on board were saved at the last minute. The loose sands at this point had claimed hundreds of ships over the years; so many that the place became known as the 'ship-swallower'. The South Foreland lighthouse, built just over the way in 1843, shone for miles over these dangerous waters. It was from this lighthouse that Marconi sent its first true wireless message, to a lightship thirteen miles out, on the very day the SS *Montrose* was launched.

The mast of the *Montrose* stood out of the water at the Goodwin Sands at low tide until the morning of 22 June 1963, when it finally broke away and was carried off to sea.

As the bus winds its way through the first hills of Argyll – ridges over 3,000 feet, jagged like animal teeth – you can see that the Highlands start here. The signs of modern tourism are everywhere: oddly familiar now, weirdly at home with other signs to do with the slow business of the past being lived out, or pulled away from. The years have seen people go from here in very large numbers: gone south mainly, or else found themselves a passport to some other place entirely. On the Argyll side of Loch Leven, the first housing scheme in the area was built for the families of those who stayed behind; it was paid for by the British Aluminium Company. The other local industry, slate quarrying, was established in Ballachulish two years after the massacre at Glencoe. But other sorts of roof cover have brought that industry down too. Those who stayed working on the land after the last war collected oats, potatoes, turnips and hay. Even as late as 1951 the town of Ballachulish could boast of eighty-seven horses, compared with twenty-seven tractors. Now the roads are mainly filled with buses covered in odd writing, crammed with people holding up cameras.

Allan Kerr worked with trees after the last war. His white bungalow looks over Loch Linnhe, up from the main road, where the buses pass. He is seventy-six years old. I came up the path that day with a map in my hand. His french windows were wide to the world. Mrs Kerr, gathering her things together for a day delivering meals-on-wheels, had the look of someone much younger than she is. Clear air and good water, a friendly doctor and an active life. As they stood by their modern window, with their pink faces, the Kerrs seemed like a living advertisement for Bupa.

'I don't know a lot about the ship's early history,' he said, 'I just know about the end of it all.' I asked him when he first saw the vessel.

'In 1939 I was nineteen,' he said. 'Nineteen, and I wanted to sign up for the war – in the navy – but when I applied they told me I'd have to go to the Labour Exchange; there was nothing for me. But then I got a letter. It said that there was a ship being refitted in Glasgow, and that I should join that as midshipman. The ship was sitting in Yorkhill Basin – I went down there in October 1939, and a lot was going on. It was the first time I ever saw HMS *Forfar*.'

Allan Kerr then trained, with other officers, in the business of naval gunnery. Nearly all the engineers on the ship were Liverpool men and all the stokers came out of Glasgow. The ship was only a short time in the hands of the workmen at Yorkhill, and gunnery trials were later carried out in the Firth of Clyde. There were a lot of cruisers and destroyers at the mouth of the river, even in those early days of the war, and many of them had been, like the newly named HMS *Forfar*, peacetime passenger liners which were converted for battle. The job of the ship was to make sure that supplies did not get through to the enemy from neutral merchant boats.

The ship's company was 300 strong. Mr Kerr brought out a photograph of the ship's officers, taken on board while the ship stood in Glasgow, on the day it was visited by the town council. The photograph is full of men in dark uniforms, and women from the council with their elegant hats and fur collars. The younger men, the junior officers, are sitting at the front, cross-legged on a worn carpet, in the ship's best place, a room filled with mirrors. There is pride and optimism in the faces of these men. The rest of the ship's company – the ratings – were to be found elsewhere on the ship, with their own expressions no doubt, but the photographs of these men are lost now, or were never taken.

Allan Kerr is very young in the officers' photograph, with his hands clasped. In his white bungalow he passed me another snap. I looked at his hands. One of them had fingers missing from it. 'This picture,' he says, 'was taken from my family house in Port Glasgow. I was on leave, and I went back to join the ship in Glasgow one morning. But the ship was just departing as I got there. So I raced after it, shooting down the road, to join it at Greenock. But I stopped off to take that snap from my house on the way.'

The picture is blurred. The *Forfar*'s two funnels look very dark against the water of the Clyde. The picture makes the ship look indefinite and misty. It looks like a ghost ship. Allan joined the *Forfar* at Greenock, just in time, and it sailed out from the Clyde estuary, out past the islands, and into the dangerous waters of the Atlantic Ocean.

Before the war, HMS *Forfar* was called SS *Montrose*. When the Admiralty took over passenger liners to employ in the war effort as armed merchant cruisers, they would sometimes change the ship's name. The reason in this case was simple: there was already a Royal Navy ship of that name. It is a long-standing custom that no two ships in the Royal Navy, or in the British Merchant Navy, may have the same name. And so SS *Montrose* became the *Forfar*, no doubt – according to a recent informant in Liverpool – because some wag at the Admiralty was in the habit of doing the football pools. Or he may just have been interested in Scottish league football. In any event, the ship that Allan Kerr joined at Glasgow was the successor to the old SS *Montrose*, by then long sunk on the Goodwin Sands.

The Fairfield Shipbuilding and Engineering Company of Govan started to build the second *Montrose* in 1920. Canadian Pacific paid one and a half million pounds for the job. It was one of the new passenger liners, set to work the very popular Liverpool to Canada tourist route, and it was a big ship, over 16,000 tons. It was launched on 14 December 1920 by Lady Rae-burn, the unsmiling wife of the then director-general of the Ministry of Shipping. When the ship sailed on her maiden voyage from Liverpool, in the spring of 1922, she had accommodation for first-, second- and third-class passengers. The best dining room was made up like a salon in a Tudor mansion: strips of wood panelling; fine tapestries hanging here and there; leather chairs, ceramic bowls filled with daffodils on long tables; black and white tiles on the floor; and acres of mirrors.

In the lounge there was a grand piano. In the children's room there was a white wooden rocking-horse. In the drawing room there was a large painting of Napoleon Bonaparte hanging above the fire. There were ornate tiles in the staterooms, but no daffodils in third-class dining. The ship was said to be busy with music and noise and children. It was a holidaymaker's place. You could dance here, and drink before an open fire, or just read quietly in a corner on your own. There was a wind-up gramophone in one of the little saloons, and newly beaded girls would primp up their hair, and swing their legs here in time to the glamorous new music. Every bed coverlet had 'Canadian Pacific Ocean Services' stitched into it.

Steam was provided by ten boilers all burning oil fuel. The two funnels were tall and widely spaced; the designers intended this to give the ship a 'balanced appearance'. But the ship – just like its sister ships the *Montcalm* and the *Montclare* – had its lifeboats suspended from some rather ugly sets of davits, the displeasing appearance of which was to be borne on grounds of safety. It was believed they could launch all of the ship's twenty-four emergency craft in two minutes.

The ship struck an iceberg in the Atlantic on Easter Monday 1928. It had been moving slowly through dense fog when the accident happened. The bow was crushed, as were two sailors, to death, when ice crashed down onto the deck. But the ship was repaired and back on duty in a matter of months. The *Montrose* became well known at the docks of Montreal and Liverpool over the next ten years. Like its predecessor, it was a trusty, untroublesome vessel, full of life and the attendant sorrows of departure. Many of the voyagers in the 1930s followed in the footsteps of the earlier *Montrose*'s passengers: emigrants, looking to a better life on the other side. The second *Montrose* would sometimes make trips from Cardiff, the valleys of South Wales being no stranger to hopefulness of that sort either.

The King and Queen, with Princess Elizabeth, sailed out for the Coronation Naval Review in May 1937. Commander T. Woodroffe made a live radio broadcast from the event, which was much listened to, and much remembered, for relaying this, the last of the grand naval spectacles before the war. It is also remembered because Commander Woodroffe was drunk. 'The splendour of the uniforms,' he said, 'and the dressing of the Royal Marines, and their steadiness, is something really to remember for the rest of one's life. I can hear the cheering of the foreign ships – the *Dunkirk*, the *New York*, the *Moreno* – as they cheer His Majesty.' Just as he says this you can hear the cheers go up from the gathered ships of the fleet. The commentator continues, as the royal yacht passes by: 'There she goes, the most lovely, swan-like thing passing by. She is an old yacht built for Queen Victoria, and she's not modern. She epitomises, I think, the English – British, I'm sorry – sea power. There is the *Enchantress*. All ships enchant you. In the dim, dim distance I can see a few destroyers, battleships, cruisers, aircraft carriers. A wonderful, great fleet, with flags flying.' The broadcast peters out on a mangled rendition of 'God Save the King'.

One of those ships in the dim, dim distance was the *Montrose*. She had been chartered that day by the Royal Empire Society, and she carried passengers from Liverpool to Spithead for that giant display of British naval power. All who were there say it was a grand day; all the more so as it was a show of greatness that would soon enough seem diminished. Within a few years so many of those fine ships would be sunk, and a great number of those who cheered for their king that day would be dead. The Second World War was to be almost lost at sea.

Winston Churchill once said that the only thing which really frightened him during the war was the U-boat peril. For several years the Germans displayed a horrible talent for sinking British ships, and there seemed at the time no obvious way around it. The German U-boat captains were thought to be fearless and brilliant: they would routinely sail into the middle of a convoy in heavy weather, firing off every torpedo they had on board, disabling one ship, sinking another, and then diving beneath the waves, dogged by depth charges, but somehow getting clear, and making off. The captains of these submarines became national heroes in their own country.

Otto Kretchmer was a dark enemy. With a devoted crew on *U-99* he ripped more than 250,000 tons of Allied shipping to bits during the war. He had a good mind for naval strategy, strong nerves, a quick eye, a kind of reckless reason and a stomach galvanised to the purpose, which was the annihilation of all enemy forces at sea. He became a Hitler favourite, though he considered himself to be merely a decent and disciplined sailor, bent to the unpleasant task at hand. He was no great lover of humanity, perhaps, but he loved the sea, and the sea-going vessels with their strange part in the affairs of the world. As a U-boat commander, Kretchmer allowed not a glimmer of mercy.

'Kretchmer had never really thought seriously of the people who manned the ships he sank,' said one man close to him. 'They were the enemy, and if they were human beings as well, it had not bothered his conscience.'

On 2 December 1940 Kretchmer was guiding his U-boat over some messy waters to the west of Ireland. At 3.15 a.m. one of his assistants wrote in the log: 'Impossible to maintain speed. Reduced to half-speed, making about five knots over the ground. Boat being pushed under water by the force of waves.' But they sailed on. At about 5.40 a 'large, ominous shadow appeared in the darkness less than half a mile away.' It was the *Montrose*, now the armed merchant cruiser HMS *Forfar*. Kretchmer went up to full speed and gave the order to fire. A torpedo dashed through the turbulent water.

The *Forfar* was hit. Kretchmer could see that someone on the ship was firing red and yellow lights into the air, trying to locate the U-boats, but he turned into an attacking position, and then fired a second torpedo, which hissed off and struck the target under the bridge. The *Forfar* then sent out a distress signal. One of Kretchmer's officers remembered the *Forfar*'s crew firing 'round after round of starshell, the lights of the flares glowing palely over the black, writhing sea'. Kretchmer let off a third torpedo, which hit the *Forfar* somewhere forward. Kretchmer was confused and surprised by the fact that the crew of the *Forfar* did not seem to be making for the lifeboats. Some of the ships he had sunk recently had survived in the water longer than they might have, thanks to the amount of buoyant material they carried. He could see oil-drums bobbing around the *Forfar*. The ship's men clearly thought they could keep her afloat.

Kretchmer went to within 800 yards. His fourth torpedo hit the stern. The *Forfar* now lay low in the water. More than an hour had passed, and daylight was coming up. Kretchmer fired one last torpedo at the stern. The ship buckled and snapped, and within minutes was engulfed. It sank reluctantly beneath the waves. Kretchmer told his officers he was shocked. He couldn't believe the ship had not lowered more of its lifeboats.

The crew of *U-99* took their last look at the debris of the *Forfar*.
They knew nothing of the ship, or of the men on board. But
later that day they sank another ship from the same group. A
junior officer climbed out to the U-boat's conning tower some
time in the evening, when they had made it to a safe distance.
He climbed up, and added another two flags to the dozens
already fixed there. Each had a horseshoe printed on it. Two
more dead ships.

Allan Kerr took me into his kitchen and served up some
soup. It was bright in there: a tiny space filled with mature
domestic application. Buffed surfaces; good order about the
microwave; small curtains boiled white. Before we lifted our
spoons, Allan put his hands together, and asked for silence
while he said grace. A flavoursome sense of the Church of Scotland sat there with us at the table. Mr Kerr had survived to live
something of an orderly life, and a thankful one at that.

On first watch the night of his ship's sinking, Allan Kerr
wrote a note in the ship's log: '2300 – parted company with
destroyer escort.' He remembers it was a black night, with no
moon, and Kerr eventually left the watch to his friend Mackay,
who waved him off at midnight. From notes Kerr wrote a week
later, we get a strong sense of what happened next:

> I undressed, said my prayers, and turned in quite happily.
> My sound sleep was soon broken by a terrific crash. Imme-
> diately I was awake. 'Torpedoed' flashed through my mind
> . . . never will I forget the eerie silence that prevailed. The
> engines had stopped and the lights were dimming rapidly.
> 'Action Stations' was sounded on the klaxons, but this
> seemed to drain the last few dregs from the dynamo, for it
> petered out and all went black . . . I can still remember being
> annoyed when one of my shoelaces broke as I pulled on
> shoes . . . In the lower chart-room I was able to assist Mr
> Broadhurst who was holding a light for the navigator, Lt
> Cdr Kenworthy, while he [the navigator] plotted our exact
> position on the chart.

'There were about twenty thousand empty oil-drums on board,' Mr Kerr said to me. 'We thought we could stay afloat with them.' But they went to their boat stations, to turn out the boats and stand by. Air was rushing violently up the engine-room ventilators by that time. The captain – a man who once skippered fishing trawlers – had bundled a bottle of whisky and a bottle of brandy into a bag. As Kerr was preparing his lifeboat, there was a crash just below them: a second torpedo. Another one quickly followed, impacting on the port side, and shower-ing these men with water. Kerr remembers shouting 'Anyone for P2?', trying to attract men to his lifeboat. But he noticed that the deck was completely deserted. It took a while for people to come to his boat. There were about twenty when a fourth tor-pedo hit below them again, and blew them into the water. Kerr thought this was the end. But he emerged on the surface, and swam over to a Carley float. He was covered in fuel oil.

The fifth and last torpedo hit the ship soon afterwards. 'There was a giant column of flame,' said Mr Kerr, 'much high-er than the main mast. And then a ghastly crunch as the after-end of the ship bent inwards, crushing the decks like matchsticks. She eventually turned over, and began to sink slowly and steadily by the stern.' There were twelve men hang-ing onto the float, and the water was freezing. As the ship went down, Kerr turned to those nearest him. 'Well, boys,' he said, 'there goes the last of the old *Forfar*.' He later wondered why he had said something so melodramatic, but it didn't seem right to him that she should make her last exit unannounced. It was a terrible scene, the end of the *Forfar*, the end of the old *Mon-trose*. Mr Kerr said he would never forget the sight of men slid-ing down from the ship as it sank, scrambling down the hull, shouting for their mothers.

The ship was gone. The U-boat was gone. And eventually, much later in the day, the survivors were picked up by a couple of rescue ships. Just under half of the ship's company went down with the wreckage. I asked Mr Kerr why, given the time the ship remained afloat, so many men were lost, and he told me one of the harsher truths. 'I'm not sure,' he said, 'but I believe some of the men below may have raided the grog shop after the first torpedo struck; I think a lot of them delayed, getting drunk in the stores.'

We sat quiet for a while by the front windows, looking down at the loch. 'I loved my old ship,' Mr Kerr said eventually. 'It was a terrible loss.' Then he picked something out of a bag, an old watch, rusted and broken. 'I was wearing this as I went down into the water that night,' he said. 'The hands are stopped at that exact moment.'

My grandfather was a good bit older than Mr Kerr, and he was a greaser in the *Forfar*'s engine-room. The last his family in Glasgow heard of him he was having his cigarette allowance docked for bad behaviour. There's no way of knowing why he didn't make it to the lifeboats: they had always said he was good on his feet. But I'd come to know that my grandfather was no longer missing: he was beneath the waves with all that broken metal.

After Hurricane Katrina

OCTOBER 2005

The sky over North Carolina was showing red the night Sam and Terry decided to leave for the South. The red clouds travelled to Smithfield from the western hills, the high Appalachians and the Blue Ridge Mountains and the Great Smokies. Sam Parham is twenty-seven years old and weighs 260 pounds. For an hour or so, right into the dark, he pulled on the starting string of an electric generator he'd borrowed from his father, until the top of his T-shirt was soaked with sweat. 'Goddamn bitch,' he said. 'This muthafucker is brand new. I want the goddamn thing to work. We're sure gonna need its ass when we get to New Orleans.'

Sam's neighbour had chickens outside his trailer and frogs were hiding in the pine trees along the drive. An American flag hung limply on the porch as Sam inspected the back of his truck with a giant torch, the crickets going *zeep-zeep-zeep* and red ants crowding in the oil at his feet. 'I just can't watch those TV pictures of children stranded and not go down there,' Sam said, while Yolande, his pregnant girlfriend, sat on the porch and opened a can of Mountain Dew and lit another cigarette.

Yolande was wearing her uniform from the Waffle House, where she works the night shift. 'You can't expect me to agree,' she said. 'But I respect you for doing it, Sam. I just think it's the government should be doing it.'

'I'm just a blue-collar guy or whatever,' said Sam. 'And I'm gonna do what I can if the country needs me.'

Terry Harper is a co-worker of Yolande's at the Waffle House. As we drove along Interstate 95 to pick him up, house-lights flared in the distance and Yolande started talking about God. 'My daddy knows the Bible one hand to the other and when he starts speaking at you it's like preachin', she said. North Carolina was the birthplace of Billy Graham and three US presidents – Andrew Johnson, James Polk and Andrew Jackson – and also, among the twinkling lights out there, you could find the uncelebrated birthplace of Thomas Wolfe, the North Carolinian who wrote *Look Homeward, Angel.* As the truck got nearer the Waffle House, someone on the radio made the point that North Carolina was itself no stranger to hurricanes – Hazel (1954), Hugo (1989), Fran (1996), Floyd (1999). It's no stranger to racism either. The Neuse river, the Roanoke river and the Yadkin river, named, like so much in the state, by the native Indian population that was cleared to make way for the twinkling lights and Interstate 95, have been known to burst their banks and flood the plains. The radio was silent on the fact that America's first ever sit-in occurred at Greensboro, North Carolina, to protest against segregation at a lunch counter.

'They're not cookin' more than $200 a night,' said Yolande, 'and I can do that on coffee and Coca-Cola if I'm tired.' She was planning to take over Terry's shifts so that he could make the trip south. Terry was mild mannered, imperturbable, sucking juice out of a Waffle House cup. He is a fifty-year-old black man with a short moustache and a gap between his teeth. He was born in Pitt County but spent his happiest days in Atlanta. Terry sat at the counter of the Waffle House waiting for a decision. It turned out he needed more than Yolande to cover his shifts, so we went in search of another worker, Ashley, who has kids on her own and needs the money. She doesn't have a telephone, but Sam found her house in the rundown Wilson area, next to a railway crossing. It was seventy-five degrees in the dark. Ashley came out from a house that flashed blue with television pictures and she jumped up and down on the porch at the prospect of having more shifts at the Waffle House. 'It's the lowest of the low works for the Waffle House,' Sam said. 'Would you look at her jumping up and down, the immaturity of her. She's got kids. Look at where we're at.' He took a long look into the bleak houses at the edge of the projects. 'My sister was

murdered,' he said. 'She was killed by an injection of liquid
crack-cocaine. They tried to say she had a drug problem but she
had no drug problem. She was killed.'

Ashley's two kids were cowering in their pyjamas in the back
of the truck with the neon of the fast-food marquees shining in
their eyes. They were delivered to a babysitter in Lenoir Drive, a
place that seemed to be exclusively black, young women sitting
on the stoop while boys played basketball on the street in cap-
sleeve jerseys. Ashley says she gets $2.85 an hour. Driving back
to the Waffle House, Ashley and Yolande were gossiping about
other members of staff. 'You know that TV show *As the World
Turns?*' Yolande said. 'Well, there's more soap in the goddamn
restaurant. We call it "As the Waffle Burns".'

Sam was using the internet as he drove at 70 mph. He kept
the laptop balanced between the two front seats, and had a
wireless connection, so he was able to look up weather and
news reports as he drove, clicking on the keypad and sometimes
using the shift key. When not on the internet, and not talking
about the shape and meaning of his life, Sam was often on his
mobile phone. He has, as he keeps saying, 'unlimited', which
means that his payment plan allows him to call anywhere in
America as often as he likes. He spent great portions of every
day on the phone to Yolande, or to his former wife, or his children, often when he was driving, and the calls often ended in
arguments. 'You know about the hurricane, right?' Sam said to
his son Zak. 'I'm going down there to help the people. It's what
we have to do. The people need our help.'

After speaking to his children, Sam would grow listless for a
while, as if love and regret were together taking their toll. He
stared into the windscreen as the night came on and his plans
fell into alignment. 'I seem to get myself into these situations
where I just help people all the time,' he said. Then he rang his
grandmother and put her on speakerphone.

'Don't run into a brawl or anything, Sammy, 'cause a lot of
those people are just crazy right now.'

By 12.10 a.m., the back of the truck heaped with chainsaw,

power generator, giant toolbox and assorted jacks, Sam and Terry had left Smithfield and before long were heading down the Purple Heart Memorial Highway. Sam split his attention equally between the road and the laptop. His love of the internet explained my presence in the back of the truck: like tens of thousands of Americans in the days after the hurricane, Sam had advertised himself on the net as a willing volunteer and I found him and followed him. 'Here,' he said, chucking Terry a carton of painkillers. 'Don't say I ain't good to you.' Terry has a bad case of gout in his right leg and it makes him hobble. When not on the phone, Sam talked into thin air, addressing himself. 'Why did the Good Lord bring Hurricane Katrina?' he asked. 'Man, it's life, it's evolution. Shit happens. But the thing that matters is what you do about it as a person. If some guy comes to rape my wife, why, this is America: I'm gonna put a cap in his ass. I'm gonna give him a hot one and let him leak.' As if to confirm his point, Sam lifted a small blue medical bag that was hanging on the rear-view mirror. It contained a gun with the clip inserted and the safety catch on. He waved the gun over the steering wheel. 'They're gonna get this in the ass,' he said.

Terry wanted to sleep a little until the painkillers took hold. And when he woke, somewhere in South Carolina, Sam was saying how much he admired George W. Bush. 'I voted for Bush last time,' he said. 'I liked the way he handled 9/11. He's a strong president. Hell, he's my commander-in-chief.' Terry gave him a long, weary look, and rubbed his eyes. Neither Sam nor Terry has ever possessed a passport and they speak of the world beyond America as if it were a hidden territory of oddness, weakness and unreality. Sam stopped the truck at a gas station.

'I feel better,' Terry said. 'I'm gonna smoke me some Turkish Jades.' And with that he hopped out of the truck and headed for the all-night window.

'He's poor as shit, man,' said Sam. 'No money at all. And he's going down to Mississippi in this bitch to help with somethin' that's got nothing to do with him.' The road south – the flashing grass, the beat of the signs – seemed to direct Sam into a landscape of clear memory. He was born in Palm Beach, Florida, and within six months had been adopted by his grandmother. His mother was an alcoholic and he was left on a window ledge in Pennsylvania in the dead of winter. That's when his grandmother came and took him to live in Maine.

'We got some of the same issues,' said Terry. 'My mother dropped me off in North Carolina when I was four years old and I never saw her again.'

'We came to North Carolina in 1984,' said Sam. 'We moved into my uncle's camper and then spent a while living in a tent. We got a house eventually. I remember my biological mother coming to the house in Greensboro and she tried to kidnap me. She took me out in the middle of the night when I was asleep. The cops came and I'd never seen so many blue lights.'

'A white baby kidnapped,' said Terry.

'Yeh,' said Sam. 'If a black kid disappeared nobody cared back then, but if a white kid was taken there would be cops crawling outta the grass.'

At the gas station, water was leaking from a drainpipe and it ran down the wall to arrive on top of a newspaper vending machine. Terry paused beside it to light one of his menthol cigarettes. The paper was out of date, but, through the glass, there was a story about the desperate situation in New Orleans. It said the government was under fire for the slowness of the rescue operation. 'It now looks like the South will be relying on volunteers. It may turn out to be one of the greatest volunteer operations this country has ever seen. President Bush said it made him proud to witness the response of everyday working Americans.' A second story said the ordeal had opened 'an old wound' about race in America.

Not far from the Chattahoochee river, Sam parked the truck in a lay-by and reclined his seat for a few hours' sleep. As he snored, Terry saw a Great Blue Heron fly over the truck and swoop down towards the interstate. 'Heading south in search of water,' he said. 'Just like us.'

Terry believes that racism has followed him all his life. He grew up only twenty minutes from the ocean in North Carolina and helped truck tobacco when he was ten years old. 'That was my first job,' he said. 'My second job was in the graveyard, burying bodies at fifty dollars a grave. I was sixteen and still at Ayden-Grifton High School. That was how I paid for everything, sports, prom: digging graves.' At school, Terry got deeply involved in civil rights actions. He speaks of a white state trooper who was cleared of murdering two young black men, the Murphy brothers. There was a dawn to dusk curfew at that time, but Terry and his friends would go out at night and set fire to cornfields. Terry says he tried to shoot the state trooper one night with a borrowed rifle. He waited all night in a ditch and when he fired he missed the policeman by three inches. Later, Terry and a group of his friends got some dynamite from a demolition company and tried to blow up their high school. Terry was detained by a teacher and so was not present when the bomb was set off. His friends were charged and found guilty. 'Yep,' said Terry. 'Those boys went down. Two of them, the Raspberry twins, got twenty years apiece.'

In the early 1970s, Terry joined the Black Panthers. A number of things drew him into the movement: his childhood experience of racist murders, an instinct for self-defence, and the charismatic influence of the Panther members from Chicago who visited North Carolina to inspire younger black men to force a change in the fabric of America and, Terry said as the truck sped forward into the Alabama sun, 'to kill a few people'.

'Cool,' said Sam. Though he'd taken a week off from his work as a cable television engineer to help with the relief effort, Sam still had to deliver his work records and invoices from the previous week. He worried about it across several states and eventually pulled into a Days Inn near Birmingham, Alabama. Terry looked up. 'This is where Bull O'Connor, the police chief, turned his damn German shepherds on those little black girls,' he said. 'Then he turned a fire hose on those poor fuckers who were marching.'

'Cool,' said Sam, parking the truck with one hand. As the

woman at the Days Inn took her time to book us into the room, Sam disconnected the internet cable from the back of her computer. 'Whore,' said Sam.

'Let's just get inside and rest a while,' said Terry.

The room was dirty and the sheets didn't fit the bed. Terry decided to call reception to complain. 'For seventy-eight dollars a person might expect hot water and fitted sheets,' he said.

Meanwhile, Sam marched into the room and put his gun down on the table and held up a bunch of papers. 'This represents fifteen hundred fuckin' dollars,' he said. 'And if I don't get them faxed to fuckin' North Carolina in ten minutes I don't get paid next week. This shit's fucked up. The bastard machine only takes three fucked-up papers at a time.' Quietly, Terry removed the clip from the gun.

'George Wallace, the governor, said over my dead body would any nigger go to school here.'

'It was them blacks that started racism in the first place,' Sam said. Sweat was dropping onto the pages he aimed to fax.

Terry wanted to stop in Atlanta on the way back to see his son, who was refusing to go to school. Terry hadn't seen his son in several years and said he just needed ten minutes. 'His black ass is on the fifty-yard line,' Terry said. 'Not going to muthafuckin' school. That's unacceptable to me. I'll kick his black ass when I get him.'

The TV was showing a movie about a police SWAT team, and Sam, his pages travelling slowly through his mobile fax machine, stuck out his tongue and made shooting noises at the screen. 'You're one dead fucker,' Terry said to Colin Farrell, the actor on the screen. 'You're gone.' As he watched the movie, Terry opened a tin of clam chowder and ate it cold with a stolen spoon, following it with a red drink called Tahitian Fruit Punch.

Terry woke up to find Sam lying on the next bed and the TV saying that New Orleans was depending on the kindness of strangers. 'It's a known fact,' Terry said, 'that the police and emergency services are, minimum, fifteen minutes slower to attend calls in black areas, so it's no surprise that they were slower to help the South when it was in trouble. If this had happened in a white area they would've been out there the same day plucking them white folks out the water.'

It had grown dark outside and we were thinking of setting off again. Sam was surfing the net for porn and talking to his ex-wife at the same time. 'I'd hope that if I was stuck up on a roof that someone would come get me offa there,' he said. 'This is America. People do their best.' His ex-wife was niggling him about family duties. 'If something terrible happens to me, you're gonna feel bad,' he said. 'Yes, ma'am. You surely are.' After a minute of silence and finger-flicking, Sam's tone changed and he seemed to lean further into the phone. 'Do you know what tantric sex is?' he asked. He was still looking at his laptop. 'It's mind-fucking!'

Terry was in the bathroom when Sam came rushing into the motel room with a giant grin on his face. 'Terry! Hey. Hot blondes outside!' Terry immediately came through and started whistling from the door. Sam laughed. 'You ain't gonna get them by whistling like they was dogs, dude.' A while later, a handsome young couple, Cory and Aimee Exterstein, arrived at the Days Inn reception desk with their two children. Cory was wearing a baseball cap that said Louisiana State University. They looked exhausted, and the children were half-asleep. Their house had been destroyed by floodwater in New Orleans and they had managed to escape with the children and a few blankets. They told the woman at the desk that FEMA was saying that evacuees could stay at Days Inn motels and FEMA would pay the costs.

'I don't know nothin' about that,' the woman said.

The young man was getting frustrated and his wife began to cry. 'We're just looking for some help here,' he said. 'We don't have anything and the boys are tired. We've been driving all day.'

The woman behind the desk suddenly grew hostile and self-pitying. 'I don't get paid enough to deal with this,' she said. 'This gentleman' – she pointed to Terry, who was standing in the foyer – 'is looking for more towels and I don't have any kind of help here.'

Mr Exterstein used the motel phone to call FEMA but things were chaotic and the person he spoke to didn't know how to help them. His wife put her elbows on the desk and sobbed behind her hands.

'Listen, man. You can have our room,' said Terry.

'What?' said the man.

'Our room,' said Terry. 'We've only been resting for a coupla hours and we're clearing out soon. Forget them: they're so rude around here. Take our room.'

When they arrived at the room Sam was combing his hair so that it sat round his head like a bowl. Delighted to see them, he gave them bottles of water and money out of his pocket. 'You guys are so kind,' Aimee said. 'It's just unbelievable, all this. And you guys are so kind.'

'That's awesome, man,' her husband said. 'We only have two hundred dollars between us and we wish we could do something for you guys.'

'All we want to do is help,' Sam said.

It turned out the young couple had worked together at a bar called the Cajun Cabin in Bourbon Street – 'the French Quarter's only authentic Cajun bar and restaurant' – a place with red-and-white check tablecloths and live music every night. But it was now under six feet of water, as was the Exersteins' house. 'It's completely destroyed,' Aimee said. 'I didn't even have time to get my framed pictures or any of the personal stuff. It's all just gone for ever now.'

'And when we went back to see if anything was salvageable,' Cory said, 'the door had been kicked down and it was obvious the looters had been there. My Xbox was gone. Aimee's jewellery. Everything.'

'They locked everybody inside the Convention Center,' Aimee said. 'It was just crazy down there. It was as if gangs had taken over New Orleans.' They put the children into one of the beds and then hugged each other in the middle of the room.

'I had to go into the bathroom and do stuff when they hugged,' Sam said later. 'It just choked me up to see them upset and it made me feel great to know we'd done something.'

On the edge of Mississippi, Sam called his girlfriend to tell her what happened back at the motel in Birmingham. 'We're finally doing something,' he said. Even in company, Sam always seemed a little lonely without his cell phone flipped out on his hand. Terry woke up and stared at the car in front. 'Oh man!' shouted Sam. 'I see the whites in the nigger's eyes! I sees the whites!'

'You're stoopid,' said Terry. 'Some things just ain't worth gettin' upset about.'

'I see the whites, muthafucker!'

Snapped branches began to appear by the side of the freeway. Then the road signs started to look ragged and the fields blasted. 'Hurricane territory,' Terry said.

The truck seemed to be moving faster as Sam began losing patience with his ex-wife. 'Listen, young lady. You're being rude! You're cutting me off. Listen, you fat pig. You fat fuckin' pig. I'm losing power here.'

She wouldn't accept that Sam was on a mercy mission. She thought he was bragging about what he had done, and she would rather he had gone back home and tended to his own business. 'Listen to me and shut the fuck up,' he said. 'I don't give a damn fuck what you put up with. You fat little piggy-piggy, stinky little pussy-pussy. Fat pig. Fat pig. Stinky pussy. I'm trying to talk, you fuckin' pig. I just want to be an American hero. Yes. That's why I wanted to be in the military. I would love to do something and be a hero.' He then hung up.

Terry and Sam talked a lot about the vehicles in front. One of the cars had a bumper sticker that said 'Yee-ha Is Not a Foreign Policy,' and Sam laughed at this at first, but then, correcting himself, he began to get excited as Mississippi Interstate 55 filled up with military Humvees. With an increasing number of bent or snapped trees lining the road, the military personnel whizzed past in the afternoon sun, wearing claret berets, designer sunglasses, and chewing gum like teenagers in an ad for American nonchalance. Sam bashed his fist on the steering wheel and whooped. 'I say praise them all,' he said. He beeped the truck's horn and shook Terry. 'Hey, bitch,' he said. 'I wanna flag. Reach out the window and grab the flag off the back of that fire truck.'

'I wouldn't touch that flag with a two-hundred-foot pole,' Terry said.

After giving his partner the finger Sam logged onto the internet, then he reached out and flipped open his phone. 'Damn,' he said. 'I ain't got a single bar on my phone. I can't call out.'

'Great,' said Terry.

'Fuck you, you black African-American bitch.'

When Hurricane Katrina grazed New Orleans, people thought the city had got off lightly. Trees were uprooted, some verandahs collapsed in the city's older districts, shutters were blown into the street, windows were shattered in a number of downtown office blocks, but that first night, people were still drinking hurricane cocktails in Pat O'Brien's bar in the French Quarter: four ounces of good dark rum added to four ounces of hurricane mix, garnished with an orange slice, a maraschino cherry, and tons of laughter into the night. It was only during the following days that the disaster put a stop to the music: the levees broke, and slowly at first, then very quickly, the bowl-shaped city began to fill up with water and then to drown in its own toxic effluent.

The worst inundations happened in poor areas. Almost a third of New Orleanians live below the poverty line – 67 per cent of the population is black – and in the most densely populated areas the water, after several days, had flooded the houses past the second floor. Relations between the New Orleans Police Department and the city's poorest citizens are notoriously bad: last year, according to the columnist Jack Shafer, when 700 blank rounds were fired in one of those neighbourhoods, nobody called the police. New Orleans's homicide rate is ten times the national average. 'Unless the government works mightily to reverse migration,' Shafer wrote, 'a positive side-effect of the uprooting of thousands of lives will be to deconcentrate one of the worst pockets of ghetto poverty in the United States.'

As the days passed, the federal and local authorities that had ignored long-standing and much-publicised warnings about deficiencies in New Orleans's system of levees took up a position that people quickly recognised as having about it the putrid odour of an old wound. Even Fox News, which found nothing particularly strange in the detention policy at Abu Ghraib, faulted George W. Bush for mouthing empty can-do-isms while the mainly black people of deluged New Orleans were gasping for breath and water. As the city was plunged into several sorts of darkness, and people without cars or gas or money or health were abandoned for days at the city's Super-dome, the president flew above in Air Force One. His symbolic flypast offered a new perspective to those keen to know what America has become; for those in the filth and lawlessness of the Superdome, or those waiting on roofs for five days with no milk for their babies and no road on which to make good their escape, it was a vision of a president who could send 153,000 troops to the other side of the world at an official cost of $205 billion. That is what people know. They also know that if a category-five hurricane hit, say, the Hamptons, then Air Force One – to say nothing of every helicopter on the Eastern Seaboard, and every public servant – would be requisitioned to save lives.

Two paramedics, in New Orleans to attend a conference, were caught up in the hurricane. 'Two days after it hit,' Larry Bradshaw and Lorrie Beth Slonsky wrote in a piece that appeared on the web a week or so after the hurricane,

> the Walgreens store at the corner of Royal and Iberville
> streets remained locked. The dairy display case was clearly
> visible through the windows. It was now 48 hours without
> electricity, running water, plumbing. The milk, yoghurt and

cheeses were beginning to spoil in the 90° heat. The owners
and managers had locked up the food, water, Pampers and
prescriptions and fled the city. Outside Walgreens' windows,
residents and tourists grew increasingly thirsty and hungry.
The much promised aid never materialised and the windows at Walgreens gave way to the looters. There was an
alternative. The cops could have broken one small window
and distributed the nuts, fruit juices and bottled water in an
organised and systematic manner. But they did not. Instead
they spent hours playing cat and mouse, temporarily chas-
ing away the looters . . . We are willing to guess that there
were no video images or front-page pictures of European or
affluent white tourists looting the Walgreens in the French
Quarter.

Eighty per cent of New Orleans was underwater by the third
day. Both the Superdome and the Convention Center were full
and hellish, and the buses that were meant to evacuate people
didn't come. Disaster relief became a matter of volunteers. In
situations of panic and urban emergency – especially when
those situations are comprehensively mismanaged – victims
can come to seem like enemies to the authorities. FEMA exists
to make sure that never happens, and yet, in New Orleans, this
became the dominant theme. And the military, when it finally
arrived, only compounded the problem. Any black person in a
supermarket was assumed to be a looter. The devastation and
chaos caused by the hurricane were understood – by FEMA, the
government, the police and the military – as a threat not to life
and limb but to law and order. People trying to set up camps on
the freeway in order to survive were treated as insurgents.

Sam and Terry were nervous when they arrived on the fringe
of New Orleans. They had seen the reports about roving gangs,
so Sam checked his gun and placed the bag around his neck as
the truck approached a checkpoint. The state troopers were
checking proof of residence and generally policing the traffic.
The city was virtually empty by this point, and, off the record,
troopers were saying that people remaining in New Orleans

were to be treated with suspicion. 'Hi, gentlemen,' said Sam. 'We've driven here from North Carolina and we want to help. I've got a chainsaw and a generator and plenty of water. Don't know where the hell to start.'

'Straight on,' said the cop.

The smell was immediate, bosky, swamp-like and dark-fumed. 'You can smell death around here,' Terry said.

'Look up,' said Sam. 'Chinooks everywhere. Look at that, man. Twin blades. Awesome.' (A lone buzzard flew underneath the choppers.) Everybody kept talking about the trees. They had been damaged or destroyed for hundreds of miles. In New Orleans, they all inclined the same way, in rows, like a cheap painting of Hawaii in the breeze. The truck was covered in love-bugs, and they swarmed outside too. Mating flies, they copulate on the wing, and Sam was having trouble making room for them amid the war-movie excitement and his wish to get things done. 'I hate these goddamn fuck-bugs,' he said. He crushed a pair with a paper tissue. 'Look,' he said to Terry. 'They died in each other's arms. Thought you'd like that.'

Terry's greatest concern in life is sex. He says so all the time. In the hour before they arrived at the flooded end of the Jeffer-son Highway, Terry said the word 'pussy' twenty-six times. At one point, waiting for gas, he rolled down the window as a young woman passed with a clipboard. 'Mmmm. Uh-huh. I like it like that,' he said.

'Excuse me?' she said, walking into the gas station.

'I like its ass,' he said in Sam's direction, but Sam was on the phone. 'I'm going in there to see what I can say to her.' When Terry came back, phone-numberless but not in the least deject-ed, Sam chucked him a walkie-talkie he got at Wal-Mart and started to speak into the voice-piece.

'Come in,' said Sam.

'Your mother,' said Terry.

'Your mother's dick.'

'And it's a big one.'

'Your mother's a crack whore,' Sam said.

Over the highway, the McDonald's giant yellow M was bent like a corkscrew. The power lines were down and the poles lay across the road or had crashed through houses. When their truck reached the first fully flooded area, Sam and Terry fell silent, as if awed by the scene or attending a church service. Sam kept his face close to the wheel as he drove the truck through the water. He stopped when he saw that to go further would mean getting stranded. Ahead of the truck, cars were floating or tipped on their sides against buildings.

The houses were cheaply built and quick to turn to papier mâché. Yet it was obvious that not all the damage was nature's work: cars abandoned at the side of the road had back seats covered with clothes still on their hangers with price tags attached. One of them had a pile of unopened CDs on the passenger seat. Terry got out of the truck and walked into the water. He met a guy called Terence who worked for the city's road crew. He was wading though the water looking for relatives whose house was near the Jefferson Highway. The man's friend and co-worker was keeping him company. He said to Terry, out of Terence's earshot, that their supervisor had already been told that Terence's family were dead. Nobody could face telling him. Sam beckoned a policeman and asked him what was happening. 'Tell you the truth,' said the policeman. 'We don't know ourselves. We don't have a clue.' He said they had pulled some bodies out from under the rubble at the corner of Cicero and Jefferson.

The boys' help was refused at most places. They went to the Ochsner Clinic Foundation and were greeted by a crimson-faced FEMA worker who was supervising the building of MASH tents outside the hospital. 'We have electricity but no water,' the man said. 'The hospital's full to capacity but we're expecting more injured, so that's the reason for the MASH tents. I don't know what to tell you. It's just so confusing.' Someone else told Terry that in one of the hospitals the patients had been abandoned in their beds as the water rose and the staff were forced to flee. (Forty-five bodies were later found at the Memorial Medical Center.) There still were people in many houses. Sam was growing indignant. He felt he was answering a historic call for volunteers, and now that he was in the embattled zone no one knew how to make use of him. At one point, with a police escort, he drove the truck to the temporary headquarters of the Fire Department. On the way they passed many houses with signs outside saying: 'You Loot, We Shoot.' The person in charge at the Fire Department was not encouraging either. 'We just had a fuckin' volunteer guy fall out of a fuckin' tree and land on a chainsaw,' he said.

In some of the graveyards the coffins had risen with the tide and popped out of the ground, returning the bones and dust of the dead to the glare of the Louisiana sun. The climate was shot to pieces, yet not so much that the night air could fail to carry the scent of magnolia, or the same breeze now and then to lap prettily on the devastating waters. Every inch of New Orleans was a warning from Faulkner or Carson McCullers. The old, bleached hotels, with rotten water seeping up through their boards and plasterwork, were a series of flashbacks from Tennessee Williams; the floating chandeliers tangled with Spanish moss were Truman Capote's; and the white-haired survivors, seeking a way out of town with their plastic bags of photo albums, were a tribute to Eudora Welty. It was the week Southern Gothic became a form of social realism, the grotesque and the biblical stepping out to fulfil an old legacy. But the aspect of New Orleans that will remain in the memory is the ghostliness: every citizen an image stranded at the centre of a civil rights mythology, a city of Boo Radleys, visible in half-light behind a series of splintered doors and broken windows, a thread of national prejudice travelling on the becalmed air and stinging the nostrils of those who once felt they truly belonged to the Big Easy.

Standing at the top of one flooded street, Terry noticed a glinting light at the far end where furniture and cars were floating among the fallen trees and a premature mud of autumn leaves. 'It's a terrible smell,' he said. The light was not a person flashing a torch as first seemed possible. It was the sun glinting off a decapitated traffic sign.

'Everyone's gone, one way or another,' said a man who came by with his wife. The man had owned a small post office behind the street. 'It's well hidden now,' he said, 'which might be lucky.' New Orleans had become the thing that geological memory knew it to be – a voluminous swamp, a lake of reeds and tangled boughs, except that television sets and teddy bears and living people had got in the way.

Sam wanted to be pulling people from the water: he saw himself as being part of American heroism, and the chaos he encountered, the lack of direction, left him stranded in doubt about the authorities and about himself. Depressed, he stayed in the truck as Terry inspected the street.

'Come back!' Sam shouted as a group of black men suddenly appeared from a house and started walking in his direction. They loitered at the edge of the water and eyed the truck. Terry walked calmly back and when he climbed into the truck he saw that Sam had his gun out and was swearing over the steering wheel. 'Let's get the fuck away from here,' Sam said.

'The natives are restless,' Terry said, opening a can of cold ravioli and eating it with a plastic spoon.

The military stopped the truck entering another part of town. 'There's a curfew,' the soldier said. 'It's not a good place to be.'

'All right,' Sam said.

Further down the road, an old man wearing a hospital wrist-band was islanded on a grass bank. 'I need help getting across there,' he said. But the water stretched out in every direction with cars submerged up past their windscreens. His house was over there, under the water. The Salvation Army office was submerged too. Sam couldn't do anything, so he tuned his walkie-talkie to listen in to the military.

'If civilians want to go in they can go in,' said the crackly voice. 'But they should know they're not getting back here if they don't have a county resident's pass. Do you copy?'

'Yip,' said the second soldier.

'Did you leave a copy of the evacuation route over there?'

'I don't know where it's at. The press are renting a boat from a guy over here and using this patch of water to get to people and their houses and stuff. Is that OK?'

'I don't think there's much we can do about that. Over.'

Helicopters were grinding away over the flooded Shell Oil Metairie Plant. 'Life is full of important choices,' said a sign on the oil plant's gates. 'Make safety yours.' Sam's head was turned up to the sky and all the helicopter activity. 'That's a Huey 204, man,' he shouted. 'They haven't used them since Vietnam. I'm tellin' ya.'

Terry began laughing into his shirt as Sam hyperventilated trying to cross a bridge over the Mississippi. 'This place has had it,' Sam said. 'It's a muthafuckin' cluster-fuck, man. Nobody knows what's going on.' After he'd made it onto a drivable part of the freeway – yellow school buses abandoned all the way down the route – he started shouting out the window at the military vehicles passing on their way into New Orleans. 'Go home, you fuckin' losers! You dumb Yankee fucks. Why don't you go back and do somethin' useful, like play paintball, you bitches!'

'They're crazy about looters,' said Terry. 'The troops shot one of them last night and they put a sign on him that said: "A thief died here."'

'He wasn't white,' said Sam. 'I haven't seen a single white person looting.'

'You haven't seen anyone looting,' said Terry.

'But it's blacks, Terry. About two hundred of them.'

'I done seen none,' said Terry.

As the truck disappeared over the broken freeway and New Orleans receded in its soup of chemicals, Mayor Ray Negin came on the radio. His only song was about the failure of Washington. He had no plans of his own, nothing to propose. Blaming Washington was the only thing that mattered. There was an almost delighted tone to his self-exculpating voice. 'Mosquitoes that are biting dead people are starting to fly,' he announced.

Sam combed his hair in the whiteness of his rear-view mirror. 'We're needed in Mississippi,' he said. 'Gulfport, Biloxi. Those folks need what we've got. I just wanna help some people.'

Terry Harper had reckoned that a good way to get away from the trouble of school was to join the air force. He forged the date on his birth certificate and gained entry that way, leaving North Carolina on 31 October 1973. He was sent to Montana, where, he says, there was a lot of racism on the base. 'The base commander threatened to have me shipped to Iceland,' he said, 'because I was fucking his daughter. I mean, there were only four black girls on the base and 140 black men and those girls charged for pussy.' He got out of the air force after ten months and went to college to study mental health technology. 'That was a fun time,' he said. 'Pussy for days, a different bitch every day if I wanted one. Me and this white guy, we had an apartment at the country club and we took women there.' But he was married by then and his wife couldn't stand his philandering so she asked him to leave. 'She threw all the furniture I'd bought out in the street, man,' he said. 'It was all just lying there in the snow.'

Terry went to live in a mobile home. 'It was a good thing Aids wasn't poppin' back then,' he says. 'Because I'd be some dead muthafucker. This stinky-assed bitch (she's a preacher now): she lied and said I was fucking her and her husband came around with a .55 shotgun in his hand and told me he'd shoot me if I fucked around with his wife any more. I took the bitch out into a field the next day and said, "Bitch, you tried to get me killed today," and I put a gun to her face and she was scared, man.'

Eventually, he went to graduate school in Atlanta. He got a Woodrow Wilson fellowship for $39,000 but dropped out because, he says, in a class of sixty-six people he was the only black. 'I had no voice,' he says. 'I just felt I was in the wrong place. This was America and I had a God-given right to be heard but if you spit on me goddammit, I go directly to your ass. Things have stayed the same in a lot of ways. A whole lot of white muthafuckers, they think they can talk to you any old way they like.' He ended up working with deprived kids. 'Hard-assed kids,' he said. 'But you can make a difference to kids like that. One of them I worked with is now a district manager for Taco Bell. He runs three Taco Bells. He's one of the most respected people I know.'

Terry has had problems with drugs and women. That's what he says. He lost a good job as a drugs and alcohol counsellor because of cocaine (he was using on the job), then he lost his career as a photographer for the same reason. 'My mother was killed by alcohol,' he said. 'From an early age I felt I had to compete with my brother. He always got everything. My sister, too. Back in the day, complexion was everything and she was whiter than me. Until recently, you couldn't get anywhere near elected office unless you were light-skinned and that's what I grew up with.'

Terry paused often when talking about his life. He wants to get things right. He wants to be honest. 'I wanna get out of the Waffle House by next February,' he said. 'Back to Atlanta. Back to photography. I'm good at that.' When he said this he hesitated and stared into the near future, then he smiled, as if there was something more essential about himself that he had not brought out. 'I once fucked fifty-eight women in one year,' he said. 'I had a contest with some guy – who could fuck the most women. And man, I even fucked his regular girlfriend. It isn't that hard if you know how to go about it. We used to strip for wedding showers. It was a good thing, you know. Two hundred dollars a pop, plus tips.'

We couldn't find a motel in Mississippi, so Sam parked the car in Hammond and we spent the night in the truck. A neon sign – 'All You Can Eat Catfish' – rasped through the early hours, and Sam occasionally woke up and bathed his face in the blue light of his laptop, typing furiously, attempting to figure out how best to reach the poor Americans who needed him. Terry propped his bad leg up on the dashboard. 'Goddammit,' he said at first light, 'I might have to get me to an emergency room.'

'Looks like we won't be taking a bath today,' Sam said, pouring talcum powder down the front of his shorts. 'Mmm,' he said. 'Feels like gittin' a whole new pair of drawers on, man.'

A woman walked by with her dog on a lead. 'She's got some ass, man,' Sam said. 'Look it, Terry. She's your colour.'

'Hot damn!' said Terry. 'She's got one of them be-donk-e-donk asses. It goes all the way down, baby. She's fine.'

'Go on, dawg! She make yo jump up and slap yo mama.'

Sam and Terry decided they might need more equipment to help the people of the Mississippi Delta, so they joined the dawn chorus at the nearest Wal-Mart, touring the near empty aisles in a couple of electric-powered buggies, the ones intended for the old and the infirm. It was the calmest they had been for days: the store Muzak dimming all anxiety as they threaded through the lanes. They chucked insults across the gaps and eventually Terry pulled up at one of the checkouts with a basketful of cheap toys. 'A dollar each, right?' he said. The girl looked at him strangely, but Terry was sure there would be children in Mississippi who had lost all their toys.

Beside the front doors, an overweight pensioner was talking to her neighbour. 'What if the Great Man Upstairs says: "You haven't learned your lesson yet, you need some more?"' she said.

'God praise the volunteers,' said the neighbour. 'That's all I can say. The volunteers are the salt of the earth.'

On the Mississippi coast, the morning seems to arrive not out of the sky but out of the trees, a golden show coming slowly until the day is bright and firmly begun. 'We're gonna do good today,' Sam said.

'We already did good,' said Terry. 'We's offering. That's all we can do and if the people wants help they'll get it.'

'Today,' said Sam. 'I'm serious as a heart attack.'

As the truck entered Gulfport, a holiday town that had taken the full force of the hurricane the Sunday before, some of Sam's general edginess was beginning to influence Terry's view of the situation. 'I wish some of them TV news stations would interview me,' he said. 'CBS, NBC, CNN, all those muthafuckers. I'd tell them like it is. They're saying: "This is needed, that is needed." Everything is here, man, they've just got to use it right. These utility people, man. They're tellin' like they're working round the clock. That's complete bullshit, straight out lies. They're not leaving their motels until ten in the morning.'

'They oughta be organised just like the military,' Sam said.

'You don't know jack shit,' said Terry.

'Don't tell me what I don't know. I work with television. I know about cable. Them boys care about people. You just got a goddamn chip on your muthafuckin' shoulder, Terry.' The boys argued often, but they would always retreat from any serious confrontation by hooking onto some shared joke, usually about a passing woman. 'I could grunge-fuck that bitch,' Sam said of a woman walking past a convenience store in Gulfport. 'She's just the way I like 'em.' On the other side of the road, a sixteen-wheeler truck full of hearses was being unloaded, hearse by hearse, in the forecourt of a gas station that had no gas.

Gulfport was struck by winds of 160 mph. The morning had started out very blue and very calm, but dark clouds broiled in the sky and Hurricane Katrina ripped over the Gulf and slammed through all the towns and villages on the Mississippi coast. The casinos that stood at the ocean front in Gulfport were gutted and several of them had ended up on top of the freeway. The devastation was still spectacularly obvious: lorries piled on top of one another; hotels pulped, with glass and mud and trees and bathroom products scattered over a massive area. Concrete had been blown apart. Metal was twisted. And for five or more streets back from the ocean, people's houses were splintered.

By the time we reached Gulfport, the military were very much in evidence, though nobody knew what to do with them. A lot of saluting took place, a lot of standing before maps of the devastated areas. As in all military zones, a great deal of attention was taken up with the troops themselves – transporting them, feeding them, briefing them, guarding them. Only sporadically were they put to work. Some people concluded that they were there to provide a show of force, a warning to looters, and evidence that the federal government now cared. Yet the real stuff of the Mississippi relief effort was being run by agencies and volunteers. It might be said that the salient characteristic of the modern American military is that they always appear homesick, they always seem alienated, and they always look bored. This may be true of any military force in any part of the world, but it was certainly true of the American soldiers who came to serve in the American South.

The Volunteer Command Post was in a school just outside the town and much of the military was stationed there. As Sam drove up he was flagged down by four young men in uniform. Three of them appeared to be seventeen years old, and the one who stepped forward to speak, the one with authority, was no more than nineteen. Sam rolled down the window.

'Morning, zug-zug,' said the officer.

'Hi,' said Sam.

'Have you any weapons, zug-zug?'

'Sorry?'

'In the truck, sir. Do you have any weapons in the truck? Zug-zug.'

Sam looked at Terry and shrugged. 'A hand gun,' he said.

'I have to check that, zug-zug,' said the officer.

He walked off to speak to a superior and Sam turned with his mouth open. 'What in fuck's name is he saying? What's this "zug-zug"?'

'Fucked if I know,' said Terry.

The young officer came back shaking his close-shaved head. 'I'm afraid we can't allow any guns on the facility. Zug-zug.' The men behind the officer were smiling now.

'What is this "zug-zug" shit?' asked Sam. The officer broke into a broad smile and his men cracked up behind him.

'It's just a joke we've got going, sir,' he said. 'Things are a bit slow out here, so he just dared me to say "zug-zug" after everything I said.'

'Oh, cool,' said Sam. 'I got ya. What I'll do is, I'll go and bury this gun and then come back. Is that all right with you?'

'Do what you have to do, sir.' Sam drove along the road and buried the gun as he said he would, right in an old pile of dirt next to an abandoned house. When he drove back the soldiers searched the car and then waved us through.

Nothing fazed Adam, the co-ordinator, nothing excited him, nothing moved him: he was a disaster professional, a young man hardened by too much experience, practical to the point of insolence. 'The thing about this situation,' he said. 'Many people downtown who look like they need help, who've suffered a lot of devastation, they can afford to pay for having trees cleared and cars towed. You don't have to do it for them. It's the poor and vulnerable ones you have to look out for. If I drive down there and I see generators outside people's houses I just drive on. That's the way it is. There are folks who need help who would be happy to see you guys. Be choosy about who you help.'

Sam had nodded through this speech, but he did not take any of its detail to heart. He had come from North Carolina because he had watched television and felt Hurricane Katrina presented a challenge to ordinary people as well as an opportunity for self-definition. He didn't mind who he helped. New Orleans had been too murky and unreal, too spooky, too inaccessible, but, here in Mississippi, Sam was going to do his bit for America. On the back roads of Gulfport he drove the truck and kept his eyes open. Power lines had collapsed and every house had something shattered or crippled about it. In one of the nicer drives, Sam spotted an old white man and his wife trying to lift a generator down from the back of a pickup truck. He hit the brakes and swerved into their drive.

Eli Myrick has lived and worked in Mississippi all his life. That day, it being hot, he was wearing light-coloured shorts, a polo shirt and a straw hat, with white towelling socks climbing up his weak legs in a style both senior and fresh. Sam and Terry got to work lifting down the Myricks' new generator. Their house had lost power and one of the walls had caved in with the force of the hurricane. They were well off, though, and had a second house out of the state, so this was all just a pest. Sam was kneeling on their patio dealing with the transfer of gas from the old generator and Mr Myrick leaned against the kitchen door, pleased but also not pleased, the eclipse of his competence almost too evident in the words of his wife. 'Oh let them do it, Eli. You'll only hurt your back. Oh, honey, let them go ahead. Step back. That's right. They know what they're doing. This young man's an engineer, Eli.'

Mrs Myrick brought pink lemonade and Spam sandwiches for the boys and told them about her years as a history teacher. 'Well,' she said. 'I was just saying to my friends the other day: with all this terrible business happening to us here in the South, it proves that the Civil War will never be over. God save us from the North.'

Terry was leaning against the truck when Sam came out. 'That sandwich she gave us sure was salty,' he said.

Sam drove on and parked the truck on the ocean front, where Chiquita Bananas lorries lay about like crumpled toys. People who ignored warnings and remained on this stretch died instantly when the hurricane hit the shore. Terry walked into the shell of an old employment centre: there was nothing left, not a paper-clip or an office chair; a spout of toxic water bubbled up from a hole in the concrete floor. In the car park outside, where huge trees lay snapped in two, a tennis ball was pushed softly by the remaining wind. Terry saw a wheelchair abandoned in the middle of the highway: earlier, he had wondered why so much of this destruction was somehow familiar, and he realised he had seen it before, like every other person in America, in *War of the Worlds*.

The streets behind the ocean were no-go areas. The army were discouraging people from entering. But Sam and Terry drove round, looking for people to save or simply to help in their struggle with the collapsing buildings. Where the houses had doors, many of them were marked with orange paint and a number, which indicated how many had died there. The sight of the devastation had a different effect on the two men: it made Sam more practical, calling out to people he saw to ask if they needed help with the rubble, had enough cold water, or were OK inside. But with Terry the dreadful sights of Mississippi brought him further into contact with his militant past. He saw the effects of inequality in the mud around him. At one point, someone said something about Jesus and Terry just shifted his bloodshot eyes. 'Let me tell you about this country,' he said. 'The Catholic Church is filled with the worst racists of them all. Some priest, he sucked two hundred little dicks and you know what happened to him? He got a raise, man. They made him goddamn archbishop. And any black priests who commit adultery get kicked out the diocese. That's it.'

'Well,' said Sam, surveying the ruins from the wheel. 'I ain't helping no black people. I just wanna see how bad they live.' Then he sang a few bars of 'God Bless America'. He saw a woman on a porch. 'Man,' he said into his dead walkie-talkie. 'You're so ugly you'd have to wear a pork chop around yo neck to get the dogs to play with you.' Terry sniggered into life.

'You're so ugly you would scare a glass of water,' he said.

The Red Cross had warned Sam and Terry that it was dangerous to drive in those areas without a military escort. One of the Humvees had been shot at earlier that day. But the military men up at the command centre didn't want to escort the boys: they didn't think it was their job. It appeared that no one had bothered to establish a chain of command between the Red Cross and the military, so the people, such as Sam and Terry, who were delivering aid were expected to take their own risks and only help people they felt they could trust.

That night, the dark in Gulfport seemed darker than the dark of anywhere else. Electricity was still only minimally available and the stars looked down with keen eyes. Terry's gouty ankle had grown to the size of a small planet, and he slept out in the open air at the back of the truck, stretched out on a long toolbox, his leg hoisted higher than the rest of him and pointing at the stars. Sam fell asleep in the driver's seat with the broken walkie-talkie tight in his hand.

When he was a child, Sam was committed several times to Cherry Hospital, a place for children with problems. 'I've always wanted my friends to come with me,' he said. 'But they never have. They never will. I don't really have any friends, to tell the truth.'

He had Attention Deficit Disorder and the doctors put him on Ritalin. 'I was always puking in the afternoon,' he said. 'I was like a zombie, but that stuff works in some way. I could rush through my lessons no problem but by 4.30 in the afternoon I'd be so angry. I've always been angry but that was too much even for me.' Sam's grandmother, who tried to look after him, turned to alcohol just as his mother had, and she spent a lot of his childhood in rehab. As a way of avoiding reform school, Sam went as a teenager to a place called Camp Ek-Su-Mee near Candor in North Carolina. It gave him a way of transcending danger and fear. 'You had daily chores,' he said. 'Latrines. Pow-wow. Making kindling wood for the fire. All that. I cried like a bitch when I had to leave that place. They were like family – you woke up with them every day. I loved it there. I used to climb trees just to breathe, man. You could see for miles up there. The hills and everything.'

Sam said he's always wanted a bigger purpose. 'I also wanted a true friend,' he said. He had two friends when he was young, Algernon and Moo-Moo, two black kids who died after being shot in separate incidents, but he always felt Cherry Hospital ruined his chances because people thought he was retarded. 'Everybody always told me I'd be in prison by the time I was twenty-one. Well, I've proved them wrong, haven't I?' Sam has made his work and his children and his truck the centre of his bid for renewal. And he always wants to make good the past. 'One day I was talking with my father,' he said. 'We were talking about education and stuff, why I'd been passed over so much and had failed so badly. He told me that the whole time I was being sent off to the mental place, they were saying: "The son will be fine, save the mother.""

Sam's story, he indicated, even asleep with the walkie-talkie in his hand, is the story of how a person might overturn anger with usefulness, if not goodness. He isn't sure that this will work but he hopes so. 'I've always had this feeling,' he said, 'that there was something for me to do that was important and the whole world would know about it. I suppose this whole trip has been about that feeling.'

At the Orange Grove Elementary School a gymnasium was piled halfway up the bleachers with donated clothes. Some of them had tags indicating they had come from Utah, from the Church of Jesus Christ of Latter-Day Saints, and others were from people in Canada, Mexico or New York. Sam and Terry stood in the middle of the gym trying to separate the great heap into women's, men's, boys', girls' and babies'. Terry found *A Bible Promise Book* in a box of tangled T-shirts. He opened the book at random and saw a quote from Jeremiah. 'I will rejoice in doing them good and will assuredly plant them in the land with all my heart and soul.' Many of the T-shirts in the box had Coca-Cola logos on the front or American flags or Disney characters. A man walked past who had lost his house in Biloxi. His name was Leroy. His girlfriend and his mother had disappeared in the flood. 'The walls of the house just opened up like a zipper,' he said. 'The tide dragged me out and then threw me back in again, just sucking me out with all the furniture and then back again and eventually I held on to a tree. Held on to that tree for fourteen hours, just waiting for the storm to pass and someone to come get me.' He looked down at the pile of skirts and bras and women's jeans. His arms were badly burned where he'd hugged the tree.

A woman in her fifties came in and lifted some clothes out of the heap. Her name was Charlene. 'All my memories floated out on that filthy water the day of the hurricane,' she said. 'Everything. I'm just gonna make a little pile here of clothes to take away.' A Red Cross co-ordinator asked the boys if they'd load up their truck and take emergency supplies to some of the outlying towns, Long Beach and Pass Christian, that had been badly hit and were not getting enough help.

'Let's get to it!' Sam said. 'They're desperate for food out there.'

They loaded up the truck with water, pasta sauce, baby food, assorted tins and military MREs – meals ready to eat. Long Beach was weirdly quiet, except for the sound of gas-fuelled generators. We stopped at the Conoco gas station and the woman who ran it clapped her hands and got her husband to help the boys unload. No sooner was the food on the ground than people were moving in to take it to their cars. 'This is great,' said the woman. Sam was like a field commander by this point: he found out what else they needed and arranged with the woman to bring further supplies, while calling Yolande in North Carolina to tell her what was happening.

'He's like a goddamn reporter,' said Terry.

Many of the doors in Pass Christian were daubed with orange paint. A terrible, plague-like atmosphere existed among the shattered houses. It didn't seem as if the hurricane had come in from the Gulf at all but had risen, instead, from the centre of the earth. Houses had simply been split down the middle or had exploded in a thousand flaws. Sam drove the truck to a drop-off point in the worst area and then felt excited. It was part of their camaraderie: whenever Sam was feeling pleased with himself he'd immediately start feeding Terry's appetite for sexual repartee and girl-talk. A young woman and her boyfriend were holding hands under a battered bridge. Sam stopped the truck to ask if they were OK and then turned to Terry as he drove away. They did it in the style of an elaborate hip-hop-style joke.

'I'd rape the fuck out of that pussy. You?'

'All the way,' said Terry.

'We could mangle the boyfriend fucker,' said Sam. 'I'd hold her down for you. Would you hold her down for me?'

'Nope,' said Terry.

'You wouldn't hold her down for me?'

'Nope. I don't do that shit.'

'Well, fuck you,' said Sam. 'There's been a lot of fuckin' rapin' down here with this disaster shit.'

A woman called Audrey asked the boys if they'd put some of the supplies into the trunk of her car. She was seventy-three years old, wearing a polka-dot shirt and flowery shorts and carrying a bottle of water. She had a tumour on her neck. 'I have terminal cancer,' she said. 'And my husband here, Mickey, he is on dialysis. We're going to New Jersey so's he can get his treatment.' Audrey began to cry when someone brought up the subject of New Orleans. 'I come from there,' she said. 'It's too terrible. I think people should just get out of there and never go back. It can never be the old way again.'

That night was Sam and Terry's last night in Mississippi. They had borrowed fold-down beds from the Red Cross and had set them up beside those of the refugees in the school library at Orange Grove. A Hispanic man had lost his identification and was worried about being able to get the $2,000 relief package that FEMA was offering to hurricane victims. He sat on the edge of his bed in the library with a copy of *The Adventures of Huckleberry Finn* on his lap. 'I found this on the shelf,' he said. The front of the book had a page with children's names written out beside the date of borrowing. The man's name was Carlos A. Garcia and he was thirty-three years old. 'That Sunday morning,' he said, 'it started raining and there was a little wind. I lived in the apartment block at 601 Joseph Fine in Pass Christian. The block had a lot of Hispanic people living there. Not everybody speaks English. The storm got up and the trees were just breaking like crackers. The trees were bent over like people praying. The cars flew past the window, man, and then the stairs of the apartment got ripped off. We ended up on the roof, we put the old people up first. The water got so high that people were just swept off the roof and some of them jumped in. Twenty-four people from the apartment are lost and I just know they died.'

The shelter at Orange Grove School had a Stars and Stripes and a Confederate flag outside, rippling in the breeze. The night was ripe with the sound of crickets and some old men sat smoking and tapping ash into a bare tin can. The red sky had turned dark and the men were worrying about a new hurricane that was said to be gathering force outside Florida. A weeping woman came wandering across the car park and stopped a state trooper. Her child was clinging to the backs of her legs and seemed frightened. 'We're here in a shelter and he's drunk. He's over in that truck drinking beer and he's drunk.' She asked the officer to give her husband a breathalyser test but he demurred. The husband walked over and the woman pulled at her hair and shouted past him into the school windows: 'If you can drink when we're homeless! If you can do that! What's the use?'

One of the old men tapped his ash several times and stared through the smoke at the other men. 'Everybody's got problems,' he said.

Sam and Terry were bonding with the local boys. 'We thought we could ride it out,' said George McCraw. 'We ended up running to the Gates Avenue Baptist Church two miles from the beach. Man, the roof was caving in and the children were screaming. The wind was poppin' so bad and it was like rotor blades going over there. The steeple was coming off the church and the light poles were scattered across the road. Sparks flyin' everywhere. You could feel the force of the hurricane move you, man. It was just like someone had dropped a bomb. You'd just never think water could do that damage. It was bad, man. We had just got on our feet down there. We found this little place and a good job and we had a car. We weren't insured, though. Everything's gone. It's just toothpicks. But the Good Lord was with us the whole time. We looked hell straight in the eye. That's what we did. We looked at hell.'

George's younger brother wondered if there was any liquor to be had in Gulfport that night. 'Not with the curfew,' Sam said.

'There's a garage up by the freeway,' George said.

Sam and Terry were told to load up as much of the supplies as they cared to take back to North Carolina. 'You guys have earned it,' said the Red Cross co-ordinator, shaking their hands. 'I wanna thank you guys. You guys are patriots.'

They loaded up the truck and looked over at the homeless young guys pushing and joking under the white light above Orange Grove. 'That bitch, woooo,' said George's younger brother. 'She comes out here, eyes poppin' like a frog.'

'I'd bend her over and fuck her like a dog,' George said.

'That's right,' Sam said. 'I hear you.'

Terry disappeared into the library to find a book and lie down with it. 'Some drivin' to be done tomorrow,' he said. 'I hope we can stop off in Atlanta. I wanna go and speak to that son of mine.'

'He's just an old dog lookin' for a bone,' said Sam. When most people had gone to bed, he walked across the car park and lingered there with a cigarette. He'd given his mobile phone to people who needed to make calls and he stood there thinking about friendship and looking into the trees. Sam looked to the very tops of the trees and then turned back to the school. There was laughter inside. 'I'm going to miss you guys,' he said.

The Faces of Michael Jackson

JULY 2006

Since being acquitted of child molestation charges last summer, Michael Jackson has been hanging out in Bahrain, enjoying the hospitality of the ruler's poptastic son Sheikh Abdullah. Jackson is said to have become a Muslim (which is sure to please his critics on *Good Morning America*), but evidence would suggest he has yet to get the hang of Islamic custom. Not long after arriving in the famously tolerant state, he caused uproar when he entered the ladies' loos at the Ibn Battutah Mall dressed in female headgear and positioned himself at the mirror to put on his make-up.

Jackson's new friend has a bit of cash, and the pair have set up a record label called Two Seas Records. Sheikh Abdullah bin Hamad al-Khalifa is also the governor of Bahrain's Southern Region, but that hasn't prevented him finding time to write a song with Jackson's brother Jermaine, 'a passion-filled song that calls for world peace and global solidarity in the face of wars and disasters'. According to local correspondents, the record already has a title, 'He Who Makes the Sky Grey', but no release date is in sight. The king's son has high hopes for the recording. He recently called a press conference in order to claim that the project 'intends to bridge the gap between East and West'. Meanwhile, Jackson is in the habit of smiling widely beside his new friend. Things are going well in Bahrain. According to the *Militant Islam Monitor*, he is planning to build a new mosque in Manama.

Some insight into Jackson's life in the Middle East was offered recently by a young man who goes by the name DJ Whoo Kid, has a radio show on the New York station Hot 97 and produces work with gangsta-rap outfits with names like

G-Unit and Lil Scrappy. According to MTV News, 'Whoo Kid says he originally connected with Bahrain's royal family when he was recommended to DJ their parties by mutual contacts, including the Prince of Monaco and Seif Gaddafi, son of Libyan dictator Moammar ("They're huge G-Unit fans," the DJ said).' The last time Whoo Kid turned up in Bahrain he found Jackson drinking lemonade by some profoundly extravagant swimming-pool. They went to supper with the sheikh that night and DJ Whoo Kid decided to give the Gloved One, the Baby Dangler, or the Prince of Pop, as he's still sometimes known, some wise advice on the fashion front. 'You can't talk to Mike all fluffy like everyone does,' he told a reporter. 'I told him he needs to cut his hair, get some million-dollar earrings, get a million-dollar watch and take all them spaceship clothes off. He said: "I have to change my whole outlook."'

Meanwhile, back at the ranch, things are getting a bit wild with Michael Jackson's finances. The star was about to be made bankrupt over a $240 million debt to the Bank of America – he was also being sued by ninety of Neverland Ranch's employees, who hadn't been paid for some time – when the bank sold the debts to the Fortress Investment Group, which has issued Jackson with a $270 million loan, saving him from bankruptcy but costing him part of his share in his greatest asset, a music catalogue which gives him rights to 4,000 classic songs, including 200 by the Beatles. Jackson bought the catalogue against stiff competition, including that of Paul McCartney, in 1985, and it is said to be worth a fortune, though perhaps it's worth more than money to Jackson, who proved by purchasing it that he was bigger than the Beatles, who were once said to be bigger than Jesus.

What explains Jackson's journey from cute little black boy with immense talent and optimism to a mutilated gender fiasco who busies himself impersonating Elizabeth Taylor in *Butterfield 8*? Jackson is a protean idea of a person, rather confused, rather desperate, but complete in his devotion to self-authorship. His every move shows him to be a modern conundrum about race and identity and selfhood. He might make us laugh, but he might also frighten us into recognising the excesses we demand of those we choose to entertain us. For my money he also constitutes a mind-boggling and vaguely uplifting example of human instability in pursuit of perfection. In a sense he is all of the show-business spectacles we have ever known rolled into one: Barnum & Bailey to James Brown, Edgar Allan Poe to Shirley Temple, and David Blaine, and Peter Pan, all the way back to Neverland. We want to see him as pop's greatest distortion of human nature, which he may be, but isn't he also the most interesting person on the planet?

Jackson's mother, Katherine, a Jehovah's Witness, has said that Michael never quite seemed like a child, that even in his nappies he 'felt' old. At little over a year and a half he would stand with his bottle and dance to the rhythm of the washing machine. Joseph, his father, was angry and ambitious, an excellent if often sorry combination in the parent of a child who wants to be successful in show business. Everything that is bad for a child might be good for a performer – including, I suspect, being locked in a cupboard by one's father – and the horrors of his childhood very soon became part and parcel of Jackson's act. In many ways the early career of the Jacksons is a classic American show-business story – the Gumm sisters with spandex trousers – except that the boys were black and suburban and they became unprecedentedly popular in white America.

Only in the early 1980s, after Jackson went solo, did he go from being a musical genius to being a genius at selfhood. He remade his nose, he started getting interested in robots and toys, he began to wear make-up every day, and he began to fashion himself as an only child and a lost boy. He began, in other words, to disappear into some region of total ambiguity. In his biography of the star, J. Randy Taraborrelli describes going to interview Jackson at his California home in 1981. Jackson's sister Janet was there and Jackson insisted that the journalist ask her his questions, then she would ask Michael, who would tell her the answer and she could then tell Taraborrelli. Here's part of the exchange:

'Let's start with the new album, *Triumph*. How do you feel about it?'

Michael pinned me with his dark eyes and nodded towards his sister. I redirected my question. 'Janet, would you please ask him how feels about the album.'

Janet turned to Michael. 'He wants to know how you feel about the album,' she said.

'Tell him I'm very happy with it,' Michael said, his tone relaxed. 'Working with my brothers again was an incredible experience for me. It was,' he stopped, searching for the word, 'magical,' he concluded.

Janet nodded her head and turned to me. 'He told me to tell you that he's very happy with the album,' she repeated. 'And that working with his brothers was an incredible experience for him.'

There was a pause.

'You forgot the part about it being magical,' Michael said to her, seeming peeved at her for not doing her job properly.

'Oh, yes.' Janet looked at me with apologetic brown eyes. 'He said it was magical.'

'Magical?' I asked.

'Yes. *Magical.*'

Jackson has what might be called a supernatural relation to his own personality, a position which, far from holding him back in the real world, led in the months after this interview to the making of his album *Thriller*, which became the biggest-selling album of all time (fifty million sales, plus seven Top Ten singles). That level of success seems both to have enlarged his sense of messianic purpose and deepened the role of fantasy in his life. He had more and more operations on his face, he went to Disneyland every chance he got, he starred in a remake of *The Wizard of Oz*, he befriended a monkey called Bubbles, he pretended to sleep in an incubator each night, his skin got whiter and whiter, he became a recluse, and he invited children to stay at his ranch.

Margo Jefferson's essay *On Michael Jackson* displays a lively understanding of black performing history. Thankfully, there is not (yet) a Department of Michael Jackson Studies at Harvard, but Jefferson makes clear the extent to which the former child star is a loose-limbed signifier for the kinds of issue that matter to cultural studies majors: black history, gender politics, the aesthetics of the closet and all that. But Jefferson is enough of a writer to convince one, rather quickly, that the big-hearted, firm-minded essay – more than the novel or the biopic – may be the place where such issues can begin to find their most open-ended resolution. She makes it clear that Jackson had a freak-making childhood, and argues energetically that his career should be seen as an emotional extrapolation of every-thing he fears about adult power and the loss of innocence:

Neverland is a happy pre-sexual island ('for the Neverland is always more or less an island') ruled by boys. Grief and loss are at its root. Peter Pan ran away from home when he was seven days old . . . and settled in Kensington Gardens. 'If you think he was the only baby who ever wanted to escape, it shows how completely you have forgotten your own young days.' The birds taught him to fly, and he settled in with the fairies and had a fine time dancing and playing his pipes night after night. Eventually he became half human and half bird, a 'betwixt-and-between'. Sometimes, though, he would visit his house and watch his mother weep; the window was always open. He liked that she missed him, and he wanted to keep his options open. But one night when he arrived expecting a welcome, the window was locked. When he looked in, she was asleep with her arm around another child. 'When we reach the window, it is Lock-Out Time. The iron bars are up for life.' Devastated, he turned his back on her, flew to Neverland, and turned himself into the island's boy-king. From that day on, he helped other children flee their parents to a life of pleasure and adventure. 'I'm youth, I'm joy,' he crowed to his enemy, the wicked, unloved Cap-tain Hook. Hook and his pirates were the only adults on the island. Peter and his band of Lost Boys killed them all. But

they never discussed fathers. Mothers, he told Wendy, were
not to be trusted.

When Jane Fonda told Michael that she wanted to produce *Peter Pan* for him, he began to tremble. He identified
so with Peter, he told her; he had read everything written
about him. Did he know that the book's original title was
'The Boy who Hated His Mother'? As Michael wrote in his
autobiography: 'I don't trust anybody except Katherine. And
sometimes I'm not so sure about her.'

In his extensive reading about *Peter Pan*, Jackson cannot have
failed to notice the recently very popular view that J. M. Barrie
was a paedophile, haunted by his dead sibling David and animated by his fascination with the Llewellyn-Davies boys whom
he met in Kensington Gardens. Jefferson does not pick up on
the parallels – the horrible accusation, the sibling psychodra-
ma, the company of children – but she has a lot of time for the
idea that we live in a culture that enjoys the oddness of child
stars behaving like adults (singing about sex) and also enjoys
punishing them for having an odd relation to childhood when
they become adults:

> Michael never admits that he is angry as well as lonely and
> sad. And yet, what better reproach to all grown-ups –
> family, siblings, fans – than to have nothing to do with them
> except as business people you can hire and fire. Or as wives
> you can marry and divorce. Or as surrogate mothers you
> can pay and dismiss.
>
> Sometimes when I think back on that infamous photo-
> graph of Michael Jackson holding his baby over the balcony
> of a hotel, I see it as a child star's act of vengeance. Holding
> a baby over a balcony is a furious, infantile acting-out –
> doing something outrageous when people are interfering
> with you. 'You follow me, you hound me, you won't leave
> me alone, you want to see me, you want to see my baby,
> fine. Here's my baby. If I drop him, if he falls, it's your fault.'

We talk about how we think, believe, suspect Michael

Jackson treats children. We don't talk about how *we* treat child stars. Child stars are abused by the culture. And what's more treacherous than when the rewards of child stardom issue from the abuse? Child stars are performers above all else. Whatever their triumphs, they are going to make sure we see every one of their scars. That's the final price of admission.

We could go a stage further, and suggest that our tabloid media have a paedophile element to their subconscious, a child-abusing energy at the heart of their own anger. The British tabloid newspapers demonstrate this every day, with their talk of 'our tots' and their enthusiastic 'revelations' about suspected child abusers and child murderers. You can't read the British papers without feeling polluted, not only by the stories but by the degree to which the writers and editors of those stories appear to want them to be true, even before the evidence has proved it. Beyond this, a carnival of sensationalism vies with a deadly prurience, matched by a creepy populist appeal to the 'common decency' of the mob. You feel that the hacks are getting off on the horrors they ascribe, getting high on the pseudo-democratic vengeance their stories might excite. 'Here's an ugly fact,' Jefferson writes. 'The sexual abuse of children largely goes under-reported. And even when it's reported, it often goes unpunished. But here's a sorry fact. We're mesmerised by such crimes: they have become a form of mass culture entertainment, and a cover story for all kinds of fears.'

This is a horrible trap for a damaged and damaging person, and if that person is famous – superstar-famous – it may be the end of him. In Jackson's case, the tabloid mentality has had a field day, thanks to his weirdness, his nose-jobs and his Neverland Ranch. Wacko Jacko was found guilty of his appearance, his little voice, his white skin, his make-up, his friendship with the young film star Macaulay Culkin: he was guilty before he was charged with anything, though every time he has appeared in court the jury has concluded that there is not enough evidence to secure a conviction. I have no information about what

Michael Jackson did, or intended to do, when he invited those young people into his bed, but nobody else has any clear information either, and we are bound to forget, as the tabloids do, that having weird hair and a strange outlook and odd abilities does not place him outwith the bounds of common justice. It was those peculiarities which made him famous in the first place, and the whole circus may actually say less about the possibility of his having a criminal nature and more about our capacity for enjoying the ruination of a public figure.

What is it about fame that can make people unbearable to themselves? In the right conditions – the wrong conditions – a dreamy and over-watched person of sizeable talent can turn steadily into a tragic being, as vulnerable to the psychically destructive forces of the age as the great heroines of the nineteenth-century novel or the doomed figures of Romantic opera. Moral captives such as Emma Bovary and Tess Durbeyfield have destruction written into their code of happiness, as does Cio-Cio-San or Verdi's Desdemona, suffocated by bad men or bourgeois custom but most effectively by a public (an audience) that loves to be complicit in the undoing of women and the aestheticising of their pain. Once you get to Judy Garland or Marilyn Monroe or Billie Holiday or Lena Zavaroni, the thrill has become a fetish, and you can see how self-change and death throes have become in a rather naked way the bigger part of their performance. Michael Jackson has all of that by rote, and is distinguished among such figures as a black man who wants to be a white woman; a person who wants to unperson himself, to become something beyond nature, something entirely concocted of private fears and public desire.

Jefferson quotes Ralph Ellison's line that the challenge for a black artist 'was not actually one of creating the uncreated conscience of his race, but of creating the uncreated features of his face'. Has this been Jackson's greatest crime: to attempt to 'pass' for white in full public view? Did this put him beyond all possibility of acceptance or belonging? An alien? In *The Human Stain*, Philip Roth showed us Coleman Silk, a black man whose whole life had been a shoring-up of a place of greater safety for himself as a member of the white intelligentsia, a person who sought to put his secret self permanently out of sight in order to live as he wanted. He thought he could 'play his skin however he wanted, colour himself just as he chose'. The world comes down on Roth's character after he is accused of racism. One can barely conceive of what the world has in store for Michael Jackson, who has appeared to flout every rule of selfhood and secrecy made fashionable or necessary by the times he lives in.

The most interesting artists are a compound of talents and shibboleths. Everything that happens to Jackson, including his unacceptableness, which has recently come to seem final (thus Bahrain), is drawn eventually into his wonder and into his madness and into his work. A few years after the first charges of child molestation were brought against him, Jackson released a song called 'Ghosts'. The video is a funny, frightening and slightly stressed response to Jackson's many alarming situations, internal, external and otherworldly, but it also shows how his work can transform his isolation into yet more public performance. I'm not sure he can do this any more. Jefferson gives an excellent description of the video for 'Ghosts':

> The parents carry torches to the castle, like the villagers in *Frankenstein*. The castle is a cavernous, Poe-like dwelling with heavy brocade curtains and suits of armour. Lightning flashes; a raven flaps its wings; thunder cracks and doors slam shut, closing the intruders in. The Maestro appears, first as a skeleton in a black robe, then as Michael Jackson in a white shirt with a single row of ruffles, a white T-shirt, black pants and black shoulder-length hair.
>
> The Mayor calls the Maestro a freak and orders him to leave town. The Maestro challenges the Mayor . . . twisting his face into masks that are part ghoul, part nineteenth-century black minstrel. 'Did you think I was alone? Meet the family,' he adds, and summons forth creatures who shape themselves into the skeletons of antique courtiers, ladies and jesters. The skeletons dance with African squats and

robotic rotating knees and shoulders, with flamenco stamps and Native American stomps up the walls and across the balcony, cluster around a golden chandelier and drift lyrically down. Then (surely a reference to the gossip about his plastic surgeries), the Maestro tears his face off to reveal a skull. Later he bends down and, starting from his feet, tears off his whole body. Now he is Mister Bones in a Walpurgisnacht minstrel show.

The music is a bit insipid and nonsensical, the dance moves freakazoid and ridiculous, the scenario grandiose and egotistical, but the whole package is nevertheless a riveting, baroque and show-stopping amplification of Jackson's fractured self-image. Whether he means it or not, Michael Jackson is a constant projection of his own nervous imagination, a showman and a shaman embedded with all the hysteria and all the ambition of the age. And to think there's a little boy in there somewhere, asking for love in the dark.

At the height of his 1980s mega-success, Jackson still attended meetings at the Kingdom Hall with this mother. Two or three nights a week he would also go door-to-door with the *Watchtower* magazine, trying to recruit for the Jehovah's Witnesses. To make things easier, he would cover his head for these outings and wear a false moustache and glasses. Wandering around the suburbs of California, he would suffer the usual abuse and door-slammings. One girl, Louise Gilmore, recalls a man coming to her house. 'Today, I'm here to talk to you about God's word,' he said, and she let him in. According to Taraborrelli, the girl didn't recognise Jackson, but noticed he was odd. 'He looked like a little boy playing grown-up,' she said. He spoke to her about his faith, then drank a glass of water and left. When a neighbour later told Louise that the visitor had been Michael Jackson she says she almost fainted. She didn't join his religion, but she kept the pamphlets he gave her as souvenirs she would treasure all her life.

England and The Beatles

MAY 2004

There is something very English in the marriage of boredom and catastrophe, and the England that existed immediately after the Second World War appears to have carried that manner rather well, as if looking over its shoulder to notice that lightning had just struck a teacup. Reading the work of V. S. Pritchett or the absconded Auden, you pick up the notion that Europe had just come through a spell of bad weather, as though the only important question emerging from the war was about how it might have affected the course of English normality. The great horror was that things would remain the same, second only to a fear that things would never be the same again. The mood is captured nicely in '1948' by Roy Fuller, a poet who happened to spend his life working for the Woolwich Equitable Building Society:

Reading among the crumbs of leaves upon
The lawn, beneath the thin October sun,
I hear behind the words
And noise of birds
The drumming aircraft; and am blind till they have gone.
The feeling that they give is now no more
That of the time when we had not reached war:
It is as though the lease
Of crumbling peace
Had run already and that life was as before.
For this is not the cancer or the scream,
A grotesque interlude, but what will seem
On waking to us all
Most natural –
The gnawed incredible existence of a dream.

England appeared then to be a country of old men, a place in which dreams were routinely gnawed down by broken teeth, while America in 1948 appeared to the English like a stately pleasure dome, housing this great new phenomenon, the teenager, and busy with every kind of plan for the future, from abbreviated hemlines to the hydrogen bomb. The compulsions of teenagers have come to so dominate the world that we might sometimes forget they used not to exist. In 1900, for instance, 20 per cent of American kids between ten and fifteen were in full-time employment and, even as late as D-Day itself, Andy Hardy represented a world where young people did useful things and had fun before going to bed alone at ten o'clock. What was the teenage market in 1945 but comic books, bobby pins, and the Toni home perm? But in 1948 the transistor radio was invented (kids could suddenly listen to music in their own rooms), and the 1948 Cadillac came with tail-fins and a radio console, a vehicle customised for teenagers and featured in a blazing new magazine called *Hot Rod*.* It was also the year of the Kinsey Report. Ed Sullivan's *Toast of the Town* was first aired in that summer of 1948 and it would eventually promise a world in which the likes and dislikes of young people in blue jeans could appear to run the culture.

In a bombed-out Liverpool, a dozen years later, new shining buildings were being erected and English normality was erupting into something of a classless, American-accented meritocracy: four cheeky lads with scuffed shoes, the Beatles, came bursting with new harmonies and even newer energies, and they appeared to be telling young people they had choices. John Lennon, quoted in *The Beatles Anthology*:

> America used to be a big youth place in everybody's imagination. We all knew America, all of us. All those movies: every movie we ever saw as children, whether it was Disneyland or Doris Day, Rock Hudson, James Dean or Marilyn. Everything was American: Coca-Cola, Heinz ketchup . . .

* For some of this information I am indebted to Lucy Rollin, *Twentieth-Century Teen Culture by the Decades: A Reference Guide* (Greenwood, 1999).

The big artists were American. It was the Americans coming
to the London Palladium. They wouldn't even make an
English movie without an American in it, even a B movie
... They'd have a Canadian if they couldn't get an American
... Liverpool is cosmopolitan. It's where the sailors would
come home on the ships with the blues records from
America.

Devin McKinney's intelligent study of the Beatles, *Magic
Circles: The Beatles in Dream and History*, finds the four in a
Liverpool coated in the grime of Empire; among the cellars,
bunkers, and backstreets of post-war Britain, they 'listened to
America and lived on fantasies of everything their culture
lacked'. McKinney listens to a tape of the sixteen-year-old John
Lennon singing with the Quarry Men, the ramshackle group
that preceded the Beatles, at a church garden fête. It is the day
Lennon met Paul McCartney. 'The music,' writes McKinney,
'though it *resembles* rock and roll, sounds as if it owes nothing
to any form, because it is so completely itself. It feels like ugly
British kids make it, and sounds as if it comes from under the
ground.'

Like most British pop groups of the time, the Beatles sang
with American accents, which shows you what Britain was
becoming in those years. Yet the group were the first to echo the
sound of America back on itself, only louder, newer, with more
screams, and their story, rightly divined in McKinney's book, is
about how they came to represent the thrill of rock music as a
high form of dreaming in the present tense of history. It is exactly forty years since the Beatles landed at JFK. What did they
bring with them apart from an instant legend of old Europe
transmogrified by America? Greeted by 'a squall of unmediated
adolescent emotion', the Beatles never questioned the meaning
of the sobbing girls who crowded around them, or of the out-
raged adults who would later oversee the burning of their
records. America was ready for something new in 1964, and the
Beatles surprised even themselves at their agility when it came to
meeting that readiness. Paul McCartney in the *Anthology*:

There were millions of kids at the airport. We heard about it
in mid-air . . . The pilot had rang ahead and said, 'Tell the
boys there's a big crowd waiting for them.' We thought,
'Wow! God, we have really made it.' I remember, for
instance, the great moment of getting into the limo and
putting on the radio and hearing a running commentary on
us: 'They have just left the airport and are coming towards
New York City . . .' It was like a dream. The greatest fantasy
ever.

Ringo Starr, the drummer, showed all the excitement of a
wallflower suddenly plucked onto the dance floor by the college
jock. 'On the plane,' he said, 'flying into the airport, I felt as
though there was a big octopus with tentacles that were grabbing the plane and dragging us down into New York.'

That madness was a fulfilment of the promise of 1948: Elvis
came first, then came the Beatles, but the Liverpudlians failed to
lose themselves in Hollywood as Elvis did, and instead they
began, after that first innocent bout in America, to travel into
the nature of their own psyches and the character of their own
time and place, journeys that still offer the most articulate def-
inition of the decade. Looked at properly, the Beatles really were
the Sixties: they started out as one thing and ended as another,
and that is the core of their story, how they changed from ultra-
melodic laughing boys to revolutionary art-heroes, making an
entire generation imagine itself differently. Another story
emerges too when you look at the Beatles' music and its reception, a story about the cultural relationship between Britain
and the United States, an odd friendship in which loyalties,
enmities, and anxieties of influence have been animated in a climate of increasing American power.

The Beatles appeared on *The Ed Sullivan Show* on 9 February
1964,* and the direct influence of that event is still being felt in

---

* The anniversary is marked by several publications and republications about the
Beatles, including Martin Goldsmith, *The Beatles Come to America* (Wiley, 2004), a
rather sweet beat-by-beat account of the band's appearance on *The Ed Sullivan Show*.

new ways. In 1961, Senator John Kerry played bass guitar in a band called the Electras. The band rehearsed in the halls of St Paul's School in Concord, New Hampshire; they cut a record and described their music as 'early surf'. Tony Blair's band was called Ugly Rumours; he played guitar and sang. Only the other day, on a tour of China, a group of students asked the British prime minister to sing a Beatles song. He blushed and looked at his wife, Cherie, who picked up the microphone and gave a rather croaky rendition of 'When I'm Sixty-Four'. John Edwards plays the saxophone and 'admires' the Beatles. Former Governor Howard Dean plays the harmonica and the guitar and his favourite Beatle is George Harrison. Wesley Clark's favourite album of all time is *Yellow Submarine* (Kerry's is *Abbey Road*; Dennis Kucinich's is *The White Album*). Who can forget Bill Clinton's saxophone solo on *Arsenio Hall*? 'There was not only a new sound,' said Al Gore, speaking about the Beatles to the editor of *Rolling Stone*. 'There was something else that was new with the Beatles. A new sensibility . . . that incredible gestalt they had.' The great exception to all this is George W. Bush. He was at Yale from 1964 to 1968, and liked some of the Beatles' first records. 'Then they got a bit weird,' he has said. 'I didn't like all that later stuff when they got strange.' Bush also told Oprah Winfrey his favourite song is the Everly Brothers' 'Wake Up Little Susie' (1957), but overall he says he prefers country music.

The Beatles are the super-boomers' house band. Even people who don't care about popular music – especially those, one might argue – are conscious of how these English songwriters may have harnessed the properties of their own time, or were

---

'Such was the nationwide fascination with the Beatles that, so the story goes, crime decreased to almost nothing while the music played . . . And evangelist Billy Graham broke his own rule of not watching television on the Sabbath, tuning in to the Beatles to try to understand his three teenage daughters. After turning off the set, he proclaimed the Beatles symptomatic "of the uncertainty of the times and the confusion about us. They are part of the trend towards escapism. I hope when they are older they will get a haircut."'

harnessed by them, down to every teenage sob and every kink of modern marketing. McKinney crunches the facts and pulps the possibilities before tossing everything into a great meta-physical soup, and his book carries sentences not unlike those Norman Mailer used to write forty years ago in the *Village Voice*:

> Despite feeling paralysed at the centre of the mania, the Beatles would draw their audience in by pushing it to new places. They would speak contentious, unprecedented words; offer upsetting, incomprehensible images of them-selves; make disorienting musical noises. Just as their music would be the best and most challenging they had yet made, their collective persona would be more provocative, richer in dimensions than ambition or circumstance had previ-ously allowed – or required. They would answer and inter-pret their suddenly hostile world in the language of symbol, the logic of dreaming; and they would, by accident and intent, seduction and aggression, tumult and meditation, sound early shots in the ferocious battle over consciousness which consumed the latter half of their decade.

If this seems a tad overheated, it's only because the writer is very close to the heat: there has never been another group so perpetually *involved* as the Beatles were, and to seek the source of their power is to interrogate the culture of then and now to a degree only just below melting point. You'll forgive the prose for being a bit drugged when you get used to its modes of per-ception: McKinney is writing about a time, perhaps the first time, that history and society were apt to be understood through the movements of its youth, and McKinney is right for the job so long as one agrees that the occasion calls for some-thing more infiltrating than the objective rigours of Hugh Trevor-Roper.

If you ask anyone what the Beatles sang about, they will say 'love' if they're thinking of 'Love Me Do' and 'She Loves You', or they'll say 'loneliness' if they're thinking of 'Eleanor Rigby' or

'She's Leaving Home'. Some people will mention drugs if they're remembering 'Strawberry Fields Forever' or 'Lucy in the Sky with Diamonds'. Those who care about, as it were, crotchets and quavers are known to compare Paul McCartney to Schumann, as Ned Rorem did when he wrote in these pages in 1968,* or liken John Lennon to Chopin. But the true, workaday beauty of the Beatles' words and the music is related to the matter of mutation – the foursome's great theme. They were a wonderful group because they truly inhabited their own ambivalence, making music that grew as it changed, songs that were loaded with an experience of contradiction and exploration. As with many of their contemporaries, they could have remained a charmingly harmonic pop band for ever; they could have scattered their perky songs like coins before the crowd and never been resented for it; they could have been Gerry and the Pacemakers. But the individual members of the Beatles spent a decade growing in and out of themselves, moving towards and apart from each other and their fame, until they finally spun into legend.

We take their innovations for granted now, as if those young men had not been real people living in a world of small, actual discoveries, but supersonic characters in a comic strip. Yet when people first bought the album *Revolver* and heard the guitars going backwards, it seemed that some sublime disjunction was taking place and that the Beatles knew something that other people did not. They knew something about their current moment and something about the fantasies of their audience and that is perhaps the largest single thing to know in show business. While the *Revolver* LP created the impression, *Sgt*

---

* 'The Music of the Beatles', *New York Review*, 18 January 1968. This was the essay in which Rorem also called the Beatles 'cockneys', a designation which thrilled the denizens of East London but caused chaos in the affections of Liverpudlians everywhere. Rorem, by the way, is still unburdening himself on such topics. See the latest volume of his diaries, *Lies* (Counterpoint, 2000): 'All art dates, from the moment it is made,' he writes. 'Some dates well, some badly. Giotto, *Le Sacre*, the Beatles date well. Beethoven's Ninth, Lautrec, the Rolling Stones date badly. (Pick your own examples: personal taste is risky, even when the argument's solid.)'

Pepper's Lonely Hearts Club Band made people feel that the group could offer not just hidden truths but a whole new way of life, and *The White Album* of 1968 seemed to millions like a rather grand echo chamber of moral concerns, from My Lai and civil rights to sexual liberation.

I was born the year that album was released, so it was nothing to do with me at the time, but the album has since come to seem to me the most that can be done with rock music. If Bob Dylan and Lou Reed were more genuinely literary, the Beatles produced more puzzling and penetrating art. 'The people gave their money and they gave their screams,' said George Harrison, 'but the Beatles gave their nervous systems, which is a much more difficult thing to give.' In their talk and in their jibes to the press, the Beatles always seemed sweetly at home in themselves, just lads from Liverpool underneath all the mania. But in fact they carried some heady enigmas into the public sphere, not least of them the bringing of English dirt and chaos into the homes of clean-living America. Their career shows a trail-blazing democratisation of cultural authority. Seventy years before them, what did it take to tinker with the old consciousness? The single-mindedness of Nietzsche? The martyrdom of Oscar Wilde? The almost private experiments of Gustav Mahler? A group of Impressionists? The Beatles had no training, no permission, and no great tradition either, but they had their own hungers and the instinct of a popular mandate. The real surprise was how they turned a mirror on that populism, song by song, album by album, in some measure showing their fans the new society that they had begun to constitute.

Four quite ordinary boys from Liverpool. In 1966, in the Philippines, the year after the Marcoses came to power, who do you think was on the flamboyant leader's wish-list of artists who could come and appear to confirm his 'democratic' revolution? Only one name: the Beatles. The band played a concert but, failing to turn up at a palace function, they were more or less deported and Brian Epstein, the Beatles' manager, had to pay back their earnings before the plane was allowed to take off.

It was perhaps the dangers of excessive populism that Lennon was commenting on when he observed that the Beatles were more popular than Jesus; he was pilloried in America for the statement, but actually he was saying something very straight-forward and real. He wasn't calling for the overthrow of religion by rock and roll but, more simply, expressing surprise at the way religion's ancient fantasia had given way to cries for the newer, more prosaic messiahs, a bunch of Merseyside vandals. Nowadays it is no big deal to notice that more young people watch *The Simpsons* than attend church, but in 1966 the insult burrowed into the heart of an American paranoia – American specifically: the comment was actually made to an *Evening Standard* journalist in London, where nobody cared – and the result was that Beatlemania found its dark opposite in people who couldn't burn their images fast enough.

In four years the Beatles had become as complicated as their decade, and by the 1966 American tour things had turned nasty. The America that had both nourished them as English kids and received them as heroes in 1964 was now beginning to buckle under the shock of the new, under the demands and freedoms that forces such as the Beatles had brought into play. Beatlemania ended at that point and something else took its place – the Beatles as soft revolutionaries and agitators, the Beatles as harbingers of strangeness and great changes to come. The songs were showing the Indian influence – also the influence of hallucinogenic drugs – and musical transformation had been the hallmark of that *Revolver* LP of 1966, with its squealing amplifier feedback and lyrical accounts of fear and death and tension.*

America behaved that year as if its innocence was being corrupted. 'One night on a show in the South somewhere

---

* Take one song, 'She Said She Said', a menacing and regretful track on that album, heralding a very different group from the one that sang 'I Wanna Hold Your Hand'. 'The antithesis of McCartney's impeccable neatness,' writes Ian MacDonald in the best account of the Beatles' music, *Revolution in the Head* (Holt, 1994). 'Lennon's anguished "She Said She Said" is a song of tormented self-doubt struggling in a lopsided web of harmony and metre . . . It draws its inspiration from the day in August 1965 when Lennon took LSD with Roger McGuinn and David Crosby in Los Angeles.'

[Memphis] somebody let off a firecracker while we were on stage,' said Lennon later. 'There had been threats to shoot us, the Klan were burning Beatle records outside and a lot of the crew-cut kids were joining in with them. Someone let off a fire-cracker and every one of us – I think it's on film – look at each other, because each thought it was the other that had been shot. It was that bad.'

Here's McKinney:

The demonstrations were, by one set of symbols, an asser-tion of white Christian supremacy. By another, they were the most extreme Beatle fantasy yet devised. They showed how far the Beatles had gone in engaging with the world, how deeply they had penetrated even its sickest and most ancient passions, and how complex were the burdens their ambitions had forced them to assume. The burnings were deplorable and stupid, but as a social and mass-psychologi-cal reaction to a certain provocation they were not without their logic. Fear of the Beatles and fear of social tolerance were not only compatible; each was implied by the other. At certain points in the '60s, the feelings people had for the Beatles and for the world around them came together and formed a circle – a magic circle, a sphere of fantasy within which mutations of thought were formed, the unimaginable was imagined, and action was taken.

This was clearly not the Sixties that everyone experienced – not the Sixties of J. Edgar Hoover, for instance, or George W. Bush – but the modern personality the Beatles promulgated is the one that broke the old culture's back. As much as John F. Kennedy, the Beatles brought a new attitude front and centre, creating at once a ferocity of love and hatred, the kind of appeal, we now understand, that sometimes finds its resolution at the tip of an assassin's bullet. The Beatles' songs got so com-plicated they couldn't be played by the band live, and the lyrics, from one album to another, grew very keen to recognise the delirium that lives somewhere inside democracy.

Paul McCartney was the more optimistic and melodic of the pair – and the more shallow, according to conventional wisdom. Lennon could be shallow enough when he wasn't trying – but generally Lennon was the more visionary, seeing terror, and some kind of resignation to terror, as one of the potential outgrowths of freedom in our time. Lennon's powerful ambivalence was four fifths of his genius: 'Half of what I say is meaningless,' he wrote in a song to his dead mother, 'but I say it just to reach you.' Lennon and McCartney found beauty in chaos, and that is rock and roll's oldest and most natural secret. But in uglier minds, such as Charles Manson's, songs such as 'Happiness Is a Warm Gun' and 'Helter Skelter' became manifestos for some of the purest and least ambiguous badness known.

America's counterculture was a dark fairy tale and it was Joan Didion's *The White Album*, a beautiful portrait of the decade's voids and erasures, which brought out, in Flemish detail one might say, the very proximity of that fairy tale to nightmare; it is a book in which the Beatles' long dance of innocence and experience is fixed and pinned like a butterfly in a glass case. Those boys who met at the church garden fête in Liverpool could hardly have imagined their lyrics would one day end up painted in blood on the walls of Sharon Tate's house on Cielo Drive. 'Many people I know in Los Angeles,' wrote Didion, 'believe that the Sixties ended abruptly on August 9, 1969, ended at the exact moment when word of the murders on Cielo Drive travelled like brushfire through the community, and in a sense this is true. The tension broke that day. The paranoia was fulfilled.'

McKinney's book maps that development rather brilliantly, and one begins to see exactly how the harmless, tuneful, teenybop band of 1962 came, quite alarmingly, over time, to conduct those discordant investigations into death and chaos and crisis in the second half of its career. Where the *Sgt Pepper* album had been a rather fey acid trip, an escape from social reality into some colour-saturated hippie nothingness, the Beatles' *White*

Album is the most perfect rock album ever made, one with a social and psychological resonance that people are still conjuring with today. Can an album of rock music do that? Well, nobody really thought so before then, but nobody would doubt it now, especially not those legions who believe so completely in their own buying power as the truest expression of the will to choose life and alter the world. Charles Manson may have been, as McKinney says, jealous of the Beatles' screams, and the band may have awakened in him, as in so many, 'a latent sense of entitlement,' the certainty 'that he had something to say that was worthy of being attended to by those awed millions.' For others, the song 'Revolution' was a denunciation of student revolt in 1968, a hymn to appeasement in the face of Mayor Daley's storm troopers. In any event, the Beatles had come to seem like moral rabble-rousers whether faced with screaming girls, Jesus freaks, leftist warriors, or the FBI. At one time or another everybody has had at least one good reason to love the Beatles and at least one good reason to hate them. 'Radical critics were wrong,' writes McKinney,

> in failing to acknowledge that the Beatles had done their bit for the revolution. Had begun doing it when they climbed their first coal wagon as the Quarry Men: had gone on doing it battling the crowd in Hamburg, banging a new sound against the Cavern walls, giving themselves to audience after audience, drawing in one here, alienating another there; and had paid for it in the rain of jelly babies and Manila fists and Jesus hysterics and mad love, in the sacrifice of their safety and the burning of their youth.

A great deal of writing about the 1960s seems to helium-huff its way into intelligibility, but McKinney is right: as journeys for artists go, the Beatles' journey into their time now appears in its own way no less surprising and world-modifying than the developments of Picasso. 'I say in speeches that a plausible mission for artists is to make people appreciate being alive at least a little bit,' wrote Kurt Vonnegut in *Timequake*. 'I am then asked if I know of any artists who pulled that off. I reply, "The Beatles did." The group's story is an inspired dream sequence about self-transformation. Lennon and McCartney were two scruffs with poor school results; they each lost their mothers very young, in those first years in England after the war. Your mother is dead, your world is bombed and dirty. What are you going to do? That's the question. And the simple answer – 'we're going to pick up our guitars and change the world' – now acts like an unconscious mantra for generations who take their entitlement for granted, including those people whose busy, Sixties-experienced shadows begin to spread over everything from the carpets in the House of Lords to those lawns just in front of the White House.

The American Way of Sorrow

JUNE 2005

Perhaps we have to thank Watergate, even Deep Throat himself, that susurrating, parking-lot ghoul, for planting us in a world where the shriek of actuality has given way to the soft lilt of fiction. To me there is a stylistic link between that great moment for the *Washington Post* and the paper's worst moment, in September 1980, when they ran a report by Janet Cooke that had everyone talking. Cooke wrote a thrilling story about an eight-year-old boy from a low-income neighbourhood of Washington who was addicted to heroin, a story for which she won a Pulitzer Prize. But the New Journalistic ethos was overstrained in Cooke's case, for her infant addict didn't exist. The young journalist got caught, the paper was humiliated, but the only element in the tale that was brand new was the level of mea culpa that seemed to invigorate all the participants.

In recent times, this level of regret has become somewhat operatic, and this can't simply be due to the fact that so many of the recent journalistic fabricators are American. Britain doesn't go in for the three-act opera so much, but this country's journalism is full of fabrications: invented sources, bogus statistics, faked opinion, and even faked photographs, although it is difficult to imagine any British reporter inventing an entire story including his notes, his quotes, his expenses and his subject. It seems we all have something groovy to learn from the Americans both in terms of souping up our stories and in terms of feeling really bad about it afterwards.

Stephen Glass, once a popular and ambitious young thing at the *New Republic*, invented email addresses and whole companies to hide his deceit, and later went on to invent a novel about the affair, *The Fabulist*, which features a not-entirely well-concealed character called Stephen Glass who invented email addresses and whole companies to hide his deceit. 'I don't know how I can demonstrate my remorse,' Glass is reported to have said to Andrew Sullivan, the editor who hired him. Sullivan pointed out, not in so many words, that taking a giant book advance and allowing a film to be made from the story of your misdemeanours might not be the subtlest demonstration of remorse. Next came Jayson Blair of the *New York Times*, whose inventions created a tidal wave of apologies, a 7,000-word explanation in the paper, and a subsequent affirmative action squabble that saw the executive editor, Howell Raines, and the managing editor, Gerald Boyd, removed from their positions.

'I hope you will agree with me that everyone should have the chance to apologise,' Blair writes in the early pages of his action-thriller-memoir *Burning Down My Master's House*. It's not that you don't feel bad for Blair (you do), or bad for his bosses at the *Times* (you sort of do), it's just that any contagion of piety eventually provokes one to laughter. A stray candle burns the cloth on a holy altar and, the next minute, everyone is wailing in a medieval way about faith and trust. Blair's book is a masterpiece of such overstatement: you get the impression he will go to any lengths to avoid simply saying: 'I was stupid. I got busted. It sucks.' He blames cocaine, he blames Johnny Walker Black, he blames overwork, he blames manic depression, he blames his colleagues, he blames his many relatives in prison, he blames the paper for not taking enough interest in the Holocaust, he blames white America, he blames black America, he blames fast food, he blames 9/11, but most of all, and with enormous flagellating brio, he blames himself, which is a little harsh, given those other things are so very much bigger than him. Blair's book is better when not describing his journalistic crimes and misdemeanours (which is a stroke of luck, given that he doesn't actually get round to describing them until thirty-four pages before the end), lighting up when he's telling us how good he was at having a good time, and also when telling the truth about how stories on the *Times* are prioritised. For much of the book Blair is having a whale of a time, with a whale of a time's attendant regrets. He is a bit like someone out of *Less than Zero*, although in America there is always a higher-than-average price to be paid for having a few drinks. Blair wants to apologise for his whole existence, and the whole of existence itself, in place of just explaining how his ambition got to run so far ahead of him. There's no doubting, though, that his basic fears say a great deal about what is happening in American journalism.

Not quite as much, though, as Michael Finkel's *True Story: Murder, Memoir, Mea Culpa*, which streaks across a firmament already glittering with apologetic precedents. Finkel was another of the *New York Times*'s ambitious young writers. He'd written a few high-octane pieces, was liked by his editors, and got into a bit of a state while trying to put together a piece on child slave labour on the cocoa plantations of the Ivory Coast. He wasn't finding enough evidence of pure child slavery, and he wasn't finding the one single experience of enforced work that would turn his assignment into a winner. He interviewed sixty or more workers, and was discovering that the 'slave story had been blown out of proportion'. He wanted to write a story that would demonstrate 'how we can sometimes see what we're looking for instead of what really exists'.

> I described my idea to Ilena Silverman, my editor at the
> *New York Times Magazine*. I was excited about its prospects;
> it had the potential, I thought, to be an intelligent, insight-
> ful, unorthodox article. Silverman, though, said she wasn't
> particularly interested in yet another story accusing the
> media of getting everything wrong. She didn't want a piece
> that might unfairly harm humanitarian agencies. Instead,
> she suggested that I present all of these issues more palat-
> ably, perhaps by telling a detailed story of one boy. Weave an
> intimate portrait of a single labourer, she said, and through
> this one worker artfully clarify the fine line between slavery
> and poverty. 'Could you do that?' she asked me.

Finkel said he could do it, but the fact is he couldn't: his notes and interviews were not up to telling his story through the experience of a single boy, but he was compelled to please Silverman, and he went ahead and made the story up. He uses the phrase 'composite character', meaning he put the detail of a number of his interviewees at the service of capturing one boy, but he was daft enough to use a real boy's name and the paper daft enough to run a real boy's photograph.

Finkel got caught. He got fired. And on the day the paper published its explanation – one of the mea culpa spectaculars that the *New York Times* now specialises in – the telephone rang in Finkel's Montana apartment. It was a reporter from the Portland *Oregonian*, asking to speak to Michael Finkel of the *New York Times*. Clinging on to the last vestiges of his old self, Finkel said it was he. The reporter from the *Oregonian* said that a man named Christian Longo, who appeared to have killed his wife and three children, was on the run in Mexico, posing as a journalist from the *New York Times* called Michael Finkel. One might choose to describe the phone call as bad timing, but only if one knows nothing about journalism and nothing about human vanity. The real Finkel couldn't believe his luck.

Longo had read a few of Finkel's articles. He used Finkel's name because the name was memorable and also because his whole life had turned into an act: real life was always battering his self-esteem and presenting a challenge to his lies and ambitions, and he imagined that being taken for a guy from the *New York Times* could make you somebody in the world. Longo pretended to the people he met that he was writing an article on Mayan mysticism, and he 'seemed like a journalist', according to one of the witnesses: 'He was taking notes, constantly writing. He talked about his other stories. I believed him.' The police caught and arrested Longo in Cancún. Michael Finkel wrote to him and he received a phone call in return. Finkel was clearly flattered by the attentions of the murderer, so flattered, indeed, that he wanted to believe his new friend wasn't a murderer at all. Longo, meanwhile, was intelligent enough to spot that

Finkel not only needed a story but needed redeeming; the journalist had found someone, albeit a possible murderer, who appeared not only to admire him but to be potentially more dishonest than he was. They took each other into their mutually phoney confidences, and then followed that modern pas de deux, where the journalist and the murderer traverse the floor by pressing one another's pressure points, each person subtly fighting to lead, in what turns out to be a rather frightening danse macabre.

We always want to know the motive for a killing, but just as interesting, in a book like Finkel's, is the writer's motive. Indeed, Finkel and Longo sometimes seem like star-crossed lovers in a screwball comedy, falling over the furniture in an effort to hide their true intentions from one another. Longo phones from prison every Wednesday night, and Finkel listens, soft-soaping and buttering up all the while, gathering material for the article or the book that might make him a respectable writer again. Longo believes in a code of mutuality and friendship that Finkel is not going to honour in the long run, not because he can't, but because he has no real interest in being admired by a murderer, and more than an interest, an obsession, in being loved by his readers and somehow forgiven by his former editors at the *New York Times*. Finkel's account of all this double-dealing is riveting, partly because one believes the writer cannot at any point really see the moral horror at the centre of his dealings with Longo. And it is this: Longo is being dishonest in an attempt to save his life; Finkel is being dishonest, as he was dishonest before, in an attempt to improve his career.

This brings me back to Michael Jackson. His child-molestation trial in Santa Monica is totemic, not only for reasons to do with race and celebrity and gladiatorial combat, but as an essay in the terrors of modern journalism. Jackson made the standard mistake of forgetting he was a subject, in his case the subject of Martin Bashir's film: he thought Bashir was his friend, and Bashir encouraged him to think that, but when Bashir and his colleagues got back to the cutting room the relationship reverted to type, and Bashir made a programme that brought Jackson's relationship with children (including his own children) into question. In other words, he shafted Jackson. The journalist relies on a sense of himself as the recording angel, the interpreter of truth about the subject, but Jackson's own cameraman also recorded part of the interview with Bashir. 'Your relationship to your children is spectacular,' Bashir says at one point to Jackson. 'It almost makes me weep.'

In *The Journalist and the Murderer*, Janet Malcolm called this kind of thing 'the Wambaugh technique'. The crime novelist Joseph Wambaugh gave evidence for the defence in the trial she writes about, *MacDonald* v. *McGinniss*, in which a convicted murderer, Jeffrey MacDonald, had sued a journalist, Joe McGinniss, for lying to gain his confidence, pretending, for the sake of access and a better story, to be his friend and an enthusiastic supporter of his innocence. At the conclusion of the original trial, McGinniss turned against the murderer and wrote a book called *Fatal Vision*, which, in the manner of Martin Bashir, throws off all pretence of empathy and understanding to provide a portrait of the subject that is both accusatory and damning.

Wambaugh, described by the defence as an 'expert on the author–subject relationship' (chosen to give evidence, along with William F. Buckley, from a list that included Tom Wolfe, Jimmy Breslin and Victor Navasky), said that a writer was always wholly justified in being untrue in his relationship with a subject. Here is how the exchange went in court:

Q: Is there a custom or practice in the literary world about whether or not an author should disclose his views to his subject?

A: I believe that one should never disclose one's views, because it may shut off further communication.

Q: Has that ever happened in your experience?

A: Yes. Frequently [subjects] would ask me questions that if I answered them truthfully would shut off further communication.

Q: And how did you answer them?

A: I would tell an untruth if I had to.

Q: Can you give us an example?

A: Yes. In writing *The Onion Field*, I can recall one of the murderers asking me if I believed him when he said he didn't shoot the policeman, and I at that time had interviewed scores of witnesses and had a mountain of information, and I did not believe him, but I said that I did, because I wanted him to continue talking. Because my ultimate responsibility was not to that person, my responsibility was to the book.

Bashir would perhaps say his only responsibility was to the film he was making. Truman Capote would say his only responsibility was to his art. What would Michael Finkel say? One has to imagine that, whatever he says, he is not familiar with *The Journalist and the Murderer*'s famous opening paragraph: 'Every journalist who is not too stupid or too full of himself to notice what is going on knows that what he does is morally indefensible. He is a kind of confidence man, preying on people's vanity, ignorance or loneliness, gaining their trust and betraying them without remorse.'

Joe McGinniss cried when his subject was convicted, just as Bashir wanted to cry when thinking about how good Michael Jackson was with his children, but each journalist, in his turn, relied on his subject's innate narcissism in order to get what he himself wanted. (For Finkel, replace 'wanted' with 'needed'.) 'When the moment of peripeteia comes', Malcolm writes, the subject 'is confronted with the same mortifying spectacle of himself flunking a test of character he did not know he was taking.' Malcolm saw a Conradian fable of moral failure in the relationship between her two subjects, just as she detected it in her own subsequent relationship with the murderer, but Finkel's story is even more complex, owing to his need to use the dishonesty of the journalist–murderer relationship to restore himself with his honesty-loving peers.

Having got Longo to think well of him, Finkel moves steadily towards the completion of his tasks:

There was one thing I wanted to get straight between Longo and me. We both knew, from the first minutes of our first phone talk, that we were spiralling around the central topic, and that it was only a matter of time before I'd have to ask him about the murders. I forced myself to remain patient during our initial phone call, and then, when I travelled to Oregon and saw him in the Lincoln County Jail, I held off through the majority of our visit. But as I sat in the booth, studying his face, the urge to broach the subject itched at me with every conversational pause . . . I gathered my nerve. I looked him squarely in the eyes. I spoke clearly and assertively. 'Chris,' I said, 'did you do what you are accused of doing?'

His face remained composed. It was as though he'd been waiting for me to ask this. He was silent for a moment, and I felt he was selecting his words carefully. 'I can't answer that right now,' he said. 'But I think you know.' And then he winked at me, winked his left eye, slowly and obviously, as if to say: Hey, our conversation might be monitored so I can't say anything directly, but there's your answer.

The relationship can be seen like the relationship between a therapist and a patient, but the journalist is a struck-off analyst who comes across this unexpected, illicit complex patient, a patient whose love (and self-love) the analyst rewards with elements of his own story, knowing all the while that the relationship might prove to be his own professional salvation, a fact that wasn't unknown to the patient from the start, although he nevertheless believes there is something salutary and long-lasting between them. Finkel and Longo are entwined in each other's desires and panics. 'When it came to my *Times* debacle,' Finkel writes, 'I was too humiliated to talk intimately about the subject with any of my friends . . . With Longo, though, I could talk freely and candidly. Compared with the crimes he was accused of, my transgressions seemed so petty that I found myself gabbing away, poking at the roots of my behaviour without hesitation or embarrassment.'

Longo's 'charm' is mentioned, his good looks, his apparent confidence, as if he had much that Finkel lacks, which he does, of course: he has a great story, and access to that story becomes part of Finkel's drive towards his own rehabilitation. The fact that Longo wants to be a writer himself only heightens the matter. Finkel becomes his writing tutor, sending stories by Alice Munro and Lorrie Moore, and buying him a copy of the *New Oxford American Dictionary* ('which cost me $45.50'), as if the gift would begin to compensate Longo for the damage the journalist was about to do with words.

It looks as though Longo may have killed his wife and his three children because he couldn't stand being thought a failure. He set up a business that went bust; he wrote dodgy cheques, cashed them, and got caught; he stole a car from a dealership and eventually got to the stage where he forged everything he touched. Longo had a pure dread of embarrassment and, as a psychologist told Finkel, 'he desperately needed to look good in the eyes of others'. Finkel, in learning all this, comes to see how it offers him a perspective on his own terrible fears and embarrassments. Through Longo's lies he begins to see his own compulsion to lie: he has lied about being able to speak French, about having a brother who died in infancy, about having read *Ulysses*, about his prowess at sports, his ability as a musician:

> I've lied to strangers simply because it was exciting to lie, or because I wanted to impress them. Perhaps people who've spent time on the internet pretending to be someone they're not can understand – that sense of risk, of power, of semi-illicit thrill. I *liked* lying . . . I always thought my journalism was immune to such impulses. I wrote creatively at times; I condensed plots and simplified complications and erased some chunks of time, but I was sure I'd always stay within the boundaries of non-fiction: reality could be shaped and trimmed, but it could not be augmented. I had no intention of ever breaking that rule. No intention, that is, until I sat down to write my chocolate-and-slaves story.

Yet, although seeing this, Finkel fails to see that his relationship with Longo is more of the same. He is still excited by the lie, still wanting to impress. It is certainly fascinating to read about, but is it possible to offer a mea culpa that is also a piece of recidivism? In the case that interested Malcolm, a witness says that he always knew the journalist had the option of not believing the murderer: what he didn't know was that the journalist had the option of not liking him. That was thanks to the efforts Joe McGinniss had put into convincing his subject that he was practically the only person who did truly like him and believe in him. 'The flaw in McGinniss's character,' Malcolm wrote, 'may be that he doesn't know how to be anything but ingratiating.'

That's Finkel's problem. But disingenuousness can't easily be allowed to stand at the centre of a man's account of his escape from the perils of dishonesty. We might find Longo, as the jury did, to be murderous, lying and manipulative, but that will not automatically relieve Finkel from his own manipulations. He was 'in' on Longo's guilt from the beginning, but chooses to be disgusted by Longo only when the trial is concluding and he needs nothing further from him. Finkel has his book, his redemption, and Longo has the death penalty. Finkel claims to have lost faith in his subject-friend when the latter gave evidence accusing his dead wife of having killed two of the children before he killed her. 'I was mortified that I'd affiliated myself with Longo,' Finkel writes, 'that I had actually cared about him.' And later:

> He was acutely aware that I was retreating from him. When Longo was leaving court . . . we'd briefly made eye contact, but I had felt so disgusted with him that my instinctive response was to quickly turn away. Longo referred to this reaction on his letter's opening page. 'I do hope that I haven't lost you as a friend,' he added.

There you go. Finkel's instinctive response was to turn quickly away, but not, he might have said, before he had his story and his fill of access to the killer. That is often the nature of the journalistic danse macabre, and how silly of Longo not to have seen where the steps would lead. Despite his ambitions, the murderer showed that he wasn't a journalist after all: he didn't have the necessary instinct. Only Michael Finkel was Michael Finkel, and he rises out of the case with a very readable book and a greatly revived sense of self. Loss of life is a relative matter nowadays, and so is betrayal – some betrayals matter more than others. To betray the editors of the *New York Times* would seem to be one of the great crimes of the moment. One would go to almost any length to make up for it. 'And so,' Finkel writes, at the end of his travels. 'The last thing I want to say about my *Times* article is this: I'm sorry.'

On Begging

NOVEMBER 1993

George Baroli and I were soaked to the skin. We sat on a wooden bench in the rain; a green bottle of sherry sat between us. George stared straight ahead most of the time, tilting the bottle up to his mouth with both hands, getting it into position, holding it there, and breathing through his nose. I tried to roll him a cigarette inside my jacket while he spoke of Newcastle, of how he thought he'd never leave it, and then telling me stories of his life now, as a beggar in London. He tapped my arm: 'Times's bad,' he said. 'but good times is just around the corner.'

George talked a lot about time; mainly he spoke of how it went too slow. He was seventy, sleeping most nights at the Bondway emergency night-shelter in Vauxhall. When he turned to me, I noticed how mottled the irises of his eyes were, how patches of white and light grey jostled for space on them in such a way as to give him a look of shock and bewilderment. He wore one of the longest coats I've ever seen; it went all the way down, ending on top of a yellowish pair of sandshoes. His face was full of crevices and shelves, shallow nicks and lines of confusion, and his lips were dark and scorched-looking. He said he was schizophrenic, that years ago, in Newcastle, he'd had injections, but that that had all stopped. He said he needed medicine, tablets, something other than what he was given now and again for 'bowel-opening'. Lunchers marched across the gardens, crouched under umbrellas, eating bananas. He puffed at my damp roll-up.

'Do ye believe Christ is the Son of God?' he asked casually.

'Sometimes,' I said, wiping the bottle. He then did something which is quite unusual between beggars: he asked me for money. I gave him some change and the rest of the Golden

Virginia. He stood up, nodded, slid his arms into the long coat and walked off. An attendant, patrolling the path, strode up and told me to get rid of the bottle. And he hoped I wasn't begging: 'This isn't the place.' I pulled my hood up and made off, slipping between the charging umbrellas, thinking to find a decent spot over the Thames.

The railway bridge by Charing Cross, I thought, might make a good begging pitch what with all those mauve scarves and coats making their way over to the South Bank Centre. I found a plastic bread-board and, placing it upside-down, sat on it at the top of the stairs on the Embankment side. I stared at the ground, soaking dirt covered with fag stubs and tickets, lifting my head just occasionally to see who was looking. Then I'd ask them for money. I'd put a hand out and ask for spare change.

This matter of sitting on the ground begging was as far from my normal point of view as any I can properly imagine. It wasn't my life and, previous to this, I knew nothing of it. Yet as soon as I folded my legs on that bridge, the moment I looked up to address some stranger with my bogus little request, I felt I was no longer part of the places I knew. I felt I'd been here for years; already I burned with resentments that normally take time to kindle. I had never been among the walkers-past, I was sure – though, in fact, I had never been anywhere but among them. Without quite knowing why, I forgot all about the conditions of journalism and the vantage points of my own life and felt, at once, that I was genuinely and irrevocably under someone else's feet. In this frame of mind, you begin to notice things about passers-by that you would never, when following your normal routines, notice about yourself.

Searching for signs of pity, I see only embarrassment. In the seconds of eye-contact, some people evidently wish the ground would swallow them up. Others, newly elevated, puffed-up and tight, looked as if they wished the ground would swallow me. In my new way of thinking I began to detect contempt and fear in the faces of most who passed. I obviously looked – and the thought made me uneasy – like I'd meant to look; people responded in the ways I knew they'd respond; in the ways I responded myself when passing a lone, wet beggar on a bridge. There were signs of sadness and disappointment in some faces, as if the promise of a pleasant evening was somehow blighted at the sight of me. There are those who tell you to get a job, to piss off or to leave them alone. And others – with their 'Sorry, mate', 'No change, pal' or 'I'm in the same boat' patter – return you to yourself a bit, speaking to you in ways you'd thought suspended by the rules of the game. But perhaps not, perhaps they're just the kind of people who can return a glance with a glance of their own, and who prefer to speak when spoken to.

People say that they hate the way beggars publicly expose themselves, expose their need and their need to expose their need. The walkers-past, on the other hand, with their maddened eyes and embarrassed shoes, their twitches and blushes and grunts, expose just about everything a beggar would wish to know about who they are. In waves of the hand and the words they choose to spit, in haughty tut-tutting and superior giggling, a great number of those who pass by express their dislike of beggars and their general scorn of any sort of in-your-face poverty. Or that's how it looked from where I sat.

The money I was given that afternoon I got in different ways. Usually, it arrived in my lap after falling through four feet of air. I'd chase coins from the flying givers all but into the Thames itself; a few coins bounced beside me and leapt through the bars of the railing, vanishing into the water. The trains might rattle in and out behind me for an hour without my gaining a penny. Then someone would appear at the top of the stairs – usually a woman – and over she'd come with a disquieted expression, a look of concern. She'd ask, was I OK, hungry? 'You look very tired . . . I'm sorry,' she'd say. She'd hand over a pound or 50p and leave with a glance backwards. I'd wonder who she was. A beggar's relationship with strangers (i.e. anyone who isn't a policeman or another beggar) is always the same: a request made and usually ignored though occasionally met. I tried begging at different spots along the bridge and was glared at by beggars who had their own territory marked out with bin liners, cardboard and sleeping bags. With the light fading and the tourists elsewhere, I leant against the railing and looked at my hand, separating the coins to count what I'd made. It came to £2.86.

In the last ten years, street-begging in Britain has become visible in ways unseen since the early nineteenth century. This has coincided, of course, with the Thatcher years, in which the idea of society as a non-thing, as a fruitless misnomer, has come into its own: with the time it has taken the word 'dispossession' to become wholly familiar to anyone who dwelt anywhere near the wrong side of the tracks. To many, the large-scale return of begging – like rises in unemployment, house repossessions and the closure of hospitals – was a sure sign that things were not going well. But the most powerful mediators in this non-society have chosen to prove it a sign of something else: that the chosen profession of scroungers and layabouts, of wasters and filthy idlers, is on the move. Such voices boom loudly these days. It's not about economic ruin, they say, it's about idleness; it's not to be called poverty, it's to be called sponging.

'Beggars were once a rare sight on Britain's streets and provoked more sympathy than disgust. But all that has changed over the last few years as the streets of our major cities have become hunting grounds – not for penniless unfortunates, but for a new breed of professional beggars. Many of them are not in need at all.' This, from a July report in the *Daily Express*, was headlined 'Scandal of the Bogus Beggars'. Two months earlier, the *Mail on Sunday* had spoken of 'a sinister and violent new phenomenon which threatens to engulf the capital and, if police fears prove correct, could break out into open warfare as the tourist season reaches its peak: aggravated begging'. It went on: 'More and more respectable people are having to run the gauntlet of intimidating beggars, blocking their path, being abusive, spitting and threatening to infect them with Aids.' According to which report you read, beggars are making so much ('Benefit cheats who gang up on victims net £1,000 a week,' roared the *Daily Mail*) that jewellers, brickies and bankers are giving up their jobs in favour of begging. 'Scruffy Dave Naylor', according to the *Daily Star*, 'has got it made. He can earn up to £85 a day – doing nothing. He just haunts a tube station looking pathetic, and people drop their hard-earned cash into his plastic cup. For dirty, greasy-haired Dave, 19, is king of the hard-faced professional beggars working Central London.'

These reports – with their penny-dreadful conflation of begging with theft, social security fraud and gang violence – have taken their toll in public wariness. People are increasingly suspicious of anyone who's asking for money. London Underground pasted up thousands of posters warning customers not to give; warning them to avoid being exploited by the increasing number of 'professional' beggars. Opposition comes from unexpected as well as extremely predictable places. Churches, once the final and surest refuge of the needy, are turning people away; some have their own poster campaigns. Father Ken Hewitt, of St Augustine's Church in South Kensington, thinks beggars are, in the main, liars and cheats: 'They're all professionals, they know what they're doing. They've actually got homes, most of them . . . I'm not aware of any part of the Gospel which suggests that Jesus casually gave money away to anyone who asked.' Hewitt claims to know of a family of beggars seen wheeling a supermarket trolley full of alcohol. He earns £12,000 a year and reckons some beggars must make around £200 a week.

Intolerance of this kind may be striking, but it is not new. Unlike, say, dramatists, beggars have never had a break from being one of the sub-groups of the great British underclass. With bards, vagabonds, rhymers, minstrels, fencers, wastrels, robbers, cripples, rioters, barrators, ribalds, sloths, rag-and-bone men, COs, gypsies, dole-scroungers, poll-tax dodgers and Avon ladies, they are more or less permanent fixtures on the mythical list of great British degenerates. Whatever was happening in British history, you can be sure that there or thereabouts was some supposed counterfeiting hedge-creeper, lying by the road with his clack-dish.

In 1362, Langland was writing about the 'loller's way of life'; about beggars 'filling their bags and stomachs by lies, sitting by night over a hot fire, where they untie their legs, which have been bound up in the daytime, and lying at ease, roasting themselves over the coals, and turning their back to the heat, drinking gallantly and deep, after which they then draw to bed, and rise when they are in the humour . . . and contrive to live in idleness, and ease, by the labours of other men'. Acts and proclamations sprouted over time, sympathetic to the idea that beggary was in most cases the favoured trade of the impotent lush and thieving bawd. Henry VIII's statute against vagrancy proclaimed that 'vacabundes and Beggers have of longe tyme increased & dayly do increase' and allowed that justices of the peace should provide the true poor with limited licences to beg; anyone begging outside these limits would be set in stocks; beggars caught without a licence would be stripped and whipped; compulsive beggars-without-a-licence would be whipped, pilloried and have an ear cut off for each of their two subsequent offences. The idea of 'licensed' begging caught on. Holinshed's chronicles tell of a proclamation of the City of London which demanded 'that all vagabondes depart the city within five days'. Some beggars, deemed truly to be in need, were given badges to wear so that they might beg legally and be allowed to buy from grocers.

Today's equivalent of these licences are the cards given to the homeless vendors of the *Big Issue*. Launched in September 1991 with backing from the Body Shop organisation, the magazine's stated objective is 'to help the homeless help themselves'. There are over 3,000 registered vendors selling around 90,000 copies a week, in Manchester and Brighton as well as in London. A separate edition is published in Scotland – launched last June – with weekly sales of 60,000. The licensees buy stock from the *Big Issue*'s distributor for 20p and then sell them at the cover price of 50p. Most of the regular vendors I spoke to shifted around thirty copies a day. Charismatic, friendly showmen sold a lot more; those who drank or looked dirty sold fewer. An old vendor I spoke to at Oxford Circus said the secret was to 'smile a bit more than usual'.

The *Big Issue* seems a very Nineties way of making begging a little more respectable; with its entrepreneurial benevolence, its 'feelgoodishness', it can at times look like the acceptable face of destitution. (In the same way the Youth Opportunities Scheme and the Jobclub were intended to make unemployment more respectable while keeping the figures down.) There's a lot of suitable talk about giving people confidence, adding to their self-esteem, helping them to 'reintegrate', to raise their heads from the ground-staring position. Someone involved with the magazine told me that selling the paper taught the vendors how to become 'like tele-sales people'. It's an independent thing, though, and it shouldn't be blamed for doing what it can (and can't). So long as homelessness and poverty are not the big issue, the *Big Issue* will provide a small-earning option for those who can't make the money anywhere else. The real difficulty is for those who, for one reason or another, do not sell the magazine. For, in line with historical precedent, the benefits accruing to the licensed are simultaneously deemed undeserved by the unlicensed, the illegitimates. People think they're a fraud.

Londoners have always been worried about being exploited by those posing as needy. A writer to the *Gentleman's Magazine* for December 1796:

> In my late walks about London and its environs, I have observed with some concern the multiplied swarms of beggars of every description ... Impressed with the idea that more of these miserable objects are beggars by choice than by necessity, I leave them with the wish that our laws, or magistrates, would at least endeavour to lessen their numbers, or by some badge or other enable kind-hearted Christians to discern their proper objects.

Visitors to the Spitalfields Benevolent Society in 1802 were exhorted to take note of the Society's newly adopted maxim 'that street-beggars are, with very few exceptions, so utterly worthless and incorrigible, as to be undeserving the attention of such a Society'. The general fear was that London workhouses were attracting scroungers from all over the country. J. C. Ribton Turner, a nineteenth-century beggarologist, recorded the graffiti on the walls of the vagrant wards of various workhouses and relayed it to a Victorian public eager for confirmation of their views on the great unwashed: 'Private notice – Saucy Harry and his moll will be at Chester to eat their Christmas dinner, when they hope Sarcer and the rest of the fraternity will meet them at the union – 14 Nov. 1865'; 'Wild Scoty, the celebrated king of the cadgers, is in Newgate, in London, going to be hanged by the kneck till he is dead, this is a great fact – written by his mate.'

Sellers of brass rings, rotten cotton and fake Windsor soap, ballad singers, china-menders, smashers (who dealt in counterfeit money), mushroom fakers (umbrella-repairers), fraters (licensed beggars who preyed on women) and begging-letter writers vied for the attentions of a London public increasingly ambivalent about the Christian duty of giving. Lurid tales of advanced conmanship filled the papers: 'Many beggars,' Francis Grose reported, 'extort charities by practising Faquir-like voluntary austerities and cruelties on themselves'; and, in *London Labour and the London Poor*, Mayhew offered a chart of 'prices of articles in the begging line':

Loan of child, without grub	0s. 9d.
Two ditto	1s. 2d.
Ditto, with grub and Godfreys Cordial	1s. 9d.
If out after twelve at night for each child, extra	0s. 2d.
For a school of children, say half a dozen	2s. 6d.
Loan of any garment, per day	0s. 6d.
Going as a pal to vindicate any statement	1s. 0d.

Extortion stories, tales of self-mutilation and child-hiring, serial dramas of beggars hiding vast quantities of money, growing rich and sailing for Jamaica; some running gangs, stashing hundreds, and throwing colossal, gin-sodden orgies for all their begging pals and their molls: it was all part of the smoggy legend of Victorian London. And that smog, long-since vanished from other quarters, has never quite unfurled from around the ankles of the British beggar.

I sat on a bleached-out walkway near London Bridge, staring into a gigantic billboard: 'Pepsi Max: Max the Taste, Axe the Sugar'. The concrete walkway sloped down from a modern block of offices labelled Colechurch House. It was the middle of the morning, cold, with hardly anyone around. I sat cross-legged with a torn piece of cardboard in front of me covered with loose change. Passers-by caught sight of me as they came round the bend; most would cross over to the other side of the slope, aiming to give me a wide berth. After an hour or so of being avoided, an elderly man came near. When I asked him if he had any spare change he fixed me with a look of boiling contempt. Almost everything he had on was tan-coloured. His shoes, his jacket, his scarf – all tan. He came right up to me. 'You should do something about this,' he said, digging a hand into trousers that were slightly darker than the rest. He pulled out three coins, tutted, and threw them on the card. 'Sitting there!' he muttered as he walked away, 'Sitting there like that!'

The tan man's 42p was what I made all morning. I was, by that time, stiff with sitting, so I walked over London Bridge, stopping here and there to look into the river. It was choppy, the air was choppy, with sirens and horns going off everywhere. I was about to start begging when I noticed a guy sitting on the other side. He looked over: this was clearly his pitch. It turned out that he was seventeen, from Leeds, and had begged around town every other day for a month. Today was bad, he was saying, only 60p the whole morning. When I said 42p, he laughed. He'd come to London looking for family he'd never seen and now couldn't find. He was a bag of nerves; and wearing a T-shirt without a jacket, clearly very cold: he'd left some clothes with someone somewhere and, he insisted, would get them soon.

I walked into the City and begged through lunch-time out-side a building on the corner of Cannon Street and Friday Street, in the shadow of St Paul's. A lot of suits went past, a lot of bad looks, seemingly hundreds of them, perhaps thousands of shoes, all clicking, all nipping off somewhere. None of them gave. Tourist buses kept stopping at the lights across from me. I felt their eyes. I laughed, imagining the guy in the bus with the microphone, the tour operator, pointing to Sir Christopher Wren's construction, on the left, and on the right, pointing to me, Baroness Thatcher's. I felt edgy at that corner, though; it was too open; I was getting a lot of looks and the City is notori-ously tight with beggars, indeed with everyone. I pulled my hood up and waited. It came at about 2.40. A lone policeman carrying a raincoat.

'Are you begging, sir?' he asked.

'No, just looking,' I said, pulling the zip up further.

'I must ask you to move on . . . on you go, go on.' I went back across the bridge, noticing that the guy from Leeds had moved on too, though he'd left his cardboard behind.

There are around thirty-five drop-in centres for the homeless in London. Mostly run by volunteers, they each have their own target groups and range of facilities. They aim to serve not only those living on the streets (not all beggars are homeless, just as not all homeless are beggars) but those living in unstable, tem-porary accommodation such as night shelters, hostels and DSS-funded bed-and-breakfast places. Almost every beggar you speak to has just come from or is just on his way to one of these places. Day centres, soup runs and night shelters give some structure to the average vagrant's day: a simple version of the structure (morning mail, breakfast, car, office, phone, lunch, shopping, dinner, date, telly, bed) those with possessions take for granted, even on days when nothing's going on.

Over the 11 years of its existence, The Passage, a day centre for over twenty-fives in Carlisle Place, near Victoria, has provided hundreds of (mainly) vagrant men – many with alcohol or mental health problems – with access to food, toilets, showers, washing tubs and driers. Other in-house services include specialist advice on DSS and housing matters as well as the offer of help from detox and drug rehabilitation projects. The London Connection in Westminster tries to attract young people aged between sixteen and twenty-six; it has television, a pool table, provides free razors and cheap lunches. The Kaleidoscope Project in Kingston upon Thames aims to serve heroin users in need of treatment. They house a medical team who run a methadone programme and needle exchange. A few of the existing drop-in centres grew out of Victorian soup kitchens or Christian missions of the 1930s, but most sprang up in the 1980s to meet a sudden need.

I stood for a bit outside the Southwark drop-in centre in Paradise Street. There were Christian posters on Day-Glo paper behind the windows, behind wire. It looked like the youth clubs I remembered from Ayrshire, like free-standing public toilets or an old-style dole office stranded at the end of a street full of small houses. It was one of the poorer centres: really just a charity hall run by a few people who believed in God. It wasn't full of driers and free condoms like some of the others. I walked in, returning the nods of some men playing dominoes at a folding table by the door. A man with red hair beckoned me over to a table in the corner, behind which he stood fixing sandwiches and sorting mugs. A giant tea urn sat on the table, drips falling rapidly from the nozzle. A bucket on the floor caught them as they dropped; the milk had been added in the urn and there was about three inches of milky – almost white – tea quivering in the bucket. I took a mug and sat down.

The sandwich-maker came over and started telling me about the mission, how it was used by a lot of unemployed people just looking for somewhere to sit down. They do two meals a week, on Tuesday and Thursday afternoons, just simple things. The tea was as sweet as it was white. While we talked, a guy over by the window – a skinhead wearing a hooded sweater, with a bangle on his wrist – kept looking up as if he wanted to come into the conversation. I asked the boss if they say prayers. 'There are services,' he said, 'but only for those who want it.' Then the skin-head got up. 'You from Glasgow?' he asked, with a Glaswegian accent. 'I thought that as soon as I heard you talking.' He sat across from me and went on about how he used to live on the street. Homeless, but not a beggar, he insisted: 'No, I could never hack that. If you're hungry later, there's this place in New Cross that gives out dinners, sandwiches and that, from the stuff the supermarkets don't sell. I still go up there myself sometimes, sling a few in a carrier bag, you know, does me a couple of days.'

He'd been resettled, as they say, out of Spur House, an all-male DSS hostel in Lewisham. He'd been there six months when he was given a local-authority flat. He said it was great at Spur, 'brilliant . . . a magic laugh . . . bevvying, smoking hash and fucking about. It was a party.' I asked him what it was like having his own place. 'Shite,' he said, 'the rent's only two quid a week, cause I'm on the broo, but I don't even pay that. To me it's just a squat. It's a right fuckin' dump.' He tells me to go to Spur House: 'You'll get in there, no sweat.' The boss goes back to tend the sandwiches and the dripping urn.

On my way out I stopped to talk to a guy with a radio held to his ear; there was shouting and booing coming out of it. He asked for a cigarette, placing the radio on the step. We squatted down.

'Some mess,' he said. The booing had crackled into a report: 'Leaders of the main political parties joined forces today in denouncing last night's victory' – it was the day after the Isle of Dogs council election – 'Derek Beackon of the BNP won the seat, opponents say, by appealing to outrage among the local white community over the allocation of council . . . Dr George Carey, the Archbish . . .' The owner of the radio was shaking his head, twisting the aerial. 'This'll be the start of it,' he said. 'They'll all be at each other's throats.' We sat smoking, listening to the reaction of the Archbishop and the news of how Home Secretary Michael Howard deplores the event.

The tube to Victoria cost more than double what I had made

all day. There was a girl at the top of the stairs when I got there. The place was packed: it was a good spot. After talking to me warily a while, she told me she'd made a tenner begging over the last three hours. She looked very pale. From Bradford, she'd come to London with nothing but a pair of tights, some knickers, and a couple of CDs in a polythene bag that she hoped to sell. She was pregnant to a guy she hated; her parents hated her and she them. She was five months gone. 'I've been here five weeks and still no dole money,' she said. Sleeping in a B&B in Holborn – rent paid by the DSS – she had to be out by 9.30 in the morning. She had started begging 'to pass the time'.

Victoria is full of police; blue shirts flitting past on every side. I stood with a group of dossers outside the station, at a bus-stop across from the theatre where the musical *Starlight Express* plays. The group was constantly separating and coming together, splitting and gathering, like a flock of pigeons, each man going off to beg and returning, moments later, with nothing in the expression to indicate success or failure. We sat on a low wall, two cans of Special Brew circulating. Some kept hold of their own; drinking, as it were, privately. One of them – younger than the rest – was drunk and agitated and kept spinning around and hassling passers-by in a loud voice. A couple of coppers walked up to him. They began to argue. As it hotted up, the others got up off the wall, pointing and shouting. I stepped around them, at this point, switching on the tape recorder in my pocket. 'Don't start all that,' says one of the cops to the jumpy one, who's trying to pull away from his grasp.

'I've been here longer than you, mate, I live around here. Piss off.'

They got on either side of him and pushed him towards a police van parked outside the station. They then came back, moving quickly through the group, prodding and shouting. 'Beat it. Move on. Get.' A very fat woman, her face painfully red and bloated with drink, sat on the ground beside the wall, bawling. She'd no socks or shoes on and the soles of her feet were filthy. She held on to a can of lager, crying her head off, while everyone around her dispersed. One of the cops flicked her arm, trying to get her attention. 'On your feet, on your feet,' he tells her over and over again. Her face stays crumpled and red, she's gripping the can, she doesn't move.

I walked towards Vincent's Square, speaking, on the way, to a girl at the corner, selling copies of the *Big Issue*. She'd sold twenty copies all day; it was late afternoon. 'Everybody's in such a big rush, you know. I haven't had any lunch,' she said. In London for four months, she'd come from Canada and just couldn't get back. 'I'm here now,' she said, 'and I've been trying to get a regular job. Sometimes I sleep in a hostel and other times I just crash down somewhere or with people I meet. I don't do very well. Some of them selling this are, like, experienced hustlers but I'm not that good.'

Round the corner, on a door of Westminster Cathedral, someone had put up a poster warning people not to give to beggars: 'If you want to give, please donate to a recognised charity.' A security guard had been taken on to keep beggars away. I folded my jacket over my arm, flattened down my hair and walked in. The smell of incense and candle wax hit me immediately, making me feel sick. I could hear the sound of a communion bell, a bell I used to ring myself, coming from an altar at the far end of the church. I almost swooned. I swiped a copy of the *Catholic Herald* and made back for the door; I dipped my hand in the holy-water font and looked out at the square. A man was lying, full-stretch, beside a bench where a number of drinkers had gathered. I stepped out with the stolen paper and unfolded it in the square, glad to have stolen something and vaguely wondering if there would be a queue for the confessionals. On the front page there was an article headlined 'Cardinal Attacks Western Values'. It was a report on Cardinal Hume's address to a Prague symposium entitled 'Living the Gospel in Liberty and Solidarity'. The Cardinal warned against 'the consumer culture' of Europe and suggested that 'the key tasks facing the Church are the need for economic justice, the moral imperative to help migrants and refugees, and the importance

of combating nationalist pressures.' I dried the remaining mois-
ture in my fingers by mussing up my hair.

Laurie McGlone lay in a doorway in Victoria Street, next to
Oddbins off-licence. His face was coarse as sack-cloth and his
eyes were puffy and wet, blinking eagerly over the passing
crowds like a pair of old salmon struggling to shoot the rapids.
The bristles on his face were grey and around his hairline ran an
angry red rash. He spoke with a strong but soft Irish accent: 'I
make very, very little money, just enough for a . . .' He nods to
Oddbins. 'How long have you been from Scotland, then . . . all
your life you say, all your life. Well it's a wild, wild life.' I asked
him if they gave him dole money.

> If I puts roots down, but I don't, you see, I just keep going
> from place to place. I've been on the trawlers now, I've been
> in Iceland, and in Germany, all over the fuckin' world. I'm
> very, very bad. I just drift from place to place. You see, I've
> got a drink problem, and sometimes I get nothing for a
> drink. Now, I've worked with Gypsies and everything . . .
> One day a tall, a very tall man comes walking down here –
> down Victoria Street there – and hit me right on the head
> with an umbrella. He got me right here, cut me, and called
> me a bastard, a lazy-fuckin'-bastard-cunt. This is a danger-
> ous, dangerous job.

He had tattoos all the way up his arm which he'd got, he said,
in Trieste in 1946.

> I worked with me brother, we worked with horses. We ran
> them and we took bets. I did that, and then I drank. A wee
> girl in The Passage, from Roscommon, she said if I wanted
> to get off the drink she'd put me in a place, a house in
> Clapham for drinkers. If I came back tomorrow she'd help
> me. She was talking to me just like you're talking to me now.
> What did I do? I met a guy from Liverpool round the back
> of the church, the cathedral there, and he gave me a couple
> of cans. So I was fucked, I couldn't go to her.

Two women came past wearing fancy hats like they were going to a wedding. Laurie grinned: 'Which one's yours?' We laughed.

'Where will you sleep tonight?' I asked.

'I couldn't care less, Jock. I really couldn't care less.'

Begging is a criminal offence in Britain. Ears are no longer cut off for it: the usual penalty is a £50 fine or three days' imprisonment. In the Charing Cross area of London, between January and June this year, 708 people were arrested for suspected begging offences. Over the same period last year, 487 were arrested. Of those arrested this year, 205 were charged and 477 were let off with a caution. In 1991 there was an energetic campaign, known as Operation Taurus, to rid the area of beggars. PC Brent Hyatt, a member of the Homeless Unit based at Charing Cross police station, seems pretty certain that the younger beggars, at least, often live on the street by choice; that arresting beggars stops them from reoffending,

A beggar I met in Leicester Square told of being arrested three times. Twice he'd been fined. Each time, he said, he had spent a few days begging in order to make up the fine. In one month this year (May) the number of begging arrests tripled. The protestations of those who oppose begging, those – including many churches, newspapers and charity organisations – who believe it has nothing to do with poverty and the ways of the economy, have had an extremely significant effect on the public perception of begging as a criminal activity. Most of those arrested in Charing Cross were between seventeen and twenty-nine. Many more under-sixteens are arrested than over-sixties. A majority of the younger ones, say the police, have come from 'a bad background': from borstals, split families, 'abuse situations' or some form of council care. On arrest, this year, the largest proportion of beggars (210) in the Charing Cross area had between £1 and £5 on them; 160 carried between £10 and £50; 130 had between £5 and £10; 95 had less than 99p; and only ten had more than £50. In other words, a substantial majority had less than £10 to their name.

A man with an acoustic guitar kept climbing on top of the parapet on Westminster Bridge the morning I went down there to beg. As l walked up, I could hear him strumming and singing the Stones song 'Start Me Up'. He strummed on as a pleasure-boat, the *Chevering*, passed underneath him, going downriver. The people on the boat looked up, many through their cameras. The high-wire guitarist was coloured red; he looked like a well-weathered Highlander or someone who'd just finished buzzing a bag of glue. He looked mad and indignant. I closed in just as two coppers did the same. 'It's beautiful, the water,' he said to one of the cops, while shaking his head, refusing to hand over the guitar or be helped down. Someone took a picture as the police brought him down and booked him.

I stood at the opposite end of the bridge, beside St Thomas's Hospital, asking for money. Almost right away, even before the crowd had fully dispersed from around the minstrel-jumper, a man in a red anorak gave me £1.20. He stuck his hand in his pocket, laughed as he handed the coins over; sniggered, shuffled and whispered 'good luck'. I tried the technique of walking up to people and moving along with them, asking on the trot. They seemed to hate that, to be more than usually offended. I made another 70p before the clock struck one, then I headed off towards Waterloo.

I got 20p off a couple holding hands on a bench down the South Bank. They sat near a slab of grey paving onto which were engraved Wordsworth's lines about the Thames:

O Glide, fair stream, forever so.
    Thy quiet soul on all bestowing,
Till all our minds forever flow
    As thy deep waters now are flowing.

Further on, along the side of the Royal Festival Hall, I was moved on; not by the police this time, but by a burly beggar twice my size who owned the pitch, or so he said. I sat down on one of the concrete connecting paths on the way to Waterloo underground station and put a handkerchief on the ground covered with coppers. People passed by. I pulled my hood up and leaned back against the wall. Battalions of suits became like one suit – the skin of an armoured multipede slithering past. I tried to imagine the levels of anxiety involved in having to beg like this almost every day. The handkerchief, for the longest hour, remained undisturbed. Then I got two pound coins in quick succession.

St Martin-in-the-Fields day centre, at Trafalgar Square, was due to open at 6.30 the evening I went. I arrived there just after five and already there were two dozen people waiting around outside. An elderly man in a grey coat, with white hair and beard and no teeth, argued furiously with a stocky woman in front of the church. They pushed each other and swore like mad, each of them looking like they were just about to start throwing punches. Beside me was a teenage guy with a pony-tail, his head pulled down so his chin touched his chest; his arms were inside his jacket, the sleeves hanging baggy and empty. Eventually he tapped me for a cigarette. The waiting crowd continued to swell; old ladies wearing numerous coats stood beside women less than a third their age. A boy dropped a puppy and the stocky woman got angry again, saying he wasn't taking good enough care of it. The centre was in the church crypt and by now there was a fat queue of people all the way down to the door.

They opened up at twenty past six. The crowd burst through, some chatting in groups, others very much by themselves. Once inside, we took our places on plastic seats lining the walls of a long corridor with a concrete floor. There was something about that subterranean corridor that made it seem very familiar, as if I'd been there many times before, with the same sort of crowd, not in life but in novels – novels written eighty or ninety years ago. I wondered about the modern journey that brought these people here; the rites of passage from the world of carpets, central heating and pedal bins – of families and furniture and everything-you-know – to the familiarity of this damp, Victorian chamber filled with ugliness and dismay and unknowable sadness.

A volunteer came round with cloakroom tickets, talking briskly with those he recognised. He started down the other end with the first ticket. I was number 76. We stood up and formed a queue down the middle of the corridor. The air was filled with the noises of scraping chair legs and shouting voices. I got to the door, handed over my ticket and gave my name as requested. Once inside, we were offered mugs of tea and a couple of biscuits: quick sugar for those who needed it. When I walked into the main room the first thing I noticed was how the place stank of piss. It was a cavernous space filled with rows of burst armchairs, most of which had people in them, eating soup or steak pie with boiled carrots. A few of them sat on a table at the back, shouting to an old geezer at the front to turn the telly over. Some were shouting for football and others for a Harrison Ford movie. The telly gave out most of the light in the room.

In the toilet, a blethering Mancunian with no socks tried to wash his feet in the sink next to me as I shaved with a razor and soap given to me by the ticket collector at the door. Other people had showers and some tried to wash out some clothes. I asked one of the volunteers if he knew of a place I could get into for the night. He told me to go up St Martin's Lane, down a certain alley, and to knock on the only blue door. I stepped out of the crypt, passing a dozen or so people on the steps: one of them was allowed in as I got out.

There was a scuffle going on in front of the blue door. The stocky woman from before was now fighting with a guy she said stole a fiver from her. 'It was all I had,' she said. 'You don't steal from your own kind. It's not right.' I followed her inside and sat by a table, across from a guy who was pulling on a pair of trousers that were way too small. The woman told me she slept on the Strand, had done for ten months, and was constantly trying to avoid plain-clothes policemen, who were always, she said, picking on beggars. She said she could not get money from the dole because she had no address. Without missing a beat, she told me she was a lesbian who'd been raped five times before she was eighteen. 'The Jesus Army always get you,' she said, 'and I say, "I'm a lesbian, how about it?" and they say, "No, God doesn't like that," and I say, "God doesn't like that? Well, God liked for me to be raped five times and abused as a kid so fuck Him!"'

A social worker came and took me to a tiny room with two chairs and a small desk that looked like a police interview cell, except for the mysterious presence of a step-ladder and an oil painting in a gilt frame. She told me what to do to get income support if I was begging, and how to see a housing officer if homeless. I could speak to the DSS about short-term accommodation. But tonight would be difficult. She gave me a map showing how to get to an emergency night shelter in Camden and brought me out of the room. Through an open door down the hall I could see an old man propped against the wall. He was in the middle of asking someone for gloves and 'maybe a jacket'.

Over the last two decades, thousands of psychiatric beds have been lost in Britain. The former patients, now decanted into 'the community', can be seen on the streets every day in a state of profound confusion, often despair; left like the members of some schizophrenic tribe to wander aimlessly about, without treatment or support. In the first twenty-eight days after discharge from hospital mentally ill men are over 200 times more likely to commit suicide than the ordinary population.

At Bondway's night shelter in Vauxhall 50 per cent of the residents are alcoholic and 20 per cent have psychiatric problems. The dormitories I was shown around were crammed with mattresses and sleeping bags, on which men – all of them seemingly over fifty-five – lay sleeping or coughing or just staring into space. Many such people, ejected from bed and breakfast accommodation first thing in the morning, will eventually just drop out of sight. Having no connections, no family, and no medical support or supervision, they will simply amble into the stew of the great urban unknown.

On Friday, 2 July this year, a man walking down Cheyne Walk, beside Chelsea Marina, noticed something bobbing in the water. The dead man was thirty; 5 feet 8 inches tall, slightly built, with brown eyes and dark-brown collar-length hair. He was clean shaven, with irregular teeth which were otherwise in fairly good nick. He had no tattoos. His face and upper body were discoloured and bloated, but he was nowhere near the point at which he would have been difficult to recognise by those who had known him. An odontologist at the Department of Forensic Medicine, Guy's Hospital, prepared a report on the special features of the teeth, for comparison with the dental records of missing persons. When found, he was wearing a navy anorak with a zipper front and distinctive purple buttons, a black T-shirt, blue jeans and black trainers. He wore odd socks. The trainers had the words 'Royal Mail' stamped on them in red, surrounded by a miniature Union Jack. He had no money, cards or means of identification on him whatsoever. His pockets contained only one thing: a tiny book of Biblical quotes, two inches by one, entitled *Golden Words*.

Without a name, the dead man is referred to by Wapping River Police as 'DB23': the twenty-third dead body pulled from the Thames this year. Drawings are made of him, posters put up, newspaper reports and advertisements are published. The Post Office records are trawled to check if a pair of company shoes were ever issued to such a man. Yet nothing: nobody seems to know of him, nobody comes forward. Thought to have been a vagrant, a travelling pauper of unstable personality and no fixed address, he remains unidentified, destined, if no one who knows this man can be traced, to be be buried at the expense of the local council, and laid in an unmarked grave. As if he'd never existed.

A woman was recovered from the river near Embankment in September; on her middle finger she wore a gold ring with three white stones set in the centre. The tide had probably carried her downriver, since bruising on the body suggested she'd bumped against bollards and bridges before being found. She was DB30. Seventy-two missing persons matched her description and, as he talked to me about her, the identification officer began to feel that she might turn out to be a young woman who went missing after being discharged from a psychiatric ward at University College Hospital. I left him in his office at Wapping, surrounded by paper and photographs and dead people's clothes, looking for the name of an attractive, thirty-year-old woman whom nobody seemed to know. There are certain kinds of vanishing which will never attract much interest; disappearances unlikely to stimulate much in the way of shock or curiosity; the by-products of a society not a society, of a time not of its time, of a country spinning hellishly backwards.

Ray Dickinson does a Salvation Army soup-run twice a week. I met him – as a helper rather than a customer – after dark, at the Regent Hall in Oxford Street, on a cold Thursday in September. He was stocking the van with soup, hot drinks and sandwiches. Also in the van was Allan, an ex-homeless guy who helps out from time to time. While Ray was sorting out the hot water, Allan talked of the trouble he was having finding a job. He had worked, years ago, in catering, and he regularly went round to the Jobcentre in Mortimer Street (which specialises in kitchen work) to see what there was. 'They sent me down for an interview to a place in Cannon Street,' he said. 'I went into this kitchen, a right mess it was, and the guy tells me to start right away. So I gutted the place, scrubbed the floor, washed up and got the place looking immaculate. Then the guy, he says, "I don't think there's much more to do, why don't you go home?" And I says, "Well, when should I come back?" The guy says, "Look, mate, don't bother coming back, there's no job for you here."' He said he was used to it, that it happened all the time.

We called at the Canadian Muffin Co. in Soho, regular donors to the soup-run of unsold stock. The rain was coming down fairly hard when we stopped in some narrow streets by Lincoln's Inn Fields, where a few people lay in doorways and in alcoves by the road. We brought them soup and sandwiches and cakes, whatever we had that they fancied. They were mostly covered in blankets or cardboard and didn't seem to me far in enough to be out of the rain. We drove on. An Indian woman appeared when we stopped in the square, asking for tea and soup and orange juice if we had it. Further up the road an old man was sipping at empty cups and sorting through wet rubbish lying in the road. He pulled his head down as we came near, putting one hand over his eyes and waving us away with the other.

After a conversation about the various strengths of tea, I asked two guys – one very young, one very old – if they begged during the day. They were lying with blankets under the arches of the Royal Courts of Justice. The older one said there wasn't much in it, it wasn't too safe, but when you had nothing else it sometimes did the trick. They both laughed, telling the story of how, one night, as they lay here, the TV games-show host Henry Kelly jumped out of a taxi and gave them a tenner. We left some muffins they could eat in the morning and drove round to Waterloo Bridge. Three men and a woman lay on a raised platform under the bridge. They had sleeping bags, and cardboard boxes to protect their heads. A lamp attached to one of the pillars lit up the area where they lay as well as a fair strip of the river beside them.

On the Strand, an old woman with whiskers came up. She called herself Mel and slept sometimes on the steps of the Adelphi Theatre. I asked her where she came from. 'Oh, the East End, I think,' she said, 'I've got asthma, it's the damp.'

'Couldn't you get into a hostel somewhere?'

'I tried being in a place. I just couldn't get on with it.' While we spoke, a youngish woman with long, straight hair drank cup after cup of hot chocolate. She had tears running down her face and screamed intermittently into the middle distance – something hard to make out about husbands and communists.

There are many soup vans in Central London. In some places, like the Strand, they very nearly queue up to serve people. But the need is astonishing and people depend on them. Everyone I saw needed what they were given, and most needed more than that. I recognised many beggars I'd spoken to, some of whom I'd sat beside in the street, but none of them recognised me. Or none of them let on. I left Ray and Allan in the rain at Euston station. It was 2.30 a.m. and they were nearing the end of the run. I turned round before I got to the corner, and saw Ray walking down a darkened slope clutching a cup of hot something or other.

The night I left the advice centre with the mystery step-ladder and the oil painting in a gilt frame, I went to Camden as the woman had suggested. The night shelter is secreted on St Pancras Way, across the road from the Tropical Diseases Hospital. It was cloudy and inky-dark as I walked up the road. The pavement was thick with dust, as if there'd been drilling going on near by. Nine men stood outside the shelter, all very different-looking, most of them familiar to each other. The building is three storeys tall; a light flickered erratically on the second floor.

Pablo, the Talker, was telling the others about his day and laying out his plans for the future. I'd noticed it before: in groups like this there's always a stable collection of types: the avid Talker, the eager Listener, the Contradictor (who's sometimes the Talker), the Loner and the Oldie (who's sometimes the Loner). Pablo was the Talker. The Listener was keen to hear the details of some fruit-picking work the Talker had heard of in Kent. 'Thirty quid a day plus food; no bed, just sleeping bags on the kitchen floor. I have blankets – many, many blankets – every time you see the Salvation Army, it's blankets. You'll be OK for blankets if you're coming with the fruit.' The Listener's eyebrows were knitted.

'How do you get on it?' he asked.

'They have a list at The Passage,' said Pablo. There's much talk of dole money: its coming, its going or its being refused. The Loner's never had a giro. A couple of the others say they can't get by on it. The Oldie sniggers. Someone, the Talker, says that Friday's the best day to beg if you can do it. If you can do it, you can make a couple of quid. The Contradictor draws his mouth into a frown. 'That depends,' he says.

The door is opened – we are now about fifteen strong. The two men on duty try, not altogether successfully, to be kind. The one standing in the door holds a clipboard. Those who were in last night get in first. You're allowed to stay for three consecutive nights. About ten men go through the door. The guy with the clipboard then closes it and we wait another fifteen minutes. The Oldie – who's obviously been a bit of a Talker in his time – introduces some disquiet by wondering aloud how likely we are to be let in. The clipboard opens the door and asks for those who've never stayed before to step up. Four of us file in. We are asked to wait in the corridor so that he can speak to us. The second guy on duty comes out of his office and joins the clipboard at the door to help explain to the old man why he's not getting in. It's clear that it's not a matter of space but of some not-forgotten incident. There's a second's disputation in the corridor about whether someone should intervene on the Oldie's behalf. No one moves. The door is closed on the old man and we hear the rules: 'No drinking or using drugs . . . leave at 8 a.m. . . . be back by 10 p.m. tomorrow night . . . must complete a Housing Benefit Form . . . go on downstairs and have some soup and toast and tea if you want it.'

Down in the kitchen, there is a non-drip tea urn, plenty of bread to make toast with and a pot of lime-green soup. The chairs round the tables are the same colour as the soup. The room smells of over-boiled veg and Domestos. Except for the Talker, few talk. Most, like the guy sat next to me, quietly eat the soup in great, overflowing spoonfuls. Rolling cigarettes and staring at the table, a couple of the first-timers speak of the 'liberty' taken with the Oldie. Back upstairs, I completed the Housing Benefit Form. The clipboard told me that – at twenty-five – I was on the border age-wise, so could I show him ID? No, well I should bring it next time. They then assigned bed numbers. I was 5B.

When I got up to the dormitory 5A was already in bed. The room had two beds, was semi-partitioned, with a small closet beside each bed. There wasn't much to it. A massive lamp

attached to the wall, like something used to light the pitch in a
football stadium, flooded the room. I took my shoes off and lay
on the bed's plastic undersheet, listening to the noise of taxis
and sirens outside. It was 11.20. You couldn't put the light out: it
was controlled, I guessed, by the clipboard. The room felt
damp. The other guy was snoring and coughing, sometimes
together. I stared at the ceiling and wondered where the taxis
were going. Everything went quiet. I turned to face the wall and,
just there, written in shaky block letters, was the single word
'GHOSTS'.

I left the night shelter at eight in the morning, nearly tripping
over ten loaves and ten pints of milk sat on the doorstep. I got
the tube to Bank and lost myself in the station's connecting tunnels. I carried a card on which I'd written 'Hungry, please help'.
I squatted in one of the tunnels with my hood up and the sign
balanced on my knees. People immediately started turning
their heads, in seeming astonishment. Some stop a few feet
from me and stare – I can't tell whether their faces show pity or
the dull stirrings of verbal abuse. I sat for an hour, and made
around £3.50. Then two Underground employees came up –
twin flashes of blue trousers and orange bibs – telling me to
beat it. I went to Moorgate and pitched myself at the bottom of
some stairs leading to the platforms. The air was cool and the
ground hard and cold. Hordes of clacking shoes went by, birling
and squeaking on the newly renovated floor.

At Moorgate, at least on the day I sat there, two distinct types
of givers revealed themselves. One is a giver-despite-himself;
he'd Federal Express the coins if he could. The other more often
than not is a woman; glad to be of help, and happy to give coins
and food and advice. She thinks there's something wrong with
a society that keeps people like this; we're losing our way; she's
concerned at the way we seem to be going. She will often give a
pound or more.

'How long have you been like this?' a woman asked me with
a pained expression on her face. I quickly made up a figure. 'I
wish I could do more,' she said, giving me a pound and some

coppers and an apple from her bag. A red-faced man with gold-rimmed glasses gave me a banana from his briefcase; a beautiful girl gave me a cheese sandwich in a plastic wrapper and some change; a sick-looking man with liver-spots on his hands and face rubbed my head and told me I was young, then he gave me 70p. Thousands of people must have passed over the hours I was there. Most of them, as usual, would ignore me or curse or snigger. But it wasn't a bad pitch at all: the hours of asking and waiting had brought £18.86, an apple, a banana and a sandwich. That was the first day I'd made more than a fiver. And it was my last day.

As I waited for the train that would take me away from there, I remembered being told by a coroner's officer at King's Cross that eighty people this year, in London alone, have died by throwing themselves in front of trains. I waited for my return passage to a world of CDs and aquarium fish and beers in the fridge. The other kind of beggar, the real kind, goes for days without money or proper food. Many are mentally ill and alone in the definitive sense; out of touch with family, social services and the network of names and phone numbers that keeps us going. A tribe of the needy and bewildered, they march – now and then stopping to make a few quid – aimless and unhelped, toward some vanishing point real or imagined.

For me, the surprise at the end of all this was my lack of surprise. Whatever the situation thirty years ago, I'd always felt – sniffling toward adulthood in the 1980s – that my time was one in which the sight of a few people eating out of bins, and begging in the street, was acceptable. It was something that happened. And it never gave pause with us the way it did with parents or others who spoke of a time when things were not this way. Two weeks after that last day at Moorgate, I stopped outside Warren Street station to buy a paper. A beggar under a blue blanket reclined against McDonald's window. While we talked, about Scotland and about Wales, he said that he knew me, or used to know me. I joked about the unlikelihood and, itching to be in some other place, found a way to say that I'd never seen him before in my life. I was back among the passers-by.

The Garbage of England

MAY 2007

By the time I worked out the style of our death the leaves were back on the trees. The journey in search of rubbish had taken the whole winter long and now I was here with the bins. The evening it was all over I emptied the latest rubbish onto some newspapers spread out on the kitchen floor – a cornflakes packet and old razor blades, apple cores and cotton buds. Looking through the stuff I felt how secret the story had been. I'd gone looking for the end but had always been brought back to this, the rubbish on the floor appearing grave and autobiographical. The seasons are like that and so is our trash: you examine their habits of repetition for long enough and you begin to think of lost time.

It began one night in Camberwell when the orange of the street lamps was fighting to show through the fog. Alf started up his van and weaved past some roadworks, dodging the cones but not the sleet that flew to the windscreen and vanished. 'My goodness,' he said, 'if this is life I don't want it.' He was talking about the way he felt when he worked as an account executive in a marketing design company. 'I finally found out that it was only worth living for love, not money.'

'What do you mean, living for love?' I said. He ran a hand through his hair and stroked his cheek.

'Putting other people's needs before my own,' he said. 'When I left that hideous job I got a sense we were all interconnected. Freeganism tries to connect with people's needs – putting community first. In 2002, I decided to devote my life to getting the message out and living as sincerely as possible. Instead of using money and all that I wanted to tread more lightly on the earth. I took everything to extremes in my old life.' Alf is thirty-three years old. His friend Martin, a fellow Freegan, popped his head through from the back of the van and pushed his glasses up his nose. Martin is thirty-six and comes from Sydney. He said he was disillusioned as a teenager by the way everyone was obsessed with money and ownership. 'You've got to take everything to a logical conclusion,' he said. 'We've given up all our possessions, because, like Mill said, if you want to bring down a corrupt system then you might want to stop buying its products.'

'Yeah,' said Alf. 'You've got to fight the greed in the world by fighting the greed in yourself. Look. Forty per cent of all food in the UK is wasted. Studies say we're the biggest wasters in the world. And the religion of economics has waste as an important component in it.'

'Yes,' said Martin. 'True spirituality overcomes the greed. What we want to do is relinquish power. Lay down your life. Share what you have.'

We passed Peckham Rye and could see blue rooms, television pictures flashing in each flat. Alf and Martin were saying that the way to live properly was to resist commerce. Their philosophy, like that of many Freegans, is a sweet-sounding blend of Karl Marx and Jesus Christ, with quite a bit of Tolstoy and Gandhi thrown in. Not using money means that they pick up food from bins: they have regular haunts, up and down the country, and they visit them when travelling around to give out leaflets. 'We feel joy at all this free food,' Alf said. 'And you also feel disgusted to see all this rubbish in the world.'

'We choose our ignorance, bro,' said Martin as Alf stopped the van in a car park behind Somerfield.

'Do you have a relationship with this store?' I asked.

'Not one they know about,' said Alf.

We sat in the van for an hour or more talking about the ethics of waste. I must have got a little tired of Martin saying that everyone should share and that we should all love one another because I asked him how he intended to deal with people who are without virtue. 'I don't believe that anyone is without virtue,' he said.

'In the spiritual realm,' added Alf. 'The greatest leader is the greatest servant.'

'Yes,' I said. 'That's all right. But Jesus had a slave's mentality.'

'We just want to save resources,' said Martin with a sigh. 'It's more of a Robin Hood model – we're stealing from the corporations. We found a bin today with fifty or sixty cartons of milk inside.'

Everything Alf and Martin own is in the van. They sleep in the back and they don't have sex with anyone. I asked Alf if there wasn't a lot of anxiety involved in living like this. He told me that the word 'mortgage' means 'death grip'. Rain was coming down heavily on the roof of the van and we sat thinking amid the smell of diesel and socks. 'Suddenly, everybody in the world needs a dishwasher,' said Martin.

We pulled up our collars and walked over to the wasteland behind Somerfield. The housing estate wasn't far away – the flashing blue light was still evident – but there was something very remote about the supermarket at that hour of the night. Alf put a torch on a band round his head. He looked like a miner as we turned to where the bins stood, then I saw other lights, and a large group of strangers. 'Bin raiders,' said Alf. 'They all come out at night.' Some of them were immigrants from Eastern Europe, who had come to London to live the dream. A man from Poland had laid out five plump grapefruit on top of a wooden palette. 'Are very good,' he said. 'Not rubbish.'

Alf and Martin dived into the bins – the Americans don't call it bin raiding: they call it dumpster diving – and pulled out bread, vegetables, ready meals, packs of mince. They offered much of it to the Polish guys, but they said they already had enough and had a long way to walk home. An old black lady in a claret hat came round and picked up items here and there. 'Very good here,' she said. 'Terrible to waste things just like this.'

'This is England now,' I said to Alf, his face lighted somewhat ghoulishly under the lamp on his head.

'No,' he said. 'This is the world, bro.'

The old lady had a large family of grandchildren and lived not far away in Camberwell. She said this was a way to get along.

The men took large clear bags of rubbish back to the van and spread some of the contents on the floor. Alf wiped the items down with a cloth dipped in bleach water and showed me them. 'Look,' he said. 'Sell-by date is two days away. This one, today. Perfectly good to eat.' Packets of biscuits were lying there and a giant heap of broccoli. Martin read out some of the labels: 'Chicken and stuffing. Yorkshire pudding. Cashew nuts. Bananas. Three chicken pies. Yesterday.' The lady in the claret hat came up to the door of the van to ask if we had any butter or bread.

'Mince?' asked Alf.

'Yes,' said the old lady. 'Yes. Now, what nice boys you are.'

'And how about broccoli?'

'Ah, yes,' she said. 'Just enough for tomorrow. That's great. Are you boys all right for rice?'

'Very much so,' said Martin, sheltering from the rain. 'We've got everything we need. Every last thing we need.'

The British government's review of its waste strategy is due from Defra at the end of this month, but the matter is as much philosophical. The question of what it means to live a good life has become the occasion for personal accounts of what one does with one's rubbish. This is the way we manage news on the subject, with a growing and often panicked sense of what our personal habits might say about our harmfulness. There are other pressing topics of course, but the environment – and the very local matter of rubbish – is the pamphleteering issue of our time. Yet none of us feels safe with it, none of us knows exactly what to think; intimate disquiet about waste is liable to spring a trap in our minds. 'Rural England is where urban England now dumps its rubbish,' Richard Girling writes in his book *Rubbish!* 'Here it tips everything from garbage in landfills to fridges in ponds, broken cars and surplus people.' The *Daily Mail* says there is a plague of rats in Britain as a result of the lack of care taken in refuse collection. The government has revealed that urban waste is growing by 3.2 per cent a year in volume – faster than GDP. 'Despite dramatic improvement in recent years, the UK still has the worst recycling record in Europe: 27 per cent of domestic waste, as opposed to Germany's 57 per cent and Holland's 64 per cent,' according to a draft policy document shown to me by the Community Recycling Network. 'The average person in the UK throws out their body weight in rubbish every three months,' says Friends of the Earth. 'Most of this could be reprocessed but instead it is sent to incinerators or landfill.'

We used to stub a cigarette out in an ashtray and never think of it again. Now we think, where will the stub end up, the ash and the tip and the paper? We grew up imagining that rubbish was taken away, only to find there is no such place as 'away'. The by-products of our desires are hidden in the earth or burned to make a toxic canopy over our heads: we are aware of that now, and that awareness has grown to feed a spirit of personal regeneration. At some level we recycle not to save the planet, but to free the part of ourselves that is enslaved to the world's goods and the body's functions.

Some people simply choose to be more sensible about separating what they throw out, nothing more complicated, and I salute them while continuing to believe that the pressing morality of rubbish – the summits, the sea-change, the plains of discourse, and the brave new worlds of anxiety – represents a powerful turn in our collective mind. At its simplest, we are now putting the Sunday papers in the recycling bin, but at its less simple we may be seeking what Emerson called, in *Nature*, 'an original relation to the universe'. The times may have become ripe for turning self-control into a form of evangelism, sensing that our wish to be the planet's saviours is also a bid for immortality. We discern a new mastery to be enjoyed over the life of everyday stuff and we consider ourselves responsible for stewardship of the ecosystem, or the egosystem.

*

High above the Brent Reservoir a fringe of red, trailing light was spread across the sky at half past five in the morning. It was still dark on the road and the houses slept as the lorries pulled into the depot. In the artificial brightness of the 'office' – a huddle of Portakabins – the binmen were gathered around a newspaper. 'Here,' said one of them. 'Have you seen the new lottery?'

'Na,' said another.

'Breast reduction, mate. Tummy tucks. That's what you win if you win the lottery: cosmetic surgery.'

Les said he liked the early start and the afternoons off. He has worked in Harrow for more than a dozen years, up early every day and out clearing the bins before anybody is awake. He now drives the truck and considers that a significant upgrade. 'I'm the gaffer,' he said, 'but not really.' Les and I tried to make jokes but tiredness got to us and the laughter came slower as we progressed along the route. Every few hundred yards I jumped down and joined the lifters as they rolled the bins from people's yards. That morning the crew were only responsible for collecting organic rubbish. 'It's a nightmare,' said Joshi, whose parents were born in Bangladesh. 'No matter how many times you give them information, or mark their card, they still contaminate the bloody recycling bins. They hide all sorts of stuff at the bottom of the organic bins – like machine parts. There's no telling them.' He showed me one of the bins outside a large house; it had grass on the top and Tesco bags full of paper underneath. Harrow has a system of compulsory recycling: green bins for paper, cans, bottles, and brown bins for organic waste, which includes garden waste and leftover food. People in Harrow who mix the stuff up, or 'contaminate', have their rubbish left uncollected, and must pay £20 to get it picked up, after they've sorted it; persistent offenders can be prosecuted and fined up to £1,000.*

Les keeps a chart of the offenders and notes down their addresses. Next to the Rayners Lane Conservative Association,

* According to BBC news reports, some boroughs are now set to employ 'recycling police', whose job will be to capture and fine people who contaminate bins or fly-tip.

he tried to reverse the bin lorry up a dark lane and Joshi came up to his window shaking his head. 'Number 9,' he said. 'Contaminated.' Les put on his handbrake and lifted his pen, turning to me at the same time.

'That's a bad one, Number 9,' he said. 'Number 63 is the same.'

There was a camera in the cabin and I could see Joshi and Sam lifting the bins of the better citizens onto a lifting device and then the stuff being tipped into the compactor. Les started telling me he drove both a BMW and a Renault and that he used to be a bodyguard for the 1970s rock groups Slade and Mud. It was clear he felt he had led a progressive life, and he seemed very composed as he pulled and hauled at the steering wheel. By then the sky had become bluer and people were beginning to queue at the bus stops, heading for Pinner. 'A lot of the old people,' Les said, 'they get worried because of recycling. They don't understand the new ways and are afraid of the fines.' As he said this I noticed an elderly lady sweeping open the curtains of a mock-Tudor house with a two-car driveway. 'But we've gone too far, too fast on the recycling,' he said.

Next to the Jewish Free School, Les beeped his horn when he spotted another veteran of the Harrow refuse system, Fred, who was driving his truck on the other side of the road. 'Spent years in rubbish,' Les said. 'He's about to retire.'

'Lucky bastard,' said Joshi.

It took the best part of six hours for the team to do their round, emptying the bins and marking the contaminators, and the morning was in full flow as Les pointed and laughed at an England flag waving over a house in Hereford Gardens. Half an hour later, we were beyond the suburban rim of Harrow and into the Middlesex countryside, heading at speed for the composting site at the extremity of north-west London.

The place smelled powerfully of rotting Christmas trees. There was smoke rising from the composting area; the process takes ten weeks from the delivery of vegetable matter to the maturation of compost, and not only is it a fulfilment of local councils' commitment to go greener, it also costs a great deal less than sending the rubbish to landfill sites. West London Composting is licensed by Defra and is the biggest facility of its kind in London, processing 50,000 tons of organic waste a year. When we arrived on the site Les's vehicle was weighed on a weighbridge; this determined the price that Harrow would receive for the load. I stood at the side of the tipping shed as other trucks arrived and dropped their material into a large hangar, where it was scooped up for shredding. Already steaming, the shredded material is then taken to the composting sheds, where its temperature and oxygen levels are controlled. At the end of the ten weeks it will be bagged and sold for agricultural and commercial use.

Les was shaking his head. The inspector who examines the material in the back of the bin lorries before it is offloaded was not happy. 'No,' said the man with the clipboard. 'Contaminated,' and then he signed a sheet and handed it to Les. Despite their efforts the gang had allowed too much non-organic rubbish to be tipped into the back of the lorry.

'The people who are serious about it are very serious,' said Les.

'And what about this load?' I asked.

'It's not good enough,' he said. 'We'll take it to Ruislip tip and Harrow will have to pay to dump it there.'

'That's a pity,' I said. 'A long morning too.'

'Never mind,' Les said, turning the wheel and smoothing his hair in the rear-view mirror. 'We won't be saving the world today.'

Whoever you speak to, in whichever corner of the waste industry, you are liable to come away with the impression that soft utopianism has taken the place of militant politics in contemporary Britain. Many of these people were born in the 1960s, which means they are not children of the 1960s – dreaming of toppling governments or teaching their uptight professors a lesson – so much as children of the 1980s, a generation all too aware of the limits of idealism. Even the Freegans, for all their hatred of corporations, take it for granted that greed is seen to be good, and their ambition is not to gather political forces but to replenish the spiritual motives of their generation. And those who have joined the establishment – the politicians, the civil servants, the lawyers – speak with energy about ethical improvements in the absence of any notion of revolution. They speak of potential and of broader choices. They speak of personhood and of lifestyle.

Among these people the question of what to do with rubbish is not about ripping up the system, much more about fulfilling your personal goals, increasing the peace, opting for harmony. They don't curse the world, they compliment it with kind acts, and their attitude to a non-recycler is rather like General William Booth's attitude to drunks. The hardcore waste community does not hate its enemies, but feels sorry for them, and in every other thing it says appears to believe a new day is dawning.

Though much slower and much less ambitious than the lobbyists would like, the government – which speaks of increasing recycling rates to 40 per cent by 2010, when Friends of the Earth wants 75 per cent by 2015 – has not dodged the bullet when it comes to enforcing penalties on big business to encourage better habits in the way it handles its rubbish. Defra recently commissioned a report from the AEA Energy and Environment Group, a private consultancy, that addresses the question of landfill and how to increase the tax on it. No British person giving an account of their life would think to mention landfill sites, but that is where most of the stuff in the average life ends up. All the bins in all our lives have gone to landfills or incinerators. We have never thought about it, and now that we are thinking about it, say the evangelists, we can never be the same.

'Final disposal to landfill is considered the least attractive option in the waste hierarchy,' says the report for Defra:

> The largely organic content of food industry wastes can contribute significantly towards the detrimental aspects of

landfill (for example, as a source of methane emissions from anaerobic decomposition within the landfill). The EC Landfill Directive sets targets to reduce the amounts of biodegradable wastes (biodegradable municipal wastes) consigned to landfill – the first target has to be achieved by 2010 (for the UK).

Where the amounts are not reduced, waste producers will be taxed to hell. The government recently announced the scale of this taxation, and it is good and punitive, with a medium to long-term rate of £35 per tonne. 'This provides a very strong driver,' says the report,

> to encourage businesses to take action to reduce their waste sent for landfill disposal. Most noticeably, the landfill tax escalator appears to have brought about an approximately 10 per cent reduction in the tonnages of standard rate waste landfilled in the two years between 2003–4 and 2005–6. This shows that a key policy, closely linked to reduction of waste disposal, is working.

Calvert landfill site lies in the most beautiful part of Buckinghamshire, snug against a former brickworks. They say that there have been quarries here since the fifteenth century, when Londoners passed their rubbish to rakers, who dumped it in the Essex marshes. In later centuries people burned most of their combustible waste in domestic fires, and the dust was taken in carts to be sieved for use in brick making. Bottles were reused and plastic was a science fiction. The nineteenth century was the age of salvage, and Victorian Britain was a recycling nation by necessity: wood was redeployed and bone was ground down; ash was spread on the land, and the only things buried were bodies and vegetable matter. But by 1875, and the Public Health Act, the regulation of household waste had become a priority, dealt with by local authorities. The act stipulated that households maintain a 'moveable receptacle' for rubbish – the birth of the bin – and a charge was made for its removal.

The 1930s saw the rise of non-biodegradable rubbish and

warnings were issued against dumping. Yet rubbish tips surrounded most urban areas and were constantly on fire. After 1956, and the Clean Air Act, domestic bins began to fill up with paper and packaging (tied to the rise of marketing), and in the 1970s chemical and electrical waste became part of the picture. Overall, the move in domestic dustbins from dust and cinders to paper and plastics has taken a little over a hundred years and has changed the air we breathe.

Calvert has been one of the country's biggest landfill sites since it opened in the 1980s. April Jennings is a tough, science-educated woman in a man's world, and nothing appears to bother her, not even the four inches of mud on her boots the day I went to see her. 'It used to be a bit of a black art, the landfill site in the 1980s,' she said, 'but the science of it has improved and we know much more about it. We can recontour the old landfill sites and extend our years.' She reckons the Calvert site may have about twenty-five years left. The great buzz-phrase in April's world is 'renewable energies' – Tony Blair loved to hear himself say it – and the people at Calvert feel good about the electricity they are able to produce by harvesting the methane gas created by the buried rubbish on their site. 'We have the capacity to produce seventeen megawatts,' April said. 'We can extract the last bit of value from what people throw away.' She seems to shrug at the view (even the government's view) that landfill is at the bottom of the hierarchy when it comes to ways of dealing with Britain's rubbish. 'Everything is checked,' she says.

Her colleague Peter Robinson chips in. 'The whole area of waste handling and management is so much more technically sound in the UK than it ever was before.' He smiles. 'This country's history of landfill has actually been quite safe; it has served us well.' On the walls of the management offices at Calvert there are pictures of green fields and of tractors moving rubbish. 'It's all changing,' Robinson said. 'We're moving from a "throw everything away" culture to one of preservation and recycling. In order to make it work there has to be a shift in how we manage our own waste and in how we handle the costs.' I asked him if there was something alien to the British mind in the idea of making a fuss about what we throw away. 'Yes,' he said. 'People don't have that understanding – but it's coming in a big way. The UK is trying to do something in a handful of years that other member states in Europe have been doing for a long time.'

Most of the waste at Calvert comes in overnight. There's a railway beside the landfill and the large cranes and the ghost trains arrive in the dark with their loads of domestic rubbish from London and Bristol. Every day, five days a week, at least four trains a day, each train consisting on average of fifty containers, each holding fifteen tons of rubbish. 'That's a lot of rubbish,' I said.

'It is,' April said. 'We have two power stations running off this site. A third of the country's renewable energy is coming from landfill.' (The trouble is that only 3 per cent of the UK's electricity comes from renewable energy sources.) We walked into the heart of the landfill area and April pointed to the trees on the horizon. 'All the way to there,' she said. The ground in between was landscaped and looked pretty much like any English scrubland, except that beneath the covering of vegetation there were hundreds of thousands of tons of suppurating English garbage. 'It's like an apple pie,' she said, 'with the clay as the base and the grass as the sugar.' I wasn't sure if this was the right image, conjuring a hot, sticky, unstable filling and a thin crust, but April said it was the best she had. Peter Robinson spoke of the 'leachate', the brown liquid that is drawn from the centre of all that old plastic and paper and general rubbish, the liquid being purified on-site and running out clear in a ditch at the end. I could also see pipes – there are 450 of them – drawing off gas that would be harnessed for electricity.

We climbed a ridge of brown sludge to reach the summit. Looking down from there was like staring into a crater of the moon, except that the colossal indentation was filled with rubbish. The sky was very blue above the ridge of sludge and the carrier bags strewn in the mud. The crater was sixty metres deep and a murder of crows swooped above us, followed by seagulls. At the near edge it seemed there were Tesco bags as far as the horizon; I looked down and saw a bottle of children's bubble mixture, a squashed box of Typhoo tea, a tin of Dulux paint, a Capri Sun fruit drink carton: the recent detritus of an average life, and in the distance there were more plastic bags trapped in the branches of a copse of trees and blowing in and out like struggling lungs. Something in the scale of the rubbish and the size of the canyon dizzied one's nervous system: a metaphysical smack came with the sight of the layers of used-up stuff, like the feeling that comes when sixty thousand people shout at a football match or a when a million supplicants crowd into Mecca. April walked off and I stood on the ridge of the landfill surveying the scene. A dumped bath, a heap of carpet, a thousand empty bottles of orange squash, a hundred thousand legs of lamb, a million bottles of shampoo: it was all the stuff of life and it was all evidence of death.

'There are four thousand landfills in the UK,' April said, as we walked through the mud and the crows dived. 'This will fill up eventually: landfill is a finite source of waste management.' For a second I wondered if April had noticed the shock and awe on my face. 'Look,' she said. 'The best thing of all would be for us to stop making waste.'

'Then you'll be out of a job,' I said.

'I'll just fall back on my chemistry.' We both laughed and I saw a seagull (or an albatross) out of the corner of my eye diving to darkness on extended wings. A plastic radio was crushed in the mud against a box of unused Oxo cubes, and I fancied the bird had spotted the shiny paper and was seizing its opportunity. 'We have a lot of pest control here at Calvert,' April said. 'You have to. We keep falcons. These seagulls are notoriously bad for carrying litter and dropping it out there.' I looked over the trees to the place she called 'out there', the villages and commuter towns of Buckinghamshire, and beyond them the cities where people sleep soundly while a train carries away the stock cubes that they forgot to use and then just simply forgot.

We have to believe that the litter of commodities melts into air, just as we do, or else we would have to live very differently in the world, much more consciously in company with the choices we make and the mess we create. Life without rubbish would mean living in a state of ethical awareness that might threaten pleasure – threaten commerce – while never releasing individuals from the facts of the past and the realities of death. We don't admit it, but the idea of absence is a comfort to the present, for if nothing is away then everything is a deposit. If nothing is away, we are suddenly not dots on a linear track of time but in some sense are constituent with all that has been, or will be. That is not convenient, and it might explain why a real engagement with recycling can come to seem transcendental. It might leave people with the impression that there is more to one's life than one's life, and that impression is powering the mood of a generation. Throwing things away has been so essential to our sense of how to live that we forget we invented the process just to increase our pleasures.

Like everything else – like health, like famine relief, like national security – the ethical impulse to minimise our waste must be rendered sensible in business terms before it can be understood to be practical in any other way. The liveliest new thinking in relation to rubbish is therefore about the great financial benefit recycling brings – there are profits to be had, and this is understood to be a motor of change. The concept was essentially invented by the Japanese, by companies such as Toshiba, who came up with a system of 'total quality management' whereby the manufacturing process would build in the possibility of zero defects. Many Japanese companies are now working on an understanding that their processes will suffer only one defect per million. 'Transferred to the arena of municipal waste,' said Stephen Tindale of Greenpeace,

> Zero Waste forces attention onto the whole life cycle of products. Zero Waste encompasses producer responsibility, ecodesign, waste reduction, reuse and recycling, all within a

single framework. It breaks away from the inflexibility of incinerator-centred systems and offers a new policy framework capable of transforming current linear production and disposal processes into 'smart' systems that utilise the resources in municipal waste and generate jobs and wealth for local economies.

At its most basic, this means that a company that aims to produce spoons will have made a plan, before they produce a single spoon, about how to source the metal ethically, how to transport it in vehicles with low carbon emissions, what to do with the metal shavings, how the water that cools the metal will be re-routed back into the system, and how the packaging will be reusable. Zero defects. Zero waste.

Zero Waste may turn out to be one of the key concepts of the post-industrial era. It will change everything: it will change what you are doing now and will do in five minutes. Robin Murray of the London School of Economics has put the matter more purposefully than most. In *Zero Waste*, his 2002 report for Greenpeace, he peels our habits in relation to rubbish to the core. 'Waste has been seen as the dark side,' he writes,

as that against which we define the good. It has been the untouchable in the caste system of commodities. The idea that waste could be useful, that it should come in from the cold and take its place at the table of the living, is one that goes far beyond the technical question of what possible use could be made of this or that. It challenges the whole way we think of things and their uses, about how we define ourselves and our status through commodities, by what we cast out as much as by what we keep in.

If the notion of Zero Waste wasn't so life-altering and revolutionary it would appear simply sensible. It relies on absolutely no discharge of toxic waste and no atmospheric damage, but it also means a new intolerance of material rubbish. From the Zero Waste point of view, a society in which a person drops a sandwich wrapper in the street would be as unthinkable as one where a person in the street pulled down their pants and shat. Everything would be understood to have an ongoing life. At its best, it amounts to a wholesale reconceptualising of our economic and moral worlds, bringing the idea of 'away' into the social sphere of 'here'. Forgetting to do the right thing with an ice-lolly stick might come to be like forgetting not to kick a dog. (Street cleaners in this country presently clear away half a million tons of rubbish every year.) You would do it automatically because that is what you do, sensing, as a form of knowledge, as a categorical imperative as opposed to a species of choice, that nothing in the world is rubbish. Our focus, then, Murray argues, would be on the material life cycle, in which it should become natural for materials to live and transform and live again. 'From cradle to cradle,' he writes, 'rather than from cradle to grave.'

A recent issue of *Resource* magazine ran a list of the 'Hot 100 Agents of Change' in the waste debate. Standing at number 28 – one above new entrant David Miliband, the environment secretary – is a man called Andy Moore, who is head of the Community Recycling Network. The first time I met him, in the bar at Paddington station, he seemed weary but refreshingly non-morose when it came to talking about rubbish. He gives the impression of having spoken to everybody and thought of everything: he gave me a head start on some of the trends, and then, several weeks later, I travelled to Bristol to see him in his element.

At the Prince of Wales pub on Gloucester Road, everybody was drinking either Weston's organic cider or organic real ale. Andy had the latter and he spares no ire on the waste companies. I asked him what his first memory of rubbish was and he spoke about an incinerator that used to exist in Chapman Street in Hull. 'I was eight,' he said, 'but what I remember was a big warehouse with a concrete floor. In the middle was the most massive hole and I knew there was a fire burning underneath. It was a horrible place, owned by the Cleansing Department.' He also remembers the rag-and-bone man, who went through the streets shouting two syllables: 'ra' bo". He took a sip from his pint and smiled over the glass. 'Where there's muck, there's brass,' he said. 'That's an old Yorkshire expression. We're all Gypsies when it comes to it, looking after the bins. It's how we used to think. "Sovereignty," Georges Bataille wrote, "is the freedom to waste." At festivals, at Christmas, and every day, we waste, we give things away, that is what seemed normal to us.'

The area around the waterway in Bristol has been reinvented. The architects have had a field day, and you detect, thereabouts, the flurry of design competitions and the late-night glow of Anglepoise lamps. People have worked hard to make the place modern, to overcome a possible downturn in West Country parts and labour, but you couldn't say the results made it the most soulful place on earth. There's plenty of life around, though, and later that night Andy Moore gathered a few of his waste-industry honchos at a restaurant sited in a former Bristol fire station. Mal Williams is great company, a round, avuncular man who lives in Wales; Iain Gulland is Scottish and quieter, though not for long. He studied ecology at the University of St Andrews. Each of the men likes a drink and is bound by a sense of social justice tailored to new realities.

'Are they going to do it?' I asked. 'Is the public going to get into the business of changing its character?'

'Of course,' said Andy. 'And business is the right word.'

Mal looked through the candles and the organic wine. 'The old paradigm was "out of sight, out of mind," but the new message is more like "you create this waste, you can stop it". We are all defining a new kind of industry now.' He made it clear – they all did – that they don't believe it will be the waste companies who lead the way. The waste companies, they say, have changed for the better but they still have an old-fashioned view of how to profit from rubbish. Bury or burn is the philosophy, and that won't do any longer because the rest of the world isn't having it.

'In Denmark in the 1970s they stuck it into education,' said Iain. 'They said, "We'll invest in the young," and out of that they developed high standards of environmental protection. And those people are now voting. Next thing we knew they want 10p on plastic bags. But we have not done environmental steward-ship before now, that's why people think the whole thing is tough and punitive. But it's happening.'

The main point of the Community Recycling Network is to get away from the kind of shoddy recycling practice I saw at work in Harrow. 'There's too much contamination,' Andy said, 'as there would be because the methods are way too coarse and are propelled by the profit instincts of the waste companies. We are talking about much finer kinds of separation: not just paper in one bin, but different kinds of paper and no commingling of different materials.'

'But the main thing,' said Mal, 'is you must put value on these things as a resource. And you've got to give the people a shove. You've got to give them the stuff to do it with.'

'That's us,' said Andy. 'Most of our people do kerbside collec-tions, and we have composters, furniture collectors. Some of them are motivated by the environment and some are motivat-ed by social concerns and for others it's just something really, really personal.'

'Like what?'

'Well, value systems. Empowering people in life. Your waste stream is really the most visible way that you impact on the world. You can see the stuff in the waste bin and you know what you're generating. The thing that makes me angry is the way waste companies have been able to con local authorities – the con-ability of local authorities itself angers me. At the moment we're trying to achieve a better system: not just minimising the waste stream but realising value from it. Do you see the differ-ence? The government's problem is that its attitude is too much "end of pipe"; it waits until the rubbish is there before it thinks of what it's going to do with it. The real task is to design society so that you're not stuck with rubbish.'

Into the night, the group talked about the transformation of personal values in Britain and the state-sponsored murder of old habits and stuffed bins. Unlike the Freegans, they didn't look to God for guidance in the wasteland, but to Europe, where a great many communities already view past mindlessness with a sort of bafflement. The men at the table had mortgages and they believed in eco-business: they foresee a future in which the profit motive will transform rubbish into American dollars, which they assume is the only way the world will listen. In the end, it may be that the Freegans go the same way as the incinerators, made redundant by the smart redeploying instincts of big business, those forces that once kept each of them burning through the dark.

You know where it all ends. But how very slowly the sense of an ending is transmogrifying into a new beginning. I was reminded of the distance to go the first time I spoke to the public relations representative at the Edmonton incinerator, or, as they prefer, the London Waste EcoPark Recycling and Energy Centre. Edmonton is responding to some of the realities I've been trying to describe – they speak of treating rubbish as a resource – but still they feel tarred with the old brush. And it would be hard not to feel that way: the plant is burning household rubbish at an absolutely colossal rate and the world doesn't like it.

'I'm just having trouble working out what it is you would like to do,' said Wendy Lord, head of corporate communications.

'I want to see what you do at Edmonton.'

'But we're quite an old facility. I could arrange for you to visit one of the newer ones.'

'I'd prefer to come to Edmonton,' I said. 'Just to see how you're coping with some of the new demands.'

'I don't know, Andrew. Whatever.'

'If you need to know more about me, that's fine,' I said.

'And how would I do that, Andrew?'

I don't know if they say so at public relations school, but extreme reluctance can be understood as a form of aggression. (As can over-deployment of one's name.) It can also signal a feeling of paranoia or shame, but none of that was in evidence when eventually I met Wendy Lord. She came striding up to me in the reception area at Edmonton wearing knee-high boots and a frighteningly professional smile, part tolerance, part indulgence. I felt that Wendy might have trained herself to spot an eco-nutter at 500 yards, but she seemed to give me the benefit of the doubt and led me upstairs, where I was invited to sit and watch a video. The fact that she starred in the video did not contribute largely to my sense of ease, but in no time I was learning about London Waste's flagship efforts to clean up and renew. The PR job was happening on an industrial scale, but that notwithstanding, many people believe incinerators are merely landfill sites in the sky. 'The problem has not been with organic waste,' Robin Murray writes, 'but with materials which give off toxic emissions when burned.' Early tracking 'of dioxins and furans identified incinerators as the prime source and even in the mid-1990s, when other sources were uncovered, municipal incinerators still accounted for over a third of all estimated emissions'.

The Edmonton centre is owned equally by the North London Waste Authority and the private waste management company SITA UK. Far from admitting to being a blight, Edmonton sees itself as a model of regulation, boasting that 'the official fireworks display on Millennium Night was equivalent to over a century of dioxin emissions from our plant'. In 1996, the plant invested £15 million in gas cleaning equipment that it claims has contributed towards the reduction of emissions to the point where they are 'negligible' and 'insignificant'. When Wendy Lord came back to find me scribbling, she started to speak like something of an eco-warrior herself. 'Nimbyism is rife in the UK,' she said. 'And we need more joined-up thinking. In Japan, they'll think about waste management before they build the town. We follow a holistic approach, where electricity is produced from residual waste, and it all requires a new way of thinking. The organic waste produced by a town can be used to "green" that town.'

If we hadn't been sitting to the side of a monstrous furnace that day, I would have sworn Wendy Lord was one of the new evangelists. 'It's about the three Rs,' she said: 'reduce waste, reuse as much as you can, and recover value from what's left.' She counted them out on her fingers. 'It's a choice you – Andrew – make,' she added. 'Be informed. Think. No one wants to talk about rubbish. It's not sexy. We're interested in shiny. You know, I have nothing in my attic but a Christmas tree. And the profile of waste management is now being raised.'

Or erased. It cannot have escaped Lord's notice that the company she represents so effectively will be put out of business when Zero Waste becomes a reality. That is the irony that lies dormant inside the volcano: Edmonton talks eco-friendly – and is, indeed, as eco-friendly as an incinerator could be – but it remains a factory for the mass immolation of rubbish and that concept is antithetical to progressive thinking in the waste-management sphere. The logical outcome of Lord's ideology is in fact the closure of her own firm, as human virtue would have rendered it obsolete, though there might always be a greatly downsized role for the plant in burning clinical waste. As she spoke of the electricity that is produced by the furnaces at Edmonton, it occurred to me that perhaps the future use of incinerators would be to burn other incinerators, keeping a few lights running to lead us out of the dark.

We walked through the building, stopping on a concrete platform like the bridge of a giant destroyer (*In Which We Serve*, with me as Noël Coward) to watch the procession of bin lorries that swept into the bays to drop off their rubbish. Outside, I could see two huge ash-heaps, the latest cinders of the twenty-four-hour fires, and beyond them the high flats of Enfield, and I wondered whether an examination of the breast-milk of the mothers who lived there might not settle a silent argument between Wendy and the world. But that's not fair: Wendy was being reasonable and professional, and much of what she said expressed a truth about London Waste's progress. The heat rose as we climbed the stairs. It rose with a notion of tension, and the scale of the fires below began to occupy my mind. The whole place seemed to thrum, as if we were standing on a great and natural instability, a fault line, a volcano, whose threatening energy was powering an industrial process.

At this point we entered an immense hangar that looked like a missile silo out of James Bond; it looked Soviet and outmoded, it looked built for massive destruction, capable of unleashing violence and deadly force on an old-fashioned scale. The air smelled sulphurous and I looked down into a number of unspeakably deep concrete canyons, with grabbing equipment hanging above them and the litter of our lives heaped at the bottom. The grabbers were truly huge; each one looked as if it could easily lift a house and a family and all their desires and all their trash too and drop the lot into the flames. 'The rubbish comes down to nothing with burning,' said Wendy. 'It's magical.' The grabber puts fifteen tons of refuse an hour into the boilers. The colossus seemed hungry for black bags and boxes. It roared and I almost toppled into the yawning canyon when thinking of the countless miles of rubbish that had passed through there since 1969. All burned. Living somewhere still. Gone but not gone. A single plastic bag fell from the edge of the canyon, and glided down, all the way down. It felt very primitive, with the smell of burning trash and the grind of titanic engines a suddenly vertigo-inducing denouement to the mad logic of commodification.

We went behind the boilers and looked at the complicated system by which the rubbish is burned, and the even more complicated system by which the resulting gases are cleaned and made to produce electricity. It would be too boring to describe, but it works. I stood behind the bank of screens in the control room and watched through thick glass as the fires were filmed by a camera. The fire is 850°C. A large screen shows the chemical make-up of the burning rubbish – substances can be added to the boiler to counterbalance some of the toxins. The electricity creation is all basic physics, but as the control room manager explained it to me my face took on the look it used to have when I was doing physics at school, and I imagined there were bigger things going on in the world. I was still dizzy from the death-in-life experience of the canyons next door, and feeling too that I had visited a scene that one day will have joined the blacking factory in our memories. 'Local people just think the dustcart throws the rubbish in and it's burned,' said one of the workers in the control room. 'But it's much more complicated than that. People see the chimney and they panic.'

I turned on the kitchen light at home and examined the rubbish lying on the newspapers. Perhaps Bataille is right and a loss of disposability will mean a loss of sovereignty, but it didn't feel like it as I picked through the things and remembered the fire. The bulb in the light overhead might have an afterlife and so might the fridge that hummed in the quiet of the small hours. The tiles under my feet might stock the foundation of a new road one day; the kettle and the clock would never die. After putting the stuff back inside the bag and closing the lid I went online to see about organ and tissue donation.

Brothers

FEBRUARY 2008

When lilacs last in the dooryard bloom'd,
And the great star early droop'd in the western sky in the night,
I mourn'd, and yet shall mourn with ever-returning spring.

Ever-returning spring, trinity sure to me you bring,
Lilac blooming perennial and drooping star in the west,
And thought of him I love.
WALT WHITMAN, 'When Lilacs Last in the Dooryard Bloom'd'

Every time you blink there are ten flashes of lightning in the earth's atmosphere. If you were to look down from a vantage point at the edge of near space, you would see constant flashes from deep inside the earth's cloud cover – red, white, red, white, blue – a fugue of lights that might seem to warn of emergencies down below. Had you been looking on 2 May 2005 you might also have seen phenomena that were new to the planet's history. In the Atlantic Ocean, icebergs larger than Manhattan were floating away from the coast of Antarctica. A hurricane season was brewing that would break all records: Hurricanes Cindy, Dennis and Emily were gathering their elements, preceding Hurricane Katrina, which would hit America's Gulf Coast and become the costliest disaster in that country's history. But on 2 May the trouble was merely stirring while US aircraft carriers travelled east through the curiously cold waters of the Atlantic.

In southern Iraq, just south of Al-Amarah, the main city of Maysan province, the British military base at Camp Abu Naji was preparing for the night. Set at the northern end of the marshlands between the Tigris and the Euphrates, the camp is now abandoned and looted, but in May 2005 it was a busy centre of military operations. Al-Amarah has seen many reversals of fortune and opinion: it was once a hideout for anti-Saddam insurgents, whom he punished by draining the marshes. He also killed many of them, and buried their bodies in mass graves around the city. But by the time the 1st Battalion of the Coldstream Guards were operating out of Camp Abu Naji, it was the British army that had become the enemy of the people. Mortar attacks on the base were just part of the general grief, a handful of dust to be thrown regularly in the face of the occupying forces.

Anthony Wakefield, aged twenty-four, had a long memory of night-time patrols. He had done any number of them in Northern Ireland. On the evening of 1 May 2005 he was talking about his children and making jokes while assembling his kit to attend a briefing from the company commander, Major Coughlin. The plan that night was to leave Camp Abu Naji and travel in a north-westerly direction, seeking to prevent the enemy's retreat from an area under Coalition control. Guardsman Wakefield was told to provide top cover in the second of two 'snatches' – a V8 Land Rover, lightly armoured – which would travel the road out of Al Amarah in the dark. Sergeant Ian Blackett was in the patrol's first vehicle and had known Wakefield for five months. There were fourteen men in the patrol and Wakefield was one of the most experienced. 'He was a professional soldier,' says Blackett. Some soldiers don't seem to do much except cheer up other soldiers, yet they surprise everyone with their readiness. 'A good lad, who was definitely up to it.'

Guardsman Gregory Shaw says they left camp at 10 p.m. Wakefield's head and shoulders were protruding from the top of the second snatch, the usual position for a soldier doing top cover. 'Everybody was fatigued,' says Shaw. 'You know it's going to be a long hot night. A lot of people are shy of work and want to do as little as possible, but he [Wakefield] was always one to muck in.' The patrol could hear bursts of small-arms fire as they made their way along the road. Over the course of the next hour or so they met other patrol groups from the company. 'We then did a U-turn on Green 9 and Green 12 [combat zones] and turned into an area known to us as "India"; says Lance Sergeant Stephen Phipps. 'We then made our way through the Al-Mukatil al-Araby district. I'm not sure if we drove to Green 5 – the streets were getting quieter.' The patrol was about forty kilometres from Camp Abu Naji and the vehicles trundled over a dimly lit road. 'It was a sort of urban area but with a lot of waste ground,' says Blackett. 'A few buildings on the road, a few shops, and very dark. Very few people. It was one of the roads leading out of town.'

'He was happy. He seemed cheerful,' says Guardsman Gary Alderson, who was next to Wakefield in the snatch. 'Seemed happy all the way round. I was facing rearwards, he was facing forwards.' Two hundred metres short of the zone called Green 6 there was a loud explosion and what some of the soldiers describe as a fireball at the right side of the second vehicle. 'Wakefield fell inside the snatch,' says Alderson. 'I went down inside as well. I was very disorientated and can't remember much.' Lance Sergeant Phipps's immediate impulse was to get the patrol out of 'the killing zone'. He instructed the driver to power ahead, but the vehicle was damaged and broke down after fifty metres. 'I could see Wakefield lying across Lance Sergeant Newton's lap,' says Phipps. 'Guardsman Alderson was injured. Wakefield had a pulse but was not breathing.' The stranded occupants just stared into the blackness at the retreating lights of the snatch in front.

In the first vehicle, Blackett saw a flash and sparks at 23:37 hrs, and told the driver to put his foot down and get out of there. Then he realised the second snatch wasn't following them and went back to help. They radioed headquarters as their snatch rumbled back to the stricken vehicle.

The regimental medical officer at Camp Abu Naji, Captain Vickers, was woken before midnight and told to come to the operations room. 'A contact had been made and we had a casualty'. The blast had come from an explosive device hidden at the side of the road, concealed in a mound of dirt with an infra-red trip set in front of the charge. The device installed in every vehicle, intended to detect and short-circuit such devices, had in this instance failed.

Guardsman Wakefield was wearing standard body armour at the time of the blast, which provides protection to the front and back of the torso. Projectiles entered his neck and upper chest, the latter through the unprotected side area of his vest. A forensic pathologist later said the neck injury severed one of four main arteries to the brain. The material passing through his chest hit a lung and the heart, causing massive internal bleeding. He had no chance of survival. Captain Andrew Cox dispatched a helicopter to pick up the injured man and bring him back to base. The helicopter carried him to camp Abu Naji where he was ventilated, but his pupils became fixed and at 0050 hrs on 2 May 2005, surrounded by medical officers, Guardsman Wakefield was declared dead.

The last day of Anthony Wakefield's life was a deadly one in many parts of Iraq. At a Kurdish funeral near Mosul, two dozen people were killed by a car bomb. American soldiers handing out sweets to children were targeted by a bomber in Baghdad. As the new Iraqi government debated the Sunni cabinet positions, home-made bombs went off all over the country in a spree that saw 120 dead. It was two years exactly since George W. Bush had announced that 'major combat operations' in Iraq were over, an anniversary marked with seventeen co-ordinated bombings in Baghdad.

Scholars of human chronology might have noticed several other anniversaries that day. It is the date of Joseph McCarthy's death and J. Edgar Hoover's. It is the date of Tony Blair's 1997 election victory and the day in 1982 on which a British navy submarine torpedoed the *General Belgrano*. Soon after colleagues at Camp Abu Naji woke up to news of Anthony Wakefield's death, Lynndie England would appear in a Texas court that day to plead guilty to charges of maltreating Iraqi prisoners.

Many servicemen, British and American, were expressing disgust that day about the crimes of England and her associated military reprobates. One who did so was Lieutenant Colonel John C. Spahr, an executive officer with Marine Fighter Attack Squadron 323, based at Marine Corps Air Station Miramar in San Diego, but serving during the spring of 2005 in the Persian Gulf on the USS *Carl Vinson*. Lieutenant Colonel Spahr was 6 feet 3 inches tall and did a memorable impression of John Wayne, which lent him his call-sign 'Dukes'. His sister Kelly told me he wasn't motivated by politics, but was driven by a keen sense of right and wrong. 'Those top pilots are all alike,' she said. 'They are not available. That's why a lot of them are single or marry late. They never really talked about what they did: there are things John did in the line of duty that I knew he would never talk about. But he said that being in the jet was like being inside his own skin.'

At 7 p.m. – eighteen hours after Guardsman Anthony Wake-field was pronounced dead – John C. Spahr climbed the ladder onto the flight deck of USS *Carl Vinson* and walked to his F/A-18 Hornet. Lance Corporal Lindsay, who did final checks on Spahr's jet that evening, said he came out onto the flight deck smiling and joking with his fellow Marines. The ship is more than 1,000 feet long and can carry 5,500 personnel; its motto *Vis Per Mare*, 'strength from the sea'. A major carrier is more like a floating town, often surrounded with smaller ships serving as warehouses. Lieutenant Colonel Spahr and his colleague Marine Captain Kelly Hinz had their orders: they would fly into south-central Baghdad and support the Marines on the ground, many of whom were fighting insurgents and taking sniper fire. Lieutenant Colonel Spahr was more than familiar with the journey. He had been the first pilot to fly into Baghdad on the night of 21 March 2003 – the first of 1,700 sorties flown by the US Air Force – at the beginning of the campaign called Shock and Awe. Launching from the aircraft carrier, 'You go from about zero to 150 miles an hour in less than two seconds,' says Captain Daron Youngberg, a colleague of Spahr and Hinz. The pilots left behind a series of signalmen scurrying on deck as each rose and tilted their $55-million plane over the empty horizon. Other pilots watched the pair ascend from the *Carl Vinson*: 'There goes Dukes', said one of them whom I later spoke to. 'He was the best Top Gun pilot of his generation, and what I would call a complete man,' he told me.

I looked at hundreds of pictures of John Spahr over the months I spent looking for his story. Many of them showed him in the cockpit of his fighter plane: one with his visor down and his thumb aloft as he waited to launch from the carrier; another in the blue sky as he saw off some Russian jets; and yet another, looking focused and fit, under a message which said, 'Do One Thing Every Day That Scares You'. On 2 May the two pilots were flying at 26,000 feet, high over fawn-coloured houses south of the Tigris, the river that stretches towards Al-Amarah. Lieutenant Colonel Hunter Hobson, who had been with Spahr at flight school and later ended up in the same squadron, the famous 'Death Rattlers' 323, told me Spahr had what few people have: 'an amazing ability in the airplane'. When I spoke to Hobson he was at the Miramar base at San Diego. 'When you're flying complex, multi-million-dollar aircraft, hand–eye co-ordination is crucial,' he said. 'You have to know how to use that machine lethally. The tangible difference with John Spahr was his athletic ability. And you know, being in charge of that machine – it's exactly where people like John and me need to be. All the training is for that moment. If you had to choose one place for it to end, it wouldn't be in a hospital: it would be up there.'

Hobson had been flying the same course as Spahr and Hinz that night but he was called back and the others went on to refuel in the air. The conditions were terrible, an ugly sandstorm, low visibility, though Hobson says the weather was better in Basra. 'There was lightning,' said Hobson, 'and after the refuelling John and Kelly lost sight of each other.' It seems that Lieutenant Colonel Spahr was behind and below Captain Hinz when Hinz's plane suddenly dropped fifty feet and slowed, at which point the planes collided. Both men were killed. Hobson and others believe that the pilots ejected, but an F/A-18 parachute was unlikely to deploy effectively at that height and in those stormy conditions. Lieutenant Colonel Spahr's life may have ended at the moment of collision, but there are signs he died on impact with the ground. He fell more than 25,000 feet to the desert, where his body lay, still strapped into his ejector seat, until it was recovered the following day. 'That night will never leave my mind,' said his sister Sabrina when I met her in Philadelphia. 'I feel I need to know exactly what happened to John so I can properly empathise with him in those final moments over Iraq.'

At the bus stop in Newcastle, people stood with damp hair and stared into space. The buses going east in the direction of Heaton were half full in the morning and nobody spoke. When I arrived at the house of Paul Wakefield I immediately saw a picture of his handsome younger brother on the coffee table. 'He was my bodyguard,' said Paul. 'He was always quite tough, but brave. He was my hero and he always will be.' Paul answered the door in his pyjamas and went off to grill some bacon. 'He was too good for most people,' he said from the kitchen. 'I don't think I'll ever meet anyone who could compete with my brother.'

The Jeremy Kyle Show was blaring on television. 'You Abandoned Your Baby When He Was Two Years Old,' it said on the screen, and all the people, audience and guests, looked angrily compliant or defiant. Paul's sitting room smelled of fresh ironing and there were plastic bags from Primark and Iceland along one wall, with Misty the cat easing around them and pawing the legs of his pyjama trousers. Paul threw a dismayed look at the TV and stroked the cat. 'It would be the best thing they ever did if they left their children alone,' he said. On the pale wooden mantelpiece, there was a Girls Aloud CD and a photograph of Paul and Anthony's late grandmother standing outside her house with a birthday cake.

'My epilepsy started when my grandmother died,' he said. The doctor gave him carbamazepine, an anti-convulsant, but

Paul is reluctant to take it because he thinks it will aggravate his weight problem. He is twenty-eight and gay, with a part-time job in Marks & Spencer. 'Anthony lived with me here when he split up with his wife,' he said. 'And it was a happy time, d'yer know what I mean? When my brother died in Iraq I think I just fell to pieces, to be quite honest. I had to take anti-depressants. It kills me to think that someone as strong and beautiful as Anthony could lose his life just like that. The army's after-care service is rubbish. At the time, they say they're going to give you the world but they don't.'

The last thing Anthony Wakefield saw in life was dimly lit waste ground, a road going out of town at the edge of Al-Amarah. But the sight could not have been unfamiliar to him: he grew up in a similar place in the north of England, in the depressed area of Walker, where he was born on 20 August 1980. Paul was almost exactly a year older, and the brothers were always 'the boys'. Their father Jimmy Wakefield died of a heart attack when Anthony was four; he'd been beaten up in the street one day and died in the armchair of their house in Walker Road, aged forty. Paul says their mother abandoned them at that time and that things have never really been right between them since. She still lives in the area. 'Anthony and I went to live with my grandparents,' he said. 'My grandmother was from Greenock in Scotland and my grandfather, he was from a mining village in Durham.' But they were really brought up by their Aunt Emily and Uncle Danny. When I went to see Emily, her house in Apple Tree Gardens was teeming with porcelain cats. 'Anthony really loved army films', she said. 'He watched *Platoon* every other day and he kept army films under his bed. My husband Danny bought him combat trousers when he was about seven – him and Paul – and you couldn't get them off him to wash them. When Anthony wore his out he stole Paul's to wear.'

Emily showed me photographs of the boys at that age. I could see from the photos the ubiquity of the combat trousers, and a certain fearfulness in Anthony's face. 'When his mam left and their dad died,' said Emily, 'I think Anthony was left with the feeling that if he got too close to people they would leave him.'

The boys were 'injured-seeming' when they first arrived, said a teacher at their old school. Anthony was the more outgoing but he was clearly troubled when his grandfather died suddenly in 1987, while queuing for unemployment benefit. Anthony liked football and was always easy and popular with everyone. The boys didn't see much of their mother (she had another family) and, as the years passed, their grandmother's people, whom Paul calls 'my family', were estranged from her. Paul was initially keen to steer me away from her, which wasn't hard, as she carefully steered away herself.

Anthony was always very good-looking, and in childhood pictures is often jumping or running. On a trip to Holy Island, Anthony is casting himself about, seeming to look for adventure or entertainment, while Paul always appears to be retiring from the scene. 'It was like he was the older brother,' said Paul. 'And eventually, telling him I was gay was just like borrowing a cup of sugar. Anthony just said, "I know. I used to share a room with you, Paul. I don't care." When Anthony was next to me I felt about twenty feet tall, d'yer know what I mean?'

Sister Josepha, the headmistress of St Vincent's Primary School, can still remember the boys coming to the gate for the first time. 'Anthony was so neat and tidy,' she said. 'Walking up with their grandmother, you could just feel the pain. I just wanted to bring them in and look after them; they seemed so small and so tentative. Anthony wasn't strong educationally. You know the way some children are . . . not shell-shocked, but frozen somehow.'

St Vincent's was built in 1932 as a result of the voluntary efforts of local Catholics. It is a small school in a difficult area, and, according to prideful lore, working men were known to have stolen building materials from the Tyneside shipyards to help with its construction. The day I went to see her, Sister Josepha was wearing sandals and a black wimple, and her eyes smiled through gold-rimmed spectacles. Behind her stood a large print of the Virgin and Child. 'There was an awakening with Anthony,' she said. 'He developed into a bit of a monkey and people wanted to be with him. It was just too sad. When I heard Anthony had gone into the army I said, "No!" His whole physique was so thin and I couldn't imagine him in that macho world.'

Sister Josepha showed me some old registers and school photographs of Anthony. His hair was light brown and the headmistress remembered the way he suddenly just burst out of his shell and became popular. 'But he wasn't the sort of boy you had to check,' she said. Listening to her talk of her fears about Iraq and compare the loss of young men to the devastations of the First World War, my eye fell on an open bible next to her. The passage was from Luke: 'Many have undertaken to draw up an account of the things that have been fulfilled among us, just as they were handed down to us by those who from the first were eye-witnesses and servants of the Word.'

Memory was the issue for Mr Simpson. A former maths teacher at the school, he now suffers from Parkinson's disease and he said he found it difficult to settle and remember things. Mr Simpson sat in a high-backed chair wearing purple pyjamas. His living room was small but it housed a great many bibles, which he sat in front of, his arms flailing and his legs jerking as he tried to clean his glasses and speak to me about Anthony. It seemed an incredible effort and I asked him if he'd like to take a rest. 'No,' he said. 'They were great dancers, the girls in Anthony's year. He never fought at school or anything like that. I think I had him as a full-back on the football team.'

Paul leaned in to Mr Simpson's chair. 'Can I ask you a question?' he said. 'Can I ask you what you thought of me when I was a kid?'

'Nice,' said Mr Simpson, rocking. 'A quiet boy.'

Brian Simpson's sister looks after him. She brought us tea and a plastic tub of biscuits. 'I remember,' he said. 'I remember' – and his hands beat a semaphore, as if guiding the words into the room – 'that Anthony would walk up at the end of the day and stand at my classroom door, showing his big smile. I remember several times he came up like that and I drew, with chalk, three stripes on the sleeve of his blazer. He seemed to like that, the stripes.'

John C. Spahr was born on 9 January 1963 at Our Lady of Lourdes Hospital in Camden, New Jersey. His mother, Eileen, is the eldest of her Irish family, the Kellys, who came to Boston from Ireland before the Second World War. Eileen married Ronald Charles Spahr of Philadelphia, the son of German immigrants, and in the late 1950s the couple moved to a three-bedroom colonial house in Cherry Hill, New Jersey, which is fairly close to Philadelphia. Everyone you ask speaks of the Spahrs as a classic American post-war family, moderately affluent and natively tough, putting great stock in education, sports, mealtimes, prayers, memories, and earning money. It is the kind of American family that knows its European origins, each generation doing a little better than the one before, while remembering where they came from. The Spahrs could always dilute conventionality with a few drinks, but overall they gleam with a sense of family duty, a common purpose, which might sometimes have chimed with the national mood.

It was obvious from babyhood that John Spahr was going to be big. He filled the crib and was often irate at first, but before he was three years old his gentleness had begun to assert itself. He was Ronnie and Eileen's first boy – their fourth child – and in all the pictures he appears placid and willing to be charming. Yet there always appears to have been something reticent about him; on his first day at kindergarten, as he left his mother and faced the new doors, he turned and said to her, 'What's my name?'

'We were the house in the neighbourhood that all the kids would gravitate to,' says Sabrina, his sister. 'I guess being the house on the street with the largest number of kids was the reason, but if you ask us, even today, we'd say it was because we were the most fun.' Dinner always happened at 5.30 p.m. and everybody remembers Eileen laying out the food on seven plates. They all said 'please' – always twice, 'Mother, may I please be excused from the table, please?' – and their father would never say much. Before the children left for the bus every day, the whole family would kneel down in a circle in the middle of the carpet. 'In the name of the Father and of the Son and of the Holy Spirit,' they said, 'Good Morning, Dear God, thank you for another lovely, happy day. God Bless Mommy and Daddy and all my brothers and sisters. Amen.' Then off they would go down the path with their satchels and lunches in brown paper bags, each with his or her name marked on them: Kelly, Sabrina, Tracy, John, and Stephen. They liked to build a snow wall in the yard at Christmas, to battle the Burcher boys across the street. And they had Easter outfits and lots of swimming at the beach in summer and every kind of sport you can imagine. It sounds like the world of the Kennedys, and not just because of their Irishness. It's that American open-air life, that instinctive response to conditions outside.

Early on, it became obvious that John was gifted at sports. He was peaceful but determined. When he was trying to learn to ride a bike, he just fell off and got on, fell off and got on, until finally he mastered it. For John's father, the great hope was that his son might become an athlete. Some of the siblings feel today that the pressure to succeed was almost too much, but Ronnie would get up with John at five in the morning and drive him down to the boathouse, just to see him row. It was Ronnie's dream that his eldest son prove his specialness that way, perhaps exceeding hopes he once had for himself.

When I turned up in Cherry Hill, the lawns were already twinkling for Christmas. It was not so much a matter of keeping up with the Joneses as showing the Joneses that some values were held in common, the wire Santas and flashing sleighs a signal of consistency. Eileen Spahr answered the door in a Chanel suit and a beautiful silk blouse; there was something rather resplendent about her looks and her Irish sense of rules. She appeared to aim for correctness – or perfection, to judge by her hair and her nails, her teeth and her sense of manners – but a merry air of devilment occasionally rises as if from her genes. Mrs Spahr made me a cup of tea and set it down in a green cup. She has lived in that house for almost fifty years, and the bustle has gone. Her husband and her elder son are dead and the others are out there prospecting for happiness, while Mrs Spahr maintains a sense of style among the lonely hours.

'Ronnie was passionate about sports,' she said. 'My husband was an intense person.' Mrs Spahr is a keen reader and she asked me several questions about books I had written and pieces I'd done. She had never allowed a writer into the house before and wanted to be sure she could handle it. She is intelligent enough to know that other people's writing can offer disclosures that may be a little difficult to bear if you are close to the subject, but the Irish in her wanted to speak and pack up her troubles. 'Oh, yeah,' she said, when I asked her if John was fixated on pleasing his parents. 'And it wasn't a burden for him. He wanted to be a good guy. He said to his brother once, "Don't you want to be all right for them?" From a young age John was focused.'

'Well, he had no choice but to be successful,' his sister Kelly said to me later, 'because my dad was always pushing. Dad was always torturing himself. But he didn't have to worry about John because John always liked to be doing something at a high level.'

When he was about twelve, John was always out on the street shouting orders at the other kids. He just had that leadership thing and all the kids respected him. 'Then suddenly,' says his mother, 'he just stopped all that. I asked him why he wasn't shouting any more. He said, "I just don't wanna be that way."' When, in junior high school, he was called out and had a fist-fight he had to tell his mother about it. She was simply pleased he had won. 'I thought it was always my job to keep them safe and on track,' she said. The boys spent a lot of the summer holidays cutting grass for money around the neighbourhood.

'That's the smell I remember,' said Sabrina. 'The boys' room always smelled like old, grassy, pre-teen sneakers. I remember opening their closet and looking down to a mound of sneakers and thinking, *Why are there so many?* And when I spoke to her in a bar at the top of a tall hotel in Philadelphia, Sabrina just kept turning over the pages of old photo albums as if they held a mystery. She'd been putting the albums together ever since John died, wanting to bind the material of his life and all their lives together. 'Ever since he was young,' she said, 'he had a coach's mentality. The kids in the street wanted to be like him. And, you know, the motto of the Marines is *Semper Fidelis*, 'Always Faithful'. That was him and always was him. Even before he was flying he loved to fly at things. We had a great childhood.'

Mrs Spahr wanted to show me around the house before we continued talking. The boys' room had an American flag above the desk. The trees outside seemed frozen and watchful, while Mrs Spahr recounted how the boys would play games up here once upon a time and share stories and laughs. It was hard not to think of soldiers all over the world who started off in small bedrooms like the one in Cherry Hill: looking up at the placid walls and the tidy small space, a certain dream seemed to rise for a moment and take hold, a very domestic dream of glory. Motivations are perhaps the greatest mystery of all.

'You know, his father hated to fly,' said Mrs Spahr. It seemed he would do anything to avoid going on a plane, including driving across the country to see John when he lived in San Diego. 'Ronnie wanted John to be a football coach and that was that. He didn't want him to join the Marines and thank God he wasn't around to see what happened to John because it would have killed him, too.' Mrs Spahr was dabbing her eyes with kitchen napkins as she spoke; they were brightly coloured, with the words 'Happy Holidays' printed the same on each one.

When I caught up with Sabrina again she seemed as if she had been thinking about significant things in the meantime. 'Even at a young age,' she said, 'he wanted to bring out the best in people and teach you what he knew. That was his gift. For my father, it was all about family. We went to church and it was always the front pew. It was a house where they would have parties, cocktails and cigarettes. It was that time, right?' Sabrina is different from the other people in her family: she worries a lot and tends to be an organiser. She will say, in quiet moments, that there is something missing in her life and that what happened to John stopped her in her tracks. Like her sister Kelly, she often starts sentences with the phrase, 'I said to my husband . . .' and she gives off a feeling of hope that family can answer all of life's demands.

Mrs Spahr played down the influence of her husband's anxieties on John's chosen path, but others felt the influence was pretty decisive. 'Not a lot of fathers in New Jersey would get up at five in the morning to drive their son to the river,' said Sabrina. I thought about that, and wondered at Ronnie's overall effect on his son's inner life. Sabrina's voice is quiet, even quieter when she's discussing their father, as if he might be listening, as if she were speaking in church, as if she were being disloyal. 'He didn't talk about much,' she said. 'My mom talked. I always wished that he had talked more.'

In May 1981 there was a story in the *Philadelphia Inquirer*: 'Spahr is New Jersey's gift to St Joseph's Prep Rowing', said the headline. 'In America, those kinds of young men are a breed apart,' said a friend of the family, 'and they're treated like gods in certain schools.' The photograph accompanying the article is of a tousle-haired, clean-limbed and smiling John Spahr, looking like a tragic hero out of Scott Fitzgerald.

> Why does one of the very best scholastic rowers in the United States go to school in North Philadelphia – when he lives in Cherry Hill? 'It was just word of mouth,' said John Spahr, who won the Junior National Singles championship last summer, rowing for St Joseph's Prep . . . Spahr, who gets up at 5 a.m. daily so that he can start practicing on the Schuylkill at 6, isn't just an oarsman. He started at quarterback for the Prep this fall, and started for the private school stars in the City All-Star Game in April.

The newspaper spread also included a picture of Mrs Spahr, elegant as ever, a believing mother, mid-life, pre-crisis, and far from the vexations of a poor Irish childhood, shouting encouragement to her American boy from the bank of the river.

St Joseph's Prep is a Jesuit school. Past a hall of portraits showing successive principals since 1966, the head rowing coach Bill Lamb sat in a room under an overactive air-conditioning system. 'To educate mind, body, and spirit,' he said, 'and show how these three components make a complete person, that is the Jesuit mantra.' Mr Lamb had a habit shared by many of the people I spoke to about John Spahr: he spoke about him in the present tense. I wondered as I listened to the coach's tough statements what effect the death of a young man had on the lives of people who lived for the vitality of youth. But Mr Lamb was circumspect: one imagines he feels, somewhere, that sacrifice is a known and regrettable part of the game. 'John is the perfect model,' continued Mr Lamb. 'To turn the skill and the confidence you learn in athletics and use that to develop as a person – and John, in a heroic way, took that complete person and recognised how he could best be of service to others. He dedicated his life to that.'

His star pupil wanted to lead and change things. He was popular and athletic, and the rowing team needed that very badly at the time, because it was feared the school might lose its position in the league. 'If we could get John to row, the rest of the kids in the school would look at rowing as something cool to do. When this started we had nine guys and by the end we had over a hundred. The best marketing is when the kids tell other kids there's value in what they're doing. He was successful at everything he ever did. But even when he was at the top level, John acted as if he was at the bottom. Out of any year, you can see there are two or three who will do outstanding things.'

I imagined Mr Lamb was a lot like Mr Tothero, the coach in the first of John Updike's 'Rabbit' novels:

> The coach is concerned with developing the three tools we are given in life: the head, the body, and the heart ... 'All those years, all those boys [says Tothero], they pass through your hands and into the blue. And never come back, Harry;

they never come back . . . Give the boys the will to achieve. I've always liked that better than the will to win, for there can be achievement even in defeat. Make them feel the, yes, I think the word is good, the *sacredness* of achievement, in the form of giving our best.'

'Some talented guys can sit back a little,' said Bill Lamb, 'but John was working as hard as the weakest guy on the team. He didn't want to risk the privilege by getting involved in some of the things that teenagers get involved in.'

'And what about his father?' I asked. 'Some people have suggested the influence was strong.'

'His father was a very, very conservative, strict disciplinarian,' he said. 'He raised all his daughters as if they were boys. It was his way or the highway.'

'Isn't there a danger in the American system,' I said, 'in creating such a platform for sterling brilliance at school that the rest of life is a struggle to maintain it?'

'Absolutely,' said Bill Lamb. 'That's our greatest challenge. We have a lot of kids who never leave high school. They're thirty years old and they're still operating as if it was St Joe's Prep, and the real world isn't like that. Some of them have a problem in applying the lessons they learned here to their daily lives. But it's about hard work. Pick up the sports pages I'll show you five of those guys. But with John it was almost as if he didn't really exist. He was the model of success, and you couldn't have drawn it any better.'

Down at the boathouse it was dark and the town's lights were reflected in the black ripples of the river. Al Zimmerman, another of John's teachers, showed me the boat that was named after John and the memorial plaque. Mr Zimmerman used to teach Latin and Greek at the school and he wrote the words for the plaque; he skirted around them when I was there, as if shy of what he had produced. The boathouse was full of expired energy and prolonged ideals. Al talked of what they tried to give John and about what he gave them. His voice lapped gently and kindly at my back as I looked out at the river, and beyond that to the merging borders of Pennsylvania and Delaware and New Jersey, wondering how many of the people out there once knew a young man called John Spahr. And what did his life say about theirs? About ours? About the lives of nations? 'He liked to roll his sleeves up and get the job done,' said Al Zimmerman. 'And that's what you really need in a crew. He applied those same principles elsewhere.'

The River Tyne is a place where famous industry appears to have given way to infamous leisure. The only ship I passed as I made my way to visit Anthony Wakefield's wife and children was one called Tuxedo Princess, a former liner now converted into a nightclub. Along the quay the flashing lights spoke of concert halls and happy-hours, while the shipyard cranes stood still against the dark. Among them, once upon a time, battle cruisers were built to order and the gatling gun was made by W. Armstrong & Co.

As he came to the end of his schooldays, Anthony kept saying he wanted to be a soldier. Living with his grandparents, he always enjoyed the stories his grandfather would tell about surviving the Normandy landings. Anthony's guardians made a rule that no toy guns were allowed in the house. But at secondary school Anthony got in with a rowdy crowd and was expelled. His childhood was transformed in that period by an adult accusation: some girls said he'd got rough with them in a park. 'It wasn't true,' said his brother, 'but it shocked him. Anthony was dyslexic and was never going to sit exams anyhow.'

The Army Careers Office in Northumberland Street turned Anthony away the first time. They said he was too small and too thin, so he got a job stacking shelves at a discount supermarket; the second time they let him have the forms. His Uncle Dan says he didn't think Anthony would pass the interview for the army because he was a little bow-legged and had high arches. Anthony accepted another job, at the twenty-four-hour Tesco in Kingston Park near the airport – where many of the staff go

round on roller skates – but right away the letter came from
the army saying he was in. Anthony and Paul's beloved grandmother was dying, but she said she wanted to hold on to hear
Anthony's news, 'Just to make sure the boys were all right,' said
Paul.

Anthony's choice of regiment, the Coldstream Guards, was
made on the basis, he said, that all the best-looking guys joined
the Guards. (The regiment performs many ceremonial duties:
the Queen's Birthday Parade, Trooping the Colour, the Changing of the Guard.) He did his training at Catterick and Aldershot and then Pirbright, where he passed out in 1998 on St
George's Day. 'We had to stand in a line for four hours,' wrote
Anthony to his Aunt Emily during his training. 'All our legs
hurt and we are all very tired and we are starving. The only
thing I've had is a Murray Mint off one of the lads. We are going
to get our hair cuts tomorrow.'

Once he got going, Anthony was getting about £250 a week,
serving first in Belize and then in Northern Ireland. When he
came home on leave, he would sometimes go out with Paul and
his friends to clubs in Newcastle. Anthony loved tanning par-
lours and dancing, so he was as comfortable in his brother's
preferred gay haunts as anywhere else. 'If anyone had come near
him I would probably have killed them,' said Paul when I asked
him about it.

'Was there anything about Anthony you didn't like?'

'I didn't like it that he smoked,' said Paul, 'or that he had tattoos. The tattoos came with the army.'

On the left side of his chest Anthony had a fairly large tattoo
of a ripped flag – a Coldstream Guards staple – and he also had
a tattoo of a kneeling girl in fishnet stockings. During his second tour in Northern Ireland, a young Catholic pulled a gun on
him but he didn't fire and Anthony was commended for standing his ground. Before that he'd already got married to Ann
Toward, a girl he'd met in the Global Video shop on Shields
Road. 'He was just dead nice,' says Ann. 'He took care of himself
and he was a laugh.'

Ann already had a little girl, Stacey, when she met Anthony. She had the baby when she was about sixteen and she has never had a job. (She is thirty-three.) She and Anthony went on to have two more children, Scott and Corey, who are aged ten and five. Anthony's Aunt Emily told me Anthony 'totally loved' having a house of his own. 'He would love making dinners,' she said. 'And he'd want everybody round. When he did that he'd clean the house from top to bottom. It was as if he just loved the idea of making a proper family himself.'

Paul has few good words to say about Anthony's widow, and she knows it. I tried to steer him away from saying too much. I told him I was writing everything down, but he said that didn't bother him. The circumstances of his childhood and his brother's loss have made Paul self-absorbed, understandably so perhaps, but he doesn't see how difficult it must be for Ann bringing up three children on her own. Paul and Anthony's difficulties with their own mother may lie behind some of this confusion. Paul was boiling with rage about his mother one night when I drove him round Newcastle. At that stage, his mother hadn't wanted to speak to me, and Paul couldn't understand why. He couldn't work out why other people didn't see the point of the story – as if it meant they didn't see the point of Anthony – and he considered his mother's refusal to be yet another rejection.

This had all been part of the chaos of Anthony's life, not just his childhood but also the time before he died, when he and Ann had split up and he was going out with a local hairdresser called Kym. The Byker Estate was pitch black the night I called on Ann, and her house seemed over-excited and over-populated, children rushing in and out of the bright kitchen. She is a pretty woman with a nice smile and a bad cough. She was looking for her inhaler but she held a pack of cigarettes in her hand the whole time I was there. I was told Scott had attention deficit hyperactivity disorder, and he certainly whirled around a fair amount, crashing into the fridge and clearly finding it hard to settle.

'My dad and me went to the lighthouse museum,' Scott said, wrapping himself around my arm. 'On my birthday my dad hided all the presents behind the settee and in the cupboards. I found five and then he told me where the other ones were. There was a hundred stairs at the lighthouse museum.'

'He died,' said Corey.

'I went in me dad's car with me friend,' said Scott, 'and we ate chewing gum and we asked Dad if we could put music on and that and he say, "Aye."'

I asked Scott what he would like to do when he grows up. 'I want to be a high court judge and work with horses,' he said. The whole family spoke with sing-song Geordie accents, the words pouring into one another.

Stacey came down the stairs wearing a Playgirl T-shirt and with her hair in bunches. She is fourteen. A neighbour told me that Anthony doted on Stacey. 'When he got home on leave,' she said, 'he was always taking her up the town to buy her phones and trainers, whatever she wanted.' By the time Stacey began to speak – it took her a while to stop chewing the ends of her hair and giggling – the living room had turned into a corner of Bedlam. Scott was thumping the Formica kitchen top with a giant stick and shooting us all with a plastic gun and Corey was blowing a whistle. 'My dad was nice,' said Stacey. 'He told jokes and he didn't shout at you. We went to the Metro Centre on my birthday. He bought us a Girls Aloud CD and jeans and everything, then we went to KFC.'

When Anthony Wakefield died, his loss animated a series of hurts and complications that might never end. 'Every Christmas, every birthday, every memory,' said Ann, 'the death of Anthony just affects the kids. To Corey his father is just in heaven. Stacey goes off on her own to her bedroom and broods about it and has her own thoughts. With Scott's problems, he often just doesn't understand. At the time of Anthony's death, Stacey would blame me, saying, "It should have been you," and things like that.'

I asked her if they had enough to live on.

'We have eight hundred pounds a month,' she said. 'Four hundred and sixteen of that goes on rent for this house, and there's another hundred a month for council tax.'

'So you and the kids have seventy pounds a week left to live off?'

'Aye,' she said. 'You've just got to get on with it.'

It was hard to speak to Ann while Paul was there: resentment made him vigilant, and he felt angry when she spent a few moments with me in the kitchen alone, 'forcing me to hear her side of the story', he said.

'There needn't be sides,' I said to him later. But I felt sorry for Paul and thought his possessiveness about his brother's memory could only be part of his grief.

'I've got these kids and I get the pension and that's what bothers him,' Ann said. 'He never comes here. Neither does their mother, the kids' grandmother. She hasn't seen the children since the day of Anthony's funeral. There's been a lot of nasty stuff, but I'm not bothered really. People might think I stole Anthony away too young and made him have kids. But it wasn't like that. We did it together and now he's gone we have to make it the best way we can.'

When I asked her, Ann said that Anthony really loved being in the army. That was his first love. 'We probably married too young,' she said. 'He only had two days' leave when Corey was born, then it was on to Iraq. It was hard and things just fell apart. But I don't think the dislike will ever end with Paul and his family. It's sad for the kids but you've just got to get on with it.'

One of Ann's neighbours in Byker is called Angela Cairns. As I walked to her house there was a crack of lightning over the estate and a roll of thunder. Angela knew Anthony and Ann when they first met. 'He had a huge picture of the singer George Michael above his bed,' said Angela. 'Everybody teased him about it, but he said, "One day I'll be famous like him."' Angela was wearing huge hooped earrings and slippers covered in hearts. Whenever she got excited she kicked an Argos catalogue that was sitting on the floor beside the front door. 'One night, when he was home from the army,' she said, 'Anthony went out on the town with my son Stephen. They went to Buffalo Joe's on the Gateside Quays – Steve was Gothic, then – and they were drunk and coming across the swing bridge. Stephen was really pissed up and he climbed onto the side of the bridge and lost his footing. He fell all that way down into the Tyne and he was struggling in the water 'cause his Gothic gear was dragging him down. Anthony dived in. The tide is strong down there and Stephen was losing consciousness, but Anthony pulled him to the side by the hair and then insisted on giving him artificial respiration. He saved Stephen's life and then Anthony was up all night crying.'

When he was leaving for Iraq that last time, it was a Sunday and he went with Paul and Kym to have lunch and then began packing his bags. 'Don't be a hero,' said Paul. And when his truck back to Aldershot broke down, Paul and Kym decided to drive him and another young squaddie all the way down in Kym's car. 'We were exhausted by the time we got there,' said Paul, 'and we all fell asleep in the one bed in his living quarters, me and Kym with Anthony in the middle. In the morning all the soldiers were pleased to see him. He had a shower and then he gave me a microwave oven to take home and a DVD player. When it was time to go he grabbed me and gave me a big hug. It was usually me that instigated that, but this time it was Anthony and it meant a lot. That was the last time I ever saw him. He just looked spotless. We were always like that when we were kids, always spotless.' We were in a restaurant at Newcastle quayside when Paul said this, and he sat back in his chair. 'We didn't have much as kids,' he said, 'and . . . that's it. We didn't have much.'

Ann and the children were asleep on 2 May 2005 when the knock came at the door. Ann was shaking as the children came down the stairs, Scott saying, 'When my daddy comes home I'm going to ask him to buy me a backpack.' Ann took all the children into the kitchen and told them there had been an accident;

'Daddy's gone to heaven,' she said. The children were screaming and Ann phoned her neighbour Angela in a terrible state – 'heartbroken', Angela said – and everyone was bewildered and disbelieving at four in the morning, the children crying and trying to imagine how it could happen. Paul says when he heard the knock on his door he thought it would be Anthony. 'He must be home.' But through the spy hole he saw it was Ann and Stephen. 'I was so stunned,' Paul says, 'that they thought I was going to smash the place up. I remember just walking around the house putting pictures of Anthony in my pocket.' Then the three of them went to tell Anthony's mother. 'It's all my fault,' is what Paul remembers her saying. 'She was throwing up her hands,' says Paul, 'shouting, "Jimmy, Jimmy" . . . shouting for her husband. She said she thought it was all her own fault because of what happened when we were little.'

Months after my first visit to Newcastle, I went back when the opportunity arose, very suddenly, to spend a little time with Anthony's mother, Sylvia Grieve. Her house on Finsbury Avenue is very neat and modest, with a sign on the side facing the street that says NO BALL GAMES. Mrs Grieve was wearing black trousers and a black top; she is a small, easily embarrassed woman, wearing a bracelet covered in gold hearts, and with eyes that seem to show some experience of what the world is like; her world, at least. 'Anthony had been a very happy baby and daft as a brush,' she said. 'I lost them when they were very young because of marriage difficulties. I was too young when I had kids. My own family background wasn't very nice so you rush into things to get a house of your own. It was mainly worries with money and his dad liked a drink. When I got the news about him I just felt guilty and wondered why it wasn't me that died.'

Mrs Grieve has photographs of Anthony on several of her walls and she appears to live a lot of her life between the gas fire and the television set.

'And did you worry about him?' I asked.

'You always have this thing in the back of your mind,' she said. 'But you could tell he was frightened the last time I saw him, before he went off. I says to him, "Just tell them your mam says you have to come back or else I'll come looking for them and I'll bash them." And when they came with the news that he'd died, I just kept hearing Anthony's voice saying to me, "Come on, Mam. You've got to say something." That's what I imagined him saying.'

Mrs Grieve was quoted later as saying that she blamed Tony Blair for her son's death. (Paul puts it differently: he says George Bush murdered Anthony.) You can tell Anthony's mother isn't actually very interested in politics, but she wishes her son had come home and she says she feels the Americans are taking all the glory. 'But I suppose Anthony wanted to go,' she said. 'He was eager. From the beginning, from the very beginning, Anthony always wanted a little limelight on him.'

As evening approached in Cherry Hill, Eileen Spahr began to tell me her own story. She has the kind of faith in comfort and progress that comes from not having known enough of either in childhood. When it comes to her children, she points out that she may not always have got things right – too much pressure, perhaps, on Stephen, the younger son, who was more rebellious; too much emphasis, perhaps, on her husband's hopes – but with all that she has a basic certainty about the values she sees her family as having tried to live by. 'You've got to have testicles,' she said to John when he was dithering at college. 'Go full force and take advantage of the opportunities in life. John was my best friend – he had this beautifulness of spirit – and we could talk about pretty much anything.'

Under his photograph in John Spahr's high school yearbook, he chose the motto, 'Good company on a journey makes the way seem shorter'. He got his degree from the University of Delaware, and he met and fell in love with Diane, who later became his wife. 'He was affable,' said his sister Tracy, 'and he had a real soft side. At Delaware he did a lot of growing up.' He came to university trailing high expectations, and he lost his football scholarship, which people say was just part of the bigger job of getting to know himself. 'I think he was quite shaken up by not quite knowing what to do,' says Tracy.

After that, he worked for a while teaching physical fitness. He also spent time teaching sports to handicapped children. 'I knew he wanted a large life,' said his mother. 'So I went down there to have lunch with him. I said, "John, what do you want to do?" And he said he wanted to fly jets, so I said, "Go do it". Ronnie had totally figured out what John should do with his life – he should go to the Naval Academy and coach football: that's the life my husband would have wanted. I don't want to be disloyal to my husband, but he knew he was right. He became more and more German every day of his life. My father was domineering, you know, and my mother's policy was appeasement.'

Three times that summer John came home to tell his father he had joined the Marines, but three times he left Cherry Hill having failed to tell him. In any event, he had entered a five-year programme to become a pilot. On 6 August 1991 Mrs Spahr wrote about John in her journal: 'On this day John called in the middle of the afternoon. And I said "why?" and he said "jets" and I said "happy?" and he said "yes".' A couple of years later there's another entry in Mrs Spahr's diary: 'John called a few minutes ago. "I am alive and I am happy – the best day of my life, winged in the Marines . . . Whatever happens, I am content. I did my best."' Mrs Spahr says that from that point on, no man was ever so proud of his son as Ronnie was of John.

'I met John as he followed his dream of becoming a Marine jet pilot at the basic school in Quantico, Virginia,' said his friend Kevin Wolfe. They went on from there to further training at Kingsville, Texas. 'Dukes stood out,' said Wolfe. 'He had the classic good looks and swagger of a Marine – he carried himself with confidence and right away you wanted to follow him and you didn't know why. He had an unparalleled work ethic: he lived in our tactical manuals, perfecting his briefing and debriefing skills. John wanted to be a Top Gun instructor, and because he had performed so well in the navy's premier strike fighter course, he accepted their invitation. It was there that Dukes would have an indelible impact on pilots throughout the navy and Marine Corps. He was funny too. My wife Heather and I were there when his daughter Chandler was born in San Diego. I remember as we all anxiously waited to know his or her arrival, John came out with a sheepish grin and said, "Well, she's a Republican!"'

John Spahr and his wife Diane worked hard at their marriage, but in the end, like so many military marriages, it didn't work out. In trying to give an account of a life fully lived, a writer wonders what is most essential and most true. In the end, what we write is not merely an account of the bare facts, but an account of our choices and of other people's: the Spahrs are a family who care about family and they speak of John's endless affection for his daughter. 'He was married to flying anyhow,' said his sister Kelly. 'It's like a vocation, and that's that.'

Lieutenant Colonel D. A. Robinson was an instructor on the Top Gun staff with John Spahr. This is the elite training school for fighter pilots in Fallon, Nevada. 'A number of his commanding officers said he was the best officer that has ever served under them,' he said. 'And a number of his own staff said he was the best officer they'd ever served under. He always had a special faith in the underdog.' At the Top Gun school, instructors would be expected to debrief rookie pilots when they returned from a training exercise. This would normally take twenty minutes or so, but Spahr's were famous for their length. Major Tim Golden remembers 'a debriefing of John's that took six hours. Nobody could believe it. The poor guy was in there for six hours and John would just go over everything in detail.'

I met Major Tim 'Nugs' Golden and Major Dan 'Knuckles' Shipley in an Irish bar in Washington, only a few minutes walk from Capitol Hill. There was a game on television as we entered, and Rich Gannon was commentating on the Miami Dolphins' performance as we ordered. 'Gannon played behind John Spahr in school,' said Nugs. 'There was always this competition between them, and many people felt that John was better

than Gannon.' This is the world these men live in – a universe
of professional self-improvement and ceaseless competition,
where being better than the next guy is a survival instinct. 'John
was the guy everybody listened to,' added Nugs. 'He was the best
instructor by far – a coach, really. And he was so competitive.
We were all out there in 2003 in the Gulf and John would be
involved in the most stressful things, then he would stay up all
night playing X-Box. I remember we all played and then turned
in for the night, and we kept calling him to get some sleep, but
whenever I woke up, all the way to six a.m., he was still playing
that damn thing, trying to get to the next level. He was up all
night.'

'And he had natural flying ability,' said Knuckles. (I noticed
these pilots liked me to use their call signs; anything else seems
too formal to them.) 'He had flown more dog fights than anybody else and was so far ahead of the action.'

'That was it,' said Nugs. 'His only fault was to push and push
and you'd say, "Hey, dude – relax, friggin relax." But he always
wanted to do more and more, which was a pressure on him and
on others as well.'

'He chose the toughest route,' said Knuckles. 'It's much more
intense being a Marine fighter pilot – six months' infantry
training, then two years' flight school. You gotta learn how to
land that thing on an aircraft carrier. Then they ask him to
come back as an instructor and he comes back and he's the best.
God, man: you wanna kick him in the nuts. But he had humility. There were people who were as good pilots as he was but
none of them had his humility.'

In training videos, you see how John Spahr would explain to
groups of elite pilots all the things that could happen while
flying his particular jet, but he kept it mainly technical. He
could draw on 3,000 hours of flying experience, but he was dis-
creet about his missions. In the 1990s and early 2000s, Spahr
had in fact spent a great deal of time in military combat, flying
sorties in Bosnia and supporting the no-fly zone in southern
Iraq. In 2003 he was aboard the USS *Constellation*, a veteran

carrier made famous during Vietnam, and it was from here that he would lead a bombing campaign in Iraq that would exceed the might and devastation of all that conflict's previous campaigns.

On 20 March 2003 the CIA received reports from Iraqi spies that Saddam Hussein would spend the night at a farm on the banks of the Tigris in eastern Baghdad. The Shock and Awe air campaign was launched at 9 p.m. local time on the following day, involving, according to William Arkin of the *Washington Post*,

> 1,700 aircraft flying 830 strike sorties plus 505 cruise missiles attacking 1,500 aimpoints at several hundred targets: palaces, homes, guard headquarters, government buildings, military bases. More targets were attacked in Baghdad in the span of one hour on March 21 than we hit in the entire 43-day air campaign in 1991, and airpower followed up reliably every day with hundreds more strikes. When the sandstorm came, when the Fedayeen arrived, when ground commanders got nervous that Iraq was not the country that the U.S. had wargamed against, when the Red Line was crossed, when the public got equally nervous, airpower continued in the background, bombing, bombing, bombing.

According to Jon Lee Anderson's account in his book *The Fall of Baghdad*, 'The sheer power and scale and precision of the attacks were at once terrible and awe-inspiring and placed us in a state of mind in which almost anything seemed possible.'

John Spahr was the first pilot over Baghdad on 21 March and the first to deliver bombs. His sister Kelly said he would never talk about what happened; 'That's what John said,' remembers Kelly. 'There are things he did that I knew he would never talk about. But John wasn't political in the way some people are: he believed in the commander-in-chief and he followed orders. That's what he did.' John told his friends that if his commanding officer said 'Go', he'd go, and personal opinion had nothing to do with it. At the end of that first mission in Baghdad, as the sun was coming up, John had his photograph taken in mid-air by one of his colleagues. For the photograph, John tilted up the bottom of the jet, to show the camera his bombs were gone.

Knuckles, another member of the Death Rattlers on those missions, told me what it's like up there in a fighter plane during a mission. 'There's anti-aircraft stuff coming at you,' he said, 'and you're working via night goggles. Your mouth goes dry and it ain't funny any more. This is what happens when you're "in-country". Time slows down to an incredible level and everything is deliberate. And you're making sure you're getting precision in the bombing. You're taking information like drinking from a firehose. You've got to be aware of your altitude; you're looking at your wingman. You're worried if you can make it back. It's literally overwhelming. It's such a frickin challenge and you know it's a son of a bitch. And then at the end you have to land this thing on a ship in the middle of the ocean in the middle of the night.' Nugs was a mission commander that night. 'You're saying, "Please, God, don't let me mess this up,"' he said. 'It's as confusing as hell out there.'

'I loved to fly with Dukes,' said David Peeler, another pilot who served with Spahr in Marine Fighter Attack Squadron 323. 'John and I had something in common in our childhoods that prepared us very well for that business. It was not a game to him. He understood that to "go to the show", as he put it, was what we all aspired to do, that is lead in combat.'

Anthony Wakefield and John Spahr were, at whatever remove, brothers in arms, but they also had brothers back home who would have to live with the glory they had sought and found. John Spahr's brother Stephen wears his own duty with a smile: he is proud of his older brother, and perfectly silent on the pressure that must always have existed for him to live up to his example. But, whatever he says or doesn't say, his burden multiplied after that fatal flight on 2 May 2005.

Their mother says Stephen was always different. She remembers him, as a boy, pouring water down from the top of the stairs onto the carpet below, an act of gleeful destruction that would never have occurred to the solid John. Stephen got into drinking and girls pretty early and his freedoms were never squeezed by his father's dislikes. He was just his own man and he still is, while knowing that his brother's example is now not only an alternative to his own life, but a hallowed ground that surrounds him. 'We stayed up late, John and I, at my sister's house one time,' said Stephen. 'We'd had a few cocktails together and were pretty drunk, and John said we were different in a way that he did what was important to make my parents happy ... going to St Joe's Prep, a stepping stone to a good career and all that. Whereas I did what made me happy. John was more focused. He didn't want to share the glory, neither would I – if you're gonna play baseball, you wanna be the pitcher. If you're gonna do crew, you want to be in a single shell. He wanted to make my parents proud.'

Stephen will always remember the boys' bedroom at Cherry Hill, the trees outside, the brothers' customary whispers and laughter, and the bus journeys to school in the morning after they'd been to the boathouse. But his abiding memory of John might be one of his last, when he visited his brother on the aircraft carrier in Honolulu. 'I was looking down and looking for his plane,' said Stephen. 'And suddenly I saw it taxiing up from the end of the carrier. He's got the full face mask on and his uniform, but I knew it was him just by his mannerisms. He gave me the thumbs up and then I saw him holding onto the dashboard – then, *phweeeewo*, he was off. He said to me one time, just before that last tour, that he was a little bit disgusted with what was going on with the war. He was getting a little frustrated with the military – I think he didn't like killing people – and it started to get to him a little bit.'

I was later briefed on a report written up by the Pentagon, and it appears John Spahr probably died instantly. It is unlikely that he ejected at the point of collision, but even if he did it appears that his parachute did not deploy and, falling five miles in a sandstorm, he would not have been conscious. He suffered a severe injury to his head and he was later found in the desert a great distance from the jet fragments, a great distance from the floating city he knew as his temporary home, and a great distance, too, from his daughter in San Diego and from the boys' room at Cherry Hill, where he once stared into the dark and dreamed of glory in the miles that were said to exist above the trees and beyond the shores.

On that day in May, two Marines came to the door at Cherry Hill and found that Mrs Spahr was in Florida. The neighbour across the road saw them and called Sabrina, who was already panicking when she saw the television news, which spoke of two pilots assigned to the USS *Carl Vinson* having gone down. 'No,' said Sabrina, 'please don't say it's John.'

In Florida, Mrs Spahr was staying with a friend and she was in the back of the house when her host shouted that two of her friends were at the door. Mrs Spahr came through and nearly passed out: she knew the meaning of two Marines standing at the door of a house containing the mother of a Marine. 'I had always planned,' Mrs Spahr told me, 'that if I saw those Marines come to the door, I would just go out of the back door and I would just run until I disappeared into the earth. That was my plan. I went to the Tomb of the Unknown Soldier with John and Chandler one time. He just wanted her to see it, and he loved it there. He was such a peaceful man. That's what you would say about him. I've been there a bunch of times but I'm not going to that place again. I just can't go there any more. When I was in Florida that time, I took a drive up to the Gulf Coast. I felt so peaceful and everything was so beautiful – for about an hour there was just this exquisite peace.'

When a soldier was clearing out Anthony Wakefield's quarters at Camp Abu Naji, he found a collection of posters stuck above his bed and they too were sent home to Newcastle, the Blu Tack still on the back of them. They included posters of John Lennon, the Sex Pistols, Adam Ant and Bruce Lee. Anthony had filled in standard MOD Form 106 – a soldier's will – saying that the contents of his savings account should be split between the three children and that all his personal belongings should go to his girlfriend Kym. These belongings made for three small boxes, and included a sandwich toaster, a gold ring engraved DAD, various CDs and civilian clothes, and a Gucci money clip, along with personal cash of £27.76. His collection of papers was not voluminous, either: some legal things, vehicle documents, a booklet from the Guild of International Songwriters and Composers and a membership card for Blockbuster Video.

A letter came to the home of Anthony's aunt Emily, the woman who had brought him up, from Lieutenant Colonel Nicholas Henderson. 'Such was his, and their professionalism,' he wrote, 'they were chosen to look after the most demanding and dangerous part of the city – in order that real progress could be made. They were having a positive effect on the Iraqis, who are desperate for peace and security, and we will continue in the same manner, partly to fulfil our mission here, but also, and most importantly, to honour the memory of Anthony.'

Anthony Wakefield's body was flown back to RAF Brize Norton and from there to Newcastle. The funeral took place at St Gabriel's Church in Heaton. Before the service, the hearse drove past his old house, and his son Scott looked out of the window and wondered what the car and the box inside it had to do with his dad. There was a large crowd on the streets around the church that day, and the coffin was taken up the aisle to 'Ave Maria', covered in yellow tulips. Paul put a card in beside his brother, saying all the things he wished he had said before; it went down into the ground with Anthony and Paul feels pleased that nobody will ever know exactly what it said.

The Benton Road graveyard was empty the day I went there with Paul. It had the look of so many English urban cemeteries, neglected in the evening traffic, more a place of forgetting than a garden of remembrance. Vandals had made their presence felt, gravestones pushed over, lager cans strewn in several areas, the remains of small fires. You could see the buses lighting up on the main road as Paul took me first to see his father's grave, and then past rows of civilians, the local people of Newcastle who had died where they were born and whose arguments had come to rest in the same place as the people they were arguing with. 'Everybody ends up here,' said Paul, except he hoped that he would not, and that a job entertaining on a cruise ship would come up before the end of the year. We stood in front of Anthony's headstone, a simple, grey one paid for by the Coldstream Guards, and I thought of Paul's letter mouldering in the local soil. There wasn't much light left at the end of the day, but enough to see other headstones just like Anthony's further along the line. 'There was nobody like him,' said Paul as we turned to go.

Lieutenant Colonel John Spahr was buried with full military ceremony, the occasion marked by the first fly-past in Washington since the events of 9/11. John's sister Tracy was involved in the second term of the Reagan–Bush administration, working as an assistant press secretary. She later campaigned for the Vice-President and had several posts in his administration. 'My friends at the White House had always wanted to know about John,' she told me. 'It was awesome to think of him up in that plane. Everybody was impressed with him, but to him it was just his calling. He accepted it and he made the sacrifice. I know that, had he survived, John would have gone on to very great things. The Pentagon was certainly on his list.' A few days after his death, a letter came to the house from her old boss the President's father, George Bush. 'Dear Tracy,' it said. 'I am so sorry that your brother was KIA. Perhaps it is of some comfort to know that this truly good man gave his life serving our great country. May God Bless him as he holds John in his loving arms. Please convey to all your family my most sincere condolences. To you I send my love.' Two hundred family and friends, and his beloved daughter Chandler, accompanied John Spahr's coffin to Arlington National Cemetery, where he was buried in a low plain made over to the American dead of Iraq.

John's sister Kelly picked me up in Baltimore and we drove to Arlington from there. 'John was timing his retirement to be when Chandler was in high school,' she said. 'Just to be with her.' As we got closer to Washington I began to notice how many of her mannerisms were just like her mother's. 'What's my point?' she would say if she got lost in talking about John. 'We went to our boys' school,' she said, 'and there was this sign hanging up and it was a kind of American motto – MEN FOR OTHERS. I just turned to my husband and said, "I think we've had enough of Men For Others, don't you?"' She told me about their beach house, where one day a few years ago, when they knew John was going to be flying past that way, they went down onto the sand and wrote in big letters, 'HELLO JOHN'.

In Arlington Cemetery there were red-ribboned wreaths in front of every grave, stretching in each direction as far as the eye could see, along a vast slope to the higher points commemorating the Union dead. When we reached the part where John is buried, Kelly's voice changed and she lay down on the ground and cried there as if the earth were merely a barrier between her and her brother. I put my hand on her back and thought of the miles, the entire oceans that spanned one human loss and another. In some ways, after searching out these lives in Britain and America, I had arrived at the simplest truth, but I felt that I tasted the complications of the Atlantic that day, as a young woman sobbed into the earth for her dead brother. Kelly stood up and gestured with her arm at the rows of graves. 'When will all this madness end?' she said. 'The last time I was here, John's row was at the end of the field, and now look.' She moved her arm over the many new rows of young men and women who had died in the fight for Iraq. Many of the graves were those of servicemen born in the late 1980s.

At the other end of the field the stones were more weathered, the beginning of the past: Vietnam, Korea, the Second World War, and on to Fredericksburg, Bull Run, Antietam. Then we left John Spahr and went to look for the Tomb of the Unknown Soldier. Anthony Wakefield and John Spahr were as different as land and air. One saw his life in epic terms, the other was more pragmatic, but their ends were the same, and they each served as part of a special relationship between their two countries, a relationship that, in its dreams and in its undoing, may be seen to mark the end of a period that started not with Churchill and Roosevelt, but with Thatcher and Reagan. As I climbed up over the manicured lawns in company with John's sister Kelly, I remembered a letter Margaret Thatcher once wrote to her dear American friend. 'Your achievements in restoring America's pride and confidence and in giving the West the leadership it needs are far too substantial to suffer any lasting damage. The message I give to everyone is that anything which weakens you, weakens America; and anything that weakens America weakens the whole free world.'

Before us at Arlington, a uniformed soldier marched up and down and we looked beyond the tombs and the urban parks to see the Washington Monument, stark as a compass needle in the distance. It seemed that summer must exist in a place behind the sky. It wouldn't be long before the smell of cut grass was back in the air, the smell of John's childhood return-ing, as fresh-seeming as the taste of Anthony's Murray Mint, to show the world that something was truly lost in all this human struggle for gain.

Acknowledgements

Most of the pieces in this collection were originally published in the *London Review of Books*, and I want to say thanks to the paper's editor, Mary-Kay Wilmers, who had many of the ideas and guided me through the stages to publication. She is that rare thing once described rather nicely by J. D. Salinger, 'lover of the long shot, defender of the hopelessly flamboyant, most unreasonably modest of born great artist-editors', and with that she is also a great friend and I couldn't have done half of it without her. I also owe a debt of thanks to the paper's publisher, Nicholas Spice, who encouraged me in a hundred different ways, and to my other friends among the staff, past and present, who succeeded in persuading me that literary journalism is worth everything you've got.

I am also grateful to Robert Silvers, editor of the *New York Review of Books*, and to his late colleague Barbara Epstein. Also to Deborah Orr, once editor of the *Guardian*'s *Weekend* magazine, as well as the editors of *Granta*, the *Daily Telegraph* and the *Paris Review*. I am grateful for help down the years from Jane Swan and my agent Derek Johns, and also from Jon Riley, Lidija Hass and Colm Tóibín, who gave me especially good advice about this collection. At Faber and Faber, I want to thank my editor Lee Brackstone – the backbone of this book – and my publisher Stephen Page. They each have shown enormous, spirited support for this work as well as my others. If there are any mistakes it is certainly their fault, but don't tell anybody.

Andrew O'Hagan
February 2008

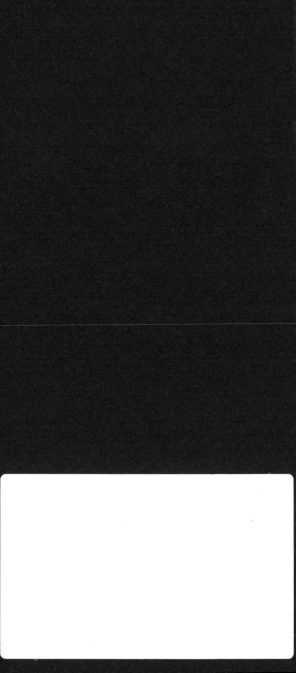